HARRIE T. LINDEBERG
AND THE AMERICAN COUNTRY HOUSE

HARRIE T. LINDEBERG

AND THE AMERICAN COUNTRY HOUSE

PETER PENNOYER
AND ANNE WALKER

Foreword by
ROBERT A.M. STERN

Principal photography by
JONATHAN WALLEN

THE MONACELLI PRESS

ACKNOWLEDGMENTS

We had admired houses by Harrie T. Lindeberg from the moment when we saw the John F. Erdmann house in East Hampton with its swelling roofs rising from the sand dunes, so we were thrilled to see the 1996 reprint of the 1940 monograph and grateful to Mark Alan Hewitt for his thorough and insightful new introduction. In journals and magazines from the period, we gleaned important views and analysis by Royal Cortissoz, C. Matlack Price, A. H. Forbes, Herbert Croly, Russell F. Whitehead and John Taylor Boyd Jr., architectural critics long gone whose voices continue to illuminate this period in American architectural history. While much of the sleuthing had already been accomplished by Hewitt, we did find new sources that vindicate our decision to reexamine Lindeberg's career. Among the surprises was a master's thesis on Lindeberg by Brian Lee Johnson at the University of Virginia in 1984. Few essays published since capture the meaning and spirit of the work of Lindeberg and his contemporaries as well.

We are fortunate that much of Lindeberg's work still stands and continues to fascinate and are grateful to homeowners who welcomed us to experience their houses and, more importantly, allowed our photographer, Jonathan Wallen, to capture them in full color and sharp focus.

Among the many people and organizations who shared information, recollections and supported our research, we are grateful to:

John Axe
Prue Beidler
David Byars
Barbara and Barry Carroll
John Casaly
At the Frederick Law Olmsted
   National Historic Site:
   Michele Clark
Stephanie and Fred Clark
Henry Christensen
Andrew Constantine
At the Greenville Country Club:
   Jim Davis
Bonnie Devendorf
Andrew S. Dolkart
Freddy Eberstadt
Steve Ells
Alice Engel
Fred Finn and Hilary McAllister
Stephen Fox
Gregory Gilmartin
Nancy Green
Catherine Havemeyer
Harry W. Havemeyer
At the Smithsonian American
   Art Museum:

Christine Hennessy
Maryalice Huggins
Werner Huthmacher
Oliver Janney
Thomas Jayne
Albert Kalimian
Michele Kearns
Mandy Lindeberg
Diane Martin
Paul Mateyunas
At PRISM:
   Kevin Merges
At the Onwentsia Club:
   Wade Miller
Heather and Scott Norby
At the American Swedish Institute:
   Robert Nicholl
Andrew Nicoletta
Nathalie and Brendan O'Brien
Kate and Timothy O'Neill
The Honorable Bruce J. Oreck
Melinda Penn
Thomas Norman Rajkovich
At Terlato Wine Group:
   Anne Ruffino and Carolyn
   Turnmire

Donna Peak
Eugene H. Pool
Ami Schulman
At the Augustana college:
   Jill Seaholm
At the National Academy
   Museum & School:
   Diana Thompson
Suzanne Tucker
Peter Turino
Millicent Vollono
Linden Havemeyer Wise
Jennifer Woods
John Yunis

We are especially indebted to Robert A. M. Stern who challenged us to write our first monograph in 2000 and has been a friendly but firm voice urging us to do our best work ever since. We thank Lucinda May for her assistance and enthusiasm; Jo Ellen Ackerman for her book design; and our editor at The Monacelli Press, Elizabeth White, who has been so supportive of our work.

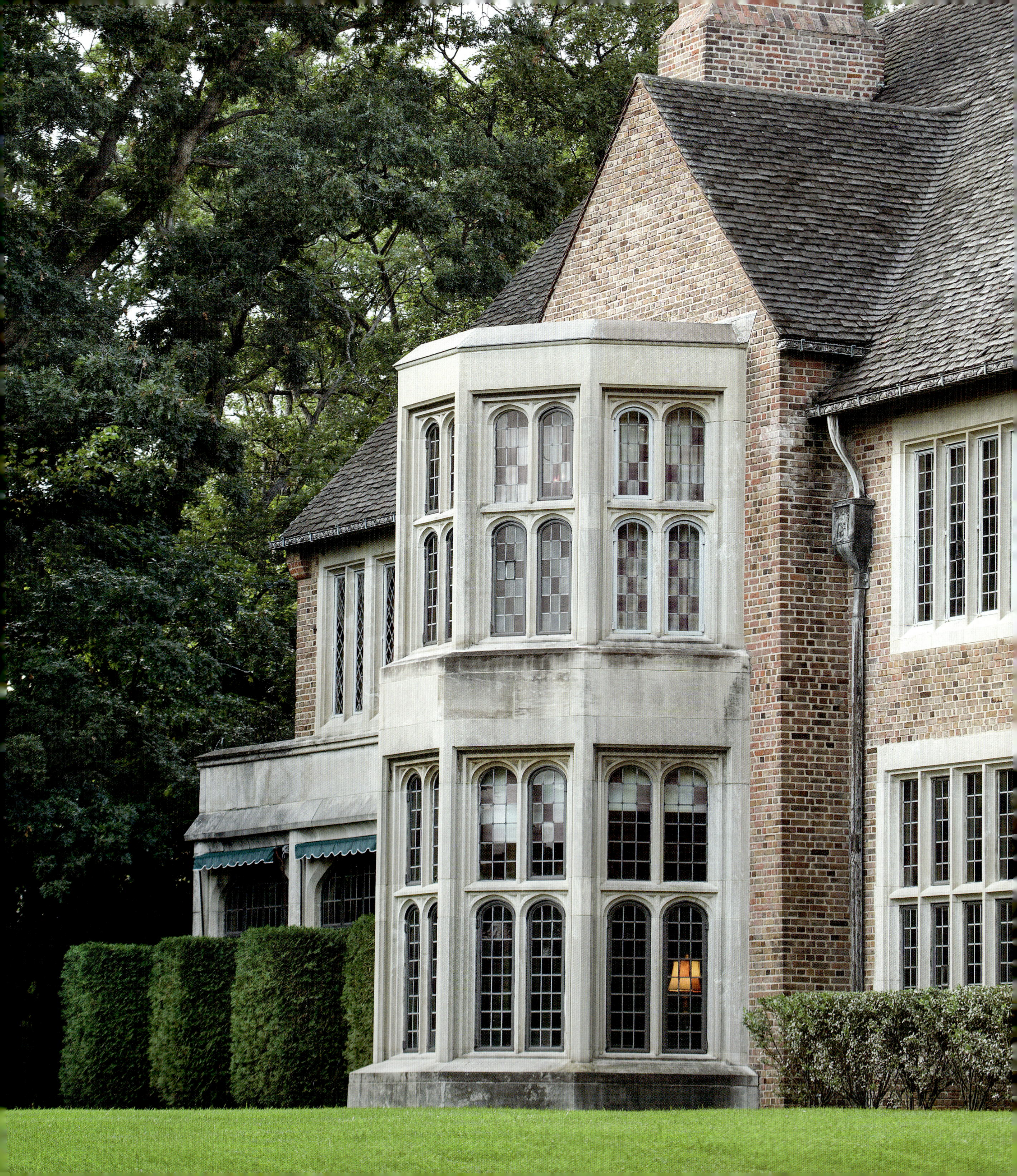

CONTENTS

8   Foreword   *Robert A. M. Stern*

11   Introduction

TWENTY PROJECTS

50   Mondanne
James A. Stillman Estate
POCANTICO HILLS, NEW YORK

56   Foxhollow Farm
Tracy Dows Estate
RHINEBECK, NEW YORK

64   Houses on Lily Pond Lane
EAST HAMPTON, NEW YORK

72   Meadow Spring
GLEN COVE, NEW YORK

80   Albemarle
Gerard B. Lambert Estate
PRINCETON, NEW JERSEY

88   Owl's Nest
Eugene du Pont Jr. Estate
GREENVILLE, DELAWARE

100   Wyldwoode
Clyde M. Carr Estate
LAKE FOREST, ILLINOIS

112   Olympic Point
Horace Havemeyer Estate
ISLIP, NEW YORK

118   Barberrys
Nelson Doubleday Estate
MILL NECK, NEW YORK

130   Shadyside
HOUSTON, TEXAS

142 Harry French Knight Estate
     LADUE, MISSOURI

148 Gray Craig
     Michael van Beuren Estate
     MIDDLETOWN, RHODE ISLAND

166 Jackson E. Reynolds House
     33 BEEKMAN PLACE, NEW YORK

172 Lowell M. Chapin/
     Francis Beidler House
     LAKE FOREST, ILLINOIS

178 West Gate Lodge
     Harrie T. Lindeberg House
     LOCUST VALLEY, NEW YORK

186 Onwentsia Club
     LAKE FOREST, ILLINOIS

192 The Church Houses
     MILL NECK, NEW YORK

204 Tangley Oaks
     Philip D. Armour III Estate
     LAKE BLUFF, ILLINOIS

214 Ruby Boyer Miller House
     GROSSE POINTE FARMS, MICHIGAN

220 United States Legation
     HELSINKI, FINLAND

227 Catalogue Raisonné

236 Appendix: Known Employees
     of Harrie T. Lindeberg

237 Notes

244 Bibliography

246 Index

248 Credits

FOREWORD
Harrie T. Lindeberg, Frank Lloyd Wright, and the New Tradition

With each new monograph in their series, Peter Pennoyer and Anne Walker push us forward to a fuller understanding of modern twentieth-century architecture in all its diversity, an understanding that necessarily must include the work of architects adapting traditional styles to modern conditions. Previous books in this series have documented tradition-inspired architects working productively throughout the first half of the twentieth century who enjoyed a broad range of commissions, from country houses to skyscrapers to infrastructural projects such as airports, while also pursuing advanced techniques in building technology and even in real estate development, making it clear that their preference for history-based form did not compromise their ability to practice as modern architects. Most of these architects were fundamentally eclectic in their approach to style, choosing a specific design tradition for each project and not seeking an overall synthesis that might lead to a new direction; nor were they interested in developing an identifiable personal style.

Today's traditionalists, like most of their predecessors of a hundred years ago, prefer to work in distinct styles such as American Georgian, Greek Revival, or Spanish Colonial—not such an easy game to play well but one that can produce very good work. Today's modernists, especially those pursuing residential projects, are also eclectic, also preferring to work in distinctive styles—typically so-called midcentury modern, particularly as it flourished in Southern California. Also an easy game to play—also hard to play well.

Harrie T. Lindeberg was not an eclectic architect working in identifiable historical styles but instead a traditional architect who drew upon diverse sources, which he did his best to conceal, synthesizing them into an identifiable personal style. In this he most closely resembles Frank Lloyd Wright, who despite his claims to not be a traditionalist also drew from the past and from the work of his contemporaries but concealed the sources of his inspiration.

At the turn of the nineteenth into the twentieth century, Harrie T. Lindeberg emerged on the scene as the taste for baronial country houses was giving way to a demand for houses conceived in response to the more relaxed, leisurely way of life favored by stockbrokers and bankers who sought modern comfort and convenience in an informal setting. Ambivalent about their relationships to big cities and to factories, which were typically the sources of their wealth, many of these clients were content to live like country squires but on relatively modest-sized suburban properties, to which they could commute from their places of business in the city. Lindeberg's genius was to extend the English Arts and Crafts approach of Voysey, Baillie Scott, and especially Lutyens, in houses that were relaxed in their massing but undergirded by the classical discipline that he acquired during his short exposure to Beaux-Arts methodology in the Atelier Masqueray and his time in the office of McKim, Mead & White. Wright, even more than Lindeberg, pursued a furtive eclecticism, allowing himself to be influenced by the English Arts and Crafts movement and also by classicizing principles through the work of J. M. Olbrich, the Austrian, and Louis Sullivan in America, and after 1910 by the pre-Columbian architecture of Meso-America. However, for the most part, Wright's houses were smaller than Lindeberg's and were truly suburban. But when he had the opportunity to spread out, as with the Coonley house, he paralleled Lindeberg in many ways.

It may seem odd to group Wright and Lindeberg together, but they were both seen by Henry-Russell Hitchcock, in his pioneering *Modern Architecture:*

Romanticism to Reintegration published in 1929, to be part of the "New Tradition," which he set in opposition to the work of the emerging generation of European modernists whom he labeled "The New Pioneers." As Hitchcock defined it, architects of the New Tradition in various countries succeeded "in blending their borrowings so subtly and in so prominently incorporating with their architecture the finest craftsmanship in building, as well as to some extent contemporary methods of engineering, that the public was persuaded there was no reminiscence of the past at all."[1] Hitchcock correctly saw in 1929 that stylistic modernism was gaining a foothold in American practice and that "the day of the New Tradition is probably coming to a close."[2] By the 1930s, he predicted, stylistic modernism would overcome traditional practice, largely because its social agenda, related to circumstances of economic depression, would make it, and not the New Tradition, seem the way to go—after all, the New Tradition, redolent with haut-bourgeois associations, was easy to dismiss as irrelevant and retrograde.

Faced with the stark economic realities of the Depression and the growing influence of abstract European modernism, some of Lindeberg's fellow New Traditionalists set out to "go modern"—think of Raymond Hood's Patterson house or George Howe's Square Shadows and Fortune Rock. After 1930 Frank Lloyd Wright also "went modern." Stimulated by his dislike for the work of the New Pioneers, he set out to beat them at their own game—think of Fallingwater as an answer to Le Corbusier's Villa Savoye, or Broadacre City as a response to Le Corbusier's various plans for Paris, or his Goetsch-Winckler house in relation to Mies van der Rohe's Barcelona Pavilion. Lindeberg, on the other hand, stuck to his guns, seemingly unable or unwilling to bend with the new wind and take the modernists on as Wright did by both word and deed. So Lindeberg's most "advanced" project of his otherwise commission-starved 1930s practice was a proposal for classically inspired small houses to be realized with metal-panel construction. Sadly also, he fell back on a narrow eclecticism in his commissions for foreign embassies and consulates, most of which were not realized.

In 1940, no doubt buoyed by the national return to prosperity, Lindeberg published a beautifully designed monograph of his work, surely in the hope that it would help his business pick up after the long drought of the Depression and that he would re-launch his career. Sadly, entrance into World War II put a stop to all nonessential construction. Moreover, the war seemed to dash any hope he might have had of pursuing his art at the level he had achieved before the crash, given that postwar clients, some of whom had patronized him before the crash, seemed to have lost interest in what he did best. His late houses were relatively conventional, with none of the authority or panache of his salad years—and the few commercial projects that came his way lacked any real distinction.

So I end with a question: why, given that Lindeberg is now so highly regarded by architects specializing in traditional work, is he not widely emulated? The same question might be asked about Wright in relation to today's modernists. The best answer I can come up with is that for each case the sources of the work are so brilliantly synthesized and so craftily concealed, resulting in so personal an approach that no next steps were left open to be followed. Close emulation of genius can only lead to parody.

Robert A.M. Stern

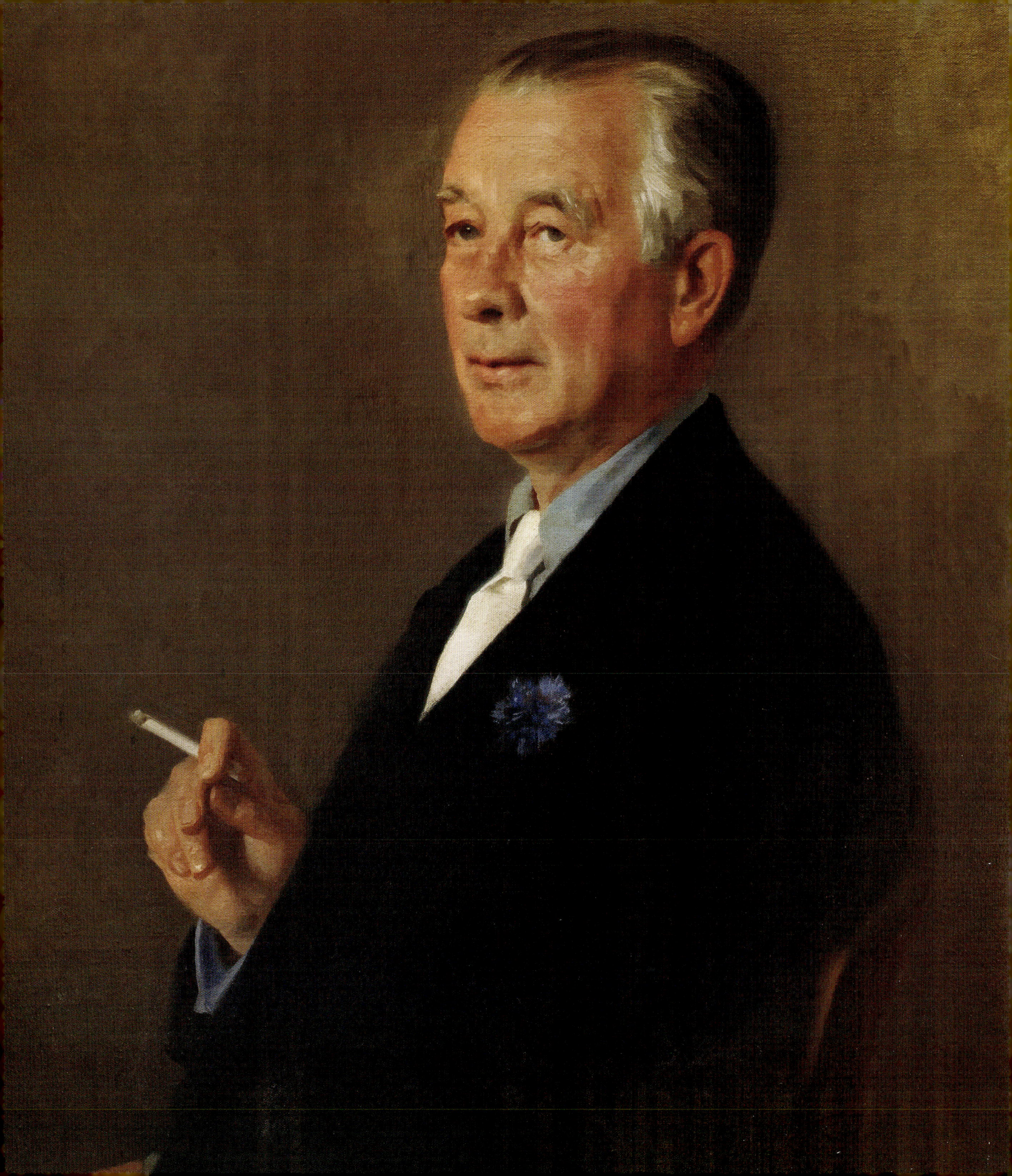

INTRODUCTION

Harrie T. Lindeberg's designs from the first three decades of the twentieth century made him famous in his day and created a legacy that sets him in the pantheon of major American architects. But along with those of many of his talented contemporaries, his accomplishments were obscured by the onslaught of modernism introduced from Europe in the 1930s. Lindeberg (1880–1959) documented his oeuvre in his 1940 monograph, *Domestic Architecture of H. T. Lindeberg*, with an introduction by Royal Cortissoz, a leading critic of his day. Many practicing architects have treasured this monograph, but the copies they acquired often bore the tell-tale deaccession stamps of libraries that recognized that the profession no longer viewed work inspired by architecture of the past as relevant. Indeed, historians starting with Henry-Russell Hitchcock had little place for architects like Lindeberg whose work was inspired by the past and whose genius was in extending the historical continuum of architecture.

As architects began questioning the orthodoxy of modernism in the 1970s and exploring, under the banner of postmodernism, the relevance of history to contemporary practice, Lindeberg's book became a treasury of brilliant designs that inspired a new generation. But it wasn't until the architect and historian Mark Alan Hewitt reissued the monograph in 1996 that a wider audience discovered his work. Hewitt's incisive essay went beyond the Cortissoz introduction, explaining the foundations of Lindeberg's career, his approach to design, his place among his contemporaries, and the essential qualities of his work.

We embarked on this project because new sources allowed us to build on the work of Cortissoz and Hewitt in telling Lindeberg's story and new color photography by Jonathan Wallen could bring his houses to life. In addition, scholarship over the past twenty years by architectural historians has illuminated the work of Lindeberg's contemporaries, expanding our understanding of the context within which Lindeberg worked.

American architects who began to practice in the first decade of the twentieth century, including Lindeberg and his early partner, Lewis Colt Albro, had the good fortune to enter a vibrant and creative period fueled by a vast expansion of wealth and opportunity. As alumni of the office of McKim, Mead & White, the premier firm of the late 1800s and early 1900s, Lindeberg and Albro had firsthand experience and exposure to the inner workings of American's most vaunted architectural practice. As the country industrialized, the rich—produced by the rapidly expanding economy—turned to McKim, Mead & White and others to create compelling cultural expressions of their wealth and newly achieved social status. Albro and Lindeberg—the primary designer—continued to forge their way as stylistic ambassadors, transforming the lessons of the practice into an architecture that appealed to the more refined tastes of the early twentieth century—a period when the flamboyance and florid archaeology of the earlier decades was becoming passé. At a moment when talent was in high demand and commissions were abundant, Americans were

Portrait of Harrie T. Lindeberg by Gordon Stevenson, 1943.

eager to convey who they were, and firms, even young practices like Albro & Lindeberg, were able to step in and influence the direction of American taste.

Capitalizing on the increased accessibility to the country created by new train lines as well as the rising popularity of the automobile, Albro & Lindeberg—and Lindeberg as a sole practitioner in 1914—chose to specialize in the design of country houses and estates. As New York's population swelled, city dwellers began to establish primary residences within commuting distance or second homes as a balance to the grind of the metropolis. Country clubs—the social hub of country life—proliferated as Americans gravitated towards leisure sports such as golf, tennis, hunting, and polo. This phenomenon was not limited to New York and its environs; Lindeberg found himself at the center of the country house movement as upscale suburbs developed around large cities across the country. His office was in New York, but he completed houses in Houston, Chicago, Detroit, Minneapolis, Terre Haute, Indiana, Dayton, Ohio, and Charlotte, North Carolina, among others. His reputation grew to the national level as his name and distinctive style of architecture garnered more and more attention—starting with the romantic James A. Stillman house in Westchester Country, New York.

Searching for a more defined American idiom, Lindeberg synthesized influences to make his houses legible, rational expressions of program on one hand and associative essays on the other. While his work captured the typical English and colonial influences that were then blossoming in American domestic architecture, his Swedish roots were visible in the houses he designed. He admired vernacular Swedish houses and their rustic attachment to the land, their simplicity having both practical and aesthetic appeal. Rural houses in Sweden were marked by an especially close association with nature, with sod roofs still prevalent in the country until the late nineteenth century. Other features he admired included steep roofs—often at a fifty-degree slope—which efficiently shed rain and snow and allowed passive ventilation to dispel heat in the summer. He was attracted to the pure forms of Swedish houses as well with their solid massing with windows as punched openings rather than as segments of a frame. Lindeberg remarked that Swedish architects did not copy old forms literally but did adhere to their native traditions.

In much the same way, Lindeberg's work pulled from tradition—sources ranging from French, English, and Georgian to colonial—but was instilled with both personality and a supreme sense of its surroundings. Seeking simplicity, even with commissions that were inspired by classical precedents, would remain one of his guiding principles. He admired the long unbroken rooflines, rhythmic groupings of windows, and low-lying masses of the English cottage vernacular—elements he incorporated into his designs time and again. He often added one-story wings to increase a project's charm and to give the effect of being low and chose brick and stone for their colors and textures, modeling what became his signature roof after those of English cottages—thatched, quarried slate, or handmade tile rich in interest. He often arranged shingles artistically to heighten the effect of their interweaving color, to soften the ridges and eaves, and to accentuate what was often a steep pitch.

Critics saw Lindeberg's approach, novel for its fresh and idiosyncratic interpretation of the past, as essentially American because it acknowledged its own time and place first and foremost. He was particularly adept at evolving a style as the appropriate solution to each architectural problem, but making that style his own. In the introduction to Lindeberg's monograph, Cortissoz described his work as having a "definite and original personality" that was also "distinctively American," writing that "a typical Lindeberg house has a fresh, newly minted quality, delightfully unspoilt by derivative influences."[1]

His work had the same poetic power and intuitive sense of massing as the work of his contemporaries, particularly the Philadelphia architects including Mellor, Meigs & Howe, Robert R. McGoodwin, and H. Louis Duhring, who took local Pennsylvania limestone as the rustic material for romantic, picturesque villas that had both classical and vernacular foundations. Likely influenced by the architect Charles A. Platt, Lindeberg saw the floor plan as inexorably

Above: Nineteenth-century houses in Södermalm, Stockholm, Sweden.

Left: Mellor, Meigs & Howe, Arthur E. Newbold Jr. estate, Laverock, Pennsylvania, 1919–25.

linked to the landscape plan, often setting his houses within rooms created by terraces, walls, and hedges to create special connections varying from intimate, tightly contained walled gardens to open swaths of land framing distant views. William Adams Delano once commented that he believed that architecture was the "most difficult of all the Fine Arts. It must serve practical needs and at the same time create an emotion, and the architect's only tools for attaining [this] are such vague qualities as line, mass, proportion and color."[2] "Well-trained architects," he believed, "can give this emotional quality" as Lindeberg manifests with his plans calibrated to enforce highly controlled, specific sequences of experience from entrances that are often through projected gabled forms in romantically asymmetrical facades to more formal and impressively scaled rooms set behind symmetrical garden facades.

Critic C. Matlack Price faithfully chronicled the arc of Lindeberg's career, marking his emergence as an important architect among the second generation of the American Renaissance. As he noted, prophetically, in 1920, "when Harrie T. Lindeberg designed the Stillman house at Pocantico Hills, it was a new sort of country house. Picturesque houses, prior to that time, had mostly been queer or freak houses, and large and important country places had always been impressively formal. Mr. Lindeberg's work at that time forecast the change in tastes and standards that now is so widely apparent.

Future historians may say that Mr. Lindeberg's work was very largely instrumental in bringing about the change in our ideals in country houses."[3] Indeed, Lindeberg's work marked something of a sea change for domestic architecture. Rather than concentrating on formal, classical, aesthetic elements, he focused on making his houses comfortable and livable. While he did not expressly criticize the École des Beaux-Arts, he felt that modern French ideals "with [their] glorification of the past, with their beauty belonging to alien lands, with their magnificence and splendor" were not well suited to domestic living.[4] Rather, his focus on the setting as the driving influence on his designs made each of his houses, regardless of style, all about the sense of place. Lindeberg stressed that architects should "build simply, whether a cottage or castle" by using indigenous materials, proper proportions, and a harmonious outline to create, in his words, "unity of design."[5] Details, such as how solids and voids were grouped, the effect of light and shadow, and even the proportions of the window mullions, played into the effect of quiet dignity. This mastery of composition was matched by an inherent sense of appropriateness that architectural historian G. H. Edgell called "the aristocratic economy of means that proudly avoids self-advertisement and as discretely glorifies the taste of designer and tenant."[6]

But it was Lindeberg's gift as an artist that gave his work an extra dimension. In 1940 Cortissoz remarked,

I have known Charles F. McKim, Stanford White, Henry Bacon, John Russell Pope, and Charles A. Platt. I have seen their genius in operation and I have seen, in each case, with what inevitability the man played into the hands of the artist and how both fused into a single force, drove first and last at the production of a work of art. How inexorable was the resolution of these men to have the work in hand made absolutely right—and beautiful! Harrie Lindeberg is like that and he belongs, on the same high grounds, in the company of the architects I have just mentioned.[7]

Lindeberg's balance of classical and vernacular forms was precisely calibrated; while there were distinct stylistic overtones—Norman, Tudor, Georgian—his blending of elements and motives prevented his work from falling into one distinct category. His houses were classic in the sense that they were logically arranged with practical plans, balanced symmetries, and architectural rhetoric grounded in tradition. But they were also characterized by an emphasis on materials, novel decorative elements—however sparing—and unfolding massing that leaned toward the picturesque and romantic. Yet, as a master of proportion, he could reconcile his low-lying volumes with his massive steep roofs and soaring chimneys, making the ensemble—often dynamically asymmetrical—appear seamless, refined, and charming all at the same time. While Lindeberg's work was deliberate—every detail was studied and executed with great care—it exuded a certain spontaneity and freshness that some of his colleagues' work lacked.

Lindeberg's work is often compared to that of his British contemporary Sir Edwin Lutyens, who was also a virtuoso at weaving seemingly disparate threads: the appealing irregularities of the romantic and vernacular and the more rigorous and logical elements of the classical tradition into his designs. Like Lutyens, Lindeberg designed with a searing insight into the essential qualities of massing and detail. As critic Talbot Hamlin observed, in the best of domestic architecture, "styles came to be inspirations rather than laws and were chosen not merely by fashion *or a priori* wish but developed from the conditions of the design itself."[8] Not an inventor by nature, Lindeberg—like Lutyens—was the consummate innovator, inspired by historic precedent to create a new and compelling feature. The expressive power of Lutyens's brickwork at the Deanery Garden or the blending of vernacular and classical, as seen at Tigbourne Court, is matched by Lindeberg's innate ability to artistically mix inspirations and make them personal, as seen in such details as the leaded repoussé sheathing at the base of an oriel window in a house on Long Island or his prominent chimney masses.

While Lindeberg's work seems most to reflect English precedent, his inspirations were diverse as evidenced by the breadth of his working library. He acquired some 350 volumes over the course of his career from the classic *Edifices de Rome Moderne* by Paul Letarouilly to later books by Frank Lloyd Wright and Le

Above: Sir Edwin Lutyens, Deanery Garden, Sonning, Berkshire, England, 1901.

Above: Sir Edwin Lutyens, Tigbourne Court, Wormley, Surrey, England, 1901.

Below: Ragnar Östberg, Stockholm City Hall, Stockholm, Sweden, 1923.

Corbusier. Ranging from the Middle Ages to mid-twentieth century, the majority of the collection focused on colonial, French, English, and Swedish architecture and French and English furniture and included many books and articles on and by his American contemporaries.[9] He was particularly impressed by the work of such European designers as Swedish architects Ragnar Östberg and Ivar Tengbom and Finnish architect Eliel Saarinen. As Henry-Russell Hitchcock observed, in the Scandinavian countries, architects like Östberg were able to "clothe new forms elegantly with subtle eclectic reminiscence of the past."[10] Östberg's masterpiece, the Stockholm City Hall, was—like Lindeberg's best work—a thoroughly symphonic essay with myriad historical and regional influences marshaled by one creative eye. For smaller-scale details, such as furniture and ironwork, Lindeberg cast a wide net including models from the Vienna Session and the 1925 Exposition des Arts Décoratifs in Paris to such designers as

Frenchmen René Lalique, Edgar Brandt, and Émile-Jacques Ruhlmann as well as Danish designer Kaare Klint. Like Lindeberg, they, too, knew how to manipulate forms and color for artistic effect.

Against the backdrop of the first decades of the twentieth century, Lindeberg's work found its place in America's canon of country house architecture—a development supported by the unbridled economic growth of the 1920s. Where Lindeberg's early work was celebrated in the architectural press for its singularly personal interpretations of historical example, his late works were designed when the profession radically rejected history. However, in Lindeberg's case, designs from the end of his career, when the nation was in the grip of the Depression and modernism had pulled the carpet from under the old guard, offer a key to understanding his entire body of work and reveal principles that underlie even his earliest projects. Lindeberg's central theme, simplicity in design, is evident throughout, from houses that look elaborate to our eyes to the spare, stripped modern approach of his last works.

The Depression halted much of the period's building boom, but Lindeberg held on with several plum commissions for embassies abroad. While house commissions were few and far between, he redirected his focus with a series of simpler "cellular" houses based on his system of modules. These pared-down houses, underpinned by classical proportioning, were Lindeberg's answer to the challenge posed by modernism as it swept the country in the 1930s and 1940s. Today, a remarkable number of Lindeberg's houses stand unscathed. Many continue to be private homes, cherished and maintained by their owners for what they are: comfortable houses with a domestic spirit, but at the same time beautifully executed works of art that reveal Lindeberg's pursuit of unity in his designs.

BACKGROUND AND BEGINNINGS

Harrie Thomas Lindeberg (né Harry) was born in Bergen Point, New Jersey, on April 10, 1880. His father, Theodore Ferdinand Lindeberg (1834–1909), a naturalized citizen, had left Stockholm in 1859 to lay down roots in the United States, eventually settling in Hoboken and Jersey City. While his grandfather, Fredric Eriksson Lindeberg (b. 1799), worked as a coachman and bookkeeper in Stockholm, many of the men on Lindeberg's side of the family had been silversmiths.[11] Many Swedes left for America during the vibrant years following the Civil War where arable land, limited in their homeland, was abundant and new industry offered employment opportunities. While Theodore Lindeberg arrived before the major wave of Swedish emigration, his exodus to America suggests that he came in search of better economic prospects. At some point, he was involved in shipbuilding on the New Jersey waterfront, but he also worked for more than twenty years as a silk importer. Throughout the 1870s and 1880s, he maintained a Canal Street business, Lindeberg & Schwab, with his partner Samuel Schwab, dealing in neckties and scarves. His wife and Lindeberg's mother, Augusta Mathilda Eleanora Österlund (1839–1896), followed Theodore to the United States in the 1860s, at least ten years before Harrie was born. But while the Lindebergs chose to emigrate, Augusta still wanted her children—Harrie and his brother, Frederick, two years older—to be exposed to the Swedish way of life. In 1884 Augusta sent the boys to live with an uncle where they attended Swedish public schools, absorbed their Swedish heritage, and internalized such qualities embodied by a thorough, methodical, and industrious approach to work and study—hallmarks of the Swedish mentality that Lindeberg embraced throughout his life.[12] Though we can't be certain about what aspects of Swedish culture impressed Lindeberg, there is evidence of attitudes that were strongly associated with the Swedish national character. His parents were Lutheran, as members of what amounted to the national church, Svenska Kyrkan. The Swedish Lutheran creed emphasized the direct relationship between the believer and God. Like their architecture, which generally eschewed overt displays of ornament and wealth, the Swedish Lutheran saw his religion as a manifestation of a national spirit of independence and ascetic strength. In both design and architecture as in their civil pageants, the Swedes reveled in their bond with nature. As a central part of their national ethos, athleticism was considered as important as intellectual development. From the mossy, rough woven roofs to the naturalistic rendering of man-made materials like brick, the Swedish taste persisted in bringing classical influences down to earth.

In the United States, the Lindebergs chose to live in Hoboken so that their sons could attend the Stevens School, the newly opened preparatory school for the Stevens Institute of Technology. The Institute, founded in 1870, provided rigorous training for aspiring engineers and the Stevens School, built in 1888 on Hudson Street, prepared potential students not only with high school subjects as Greek, Latin, and French but also important prerequisites such as mechanical drawing and mathematics.[13] Lindeberg's slight stutter and Swedish accent made his early school years difficult but, excelling in drawing and sketching, he found a refuge in skills that would serve him well in his career. Both boys were artistically inclined: while his brother showed promise playing the piano, Harrie, at the age of seven, began covering the walls of his family's house with drawings of flowers, people, and houses.[14] To encourage his sons' talents, Theodore Lindeberg brought Harrie and Fred to visit the famous Swedish-American engineer John Ericsson just before his death in 1889. The call on Ericsson, inventor of the first screw-propeller steamer, the *USS Princeton*, and the first armored ship with a rotating turret, the *USS Monitor*, at his house on Beach Street was one of Lindeberg's most vivid childhood memories. While showing the boys his workshop filled with sketches and plans for various inventions and machines, Ericsson talked at length about the value of training, the importance of the brain and hands, and how the ability to accurately convey ideas with the hands was a key to success, particularly in the realm of art, science, and music.[15]

When Harrie was eleven, his father began to experience business setbacks and the boys, aware of the family's financial reverses, attempted to help out. Ever resourceful, they bought ice at wholesale from the barges on the New Jersey riverfront and sold it for a small profit to tenants in their building. Since many neighbors were professors at the Stevens Institute, they were brought into contact with many of the brightest thinkers in the area. Despite the hard work, Harrie found time for hobbies and fun. He was interested in boats and built a beautifully crafted small cruising canoe, which he would sail down the Passaic River, through Newark Bay and across to Sandy Hook. There, he would moor his canoe to the houseboat of Van Dearing Perrine, an American painter and educator.

Frederick and Harrie Lindeberg.

After high school, Harrie decided to pursue architecture—a discipline that satisfied his love of drawing and his aptitude for engineering and draftsmanship. At seventeen, he started working for George A. Freeman, an architect of large houses, many of which were designed for members of the Whitney family, a prominent clan at the center of New York social and business circles. Although he was young and inexperienced, the fastidious and industrious Lindeberg made a strong impression on clients of the firm. In 1898 he was sent to inspect the foundations of a ballroom addition in Southampton for Charles T. Barney, president of the Knickerbocker Trust Company and brother-in-law of William Collins Whitney. When Lindeberg arrived in

Long Island to do his job, the builder refused to show him the foundations. Lindeberg waited for the builder to leave for the day and took a shovel and pick and uncovered the foundations himself, revealing that the pier footings had been improperly installed. In the midst of this discovery, Barney arrived at the house, and Lindeberg was forced to explain what had happened. The aspiring architect's meticulousness won Barney's confidence; later, Barney asked McKim, Mead & White to assign Lindeberg to supervise the construction of his house at 67 Park Avenue.[16]

In 1896 Lindeberg started night classes in the Antique School at the National Academy of Design and worked for Freeman during the day. In the Antique School, students learned to draw from plaster casts in the Academy collection, which included reproductions of nearly all of the most important works of ancient sculpture. During this period he also studied in the Atelier Masqueray, a studio founded by Emmanuel L. Masqueray, just down the block from the Academy at 123 East 23rd Street. The French-born Masqueray had studied at the École des Beaux-Arts under classicist Charles Laisné and the more romantic Neo-Grec designer Léon Ginain. He came to the United States to work at Carrère & Hastings—both John Carrère and Thomas Hastings had been in Paris with him—and later Richard Morris Hunt. In 1892 he opened his own atelier to provide aspiring architects unable to go to Paris the option for serious study. The curriculum was based strictly on the Beaux-Arts system and open twenty-four hours a day, exposing students to the competitive environment and hard work of its Parisian model, where progress was measured in terms of *esquisses* and *projets*. Known as a capable designer and educator, Masqueray assigned problems and came in twice a week to offer criticism.

Lindeberg began working at McKim, Mead & White in 1901 after Charles McKim discovered his skills as a designer and supervisor—perhaps through Charles T. Barney or Masqueray's atelier. At the turn of the century, the firm was at its peak, employing upwards of 150 draftsmen turning out one successful project after another. A stint at McKim, Mead & White was a highly coveted position for an aspiring

McKim, Mead & White, Addition to the rear of the Harvard Club, West 45th Street, New York, 1905.

architect, and the principals were very gifted at hiring exceptionally skilled designers to carry out much of the work. As H. Van Buren Magonigle, who primarily worked for Stanford White, recalled, "White's way was to load a job on us youngsters way beyond our powers and force a result out of us if it could be squeezed out—sometimes it couldn't. But it was wonderful training if you didn't crack under the strain—it made a man of you—or it didn't."[17] McKim was known as the perfectionist of the partners, laboring to achieve the best possible results and proportions in every design. But regardless of the partners' differing styles, the office provided rigorous training with the principals cultivating the talents of its employees, in turn molding the next generation of architects and firms, including Carrère & Hastings, York & Sawyer, and Henry Bacon, to mention just a few.

In addition to supervising the Barney house on the corner of 38th Street and Park Avenue, Lindeberg oversaw the addition of Harvard Hall to the firm's 1894 clubhouse on West 44th Street. This was no small feat

Above: McKim, Mead & White, Thomas Jefferson Coolidge Jr. house, Marble Palace, Manchester, Massachusetts, 1902–4.

Right: McKim, Mead & White, James L. Breese house, The Orchard, Southampton, New York, 1898–1907.

for Lindeberg, a 24-year-old with no college degree whom McKim put in charge of four older graduates of the Harvard School of Architecture. Challenges notwithstanding, Lindeberg rose to the task. At the opening of the addition in 1905, James K. Higginson, speaking on behalf of the building committee, showered Lindeberg with praise, declaring:

When I speak of our architects, I have in mind the young gentleman, a member of [McKim, Mead & White's] staff, to whose special care this work was entrusted. I mean Mr. Harry [sic] Lindeberg. He it was whom we always saw. He was never too busy to meet us. Every suggestion that we made was carefully considered and where possible adopted. Crammed to the mouth with the details of the work, he could answer any question at any moment. I used to half bother his life out by asking the same question over and over again, for I confess too much thick-headedness in such matters, and I found it difficult to understand the plans. But Mr. Lindeberg was patience itself and never wearied of explaining and re-explaining until we all understood. I wish to give Mr. Lindeberg my warm, grateful thanks, and I want you, brothers, to do the same.[18]

During his tenure at McKim, Mead & White, Lindeberg worked on Thomas Jefferson Coolidge Jr.'s Marble Palace in Manchester, Massachusetts, an elegant Georgian house inspired by such Southern masterpieces as Monticello—the country seat of Coolidge's direct ancestor—as well as the brick houses of Portsmouth, Newburyport, and Salem. McKim, a close family friend of the Coolidges, assigned

Lindeberg onto the project. Under McKim's tutelage, Lindeberg also worked on The Orchard, financier and photographer James L. Breese's house in Southampton, Long Island. While both McKim and White had a hand in its design, which stretched between the years 1898 and 1907, McKim was primarily responsible for the exterior, inspired by Southern colonial architecture, particularly Mount Vernon, while White designed the interior. By 1903, as Lindeberg began working on Breese's house, he was already enmeshed in several other projects. As McKim explained to Breese, "I have made arrangements to have Mr. Lindeberg,of our office, undertake your work. There is a heavy load on his shoulders, and I trust that you are not in such a hurry about it, that the work will have to suffer."[19]

In 1904, while still at McKim, Mead & White, Lindeberg joined Horace B. Mann and Perry R. MacNeille in practice to form Mann, MacNeille & Lindeberg. With Mann and MacNeille, he worked on a group of Elizabethan residences for professors of the University of Chicago, a Georgian townhouse in Chicago for E. F. Robbins, a Colonial Revival house in Glen Ridge, New Jersey as well as a subdivision in Rochelle Heights, New York.[20] This partnership endured until March 1906 when Lindeberg forged out on his own with another colleague, Lewis Colt Albro.

According to the firm records, Albro began at McKim, Mead & White in 1895 at the age of 19. Born in Paris to Princeton-educated Lewis K. Albro from Elizabeth, New Jersey, and Mary Colt Albro, Albro was raised in Pittsfield, Massachusetts—his mother's hometown—where his father worked as a lawyer. After he attended the Metropolitan Art School at the Metropolitan Art Museum—part of Columbia University—he joined McKim, Mead & White, becoming a seasoned assistant. He worked closely on the designs for the new campus at Columbia University, particularly its centerpiece Low Library. Through his work on a Colonial Revival townhouse at 127 East 73rd Street, Albro forged a friendship with its owner Charles Dana Gibson, the well-known illustrator.[21] It was not uncommon, during this period, for young architects to carry out projects on the side and Albro continued to

McKim, Mead & White, Charles Dana Gibson house, 127 East 73rd Street, New York, 1902–4.

work for Gibson. In 1903 he designed a shingle style summer house, Indian Landing, on 700 Acre Island in Maine; he also traveled through England, France, and Italy. Similarly, several years after the completion of Marble Palace, Coolidge called upon Albro & Lindeberg to rework the loggia, a semi-detached wing, which they transformed into an enclosed summer living room lined with trelliswork and centered on a large fireplace.

For Lindeberg, 1906 was a year of both triumph and tragedy. In April, a month after opening the practice, he married Eugenie Lee Quin, a daughter of his landlady, Mrs. Joseph P. Quin. Along with several other artists and architects, Lindeberg had rented a room at the Quin family's brownstone at 16 West 9th Street. Lindeberg's colleague from McKim, Mead & White, artist James Wall Finn, known for his ceiling murals in the reading room at the New York Public Library and librarian's room at the Morgan Library, was also a boarder. In 1905 Finn married Florence Lee Quin, Eugenie's younger sister, and Lindeberg soon followed suit, only to lose his bride six months later to tuberculosis.[22]

Lindeberg riding at Foxhollow Farm, Rhinebeck, New York, 1912.

Around 5 feet 8 inches tall and of medium build, Lindeberg had brown hair and hooded blue eyes. As a young practitioner, he had almost a boyish quality about him—perhaps due to his height. In his twenties, he joined the Cavalry Troop of Squadron A and also moonlighted as a jockey, but a bad fall during a steeplechase in Virginia in 1913 ended his riding career. However, as Lindeberg grew into his profession, he became a more commanding presence, with a quiet confidence and air of authority. Affable and approachable, as one relative recalls, he was also articulate and soft spoken—never pushy.[23] But professionally, if he felt he was correct, he could be insistent and persuasive—almost imperious.[24] One interviewer wrote, "There is much of the artist—the portrait painter—in the man's own appearance and in his quick, deft movements."[25] Lindeberg was very precise in his appearance, often wearing ascots and tweed jackets and, later in life, brushing his hair—then a bright silver—straight back. He even came up with the idea of the "four-pointer," a sartorial invention that one article accurately described as "defying classification."

Fed up with traveling and packing with limited space, he designed a shirt with a collar, built–in tie and shorts all in one piece. The "four-pointer" drew the attention of gossip columns and even *The New Yorker* but Lindeberg downplayed his invention, claiming that "architects are always interested in functional design."[26]

By the time Lindeberg had completed his tenure at McKim, Mead & White, he had transcended the challenge of his modest background and found a secure place among his peers. With his dignified carriage, genteel manners, and polished way of dressing, Lindeberg came to embody the image of a gentleman architect. He was elected into the American Institute of Architects in 1939 and the National Academy of Design in 1949 as one of its twenty-five architect members. In 1948 he became one of "America's Immortals" as a member of what was then known as the National Institute of Arts & Letters.[27] Because only members could select new fellows, election to the National Institute was long considered the highest formal recognition of artistic merit in the United States. He supplemented his professional associations, such as the Architectural League of New York and the Beaux-Arts Institute of Design, with social clubs including the arts-oriented Players and Coffee House and the more stalwart Knickerbocker and River Clubs. With friends ranging from artists, writers, architects, playwrights, bankers, executives, manufacturers to professors and physicians, his circle reflected, as one biographer commented, "his innate sociability and lively intellectual curiousity."[28]

ALBRO & LINDEBERG: 1906–1914

The firm's first major commissions, the James A. Stillman house in Pocantico Hills and the Tracy Dows house in Rhinebeck, New York, came through connections the partners formed at McKim, Mead & White. Stillman's father, James J. Stillman, chairman of National City Bank, had been a client of the firm during the period when Lindeberg was working under McKim, while the Dows commission came through Albro's association with Charles Dana Gibson, who recommended the architect to his good friend Tracy

Dows, the son of one of the country's most successful grain merchants, and his wife, Alice.

The division of responsibilities between the partners was set early on: Lindeberg took charge of design and the drafting room, and Albro oversaw construction and the business end of the practice. They leased office space at 481 Fifth Avenue in a Rogers Peet & Company building, where the well-known men's clothing company operated a store at street level. In 1906 the New York Public Library was rising across the street and Grand Central Terminal and its associated buildings was just underway to the northeast. As Lindeberg threw himself into the early commissions, the young firm found its niche, and swift success, in the realm of country house design. And when the Stillman and Dows estates, known as Mondanne (see pages 50–55) and Foxhollow Farm (see pages 56–63) respectively, were completed around 1910, they received widespread critical acclaim in the architectural press.

Unlike any house the critics had seen before, Mondanne was regarded as almost a work of genius and a clear break from the more academic eclecticism of the first generation of the American Renaissance. Architectural critic A. H. Forbes thought that it "seem[ed] especially curious as the work of men fresh from the McKim, Mead & White office," writing in *Architecture* that he "imagine[d] that was the result of the reaction of a brilliant and original mind, long trammeled within the limits of the careful formalism of that great firm."[29] In 1922 architect Aymar Embury II commented: "I do not think that the best modern work is any better than the best work of fifteen years ago. I do not recall any country house more beautiful than McKim, Mead & White's Breese house at Southampton, or Charles Platt's Manor House at Glen Cove or Harr[ie] Lindeberg's Stillman house at Pleasantville."[30] Notable for its almost organic connection to its landscape, Mondanne represented a sculptural approach and the first form that would become the archetype that would be known, by the 1920s, as "the Lindeberg roof."

While its design was more conventional and formally Georgian, Foxhollow Farm was heralded as a modern and tasteful country retreat and named one of the twelve best houses in America by *Country Life in America* in 1916. Lindeberg anchored the symmetrical entrance facade with a broad colonnade of eight tapered Doric columns, a design approach he used in later projects.[31] But despite diametrically different architecture—a testament to Lindeberg's skill and range—Mondanne and Foxhollow Farm manifested similar traits: the Lindeberg roof (at Foxhollow laid in shades of green and gray), sturdy rhythmically placed chimneys, and an air of age and engagement with the landscape. Built beneath a canopy of existing elms, the manor at Foxhollow Farm—like Mondanne—seemed thoroughly embedded in its surroundings. As the architectural critic Russell F. Whitehead noted:

Each house was a complete success in its way, although they were about as different as it is possible to conceive that houses of about the same size, and built not many miles apart, could be. Especially was this amazing because each seemed so absolutely appropriate to its site, the easy graceful Stillman house to the soft, rolling, treeless hillside on which it is placed, and the simple and formal Dows house to the level lawn, shaded by great elms, which made its setting.[32]

For the most part, however, the firm's early houses were smaller than these two great estates. In their eight years of practice, Albro & Lindeberg designed a series of houses—both suburban and summer —in such

Above: James A. Stillman estate, Mondanne, Pocantico Hills, New York, 1906–10.

Right: Tracy Dows estate, Foxhollow Farm, Rhinebeck, New York, 1906–10.

Opposite: Lindeberg in Tracy Dows's office at Foxhollow Farm, Rhinebeck, New York, 1913.

places as Hewlett, New York, the Fieldston section of the Bronx, Forest Hills Gardens in Queens, and Short Hills, New Jersey. As Lindeberg noted in 1909, "The increased desire for country life, and outdoor living, has given rise to a demand for modest homes designed with the same high standard of work and care in detail that the architect gives to his larger [projects]."[33] By today's standards, most of their houses are quite sizable, but they were much smaller than the Gilded Age mansions designed by McKim, Mead & White. Modest and well-designed, they were indicative of a widespread revival and interest in domestic architecture or, in Lindeberg's words, "an immense upspringing of individual delight in home construction."[34]

In 1907 the Hewlett Bay Company purchased a 650-acre tract of land on the south shore of Long Island between the villages of Hewlett and East Rockaway overlooking Hewlett Bay. The directors of the company saw the potential of the land—formerly owned by attorney Joseph Auerbach and originally farmed by the Hewlett family—as the grounds for an enclave of luxury summer houses. The group developed

Above: Carleton Macy house, Meadowwood, Hewlett, New York, 1907.

Right: Tracy Harris house, Wisteria Lodge, Hewlett, New York, 1907.

plans for a new train station and brought in landscape architect Thomas W. Sears, an alumnus of Olmsted Brothers, to lay out a series of five-acre lots. All of the directors of the Hewlett Bay Company commissioned Albro & Lindeberg houses. For company president Carleton Macy—also president of Queensborough Gas & Electric—the firm designed an Italian-inspired stucco villa with a two-story circular bay, large piazza, and a series of comfortable and conveniently planned rooms.[35] Meanwhile, the firm used Colonial Revival vocabulary for attorney and real estate developer Tracy H. Harris's cottage, Wisteria Lodge, and for G. D. Gregory's house, which included symmetrical loggias extending from the garden front. Twin Gables, for Macy's cousin, financier Valentine E. Macy, was a formal brick Tudor house with two gables on the garden facade. In total, Albro & Lindeberg designed eight houses in Hewlett Bay Park and the neighboring town of Woodmere, another development connected to Carleton Macy.[36] While the designs drew on a variety of stylistic sources, they shared a similar form, incorporating loggias and steeply pitched roofs with artistic shingling and presenting an asymmetrical entrance front with a more symmetrical approach for the garden facade. The houses for the Hewlett Bay Company, built between 1907 and 1912, reflect the aesthetic of the early summer cottages they designed in East Hampton, the north shore of Long Island, and Westchester.

Above: Albert H. Marckwald house, Short Hills, New Jersey, 1908.

Right: House developed by Crestmount Reality, Montclair, New Jersey, c. 1910.

In Short Hills, New Jersey, Albro & Lindeberg designed several houses as part of Stewart Hartshorn's garden suburb. Starting in the 1870s, Hartshorn, a wealthy investor and manufacturer who invented the spring-roller window shade, set about creating a residential park in the rolling hills of Millburn near his house, in commuting distance of the city. Setting the architectural bar high, Hartshorn commissioned McKim, Mead & White to design a shingle style music hall near the train station to lure buyers, and he reviewed all designs to ensure that the houses were interesting, tasteful, and well-suited to the area. During the 1890s and 1900s, Short Hills grew into an established town with Hartshorn continuing to attract buyers with building lots. Albro & Lindeberg designed two houses in 1908. Their large stucco house for bond broker Albert H. Marckwald incorporated a half-timber entry and a gable front containing the stair hall lit by a double-height casement window—a design element the firm used frequently—as well as a boldly raking roof pierced with dormers, an angled library wing, and a more formal and symmetrical garden front. Banker Charles E. Van Vleck Jr.'s stone house featured a similarly dramatic roofline, wood timbered details, several sleeping porches and shuttered windows. Meanwhile, the clapboard house the firm designed in 1911, known as Hartshorn House #77, was more idiosyncratic. Its design was dominated by a hipped

Hugh Mullen house, Forest Hills Gardens, New York, 1914.

Boardman Robinson house, Forest Hills Gardens, New York, 1914.

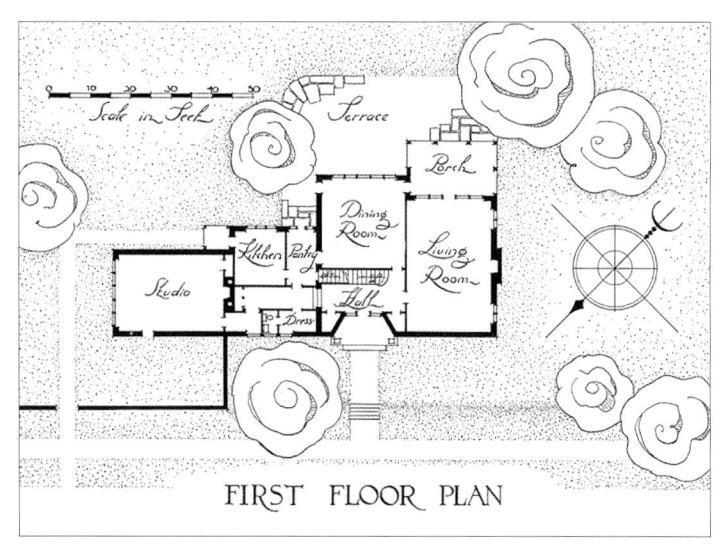

Plan of the Robinson House.

roof sweeping down to the ground and displaying an amalgam of Georgian and picturesque details, including a hooded stair hall window. Experimenting with various styles and forms, the firm executed a similar design in nearby Montclair for Crestmount Realty on a hillside site. Here, the low sweep of the roofline of the English-style stucco house was amplified by side porches which, as one critic noted, made "the structure seem to settle down snugly to the ground," an attribute that would frequently mark Lindeberg's work.[37]

In Queens, the Russell Sage Foundation was in the process of developing Forest Hills Gardens, a planned community built in conjunction with the opening of the Pennsylvania Railroad's tunnel under the East River, which connected midtown Manhattan to the Long Island Railroad. The foundation, established by Margaret Olivia Slocum Sage, conceived Forest Hills Gardens to demonstrate that a well-planned, tastefully designed, and economically accessible suburban village could improve the living conditions of those of modest means and, in turn, present an influential model to guide future development. Grosvenor Atterbury designed a picturesque village square with an inn centered on the train station and a series of artistically conceived houses, semi-detached houses and row houses carried out in a combination of textured lammie brick, red and brown shingles, and cast concrete details; Frederick Law Olmsted Jr. designed a curvilinear street plan radiating out from the station square. While Atterbury designed most of the early buildings, in 1910 the foundation invited other architects, including J. T. Tubby, Wilson Eyre, Aymar Embury II, and Albro & Lindeberg, to design groups of houses to create an "agreeable variety . . . from different methods of treatment."[38] Sympathetic to Atterbury's design aesthetic, Albro & Lindeberg's group of semi-detached stucco houses on Puritan Avenue featured characteristically steeply pitched roofs with dormers and half-timbering details. The firm's detached houses included Hugh Mullen's center hall Colonial Revival house with several loggias and for the artist Boardman Robinson, a sturdy gray stucco house with an indented entrance, large studio, French-blue trim, and a roof shingled in shades of mottled red, blue, and black.[39]

Clayton Cooper house, Riverdale, New York, 1913.

Just north of Manhattan, in the Fieldston section of Riverdale, the firm designed several houses for the Delafield Estate. Comprising 250 acres—originally acquired by Major Joseph Delafield in 1829 and named after his ancestral estate in England—the tract of land became increasingly attractive when the city's first subway, the IRT, was extended to 242nd Street in 1908. As a result, the Delafield Estate began to slowly develop its land into a private residential park or "country in the city" as one promotional pamphlet proclaimed.[40] Engineer Albert E. Wheeler laid out the street plan, and the rugged rocky terrain, which had impeded development up until the 1900s, inspired a range of imaginatively conceived houses that absorbed and enhanced the site's natural landscape. The first lots were sold in 1910, and by 1914, eighteen houses were up. Eight years later, there were eighty. Stylistically, Albro & Lindeberg's (and later Lindeberg's) work incorporated fieldstone and stucco as a reflection of the rock outcroppings and were picturesque in an English cottage manner. For the most part, the houses—four in all—reflected Lindeberg's affinity for steep roofs, heavy chimneys, overhanging eaves, and loggias. Completed between 1913 and 1915, they reflected the architectural tenor of Fieldston during the first years of its development.[41] One house, developed by the Delafield Estate and sold to Elizabeth and Clayton Cooper, won an Honorable Mention for the House of the Year in 1913 by *Country Life in America*.[42]

For the most part, Albro & Lindeberg's houses displayed similar design attributes despite their varied stylistic guises. Frequently, Lindeberg extended the service wing to the north off of the front facade, creating a more informal, asymmetrical approach, and oriented the formal rooms to the south, where sunlight and breezes prevailed. He then composed the garden front in a more symmetrical manner, balancing it with loggias on either end. The repetition of this organizational technique was masked by Lindeberg's use of materials and architectural expression—which one critic described as "a free collection of the required material from whatever source it may have been derived, and the assemblage of the further parts into a beautiful and unified and above all a coherent whole."[43] His early 1910s houses for banker Orville Babcock in Lake Forest, Illinois, financier Thomas H. Kerr in White Plains, New York, stock broker Arthur W. Rossiter in Glen Cove, New York, and businessman Philip B. Jennings in Bennington, Vermont, owner of the Knickerbocker Watch Company, were strikingly

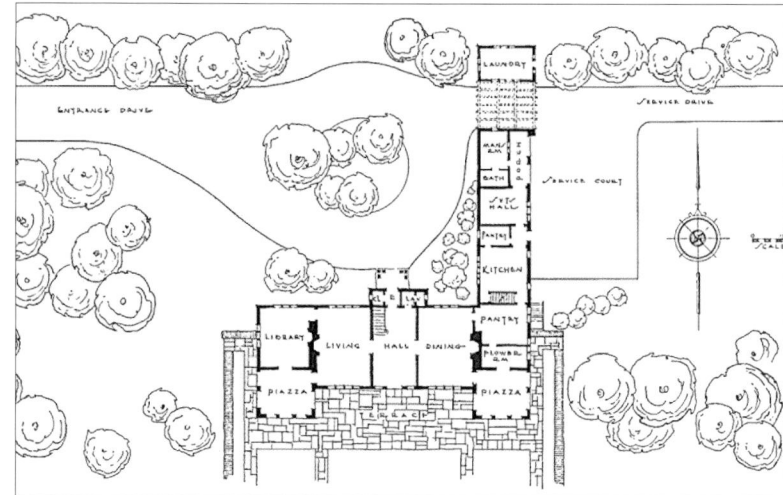

Above left: Orville E. Babcock house, Two Gables, Lake Forest, Illinois (later known as the Laurance Armour house), 1910.

Above right: Plan of the Babcock/Armour house.

Right: Thomas H. Kerr house, White Plains, New York, 1910.

Below left: Arthur W. Rossiter house, Cedarcroft, Glen Cove, New York, 1911.

Below right: Philip B. Jennings house, Wayside, Bennington, Vermont, 1912.

Left: J. Langdon Erving house, 62 East 80th Street, New York, 1906.

Center: Edward T. Cockcroft house, 59 East 77th Street, New York, 1907.

Right: Mary Hale Cunningham house, 124 East 55th Street, New York, 1909.

similar in plan.[44] However, the brick and half-timber Babcock house was vernacular and picturesque, the stucco and tile-roofed Kerr house was more Mediterranean in inspiration and the Rossiter house seemed vaguely Italian. Meanwhile, the white clapboard Jennings house reflected the character of the colonial architecture in rural Vermont. Lindeberg's ability to combine the more formal elements of classicism with picturesque aplomb made his houses seem novel and modern, natural and almost inevitable.

Lindeberg designed most of his city houses during his partnership with Albro. In the first decades of the twentieth century, architects were kept busy transforming the tired midblock stretches of brownstones, most of which were built in the 1870s and 1880s, into stylish and modern townhouses with English basements. As the architecture of monotonous row house strips fell out favor, it became increasingly popular to renovate them—as opposed to building anew—as a means to create up-to-date single-family houses more affordably. In many cases, these projects were considered alterations because the party walls of the brownstone were left intact while the stoops were removed and the street facades were extended out to the lot line. The interiors were reworked to reflect the relocation of the stair to the center of the house, a measure to maximize the window spans to the north and south.[45] Most of Albro & Lindeberg's townhouses fell into this category. In 1906 they began reworking a house for J. Langdon Erving and his wife, Alice Rutherford Erving, at 62 East 80th Street. The Colonial Revival townhouse, which the architects organized with a series of string courses, was reminiscent of the Charles Dana Gibson house. One year later, Viola and Edward T. Cockcroft,

Richard M. Hoe garage and apartment, 163 East 69 Street, New York, 1909.

the son of wealthy landowner John van Voorhees Cockcroft, asked the firm to transform 59 East 77th Street from a nondescript brownstone—one of a row of eight from the 1870s—into what was ostensibly a Federal-style brick townhouse. A friend of Albro's, Cockcroft had also recently enlisted the firm to design Little Burlees, Albro & Lindeberg's first summer house in East Hampton (see pages 64–71). For the couple's New York house, they incorporated the second and third floor windows into a larger opening to organize the facade and combined Italianate elements, such as a tiled roof and heavy denticulated cornice, to create a more eclectic effect. They used this strategy again for their renovation for Mary Hale Cunningham, a wealthy widow with four children. Albro & Lindeberg designed a new Tudor facade for an existing French flat at 124 East 55th Street with a monumental frame unifying the second- and third-floor windows and terra-cotta spandrel panels, creating one colossal element. Lindeberg mixed Tudor

details, such as the brick gable, narrow multi-pane windows, and rough-faced purple brick with more classical elements like the paired Doric columns at the base.[46] Meanwhile, the Colonial Revival character of the garage and apartment that the firm designed at 163 East 69th Street for banker Richard M. Hoe—the brother-in-law Tracy Dows—was more straightforward with shuttered windows, blind arched windows on the piano nobile, and keystones.[47]

By the end of 1913, when the partnership was only eight years old, Albro & Lindeberg had completed more than fifty substantial projects, many of which had been featured in the architectural press. In 1912 both *The Architectural Record* and *Architecture* dedicated an entire issue to their work, and the firm produced *Domestic Architecture*, a book featuring their houses. Lindeberg was only in his early thirties, but his work had come to be recognizably "Lindeberg" by this time. As C. Matlack Price observed, "It is a significant fact that Mr. Lindeberg's houses very soon became recognizable, even to the lay observer, as his work, and this is because there may be said to exist, in all of them, a dominant note which can only be called 'personality.'"[48] Nonetheless, in January 1914, Albro and Lindeberg opted to dissolve their partnership. Both men retained offices at 2 West 47th Street, where the firm had moved in 1912, but Lindeberg operated his own practice and Albro became associated with Paul Phipps, an architect who had trained under Lutyens and was the brother-in-law of his good friend Charles Dana Gibson.[49]

Though there is no record of the reasons for the separation, the change did offer Albro who, as the minder of the business side of the firm, had had no opportunity to design, the chance to exercise his creative talents. Indeed, during the next ten years, before his death in 1924, he put his stamp on several commissions. In 1916 he married Mary Pace Groner, the daughter of James B. Pace of Richmond, known then as the "tobacco king" of his day. This connection likely led to the commission for Hillbrook (1916) in Rye, New York, the estate of George Arents Jr., a Virginian involved in the American Tobacco Company who eventually patented cigar and cigarette rolling machines. Over the next decade, Albro designed a number of houses in Albany,

30

New York, Kentucky, Ohio, Westchester County, and Connecticut as well as Cedar Brook Farm—an old farmhouse he modernized and restored for himself and his wife in Webotuck, New York.[50]

HARRIE T. LINDEBERG: 1914–1930

By 1914 Lindeberg's social circumstances had changed considerably. In July of that year, he married Lucia E. Hull (1885–1978), the younger daughter of George Huntington Hull, president of the American Pig Iron Warrant Company. A native of Louisville, Kentucky, Lucia relocated to New York in the 1890s, where her parents took an apartment at 21 East 82nd Street and began spending time in Tuxedo Park. One newspaper reported that the couple met in Newport when Lucia was a debutante, which may be true, but it is likely that Harrie met Lucia through Tracy and Alice Dows and their circle. During and after the construction of Foxhollow Farm, Lindeberg spent time with the Dowses and their close friends and Rhinebeck neighbors, Helen and Vincent Astor. In turn, the Hulls were old family friends of Helen Astor, who married Lucia's brother, Lytle Hull, after divorcing Vincent Astor.

Free-spirited and social, Lucia Hull was a poet and a photographer and was reputed at one point to have almost eloped with Mark Twain.[51] She and Harrie had two children, Linda and Lytle, but the couple divorced in 1925. After their marriage, the couple began spending time in Locust Valley at a cottage called Wisteria Lodge, and Lindeberg, who was a member of The Players and the Riding Club at the time of their marriage, joined several more clubs, including the Seawanhaka Corinthian Yacht Club, the Piping Rock Club, and the Nassau Country Club. In 1926 Lindeberg designed his own house, West Gate Lodge, in Locust Valley, set on eight acres next to the Piping Rock golf course (see pages 178–85).

Through Lucia's social position, the new club connections, and his own reputation, Lindeberg's prominence as an architect continued to expand. Two West 47th Street, a new loft building and the first commercial enterprise on a street still populated by brownstones and front gardens, became something of an architectural center. In addition to mantel dealer W. H. Jackson on the ground floor, Elsie de Wolfe operated a two-floor studio in the building and architect Bertram Grosvenor Goodhue's offices were in the penthouse.[52]

As a sole practitioner, Lindeberg quickly garnered a string of substantial house commissions in New Jersey, Connecticut, and Long Island as well as in Lake Forest, Illinois; Greenville, Delaware; and Orono, Minnesota. However, with the onset of the war, it wasn't until the 1920s that Lindeberg's office was fully established. During this period, he engaged a sizable staff of talented architects to manage the projects, which could require the attention of up to six associates at a time. Belgian-born draftsman Daniel Neilinger and Herman Brookman, who went on to a successful practice in Oregon in the 1920s, were associates of longstanding, and many other architects soon joined the ranks.[53] Like McKim, Lindeberg seemed to attract talent and, in turn, he nurtured and encouraged that talent. Both Alberta Raffl Pfeiffer, who later practiced in Old Lyme, Connecticut, and John F. Staub, who became Houston's most acclaimed residential architect, were initially drawn to Lindeberg's office because his work was of the highest caliber they had seen published.

Maurice Fatio, a young Swiss architect, spent time in the office in the early 1920s before forming a practice in New York and Palm Beach with William A. Treanor, an executive architect who had been with Lindeberg for ten years. In letters to his family, Fatio wrote that his "work [was] very interesting. [Lindeberg] g[a]ve [him] a lot of freedom, and seem[ed] in general quite satisfied with [his] tastes and ideas."[54] Lindeberg also encouraged him, as Fatio noted: "Lindeberg is very interested in my work; he often asks me why I don't want to establish myself in America."[55] Meanwhile, Pfeiffer, one of the first women to graduate from the University of Illinois School of Architecture, noted he was very accommodating, letting her go for six months in both 1928 and 1930 to travel to Europe and England and welcoming her back each time.[56] In 1925, however, as Pfeiffer recounted, Lindeberg's office was unprepared for female architects. Lindeberg put her in the library, away from the swearing in the drafting room, but eventually moved her in with the men. Seeing her talent and industriousness, Lindeberg gave Pfeiffer more work than some of her male colleagues, and after she left in 1931, he was happy to hire female architects seeking work in the office.[57]

Lindeberg's salaries were miserably low, but the experience gained was valuable. When Fatio spoke to the chief designer about potentially increasing his compensation, he was told that "all the employees were paid very little, but that they consider this to be an office where one can acquire the best experience for later on, and that it is a very desirable place to work."[58] Pfeiffer agreed, writing that she "learned more about construction, detail drawings, specification, than [she] had learned in 4 years of school."[59] In addition to Pfeiffer, Staub, Brookman, Fatio, and Treanor, many others went on to form successful practices in various parts of the country including William Warren in Birmingham, Alabama, and J. Byers Hays in Cleveland, Ohio.[60]

Like some of his contemporaries—including Delano & Aldrich—Lindeberg took a comprehensive approach toward the interiors, producing special designs or selections for mantels and light fixtures as well as specifying furniture, rugs, and decorative fabrics. Ernesta Beaux, the niece of artist Cecilia Beaux, worked in Lindeberg's decorating department in the 1920s before going on to decorate the lobby of River House and the rooms of the River Club for William Lawrence Bottomley.[61] Subsequently, Lindeberg's daughter, Linda, managed interior design for her father. During the 1930s, she designed much of the furniture Lindeberg produced for clients and also put together the 1940 monograph.[62] Linda, later an accomplished abstract artist married to Giorgio Cavallon—also an artist—went on to decorate Gracie Mansion in the early 1940s for Mayor La Guardia under the direction of Aymar Embury II. Her brother, Lytle, became an architect and worked for his father before moving to Washington State, where he settled with his family and found success designing houses as well as the interiors of the Federal buildings in Seattle.

While Lindeberg designed several houses in the Midwest during the 1910s, it wasn't until the 1920s that his practice really expanded beyond the Northeast. In 1921 he opened a Houston office and placed John F. Staub, a Knoxville-born architect with a degree from MIT, in charge of the six commissions that materialized from various Texan businessmen and industrialists. Staub began working for Lindeberg in 1916—with a break while he served during World War I—and stayed on in Houston to practice independently after Lindeberg closed the office in 1923.[63] Meanwhile, in Lake Forest, Lindeberg enjoyed a flurry of commissions after the completion of the Norman style house he designed in 1916 for Clyde Carr, president of Ryerson Steel (see pages 100–11). In 1927 he went on to design a clubhouse for the Onwentsia Club—the nexus of Lake Forest society—as well as several other houses for club members, including Philip Armour, Robert Gardner, Dexter Cummings, and Earle Reynolds. At the same time, he was also invited to work on projects in the Midwest (Ohio, Missouri, Indiana, and Michigan), the South (Virginia, North Carolina and Tennessee), and the West (Washington and California).

Lindeberg continued to evolve his mastery of precedent, and his singular imagination led him to new and intriguing designs. In 1915 C. Matlack Price remarked that his work "very clearly shows that he has gone on thinking, and has never from the first allowed the personal and living spontaneity of his design to become petrified into anything so final or uncompromising as mere thought."[64] Lindeberg's inspiration from precedent—both classical and picturesque—were neither fixed nor rigid. As Russell F. Whitehead noted in *The Architectural Record*, "Mr. Lindeberg's work . . . is like a pair of intertwined chains, one of houses of classic origins and one of romantic; but just as it is difficult to distinguish the continuity of the links of intertwined chains, so it is difficult always to be sure of the types to which Lindeberg's houses belong."[65]

This stylistic freedom and integration of what would seem to be competing motives became increasingly pronounced in the 1920s as Lindeberg became even more adept at synthesizing seemingly disparate styles into a well-integrated whole. His ingenious handling of building materials matured as he continued to use brick, stone, tile, slate, iron, and wood in expressive and flexible ways, emphasizing the virtues—the colors, textures, and size—of the materials themselves. He extended great care to every aspect of the design. As Gerard Lambert recalled, "We set up slate from four quarries on the front lawn to study the colors for the roof" while designing Albemarle, his house in Princeton, New Jersey.[66] But although Lindeberg's work was studied and meticulously executed, the overall impression it gave was more spontaneous and free than labored. Rather than using newly planed wood, he incorporated half-timber details bearing the marks of the craftsman's tools, lending each house additional character and authenticity. On one occasion, he chastised wood carvers for carrying out their work too well, remarking, "Oh, it's too perfect—I don't want it so perfect."[67]

Lindeberg focused on the artistic dimension of his work, lavishing attention on the ironwork details. Initially, he produced full-scale drawings for the artisans, and after they were revisited and revised, he examined the various grilles and wrought iron flourishes in fabrication before approving them. While Lindeberg worked with a number of ironworkers and companies, including Samuel Yellin, B. J. Hasselman, Renner & Maras, and Marie Zimmermann, his collaboration with the German-born craftsman Oscar Bruno Bach produced some of the most elegant and imaginative details.[68] With a formal education in painting and the metallic arts from the Royal Academy and Imperial Academy of Art in Berlin, Bach established his business in the United States in 1913 after working as a successful metalsmith throughout Europe.

Lindeberg provided Bach with some of his first projects in this country, starting with artistic metalwork for the Eugene du Pont estate in Greenville, Delaware (see pages 88–99). Ironwork, often featuring natural forms and animals and birds in free-flowing fancy, was typically reserved for entrance details and doorways, radiator grilles, light fixtures, and exterior embellishments. Lindeberg was partial to the form of the peacock, a symbol of eternity, integrity, beauty, nobility, and protection. Above all, Lindeberg never let a decorative element upstage the architectural composition; indeed, he was known for seamlessly integrating them into his designs. As Price noted in 1920, "In

Drawing of a radiator grille in the Hugo V. Neuhaus house, Shadyside, Houston, Texas, 1920–22.

themselves architectural details may be very interesting" but in Lindeberg's hands, "their real merit is proven when they are so combined . . . to make the completed house harmonious."[69]

Whether the project was large or small, Lindeberg strove for intimacy, creating houses meant less as impressive statements of status and more for comfortable living. As he had in partnership with Albro, he often designed the entrance front more informally with low sweeping rooflines to minimize size and impact. On the garden front, he frequently used a more classical and symmetrical approach, a synthesis he further developed at Thomas Vietor's house in Rumson, New Jersey; Olympic Point for Horace Havemeyer in Islip, New York; and Southways for John S. Pillsbury on Lake Minnetonka in Minnesota.

In effect, the sprawling, low-lying Vietor house was a Tudor variation of Clarence Alcott's Cotswold-style cottage in East Hampton, completed simultaneously (see pages 64–71). Lindeberg arranged the entrance facade around a large gable with a chimney extending up through its center, added multiple dormers, and extended the kitchen wing laterally to the east. To the rear, he opened the facade to its full two stories and arranged two symmetrical wings around a terrace. His collaboration with Oscar Bach produced subtle yet striking effects, including bronze window grilles featuring peacocks with long sweeping plumes.[70] At Olympic Point (see pages 112–17), Lindeberg took this technique one step further, combining the entry facade—a romantic rhythm of bays, windows, and dormers—with a symmetrical and more imposing waterfront elevation and pairing whitewashed clinker brick with spare stone window frames—an approach that could not be categorized as either classical or picturesque. Here his architecture reached a subtle synthesis of influences that made its allusive qualities as powerful as its sources were obscure.

Southways for grain producer John S. Pillsbury and his wife, Eleanor, a summer house on Bracketts Point on Lake Minnetonka outside Minneapolis, was among Lindeberg's most imposing houses. Designed in 1916 but not completed until 1920 because of the war, it was built of antique brick with an asymmetrical half-timbered entrance facade and a formal—almost severe—elevation fronting the lake. Although Lindeberg and Eleanor Pillsbury disagreed on several important points, she admitted that "he was excellent on the details," which included a living room floor of curly pine from South Africa, individually designed fireplaces, a wrought-iron front door by Samuel Yellin

Above left: Thomas Vietor house, Rumson, New Jersey, 1915

Above right: Bronze window grille with peacocks, Vietor house.

Opposite above: John S. Pillsbury estate, Southways, Lake Minnetonka, Minnesota, 1916–20.

Opposite below: Plan of Southways.

with a scrolling peacock, and carved owl posts on the main stair.

On the other hand, he could be impervious to his client's preferences. Mrs. Pillsbury wanted her living room to be painted rather than paneled in butternut as Lindeberg specified. As a result, Lindeberg went ahead and paneled the room but then painted over it in Mrs. Pillsbury's chosen color. He later relayed this fact, saying, "You have chosen a marvelous color. But I will tell you something you don't know. I have built these walls of butternut wood, and some day people are going to scrape off this paint and find the very special wood underneath." Lindeberg was adamant that the style of his house not be categorized. As Mrs. Pillsbury recalled, "Although I appreciated Lindeberg's talents, I thought him rather a vain man. When Southways was finished, I asked him exactly what style the architecture was and he answered, 'It's a Lindeberg house!'"[71]

Inside, Lindeberg shifted the axes established on the exterior at his discretion, creating complex plans that did not follow any formal ordering system preordained by the facades.[72] As Royal Cortissoz observed, he was "predisposed toward an asymmetrical plan, one which nominally rambles, but in truth the characteristic thing about a plan as he frames it turns out to be its lucidity and convenience, the happy arrangement of rooms . . . and the wise provision made for circulation."[73] Within the Pillsbury house, Lindeberg extended an unexpected axis—or gallery—against the entrance facade leading to library and loggia and culminating in the sunroom and garden beyond. As Mrs. Pillsbury recollected, "Lindeberg did not believe in going from one room to another room. He said you have to have a hallway."[74] Always interested in producing comfortable and livable interiors, he felt that the real builders of homes—himself included—were "thinking first of the charm and the beauty of the interior, of the fireplaces and the windows that will admit sunlight, of the opening of one room into another, making the hall light."[75]

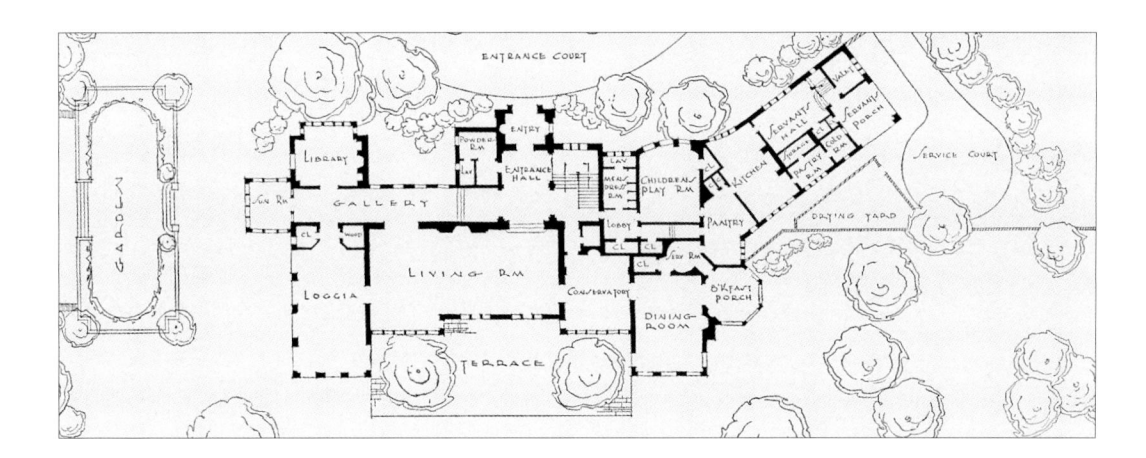

Lindeberg's work became increasingly spare and stripped down throughout the 1920s, the simplicity of the facades often masking the complexity of the plan. Indeed, the architect found the idea of simplicity—"the acme of artistic accomplishment"—more and more compelling.[76] In each new design, he reveled in the study of simplicity, or elimination of anything extraneous, whether it be unnecessary breaks in the roofline or columns that would have been needed to bear weight. But as Lindeberg's work became more severe and powerful, his propensity for clearly delineated volumes, powerful clean lines, and judiciously placed ornament emerged vividly beginning in the late 1910s.

Top left: Frederick L. Lutz house, Laurel Acres, Oyster Bay, New York, 1917.

Top right: Amasa Stone Mather stable group, Gates Mills, Ohio, 1919.

Above: Amelita Galli-Curci house, Sul Monte, Fleischmans, New York, 1922.

Lindeberg was clearly influenced by the work of British architects C. F. A. Voysey and Sir Edwin Lutyens as well as H. H. Richardson, whose simplified use of bold arches and massing forms were lessons in effective abstraction. His gable-end entrance facade for Laurel Acres, silk merchant Frederick Lutz's house in Oyster Bay, Long Island, was utterly compelling in its simplicity.[77] Here, Lindeberg arranged a central door, a band of small windows above and attic casement within the bold outline of the gable end and chimney stack at center. Symmetrical leader heads, a half-timbered arch, stepped brickwork, and ornamental ironwork at the arched entryway only added to its spare abstracted quality—in retrospect almost postmodern in nature. Similarly, his stable group for iron magnate Amasa Stone Mather in Gates Mills, Ohio, was stripped of any ornament—save the side door lanterns and clock—deriving its impact from the crisp outline of its central stucco gable.[78]

Above: Frederick B. Patterson house, Far Hills, Dayton, Ohio, 1925.

Right: Dining room at Far Hills.

In the 1920s, the characteristic elements of Lindeberg's work became increasingly pronounced. Sul Monte, his house for well-known Italian-American soprano Amelita Galli-Curci in Highmount, New York, revealed the architect's appreciation for the special qualities of place in shaping his design. Located in the Catskills near Fleischmanns, the house was built into a mountainside, wrapping the site to the northeast to emphasize sweeping views to the southwest. Like Mondanne, the stone, stucco, and half-timber house was long and rambling with a taller central mass and angled wings that gave the impression that it was firmly planted in the landscape. With little extraneous ornament, the success of the design relied on the balance of the chimneys, the pattern of the windows,

37

and the manner in which the massing unfolded in response to the topography. In Lindeberg's hand, the Tudor style became something abstract and more personal. The interiors, carried out with hand-applied plaster and hand-hewn timber, included a double-height studio and music library with its own entrance for recitals.[79]

Lindeberg's design for Far Hills, Frederick B. Patterson's house in Dayton, Ohio, was equally powerful. Built on a grand scale—Patterson was president of the National Cash Register Company—the massing was a series of crisp unfolding brick volumes—angled, turreted, rectilinear—all settled amicably under one great roofline composed of hand-hewn Scottish slates.[80] The main entrance was off center within a gable balanced with a turret on the opposite side of the central block. Angled walls and a shallow arching brick lintel marked the entrance with an oriel window above. Ernesta Beaux decorated the formal interiors, which featured early English and Spanish paneling, stained glass from a mid-sixteenth-century Spanish castle, and, in the front hall, paving from a London street.

Gray Craig, Michael van Beuren's estate in Middletown, Rhode Island (see pages 148–65), shows

Above: Michael van Beuren estate, Gray Craig, Middletown, Rhode Island, 1924–26.

Opposite: Ruby Boyer Miller estate, Penguin Hall, Wenham, Massachusetts, 1930; Library at Penguin Hall.

the influence of Lutyens, displaying Lindeberg's full mastery of both the classical and picturesque. In designing his most sophisticated and refined project, he oriented the formal Georgian-inspired house south toward a vast lawn and ocean beyond, designing a spare, symmetrical facade of indigenous pudding stone, with large openings reflecting the public rooms within. However, the symmetry was only one room deep. Lindeberg set the entrance inside a colossal arched porte cochère at one end of the house leading to a series of galleries that extended in enfilade behind the entertaining rooms. At Gray Craig, Lindeberg's handling of the plan and elevations revealed a singular ability to fuse the formal qualities of classicizing architecture with the more domestic and picturesque qualities of a romantic approach. His attention to the execution of the stone walls, sandy limestone details, and variegated roof tiles added to its artistic effect.

In 1930 Lindeberg completed Penguin Hall in Wenham, Massachusetts, for Detroit resident Ruby Boyer Miller, a daughter of inventor Joseph Boyer, president of the Burroughs Adding Machine Company. Formerly married to lumber executive William A. C. Miller, Ruby Miller spent her summers in Wenham on a 53-acre estate with her alleged—and married—paramour Admiral Richard Byrd. At Penguin Hall, Lindeberg presented a stark formal entrance front, mitigating the size of the stone house with outreaching one-story wings that framed the forecourt. Meanwhile, the south facade unfolded romantically as a series of bays, chimney stacks and half-timbering. Decorative touches such as the bronze penguin statues by Beverly Lothrop, a gift from Byrd, marking the forecourt—a nod to Byrd's Antarctic explorations—a delicate iron-wrought spider web screen door and signs of the zodiac around the front entrance added a subtle whimsy to the austere design.

The interiors of Penguin Hall featured long galleries, a large stair hall, and expansive rooms with linen-fold paneling, molded ceilings, and stone detailing.[81] Typical of Lindeberg's approach, its formal rooms—the living and dining rooms and library—were carried out in a more traditional manner with the classical arrangement of base, chair rail, and crown, the Georgian and Tudor styles prevailing. He incorporated antique mantels and designed new ones, including a modern Georgian model in the living room—a design he repeated in some of his later commissions. In many of his houses, including Penguin Hall, a great room rounded out the plan. These double-height spaces—one of which Lindeberg incorporated into West Gate Lodge—were more rustic or astylar in nature with exposed rafters, stone or rough plaster walls, and large bay windows.

Like most architects practicing in the 1930s and 1940s, Lindeberg confronted a drastic reduction in the number and size of commissions coming through his office. While the 1929 crash affected the 1930s, World War II eliminated virtually all private construction, and the economy was slow to recover during the 1950s. However, although the heyday of the country estate

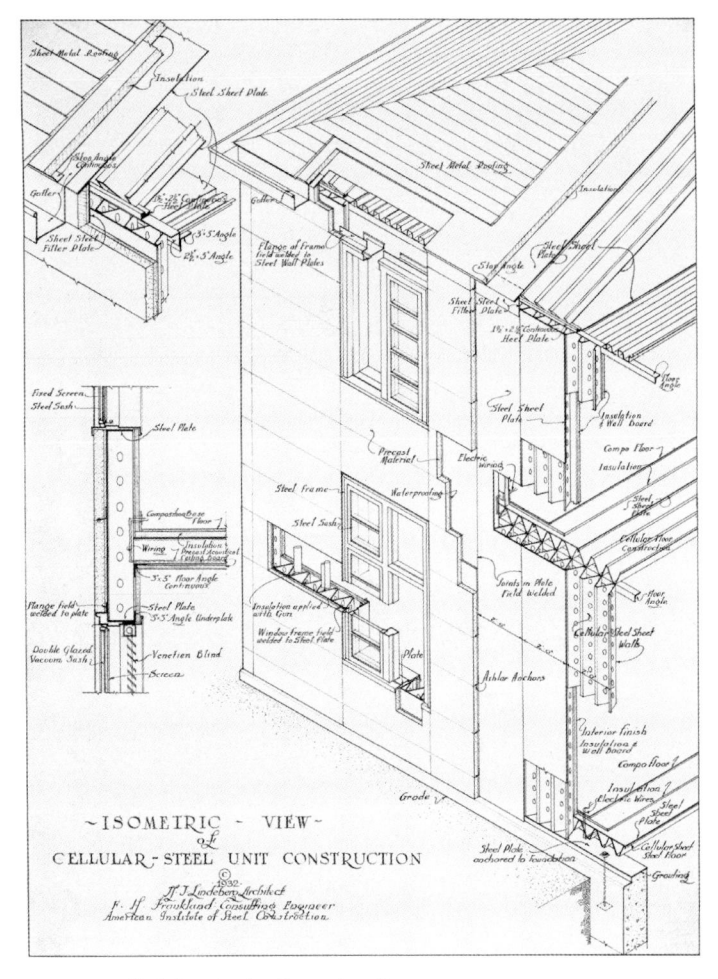

Cellular steel unit construction, 1932.

passed abruptly with the market crash, Lindeberg adjusted to the reduced conditions of the period, and he was fortunate enough to find government work to compensate for the lack of house projects.

LATE CAREER: 1930–1959

In the depths of the Depression, twelve years after his divorce, Lindeberg remarried. He had met his third wife, Angeline Krech James (1896-1971), the daughter of the late Alvin W. Krech, former chairman of the Equitable Trust Company, when she was a client married to attorney Oliver B. James. In the early 1930s, Lindeberg designed furnishings for the James townhouse at 133 East 62nd Street. After twenty years of marriage, Angeline divorced James and on August 12, 1937—just two days later—married Lindeberg, seventeen years her senior. James, who also remarried in 1937, moved to Phoenix, Arizona, in the 1940s; Angeline and her five children, then ages 9 through 18, lived with Lindeberg at their apartment at 333 East 57th Street and at Lindeberg's house in Locust Valley. Relatives and family friends recall Angeline and Harrie as an urbane and polished couple, both very well dressed and precise in their appearance. They enjoyed entertaining on the terrace of West Gate Lodge, and Lindeberg, an expert at mixing his favorite cocktail, the southside, always designed his houses—including his own—with a bar close at hand.

In the early 1930s, as the Depression deepened and house commissions dwindled, Lindeberg examined his own practice and thought about his future. As with every challenge in his career, Lindeberg—ever the problem solver—took the collapse of private work as an opportunity to analyze the state of architecture. Well aware that he occupied a lofty position on a sinking ship, he chose to extract the principles that he had followed in design and posit the position that the essentials of good architecture remained universally relevant. His essay "A Return to Reason in Architecture," published in *The Architectural Record* in 1934, was a manifesto of sorts—a confident tract demonstrating that systems of proportioning, revealed by the overlay of grids on buildings he admired, could be successfully applied to a new architecture devoid of ornament and shorn of historically based references.[82]

He began to explore his ideas about proportioning in designs for panelized steel houses based on a two-foot module. Lindeberg, like other architects before him, believed that there must be less costly alternatives to conventional wood-frame construction. His solution involved a modular steel-panel system that he was convinced would make robust, affordable, fire-proof housing. By applying the modules according to a system of correct classical proportions, he was confident that his prefabricated houses would have architectural integrity. His system called for prefabricated light-gauge steel sheets, flanged for joining and increased strength, to be used for exterior walls, roof, and floors, that would be welded together and attached to a base plate on top of a concrete foundation. Conventional materials such as stucco or brick could be used on top of the steel and

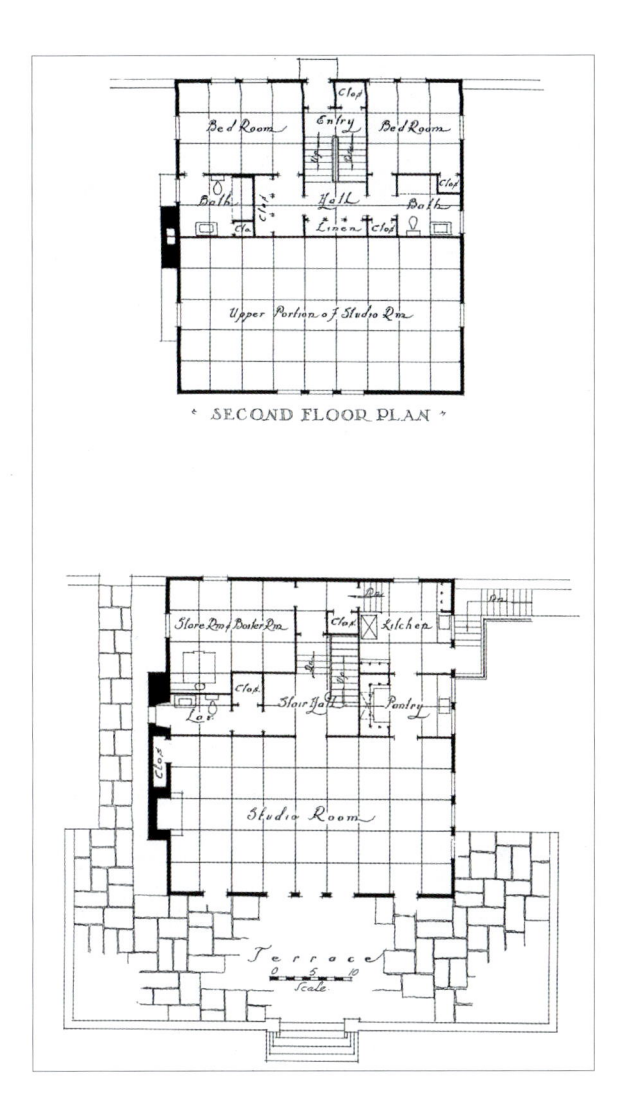

Preliminary study and plan for a hillside studio, 1932.

could express any number of architectural styles ranging from Georgian to spare modern. Approved by the Institute of Steel Construction, Lindeberg's new method was the basis of the design of one house in Virginia with engineer F. L. Frankfort.[83] Throughout the 1930s, Lindeberg worked out a number of different schemes incorporating modular steel panels, from five-room houses, Florida bungalows, and hillside studios to row houses, although it is unclear how many—if any—were built. Most of these designs were extremely spare—a response to mediating tradition to the rising tide of modernism—but their underlying proportions reflected a compelling classicism. As Mark Alan Hewitt has noted, some of the designs evoked the 1920s work of André Lurçat, Eileen Gray, and Adolf Loos.[84]

Unlike Grosvenor Atterbury's contemporary work in concrete, Lindeberg's cellular steel housing was not primarily driven by a sense of social purpose. While Atterbury invested significant time over the course of his career in a quest to use precast concrete panels in building affordable housing, Lindeberg was more concerned with prefabrication as a means to make his designs more affordable to his own clientele. In fact, many of his schemes depicted larger houses, replete with multiple bedrooms, sun porches, and garages. These house schemes never gained traction, but Lindeberg was nonetheless energized by the effort. In the early 1940s, the system was used on a larger scale for industrial buildings such as the printing plant for Doubleday & Company in

Above: Doubleday & Company, Hanover, Pennsylvania, 1946.

Left: House for the Weyerhaeuser Sales Company, St. Paul, Minnesota, 1938.

Hanover, Pennsylvania, and the Country Life Press in Garden City, Long Island.[85]

In 1938 Lindeberg was challenged to bring his modular approach to domestic design to the growing problem of housing for working-class families. The Weyerhaeuser Sales Company, a timber company based in St. Paul, Minnesota, commissioned model houses to promote the use of their 4-Square lumber, a brand of seasoned, dimensioned wood used for home building. While these houses were very small, they were planned with good circulation, light, cross-ventilation, storage, and maximum wall space for furniture.[86]

Meanwhile, more substantial projects from the Foreign Service Building Commission (FSBC) kept Lindeberg's office busy during the leaner years of the Depression. In the aftermath of the United States entry into the international arena during World War I, the State Department realized that the country's embassies and consulates should project a national image through purpose-built facilities rather than the retrofitted buildings, usually historic mansions, that had previously been used. With the establishment of the FSBC in 1926, the government began to make a concerted effort to design buildings reflective of American democratic principles but also sympathetic to local traditions. In Tokyo, H. Van Buren Magonigle, with Antonin Raymond, designed a concrete building with white stucco facades embellished with ornament drawn from Japanese precedents; its copper roof was reminiscent of local Shinto shrines. Delano & Aldrich's American Government Building in Paris adopted the massing, fenestration, and cornice heights of Jacques-Ange Gabriel's original buildings on Place de la Concorde. The building fit in so well that it became barely distinguishable from its historic Parisian context despite its subtle ornament of sculpted eagles and seals of the United States of America. Under the direction of President Franklin D. Roosevelt in the 1930s, the State Department's construction programs were carried out in conjunction with the office of the supervising architect, an agency within the Treasury Department, headed by Louis A. Simon. Believing that America had to project its values and history through its diplomatic architecture abroad, Roosevelt urged the use of historical models that upheld the image of America's democracy.[87]

In 1934 William C. Bullitt Jr., the first ambassador to the Soviet Union, and Lindeberg began working on the U.S. legation in Moscow.[88] Diplomatic relations between the United States and U.S.S.R. had warmed with Roosevelt's recognition of Stalin's Communist government and a newly negotiated trade agreement between the two countries. Stalin promised Bullitt what Bullitt described as the "best site in the entire Soviet Union"—a 15-acre wooded plateau in Sparrow Hills, one of the highest points in Moscow, overlooking the Moskva River—for the United States to build its compound. Together, Bullitt and Lindeberg came up with a Jeffersonian Colonial scheme based on the University of Virginia—an approach that Roosevelt embraced, saying "I like the idea of planting Thomas

Bird's-eye view of the United States Embassy, Moscow, Russia, 1934.

Jefferson in Moscow."[89] In May 1934, Lindeberg traveled to Moscow and prepared sketches and blueprints. His proposed design detailed a group of wine-colored brick buildings arranged around a quadrangle and linked by an arched cloister. The Ambassador's residence and chancery, inspired by Westover on the James River in Virginia and the Hammond-Harwood House in Annapolis, Maryland, respectively, terminated the long axis to the north and south while living quarters for the Foreign Service officers, military attachés, and staff made up a series of pavilions, articulated by colonnaded porticos, to the east and west. Lindeberg oriented the great portico of the Ambassador's residence toward the river with views out over the city.

Lindeberg completed the plans and detailed specifications for the American campus and planned to sail for Moscow in April 1935 to oversee its early construction. However, by that time, the embassy's future had started to look shaky with the collapse of international debt negotiations. On top of that, Bullitt was finding construction in the Soviet Union increasingly frustrating due to differing building methods and, as Lindeberg realized, the lack of seasoned lumber, good

Above left: Study for the United States Consulate, Shanghai, China, 1936.

Above right: Study for the United States Legation, Managua, Nicaragua, 1937.

millwork, window glass, and rolled steel. All Bullitt's requests for imported materials and American foremen were denied, and to purchase resources from Russian suppliers at the official exchange rate would render the project, slated to cost $1,165,000, entirely too expensive. Eventually Bullitt was forced to abandon his plans, and Lindeberg's ambitious scheme was unrealized.[90]

Lindeberg's design for the United States consulate in Shanghai, the financial and commercial capital of Asia, also remained on the drafting board. Planned for a site on the banks of the Huangpu River, the design reflected the spare stripped classicism that was becoming popular in Shanghai and was codified in contemporary buildings such as New York's Rockefeller Center. Entirely modern, it featured a bold central tower with windows bays organized in severe vertical strips and side wings with colossal arcades facing the river. In the only nod to its context, Lindeberg capped the buildings with red-tiled hipped roofs that, while not explicitly Chinese in inspiration, softened the imposing monumentality of the complex. In his most understated diplomatic design, Lindeberg proposed a legation complex in Managua, Nicaragua, as a stripped-down plantation-style house flanked by service wings arranged around a central patio. With its simple construction, hinged shutters, and cross-ventilation, this unrealized project demonstrated Lindeberg's ability to adapt local building customs and tailor his design ambitions to budget and local conditions.

Lindeberg's embassy and chancery in Helsinki, Finland, was his only commission from the FSBC to be built (see pages 220–25). Completed in 1940, it was a modest version of the Moscow scheme with the Ambassador's residence based on Westover and two outstretched wings, containing the chancery and the garage, organized around a central lawn. The building contained restrained Georgian interiors and paneling of rare figured Karelian wood—a material that was wiped out after the Soviet Union assumed control of the Karelian peninsula soon after the compound was completed. This spare version of the Jeffersonian campus left an indelible mark of American democratic architecture in the capital of Finland. As a State Department building based so explicitly on a historical model, this was the last United States outpost that was designed to reflect Franklin Roosevelt's vision for American architecture as emblematic of democratic values.

By paring and editing his designs, Lindeberg was essentially following the emerging trends of modernism, in the same vein as his fellow traditionalists Delano & Aldrich and the French-born Philadelphia-based architect Paul Cret, who also produced exemplary spare modern classical buildings. While the houses that Lindeberg designed during the 1930s and 1940s still evoked classical and picturesque sources, they were smaller and simpler. His house for Ruby Boyer Miller in Grosse Pointe Farms, Michigan, was stripped of any extraneous ornament and featured two flat-roofed, low-lying wings housing the garage and servants' quarters framing a forecourt of sorts (see pages 214–19). Nonetheless, its gracious proportions, symmetry, flanking chimneys, and center entrance gave it a modern classical appeal. His winter cottage for banker Sidney A. Mitchell in Brookville, Long Island—a stone's throw away from West Gate Lodge—was a simple whitewashed brick house built into the slope of a hill with a central door and a fanlight and side lights finely detailed with geometric iron-wrought patterns. Lindeberg did receive several sizable estate commissions, the largest for chemical manufacturer Robert T. Vanderbilt in Greens Farms, Connecticut, overlooking Long Island Sound, which included an expansive Tudor-inspired house, garages, and greenhouses.[91] He also designed a three-story Georgian townhouse for Major David S. Barry Jr. in the prestigious Kalorama-Sheridan section of Washington, D.C. The house fit well into the historic neighborhood, but it also featured several Lindeberg flourishes, such as iron-wrought leader heads and an attic bull's eye window set within the chimney shaft. Lindeberg's interiors were grounded by essentially classical proportions and included dentilated cornices, shallow panel moldings and stone bolection-form mantels abstracted to a degree so that they became stylized versions in the Deco spirit. In the drawing

Sidney A. Mitchell cottage, Brookville, New York, 1939.

room, Lindeberg incorporated a pair of paneled doors featuring a typical Greek key motif but enlarged to the full width of each panel—a powerful and stylish statement of Art Deco verve.

The firm had considerable success designing domestic furniture, aptly adapting historical precedents as they had done with architecture. During the 1930s, Lindeberg's daughter, Linda, produced a number of sophisticated pieces for such projects as the James, Miller, and Barry houses. Remarkably competent, they pulled from a wide range of inspirations—Georgian, Regency, Swedish, Vienna Secession, and Art Deco sources—and offered a fresh interpretation rendered with a delicate scale. For example, a secretary designed for the Angeline and Oliver B. James house took the overall form of a Georgian piece, its base specifically referencing similar furniture under George III. But Lindeberg wove together a number of different elements, including two large circular panels, wire-front cabinet doors and a rounded-top profile, reflecting Biedermeier, Federal and Moderne influences, that gave it a modern appeal. Approaching interiors in the manner of British interior decorator Syrie Maugham, known for decorating rooms entirely in white, Lindeberg employed his conservative but highly abstracted traditional architecture as a backdrop for a mix of more modern furniture with period pieces as accents.

Top: Robert T. Vanderbilt estate, Green Farms, Connecticut, 1939.

Above: Major David S. Barry Jr. house, Washington, D.C., 1939.

Opposite left: Secretary for Angeline and Oliver B. James at 133 East 62nd Street, New York, 1932.

Opposite right: Chairs, sofas, and tables for Major David S. Barry, 1939.

Lindeberg's commissions dwindled in the 1940s and 1950s as he wound down his practice and worked exclusively from his apartment at 277 Park Avenue and his studio in Locust Valley. Sunnyridge Hall for sportsman and lawyer Devereux Milburn Jr. in Old Westbury was one of the last houses he designed. Milburn, who inherited eleven acres from his grandmother Mrs. Charles Steele, commissioned a simplified Georgian-inspired house with two projecting wings. The interiors were both comfortable and refined with carved paneling and antique Federal-style fireplace mantels throughout the rooms. In the 1950s Lindeberg also designed several houses for his stepdaughter Angeline and her husband, Dr. James Pool, in both Alpine, New Jersey, and North Haven, Maine, as well as several houses in conjunction with William Russell on the North Shore of Long Island.[92]

In his later years, Lindeberg found deep satisfaction in pairing down his work to its most fundamental forms. His hand may have been forced by the joint realities of reduced expectations following the Depression and the force of modernism, but he was convinced that the underlying geometries expressed in classical proportions and harmonious plan arrangements could be adapted from important examples of historic architecture and applied to contemporary practice, even underpinning designs for more modest houses. In light of the modern movement sweeping the architectural arena from the 1930s on, the final chapter of his career could be seen of something of a disappointment, but that reading underestimates the profound influence his work and mentorship had on American architecture. As a leading member of the second generation of the American Renaissance, he produced designs that stood apart as examples of the power of creative synthesis. In a range of styles, his houses responded to the specifics of place and reflected his mastery of taste and composition. Many of the architects who passed through his office went on to define residential sections of cities throughout the country, spreading Lindeberg's methods beyond just the buildings he designed. There is no doubt that he made his mark as a domestic architect during the first three decades of the twentieth century. His work and his artistic legacy continues to be enjoyed and revered by many one hundred years later.

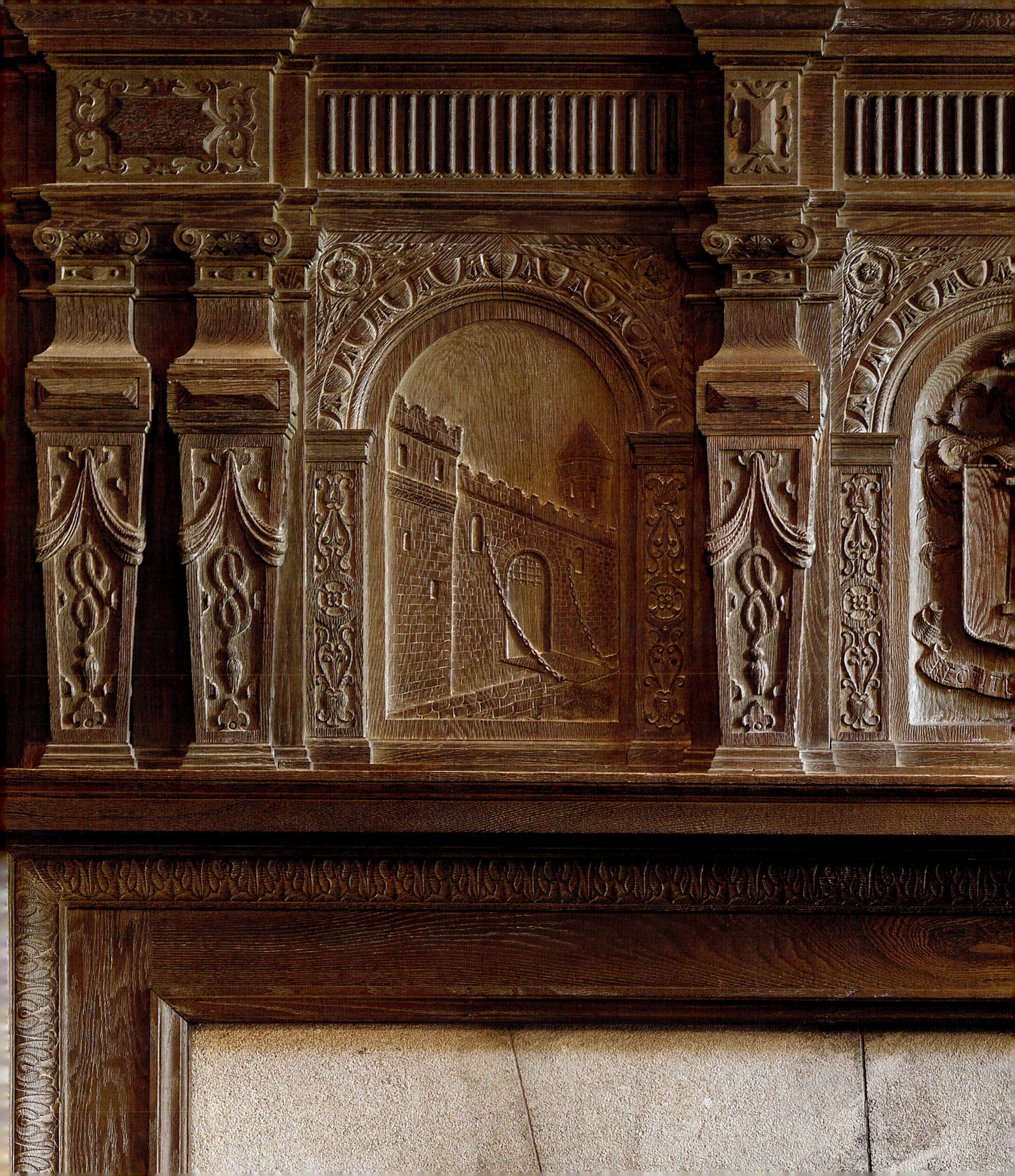

TWENTY PROJECTS

MONDANNE
JAMES A. STILLMAN ESTATE

POCANTICO HILLS, NEW YORK

1906–10

Albro & Lindeberg's first major project, the uniquely charming Mondanne for James Alexander Stillman (1873–1944) and his wife, Anne "Fifi" Urquhart Potter (1879–1969), propelled the young firm to prominence. Soon after its completion in 1910, the picturesque half-timbered main house and romantic outbuildings garnered the attention and praise of the architectural community. As critic Royal Cortissoz later recalled, "I can remember as though it was yesterday the sensation [Lindeberg] gave me when he erected the house for James Stillman at Pocantico Hills... I knew at once that a new talent had arisen and ever since I have observed its evolution and progress with particular sympathy."[1] While other firms had explored the architectural language of the English cottage style, none had brought the deft hand that Lindeberg displayed here.

James A. Stillman was the oldest son of James Jewett Stillman, a Texas-born railroad industrialist and chairman of National City Bank. Stillman's introduction to Lindeberg came through his father. In the early 1900s, the elder Stillman had been a client of McKim, Mead & White's when Lindeberg was working under Charles F. McKim. Following the acquisition in 1899 of the former Merchants Exchange at 55 Wall Street, Stillman engaged McKim to transform the building into the headquarters for the bank. The firm also designed a house for Stillman on the northeast corner of 72nd Street and Fifth Avenue, which was never built.

The younger Stillman graduated from Harvard, where he was a varsity baseball pitcher, in 1896, and he started at the bottom of the ladder as a clerk at National City Bank. In 1901 he married Anne Potter, daughter of James Brown Potter of Brown Bros. & Co. Stillman's career at the bank culminated in his brief tenure as president from 1918 to 1921 when he resigned amid sensationalized divorce proceedings involving affairs and illegitimate children. While the Stillmans briefly reconciled, they eventually divorced, and Anne married Fowler McCormick, twenty years her junior, a grandson of John D. Rockefeller as well as a close friend of her son.

The Stillmans' Pocantico Hills property was adjacent to the vast estate assembled by John D. Rockefeller in the 1890s, which was centered on Kykuit, his own mansion, and close to the property of his brother William Rockefeller, a friend and business associate of the senior Stillman. The Rockefellers had been drawn to the Hudson River Valley, an area that had enthralled artists like Frederic Edwin Church since the middle of the nineteenth century, for its rolling hills, verdant pastures, and the dramatic views of the river itself. The Stillmans' land shared all these qualities with dramatic topography bracketed by woodlands.

An ingenious reinvention of a picturesque English cottage style, the house, known as Mondanne or "Anne's World," and its dependencies displayed singularly sculptural roof forms that captivated the architectural community. Sprawling across a high ridge nearly a half mile from the entrance gates, it seemed firmly embedded in the landscape—an effect enhanced by its 300-foot breadth, its brooding horizontality, weathered fieldstone facades, and great unbroken roof surfaces—that critics could not quite believe it was in Westchester County. As A. H. Forbes, writing for *Architecture*, later marveled, "Perhaps nothing that

Entrance facade.

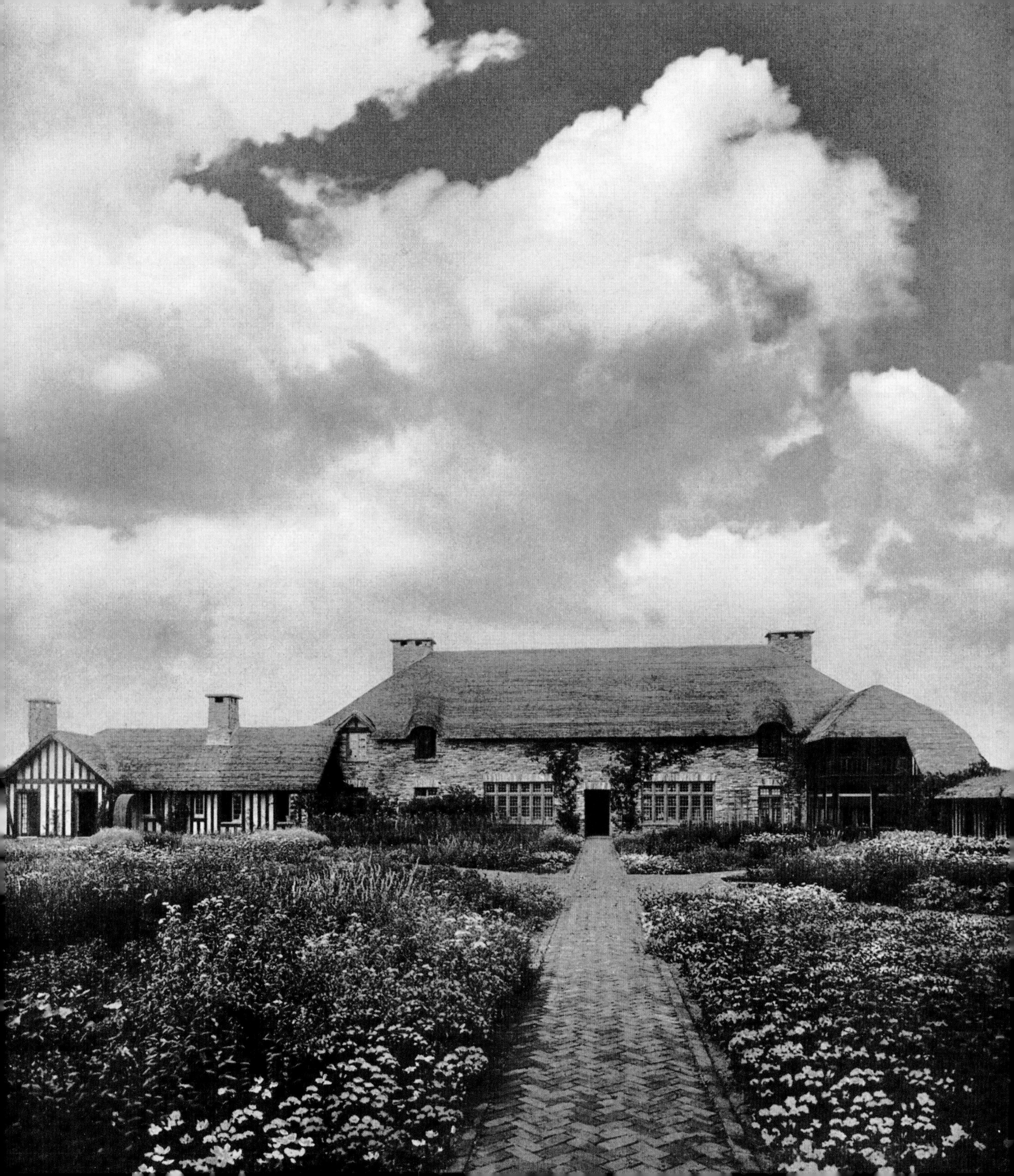

Above: Rendering of the north facade showing how the service wing fits into the slope of the ridge.

Albro & Lindeberg have ever done is more exquisitely lovely than the superintendent's cottage . . . or more filled with real personality and power than is evidenced by the garden front of the Stillman house."[2]

The more unusual aspects of the design, especially the gardener's cottage suggest, that the architect had the kind of latitude that only emanates from a trusting and inspired client. According to Tom Pyle, a longtime gardener at both Mondanne and the Rockefeller estate, the red-haired Fifi Stillman was fiery and unpredictable. "She was a curious mixture: at times thoughtful and generous, at other times she was a wild and imperious tiger cat who could frighten mature men." She supervised the construction of the house which Pyle described as "a reflection of [her] capricious, but withal excellent taste."[3] From the entrance gates, the drive curved over a moss-covered stone bridge past the gardener's cottage (or red cottage) and other outbuildings to a fork, where the right road continued to the main house and gardens and the left led to the greenhouse and pump house.

Lindeberg's entrance sequence skillfully intensified the experience of discovering the full breadth of the powerfully unconventional garden facade. Masked by the garden wall, the house was not fully revealed until visitors ascended the entry stair—secreted away by the kitchen court—and emerged half a level up in the entry porch. A short run of steps set against the garden wall along the eastern facade led up to the front entrance porch, tucked inconspicuously under a sleeping porch set into the angle of the roof. This opened into an entrance hall that in turn opened into a double-height great room with a massive stone fireplace and decorated with moose and elk heads and grizzly-bear-paw match containers as well as paintings, tapestries, and antiques. Here, a stair led to an upper floor gallery and three bedroom suites. Meanwhile, a low-lying bedroom wing extending to the west housed Fifi Stillman's private quarters, which were decorated in more delicate whites and golds. The kitchen wing angled out to the east. Lindeberg set a covered passageway and the servants' quarters into the slope of the ridge so that the wing sat inconspicuously one level below.

The form of the main roof is early evidence of Lindeberg's skill at sculpting architectural massing.[4]

KEY TO SECOND FLOOR

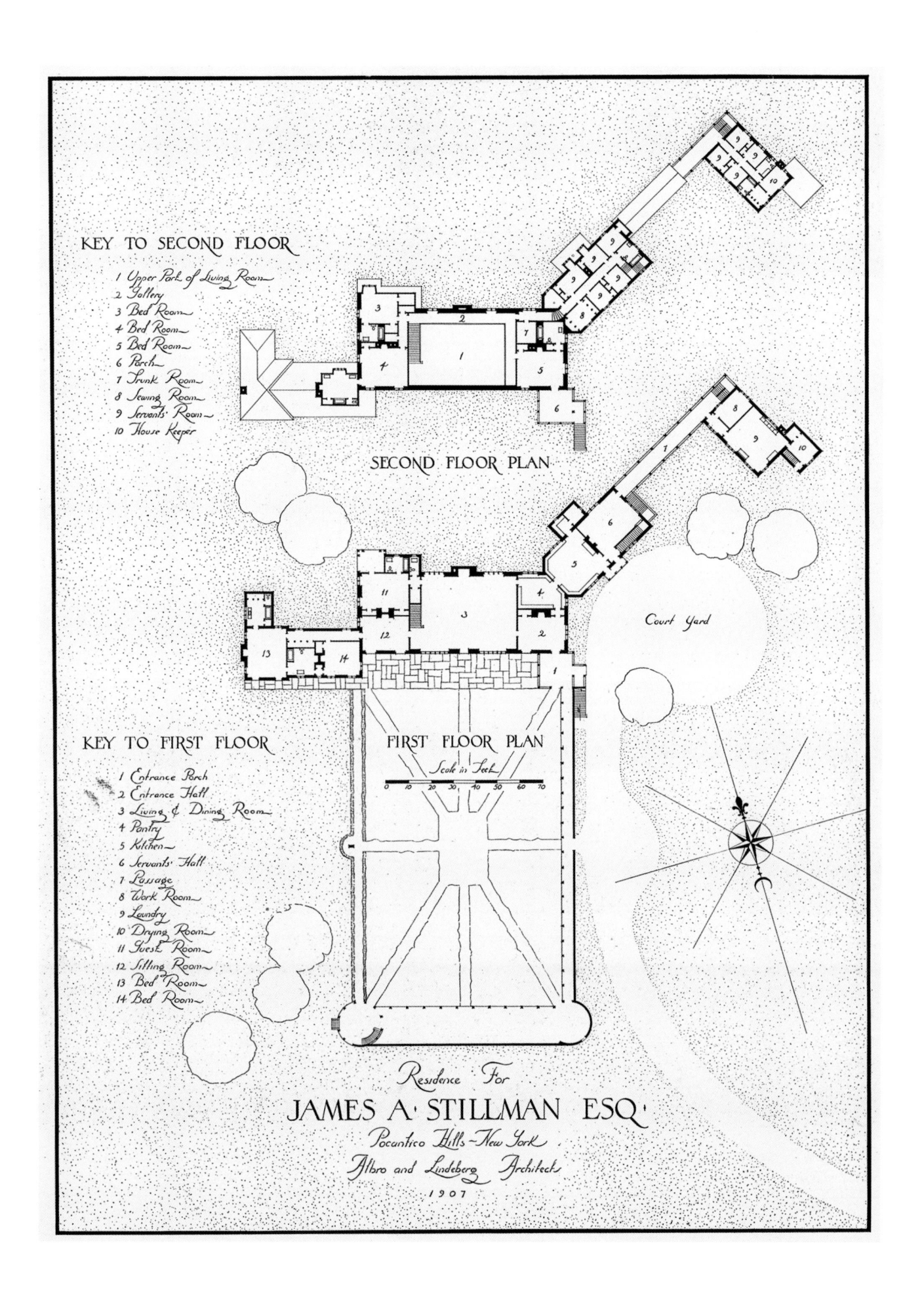

1. Upper Part of Living Room
2. Gallery
3. Bed Room
4. Bed Room
5. Bed Room
6. Porch
7. Trunk Room
8. Sewing Room
9. Servants' Room
10. House Keeper

SECOND FLOOR PLAN

KEY TO FIRST FLOOR

1. Entrance Porch
2. Entrance Hall
3. Living & Dining Room
4. Pantry
5. Kitchen
6. Servants' Hall
7. Passage
8. Work Room
9. Laundry
10. Drying Room
11. Guest Room
12. Sitting Room
13. Bed Room
14. Bed Room

FIRST FLOOR PLAN
Scale in Feet

Court Yard

Residence For
JAMES A. STILLMAN ESQ.
Pocantico Hills — New York
Albro and Lindeberg Architects
1907

Dominating the south-facing entrance facade which fronted meadow-like gardens, the roof had a rustic texture and thatch-like appearance that were achieved by the artistic handling of the cedar shingles. These were woven together in varying exposures and steamed and rolled to achieve soft ridges, valleys, and eaves. Combined with the heavy fieldstone, widely spaced windows, and spreading one-story wings, the roofs gave the composition a low-lying and guarded quality. Hooded dormer windows, interspersed sparingly under the eaves, added to the mysterious quality of the house.[5]

Lindeberg designed all of the accessory buildings in fieldstone, stucco, and timbering to complement the main house—even the gates and garden walls were thatched. Their alluring, seemingly age-old charm led critics to draw comparisons between them and the Hameau de la Reine at Le Petit Trianon. Certainly the most idiosyncratic was the gardener's cottage. Lindeberg built it around an old apple tree, and its branches protruded through the roof, a conceit that suggested that the tree had literally grown through the cottage.

Stillman deeded Mondanne to his ex-wife after her marriage to Fowler McCormick in 1931. In May 1932, a fire—which started in the housekeeper's suite—ravaged the house while the family was away and servants were preparing the house for the arrival of one of the Stillmans' sons.[6] The firefighters could not save the main house, but they were able to prevent the fire from spreading to the outbuildings, most of which survive today as private residences.

Above: Gardener's cottage built around an apple tree.

Opposite top: View from the garden of the south facade and entrance porch.

Opposite below: Stair leading from the courtyard up to the entrance porch.

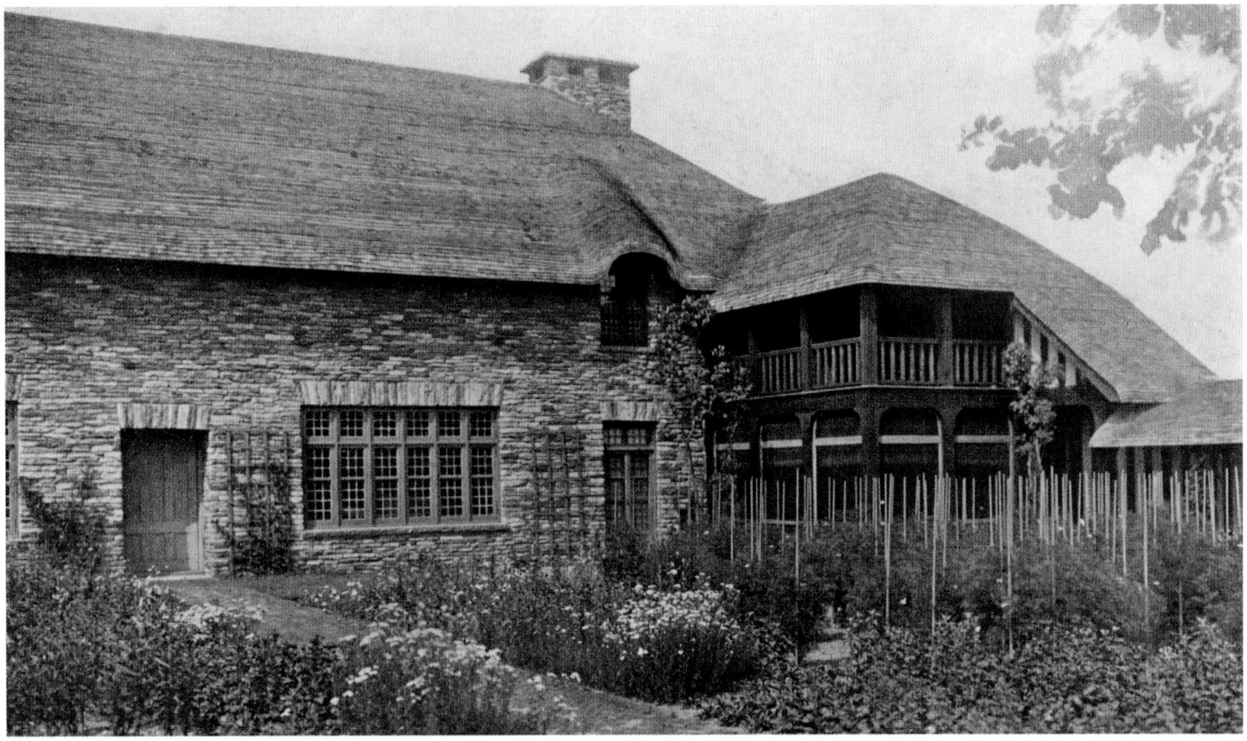

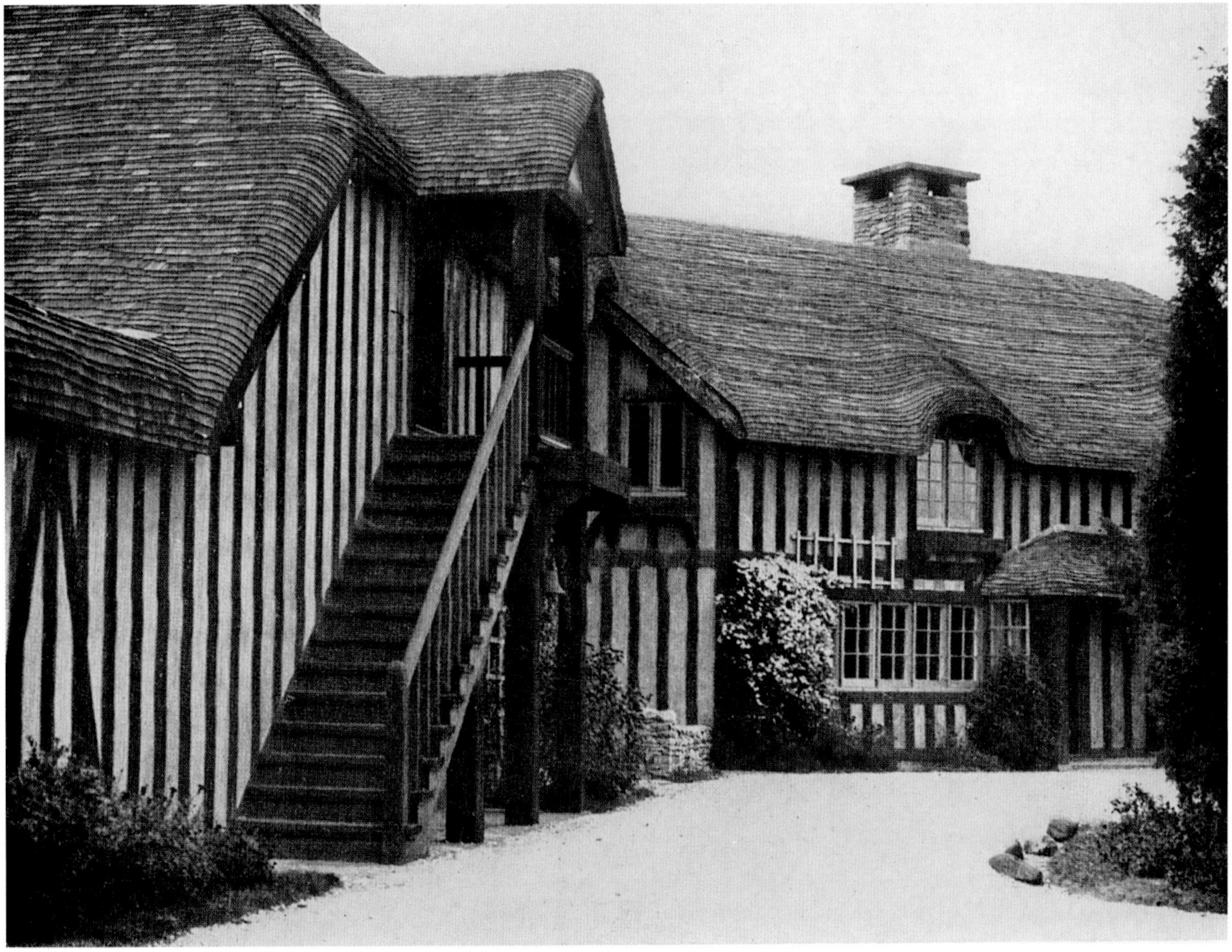

FOXHOLLOW FARM
TRACY DOWS ESTATE

RHINEBECK, NEW YORK

1906–10

Albro and Lindeberg began working on Foxhollow Farm at the same time they were designing Mondanne. In fact, the Stillmans were close to Tracy Dows (1871–1937) and his wife, Alice Olin Dows (1881–1963). The Dowses' friendship with artist Charles Dana Gibson was Albro & Lindeberg's path to the commission. In 1906, based on Gibson's recommendation, Tracy Dows hired the young firm to design a new house, which the partners began drawing before their official departure from McKim, Mead & White. Albro was the primary contact, but the Dowses embraced Lindeberg as a friend, and he was a frequent guest at Foxhollow Farm, both during and after construction.

As with the Stillmans, the young partners were fortunate to have a client with both great wealth and extraordinary land. Tracy Dows, an 1893 Harvard graduate, was the son of David Dows (1814–1890), one of the country's most successful grain merchants. Because Dows chose to limit his business interests to managing the trust left to him by his father, he could pursue the leisurely life of a country gentleman. The Dowses chose Rhinebeck as their primary residence, opting to rent quarters in apartment hotels for their stays in New York City. By 1906 they acquired several farms in the Hudson Valley, amassing eight hundred acres adjacent to Glenburn, Alice Olin Dows's family home. To make way for their new manor house on the best site on the land, they tore down Linden Hill, a Gothic villa designed by Alexander Jackson Davis in 1842 for Dr. Federal Vanderburgh, a pioneer of homeopathy.

Designed as a working farm, the estate grew to contain a series of buildings, including barns, stables, cottages, a playhouse, and a water tower. Dows brought in farm designer and agricultural advisor Edward Burnett, who had previously worked on the farms at Biltmore, George Washington Vanderbilt's estate in Asheville, North Carolina, and his associate Alfred Hopkins to design the barn complex. Unlike Mondanne, where the young partners had free rein on landscape planning, at Foxhollow Farm they were required to collaborate with John C. Olmsted, whom Dows hired to advise on building siting, the approaches, the trees, and even the orientation of rooms vis à vis the views and breezes. Where the two firms disagreed, the record shows that the architects prevailed.

Dows decided to build the estate in stages to manage expenditures, and the design of the main house was protracted. Albro reported that during the lengthy process, their clients changed their brief. At one point, Dows called for a "larger and perhaps more formal scheme than what [he] at first intended. One of his first requirements was a portico, or outdoor room, which could be used in summer, and yet enclosed with glass in winter. He also wished a formal Georgian type of house."[1] As first designed, the house included a two-story porch with columns along the southwest elevation with the second floor overhanging a loggia to the south. In the end, it became a "much less formal type than previous plans."[2] While the house was new, the landscape retained features from Linden Hill, including spreading elms that anchored the building to its perch overlooking a cove on the Hudson River.

While the main house was under construction, the Dowses lived in Albro & Lindeberg's farm house, completed in 1907. This substantial center hall colonial,

A wall fountain and sculpture of Pan by Henry Hering masks the kitchen wing.

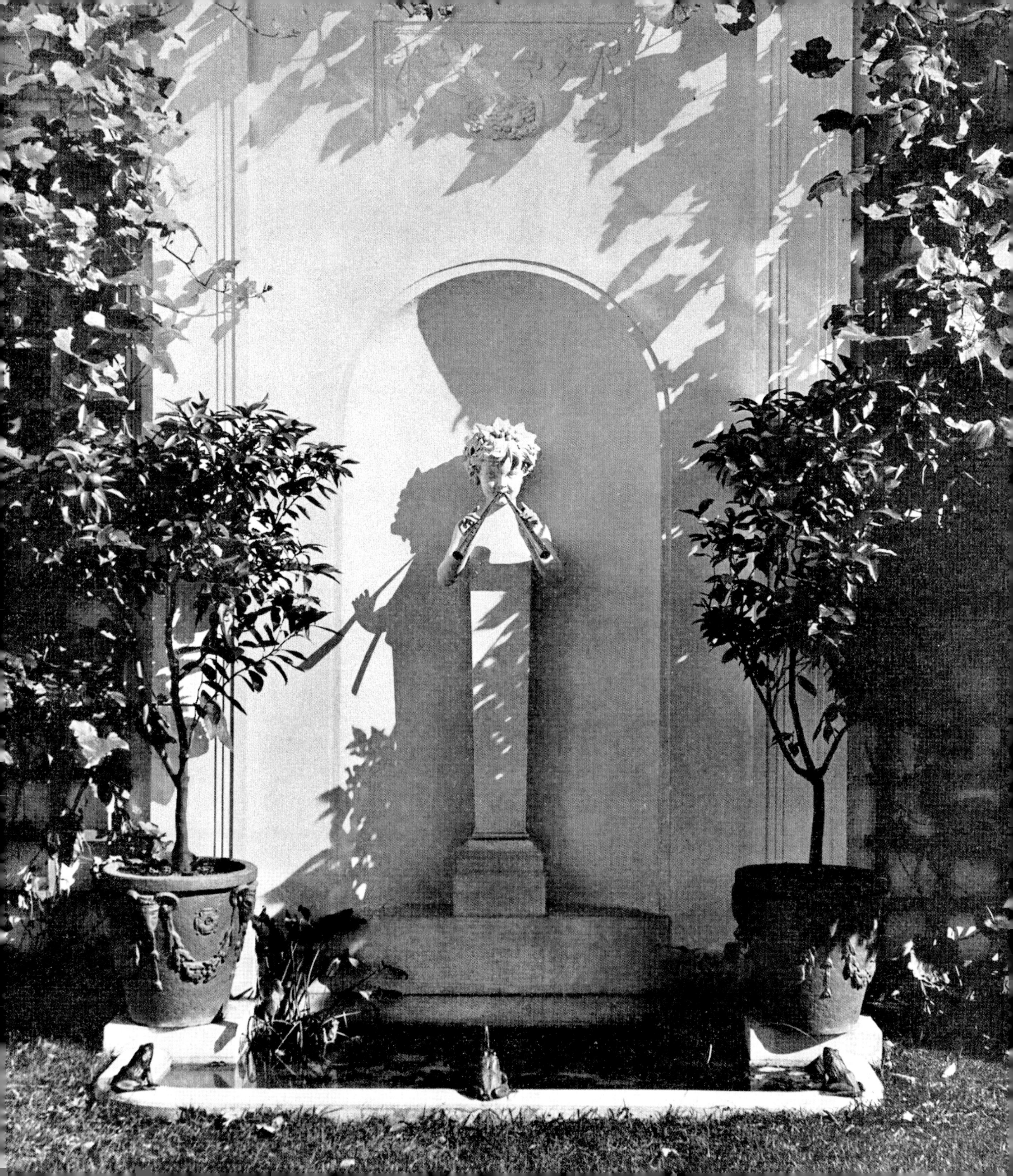

Above: Entrance facade.

Opposite: Southwest facade overlooking the Hudson River.

which later became the caretaker's house, was built of weathered stone laid up Germantown style in white mortar with two story-and-a-half wooden wings and a diamond-patterned rooftop balustrade. Both its style and materials closely linked the farm house to its place—indeed, the stone was taken from the ground not far from the house and the rough-hewn faces gave the impression that the house had been on the land for generations. Albro & Lindeberg's U-shaped stone carriage house and several of Burnett's barns were completed soon afterward.

Like Mondanne, Foxhollow Farm was heralded in the architectural press, although it could not have been more different. Lindeberg's skill at distilling a style and form that was appropriate to each place meant that even though the nearby Stillman estate was a completely different architectural expression, it is clear that each commission was designed to be an inevitable outcome of the land it inhabited. A Hudson River showplace, Foxhollow Farm embodied the spirit and substance of a modern, twentieth-century home, at the same time drawing inspiration from Mount Vernon and the James Breese house in Southampton—a Lindeberg project during his time at McKim, Mead & White. A broad colonnade of eight tapered Doric columns capped by a distinctive balustrade gave the stucco entrance facade grace and dignity while the southwest facade, with views of the river, featured two projecting wings—a loggia and the kitchen—that embraced an outdoor living space where Tracy and Alice Dows, their three children, and their friends liked to congregate. Though Lindeberg sited the house to take full advantage of the views, he and Olmsted never were of one mind on its exact position and form. As Olmsted recalled,

"In our opinion the effort of the architect to obtain symmetry in the general plan and masses of the house on the southwest front, is carried much too far. The result is that the views from the dining room, the central hall and the living room, but especially the dining room, toward the south are very much interfered with and the principal living rooms, aside from the sun room, are given a cramped and pocketed effect."[3]

However, it was the Dowses who had suggested projections on either side of the living terrace for protection from the Hudson winds. They were not concerned about views from the dining room since they rarely used it, except by lamp light, preferring to take meals out-of-doors. It is interesting that Albro & Lindeberg's design would be condemned for its "symmetry of outline [carried out] to such an extent as to radically injure the comfort and satisfaction" of the residents since their houses were rarely symmetrical and often praised as comfortable and livable.

On the terrace, a fountain with a sculpture of young Pan, god of the fields, by Henry Hering—Augustus Saint-Gaudens's former assistant—masked the kitchen wing and created a secondary axis through the outdoor living room to the loggia. A series of substantial square chimneys and dormers, rhythmically spaced, punctuated the steeply pitched gray-green slate roof, adding further interest to the roofline. On South Mill Road, a stucco gate lodge incorporated into the slope of the rise along the Landsman Kill signaled the entrance to Foxhollow. With its long low roof lines and Dutch Colonial charm—including two-part Dutch doors—the small cottage set the stage for the various outbuildings extending to the northeast beyond the main house. The estate provided accommodations for fifty—the Dows family and a retinue of staff, that included household servants, coachmen, gardeners, farmers, the superintendent, bookkeeper, and their families.

As critic Phil M. Riley proclaimed, "Unlike many estates of to-day, in their architectural display of wealth, this country place breathes the very welcome sweet simplicity of the farm. The whole impression is that of good taste, and comfort."[4] Inside, the architects used a sparing touch, using white-painted paneling and

RESIDENCE, TRACY DOWS, RHINEBECK, N.Y.   ALBRO & LINDEBERG, ARCHITECTS

Above: Gate Lodge.

mahogany touches to create an impression of luxurious simplicity. Bookshelves on all the walls of the English oak-paneled living room, which occupied the entire depth of the house, were both practical and decorative. A globe-shaped crystal on the newel post of the main stair added an element of whimsy.

Lindeberg also designed the light fixtures throughout. The Dowses' first design mandate, the loggia, became the family's favorite room; a large bright space, it was flooded with light from windows on three sides, had green-tiled floors, a giant fireplace, and a decoratively beamed ceiling. Not only was Foxhollow Farm regarded as the epitome of the modern and tasteful country retreat, but it also was heralded by *Country Life in America* as one of the twelve best country houses in America.[5]

Lindeberg's close friendship with the Dowses led to many commissions, especially early on in his career. While he was working on Foxhollow Farm, Albro & Lindeberg remodeled nearby Glenburn for the Olin family. Simultaneously, Alice Olin Dows's father, Stephen H. Olin, a trustee and member of the building committee at Wesleyan University (Alice's grandfather had been its third president), brought the firm the commission to rebuild North College. This project—awarded just three months after Albro and Lindeberg formed their practice—involved replacing an 1825 dormitory that had burned down with a more neoclassical design that still meshed with the school's original row of stone buildings. In New York, Tracy Dows's sister and brother-in-law, Mr. and Mrs. Richard Hoe, commissioned a Colonial Revival garage and apartment at 163 East 69th Street. Lindeberg went on to design several branches in the 1910s for the Corn Exchange Bank, a bank organized by David Dows with which Tracy Dows was associated, and to remodel the

Above: The sunroom opened to the terraced sitting area.

Left: Lindeberg and Tracy Dows in the sunroom, 1914.

Opposite: Living room.

historic Beekman Arms in Rhinebeck for Dows, transforming it from a brick gambrel roof structure into an up-to-date hotel with a classical facade.[6] The Dowses, Lindeberg, and Vincent and Helen Astor socialized frequently at Foxhollow Farm; for Astor, Lindeberg would design Holiday Farm, a convalescent home for children, and the stone barns at Astor's estate, Ferncliff, later built by Charles A. Platt.[7] It is likely that Lindeberg met his second wife, Lucia Hull, through this circle of friends: Lucia's brother Lytle Hull was a friend of Helen Huntington Astor as well as Vincent Astor's business associate.[8]

In 1930 Tracy Dows closed up the house and moved to England. At this time, the Foxhollow School for Girls was established on the estate, adopting the name of the property, but the house soon returned to residential use. In 1938 Vincent Astor's company Harbor Acres Realty bought Foxhollow, and it was occupied by his half-brother John Jacob Astor V. It changed hands again in 1941 when real estate investor and former Lindeberg client Duncan Harris purchased the property. Harris had commissioned Lindeberg to design his house on Wilson Point in Norwalk, Connecticut, in 1921 when he and a partner developed the 154-acre property overlooking Long Island Sound. Subsequently, the Rhinebeck Country School took over the buildings, and since the mid-1980s, the Samaritan Daytop Village, a drug rehabilitation center, has occupied Foxhollow. All the buildings—some altered, some in decline—survive.

HOUSES ON LILY POND LANE

EAST HAMPTON, NEW YORK

LITTLE BURLEES
EDWARD T. COCKCROFT HOUSE, 1906

DR. FREDERICK K. HOLLISTER HOUSE, 1908

COXWOULD
DR. JOHN F. ERDMANN HOUSE, 1912–13

CLARENCE F. ALCOTT HOUSE, 1914

Prior to 1896, the year service on the Long Island Railroad was extended to Montauk, East Hampton was a sleepy farming community, consisting of a main street surrounded by swaths of open land of crop fields and pastures. While the charm and allure of the seaside village had been discovered by a group of enterprising artists in the late 1870s—Winslow Homer, Julien Alden Weir, Edwin Austin Abbey, and Robert Swain Gifford among them—East Hampton and its nascent summer colony grew primarily as a result of the new access from New York. Tracts of farmland became ripe for development as the village began to experience a transformation similar to that of Southampton a decade earlier, and the Great Plain stretching between Hook and Lily Pond grew into what was the original summer colony as shingle style cottages began to materialize along the dunes. Clustered together, Albro & Lindeberg's four houses were at the heart of this burgeoning enclave, a community made up largely of affluent professionals, such as doctors, lawyers, and bankers—as well as artists—as opposed to the robber barons and industrialists who gravitated toward the social rigor and formality of Newport. While the shingle style flourished in East Hampton well into the twentieth century, Albro & Lindeberg helped to establish the English vernacular style with these four houses on Lily Pond Lane. As architect Aymar Embury II noted, Lindeberg's designs on the East End heralded in the "revival of good taste in the early 1900s."[1] In each of them, Lindeberg transformed English precedents into a style that was so complete a synthesis as to create strongly allusive architecture that conceals its direct sources.

One of the Albro & Lindeberg's very first commissions, Little Burlees, came from Edward Truesdell Cockcroft (1871–1951), the son of wealthy New York landowner John van Voorhees Cockcroft and a close friend of Albro's—the architect had been an usher in Cockcroft's wedding to Viola Baker in 1904. The firm designed an informal stucco house with a large living room and dining room that flowed directly into one another.[2] Intended to exploit the temperate summer climate, the house featured an expansive loggia and pergolas. The stair, leading up to six bedrooms, which more typically would be a major feature, was set unobtrusively behind the living room. Local sand mixed into the stucco gave the facades a warm buff color that Lindeberg accented with pale-green trim and shutters. Meanwhile, the rounded shingles used at the corners softened the roofline, giving the striking impression of thatch—a roof that would come to define Albro & Lindeberg's work. Highly publicized in the architectural press, Little Burlees represented a relaxed and informal alternative to the shingle style. As work on the house progressed, the Cockcrofts asked

Entrance of Coxwould.

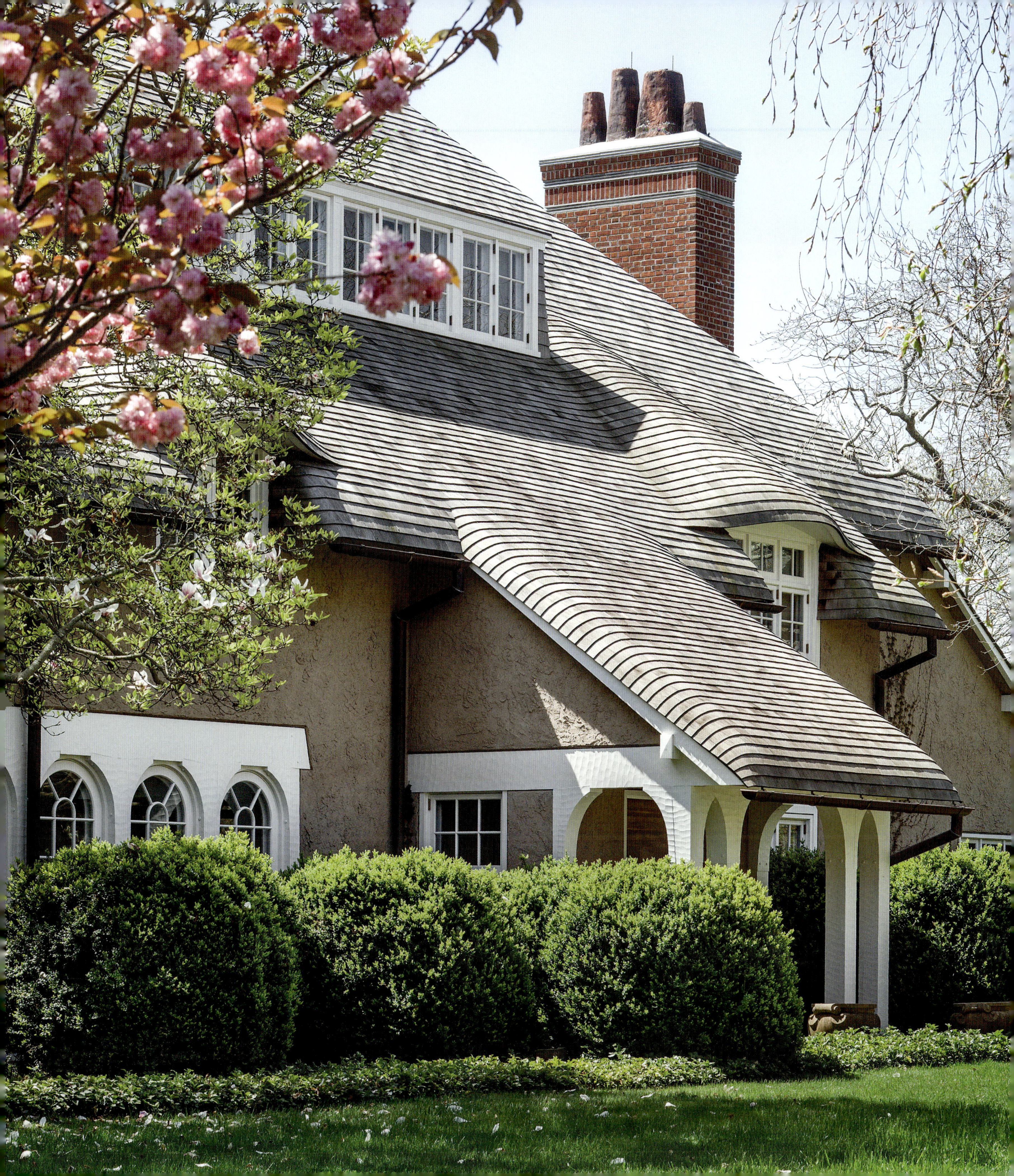

Above: Entrance facade of Little Burlees.

Left: Dr. Frederick K. Hollister house.

Opposite: Entrance facade and plan of Coxwould.

the firm to renovate their brownstone at 59 East 77th Street in 1907.[3]

In 1908 Dr. Frederick Kellogg Hollister (1868–1934) commissioned Albro & Lindeberg to design a cottage just east of the Cockcrofts.[4] Dr. Hollister, a physician and lecturer at Flower Hospital, and his wife, Harriet Shelton Hollister (1875–1965)—the daughter of his partner, Dr. George G. Shelton—had been summer residents of East Hampton since 1901. With its low pitched hipped roof and vine-covered pergolas and porches, the Hollister house embodied, as Robert A.M. Stern has pointed out, the spirit of Charles A. Platt and was influential in shaping the work of other local architects.[5] The plan followed the informal arrangement found at the Cockcroft cottage, with the front door opening directly into the living room, which in turn opened into dining room. The interior finishes were simple, and the stair was tucked discreetly to the side and the kitchen wing to the rear. Much of the house's floor area consisted of loggias and porches.

While the more conventional Cockcroft house was characteristic of Albro & Lindeberg's early work, the design of Dr. John F. Erdmann's house, just across the street, revealed Lindeberg's uncanny ability to create facades that were at once balanced, asymmetrical, and inviting. Erdmann (1864–1954), the son of a merchant tailor from Chillicothe, Ohio, rose from humble beginnings to great success as professor and director of surgery at the New York Post-Graduate Medical College and Hospital (now part of NYU). He performed surgery well into his 80s, claiming "a busy surgeon has to keep up or he won't be a busy surgeon." He had a long roster of famous patients, including President Grover Cleveland on whom he helped perform a covert operation on a yacht in Long Island Sound to eradicate cancer in his mouth.[6]

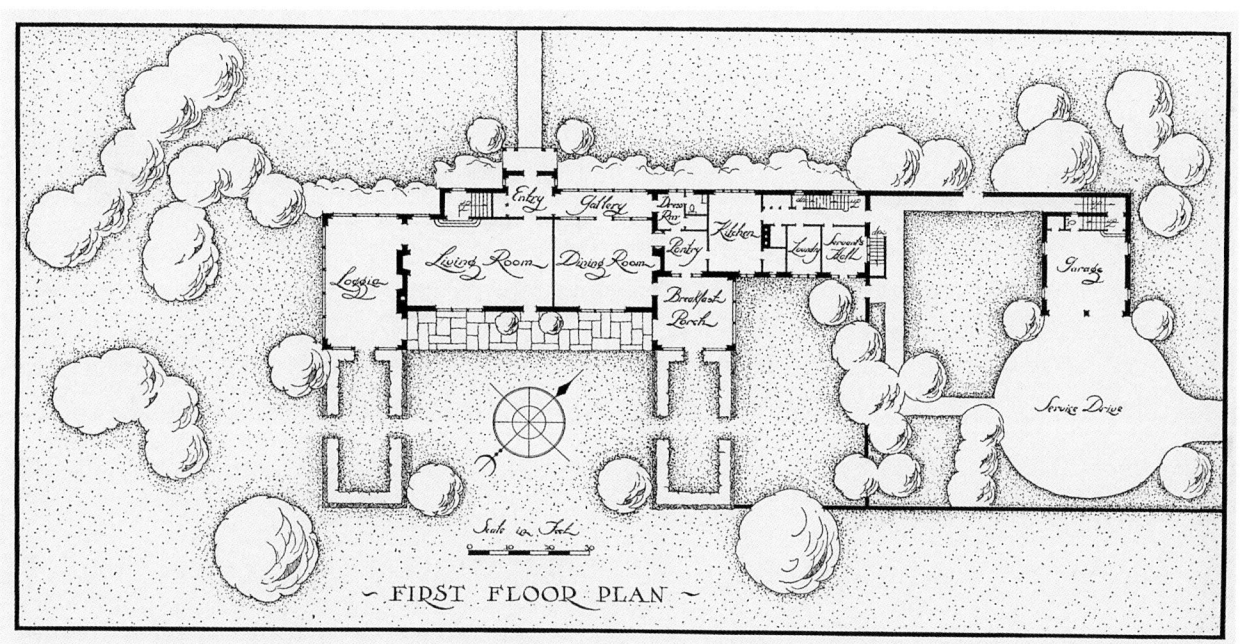

Erdmann and his wife, Georgiana Wright Erdmann (1868–1952), commissioned Coxwould, a low-lying English-inspired house with an imposing roof with shingles laid to simulate thatch. With much of the second floor expressed as dormers just peeking up through the eaves and the front door sheltered by an overhanging entrance porch, the house had a hooded, almost closed, quality. Lindeberg extended the kitchen wing, garage, and walled service court to the east, emphasizing the long low-lying mass of the north facade. However, to the rear, he incorporated two loggias on either side of the central block which opened onto gardens, giving the south facade the impression of symmetry. At the time, the Erdmanns owned the entire tract of land extending south to the beach so that the water would have been visible from the house. For the most part, the plan echoed that of the Cockcroft and Hollister houses, with the exception of a sunlit gallery leading from the small entrance foyer to the kitchen wing.

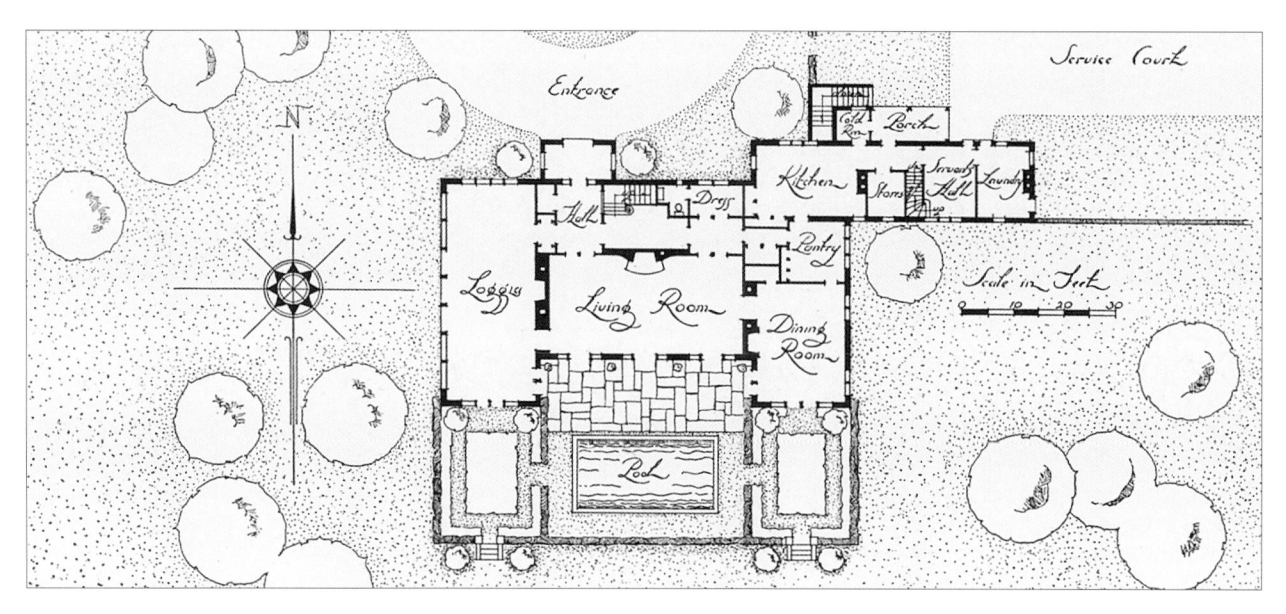

Even more English in spirit, Lindeberg's picturesque house for Clarence F. Alcott (1885–1957) and his wife, Lucie Burke Alcott (1885–1961), was dominated by the great sweep of its flared roof.[7] Alcott, had been captain of the Yale football team and selected as an All-American in 1906 and 1907. While he chose a career in investment banking after college, he would also return to Yale to coach football periodically. For

Above: Entrance facade of Coxwould.

Right: Garden facade of Coxwould.

Opposite: Garden facade and plan of the Clarence Alcott house.

the Alcotts, Lindeberg—now a sole practitioner—chose a grayish tan stucco and paired it with the same pale-green for shutters as he had used on the other houses. This muted palette, typical of Lindeberg's color sense, bound the house to natural tones of the landscape. As the most prominent element of the design, the roof was framed to create the buckled appearance of age and was carried out in variegated moss-green tiles that extended down—and almost fused with—the greenery surrounding the house. Like Coxwould, the house presented an asymmetrical entrance facade, this time anchored by a large central gable and chimney with hooded shingled dormers peeking out of the expansive roof. But again, on the garden front, Lindeberg created a semblance of symmetry with a loggia and dining room extending out under the sweeping roof toward boxwood gardens that originally framed a pool.

The Cockcroft house, later occupied by Jacqueline Kennedy Onassis's aunt Winifred Lee d'Olier and her husband, Franklin, was destroyed by fire in 2008 and rebuilt on the same footprint. Both the Hollister and Erdman houses have been recently restored while the Alcott house remains much in its original condition, with the half-timber details now painted brown.

Above: West facade of the Alcott house.

Opposite above: Entrance facade.

Opposite below left: An asymmetrical composition of gables and dormers marks the entrance.

Opposite below right: A bank of windows provides natural light to the stair.

71

MEADOW SPRING

GLEN COVE, NEW YORK

1911

WILLIAM NELSON DYKMAN/JACKSON ANNAN
DYKMAN HOUSE, 1911

HENRY C. MARTIN/WILLIAM NELSON DYKMAN
HOUSE, 1914; REBUILT 1923

GEORGE GALT BOURNE HOUSE, C. 1915

Meadow Spring was an early development in Glen Cove initiated by Henry Lewis Batterman (1876–1961) through his company Barwin Realty. Batterman's father, Henry Batterman (1850–1912), was a successful Brooklyn merchant, president of the Broadway Bank, and heavily involved in the life and culture of Brooklyn. His son did take on the presidency of the family department store, but he eventually sold it and moved on to real estate. Barwin Realty, initially located on Montague Street in his native borough, specialized in Brooklyn real estate, but the office moved to the more central location of 50 East 42nd Street when Batterman moved to Manhattan. Batterman, a member of the Nassau Country Club, was one of several Brooklyn men who began summering in Glen Cove in the 1900s. As the *New York Times* reported in 1907, Glen Cove was prospering because the club, founded in 1896, was attracting new cottagers to the village.

Meadow Spring was conceived as a cohesive development that would allow purchasers some latitude in architectural styles while guaranteeing homogeneity of ownership through restrictive covenants. With twenty-four lots arranged around an informal and rambling loop with a main entrance off Town Path (now Duck Pond Road), the plan reflected garden suburb designs of the era. Batterman brought in Albro & Lindeberg to design several of the first houses as well as a caretaker's cottage, accessible by the service drive from Elm Avenue, with an arched drive-through. Old-growth trees and landscaping gave Meadow Spring a sense of privacy and almost a rural character despite its relatively small lot sizes and a central location near the Glen Cove train station and the Nassau Country Club. Conveniences like Peekskill gravel roads, water mains with fire protection, electricity, telephones, and independent service drives, as advertised in *Country Life in America* and the *New York Times*, were selling points.

Lindeberg's first house on lot 3, a two-acre site, was completed in 1911. The white-shingled house consisted of a central block framed by two solid chimneys and a center door. This straightforward design was given a touch of individuality through a projecting loggia, steeply slopping roofs, and attic dormers. Inside, a center hall encompassed a square stair that climbed up to the third floor.

Lindeberg's second house on the slightly larger lot 2 (three acres) was completed by 1914 and located to the north inside the loop. A larger stucco house with a half-timbered service wing and loggia angling out to the southeast, it was more picturesque than the house on lot 3. Much like his houses in Hewlett, New York, it featured a large arched window on the front facade that lit the stair hall. Advertised as a "splendid example of the modern country house," it enclosed an "unusually practical plan for convenient management. Rooms [were] large, light and airy with every modern appointment."[1] To the rear, a sunken walled garden with an

Entrance of the William Nelson Dykman house, White Acre.

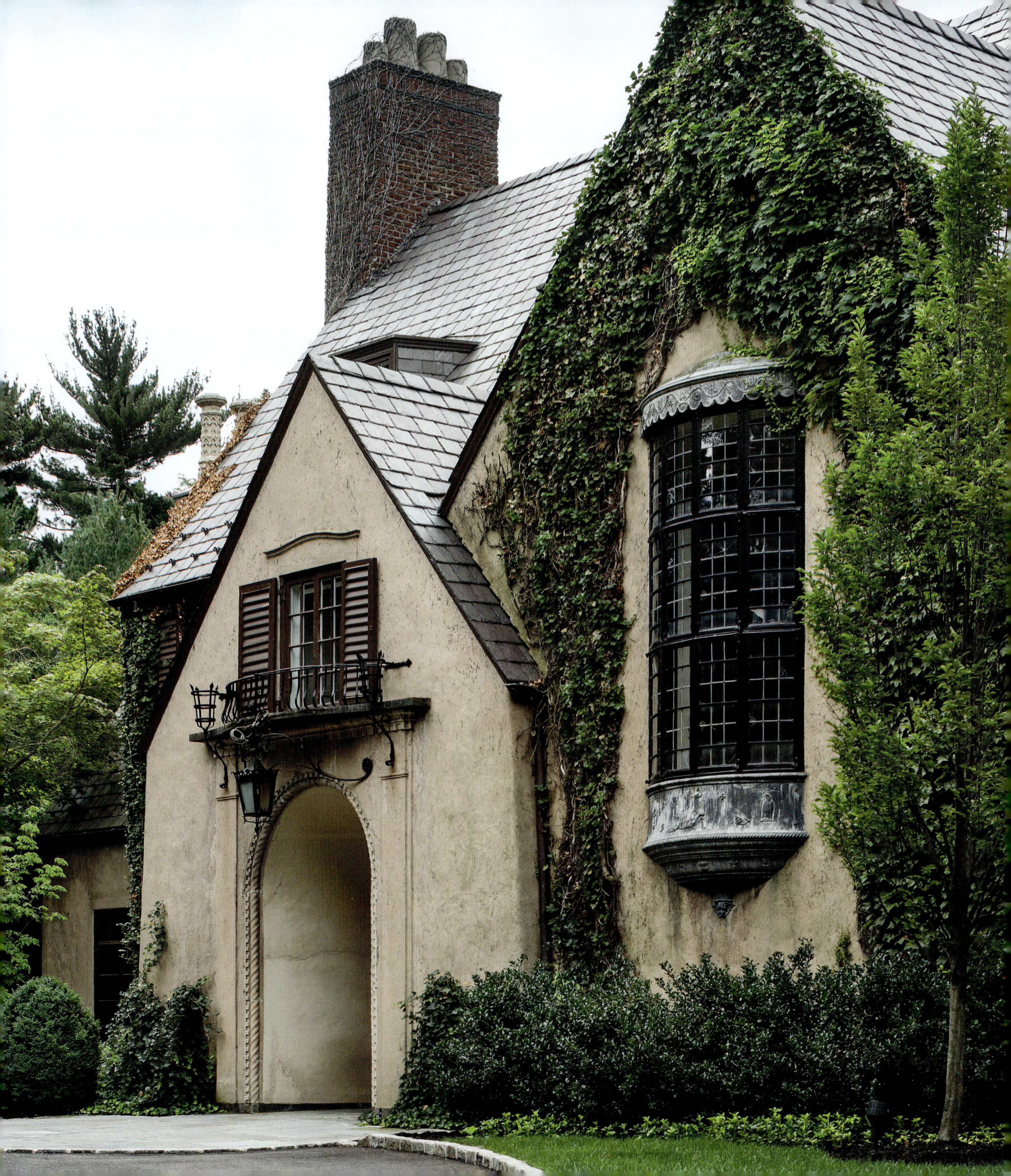

Above left: Henry C. Martin house on lot 2.

Above right: Jackson A. Dykman house on lot 3 with its original shingling.

abundance of flowers carried out by garden designer Charles Galanti stretched to the south; the property also included lot 6. Montague Flagg rented the house until cotton goods broker Henry C. Martin (1882–1948) and his wife, Elfrieda Weber Martin (1887–1979), bought it. They sold it to well-connected Brooklyn-based lawyer William Nelson Dykman (1855–1937) in 1923. At that time, an unchecked fire, started by sparks from the chimney, ravaged the house and garage. As the *New York Times* reported, "smoke and flames from the burning building could be seen for miles and brought to the scene virtually the entire population of the fashionable district."[2] In the fire's aftermath, Dykman and his wife, Isabel Annan Dykman (1864–1941), asked Lindeberg to rebuild. While the house more or less occupied the same footprint, Lindeberg upgraded the long rambling mass with leaded glass windows and ironwork details by Samuel Yellin and designed a double-height oriel in the front gable with details of a squirrel, an eagle, wingless griffin, a fleur-de-lis, and a cupid. He also incorporated iron valences wrought with grape vines and a bracket over the front door for a lantern with birds. The interiors were carried out in paneling as well as rough plaster and featured a large circular stair and center hall that extended through to the garden front. The attic level, a substantial volume given by its steep pitch and myriad dormers, contained two bedroom suites with fireplaces in addition to the five bedrooms on the second floor and series of servants' rooms above the kitchen. It is likely that the Dykmans initially purchased the house, which they named White Acre, after moving from Lindeberg's first house on lot 3. Their son Jackson Annan Dykman (1887–1974) and his wife, Susan Merrick Dykman (1893–1969), who married in 1915, later occupied lot 3.[3] Both the Martins, another prominent Brooklyn family, and Dykmans would have been well acquainted with the Battermans through Brooklyn circles. Jackson Dykman, a lawyer at his father's firm Cullen & Dykman, also became the Chancellor of the Protestant Episcopal Diocese of Long Island.

Lindeberg's next house, completed around 1915 on lot 8, was originally occupied by George Galt Bourne (1888–1945) and his wife, Helen Whitney Bourne (1890–1974). The son of Frederick G. Bourne, the head of the Singer Sewing Machine Company, George Bourne took over as president after his father's death in 1919. Located in the center of the loop, the brick cottage, originally whitewashed, was dominated by a steeply pitched hipped roof that swept down to the ground on

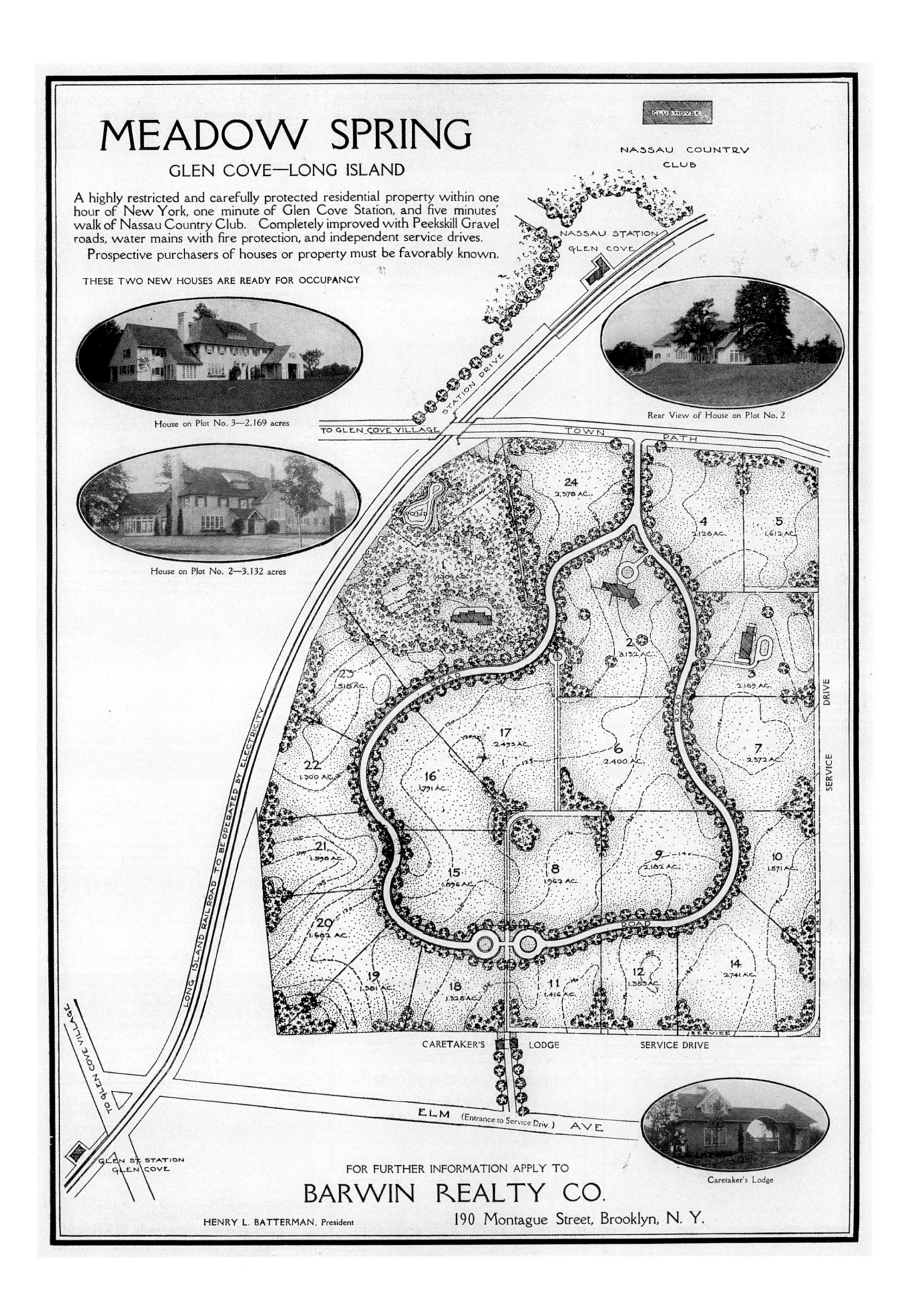

MEADOW SPRING
GLEN COVE—LONG ISLAND

A highly restricted and carefully protected residential property within one hour of New York, one minute of Glen Cove Station, and five minutes' walk of Nassau Country Club. Completely improved with Peekskill Gravel roads, water mains with fire protection, and independent service drives.

Prospective purchasers of houses or property must be favorably known.

THESE TWO NEW HOUSES ARE READY FOR OCCUPANCY

House on Plot No. 3—2.169 acres

Rear View of House on Plot No. 2

House on Plot No. 2—3.132 acres

Caretaker's Lodge

FOR FURTHER INFORMATION APPLY TO

BARWIN REALTY CO.
190 Montague Street, Brooklyn, N.Y.

HENRY L. BATTERMAN, President

Above: Dykman house.

Opposite above: George Galt Bourne house on lot 8.

Opposite below: Bourne house with its original whitewashed brick exterior.

either side.[4] Smaller than the other houses in the development, the charming cottage was just one room deep with an intimate stair hall and a gable-front entry porch. The Bournes stayed briefly, moving to Locust Valley in the early 1920s. By 1922, James Blackstone Taylor Jr. and his wife, Aileen Sedgwick Taylor, lived in the cottage, christening it Little Waddingfield.

Henry Batterman set Meadow Spring up as a corporation, and residents originally owned shares in proportion to their lot size. While the Dykmans and the Bournes lived in Lindeberg-designed houses, other residents, such as banker Clarkson Runyon Jr., opted for different architects—in his case, Mott B. Schmidt. Later, Henry Batterman's daughter Marian, married to Horace Ridgely Bullock, lived in Meadow Spring. Batterman himself, a breeder of prize Guernsey cattle, chose to live in nearby Mill Neck on an 81-acre estate. In 1910 he purchased property and commissioned a stately Southern Colonial house from Albro & Lindeberg. Completed in 1914, it was known as Beaver Brook Farm.[5] "It is not difficult" one article commented, "to imagine this Batterman house becoming, with time, as distinguished a monument of sincerely American architecture as Westover, for one of the most delightful qualities of genuine architecture is the grace and dignity with which it ages."[6] Beaver Brook Farm was torn down in the 1950s and only a caretaker's cottage remains. Meadow Spring, on the other hand, remains the bucolic enclave it was when it was originally designed. All of the historic houses have been well maintained, and although additional houses have been added over time, some of the original lots remain open and the serene pocket of development off Duck Pond Road continues to feel quiet and private. There is no longer access from Elm Avenue and the caretaker's cottage has been absorbed into the adjoining neighborhood.

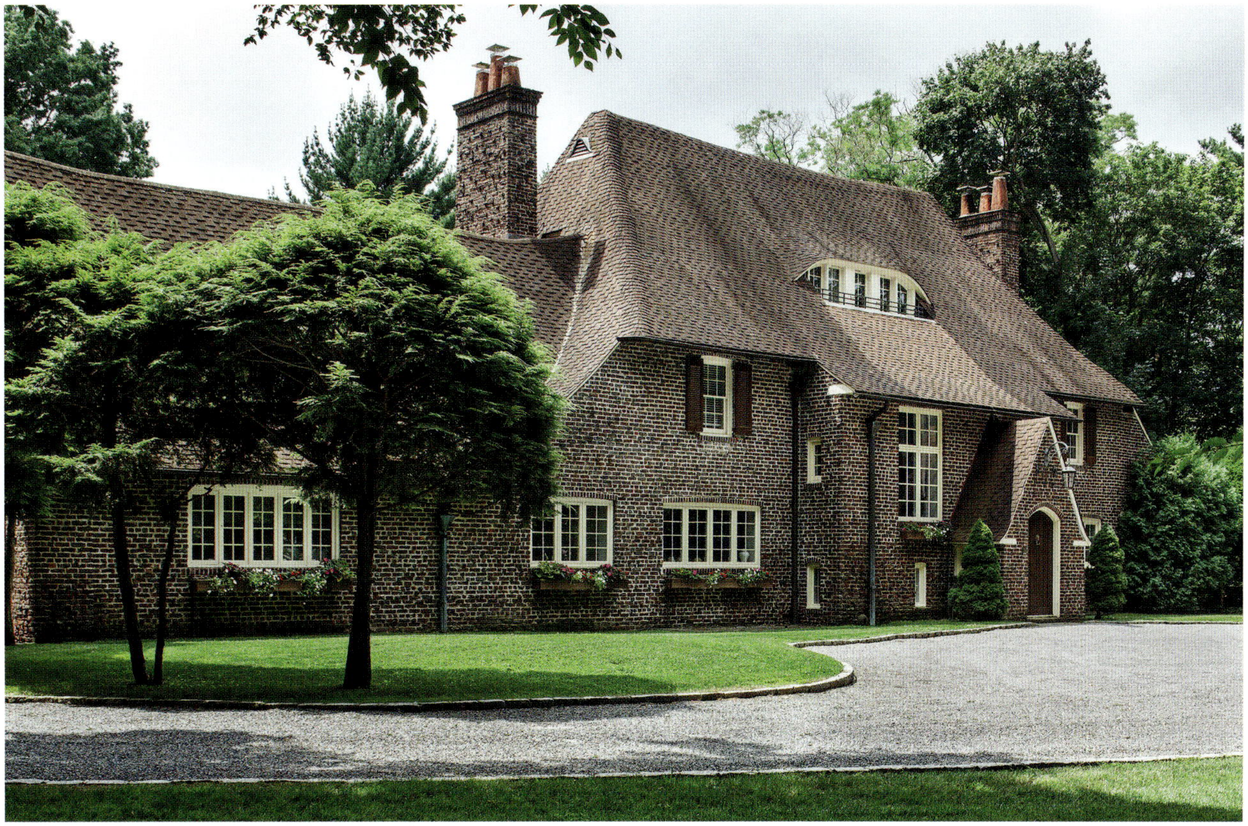

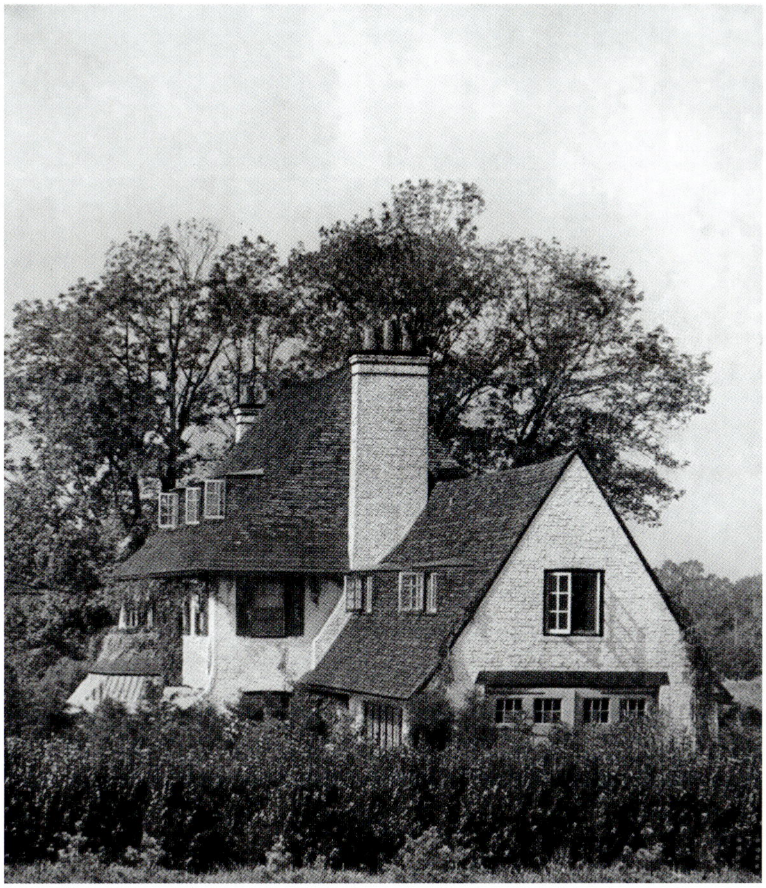

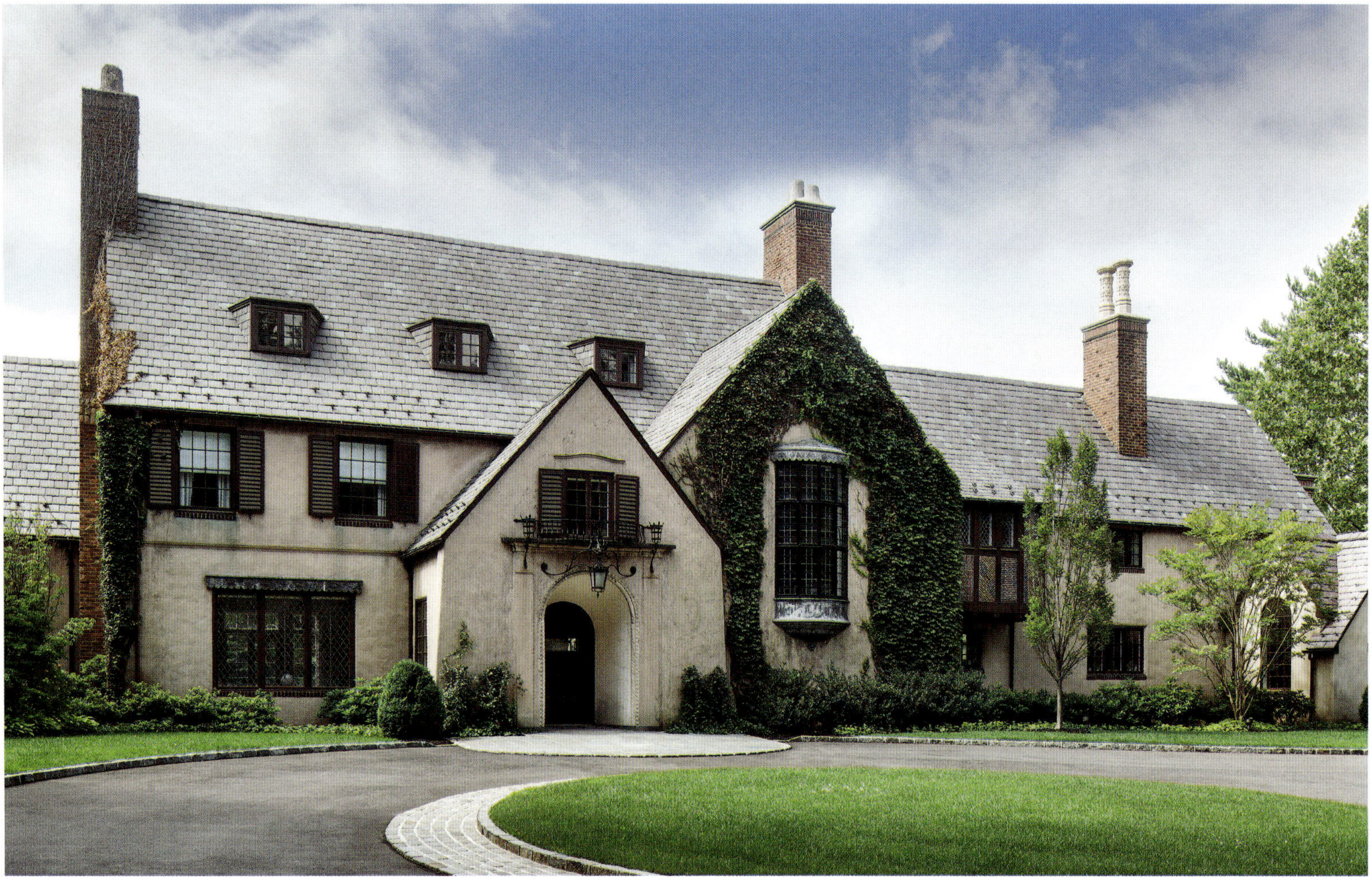

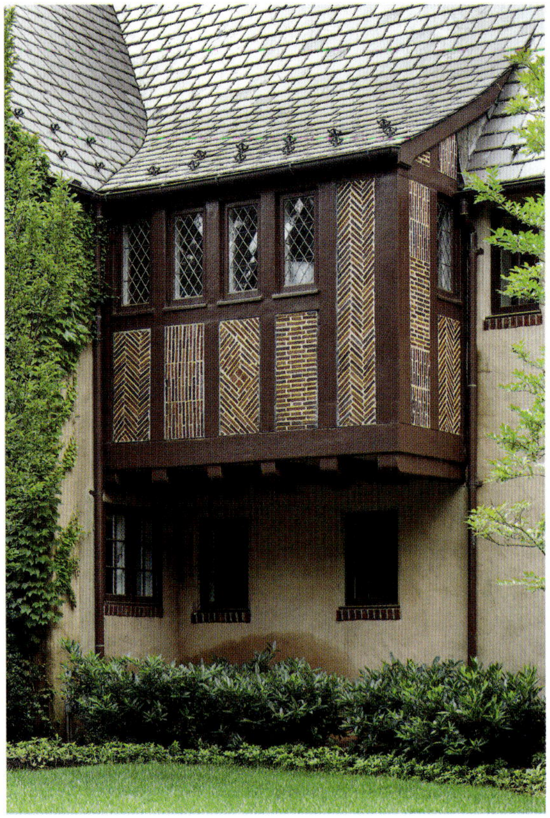

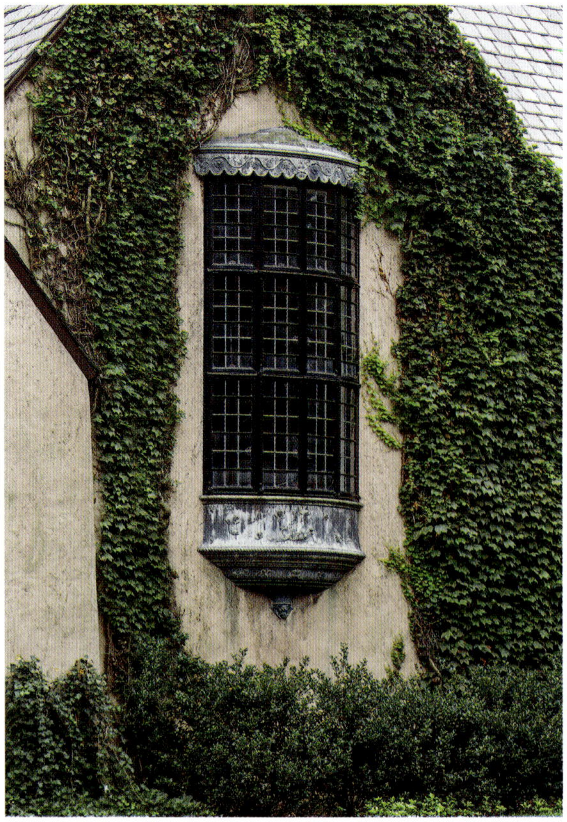

Opposite above: Entrance facade of White Acre.

Opposite below left: Half-timbered detail.

Opposite below right: Oriel window with details of a squirrel, eagle, wingless griffin, fleur-de-lis and cupid.

Above left: Stair.

Above right: View from the front hall into the dining room.

79

ALBEMARLE
GERARD B. LAMBERT ESTATE

PRINCETON, NEW JERSEY

1913–17

In 1913 Gerard and Rachel Lambert bought four hundred acres in Princeton. Gerard "Jerry" Barnes Lambert (1887–1967), who had graduated from Princeton University in 1908, was familiar with the area and had been lured by friends to buy land there instead of Long Island, where the couple had had an option to purchase property. Lambert's father, Jordan Wheat Lambert (1851–1889), had developed the all-purpose antiseptic Listerine after a carbolic acid concoction invented by British surgeon Joseph Lister to use on operative wounds. This was reformulated as a mouthwash that his father's company Lambert Pharmacal Co. (later Warner-Lambert Pharmaceutical Co.) produced and sold. After Lambert's parents died, he and his siblings were left as wealthy orphans and raised by various aunts and uncles.

After spending two years studying architecture at Columbia University, Lambert joined his father's company. In the 1920s, as president, he formulated an advertising campaign around the fear of halitosis, prompting people to worry about a newly identified problem. Its effect increased Listerine profits sixty-fold. Lambert sold his portion of the business in 1928, clearing $25 million, and he was unscathed by the Great Depression. He then made a second fortune by reorganizing and turning around the Gillette Safety Razor Company. Something of a Renaissance man, Lambert was an author, an international yachtsman, an amateur archaeologist, in addition to his training in architecture. In 1910 he filed a patent claim for a drawing board with manually operable members to stretch the paper.[1]

Lambert married Rachel Parkhill Lowe (1889–1978), the daughter of Arthur Houghton Lowe, a textile manufacturer and former mayor of Fitchburg, Massachusetts, in 1908, and they had three children. Their eldest daughter Rachel, or Bunny as she was nicknamed by her mother, later married Paul Mellon and became a well-known horticulturist, philanthropist, and art collector. After purchasing the Princeton property, Lambert—then with a young family—immediately contacted Lindeberg; the couple had previously rented one of the houses he had designed in East Hampton. The Lambert house, more than any other commission, was a collaboration between architect and client, yet Lindeberg's strong vision is clearly legible in the completed building. The men spent two years designing the house, studying every element in detail. As Lambert recalled, "We would put up a column and take it down and remove half an inch in diameter, and then keep on doing this until the column was right. We set up slate from four quarries on the front lawn to study the colors for the roof. We argued for weeks over a molding for a doorway. I was enjoying this, and my study of architecture at Princeton and Columbia came in handy. Harrie Lindeberg is by far the most brilliant architect I have ever known and since those days he has done many jobs for me. We loved the problems and did not rush things."[2]

Lambert named the estate Albemarle after the county in Virginia where he grew up. As inspiration, the two men looked to McKim, Mead & White's Colonial Revival house for James Breese in Southampton and its prototype, Mount Vernon.[3] However, Lindeberg incorporated eight slim round columns instead of the thin wooden square ones used at George Washington's residence. At three stories tall and 192 feet long, it was a

Entrance facade.

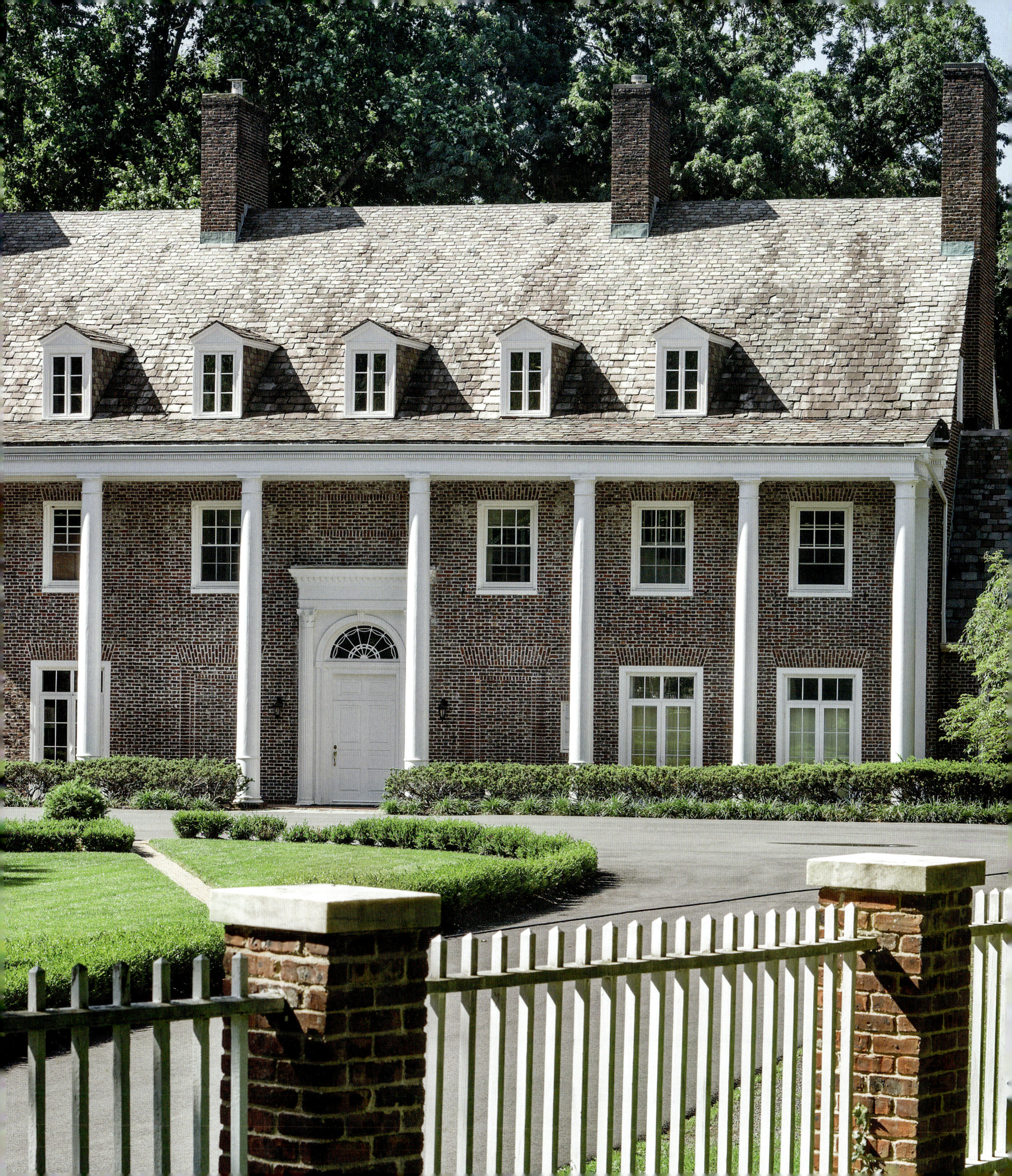

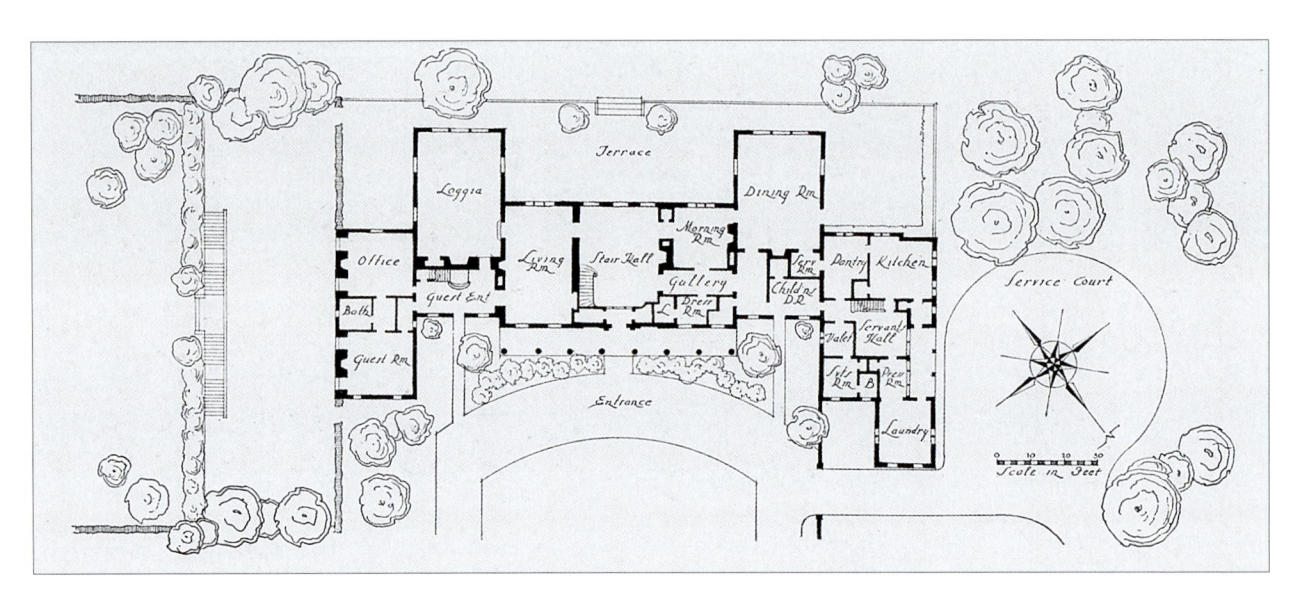

large house, but Lindeberg and Lambert tempered its size with huge doors and windows, creating a more intimate sense of scale. As Lambert recalled, "Harrie Lindeberg and I worked very hard to obtain this optical illusion."[4] The front door, for example, is massive, rising up well into the second floor. The rough uneven brick, painted white, appeared weathered, giving the house the instant patina of age. The two years of design were followed by two years of construction, and the house was completed in 1917.

The entrance passed under the stair that curved against the front facade into a large hall overlooking the south terrace, a sequence designed for entertaining. To the east lay the drawing room, paneled living room, secondary stair hall, office, and guest room. A morning room, linen-fold-paneled dining room, and wide gallery with a "withdrawing room" for the ladies as well as the kitchen wing extended to the west. In the interstices between the curving stair and the north facade, Lindeberg inserted windowed alcoves on the

Opposite: Entrance facade

Above left: Linen-fold paneling in the dining room.

Above right: Living room.

Overleaf: Entrance facade.

upper level. Family and guest bedrooms filled out the second floor and the full attic.

The gardens grew over time. In the late 1920s, the Lamberts hired Olmsted Brothers to carry out the grounds. Lambert, who was very interested in grasses, focused on obtaining smooth expanses of green around the house. In front, a tapis vert, as he called it, stretched two hundred feet toward the forecourt gates with ancient apple trees and boxwood creating an entirely green effect. As Lambert recalled, "The enclosure of this inner court seemed to wrap the arriving visitor within its cool green arms."[5] Off the east side of the house, a bowling green where family and friends actually bowled featured a flawless swath of creeping bent, a specialty grass primarily used for putting greens and lawn tennis courts. Beyond the bowling green, Olmsted Brothers designed a vista garden to the east with a long view down the hillside to the woods with a brick retaining wall and two sets of stairs descending to the formal flower garden with a picturesque gazebo set off to one side. The Lamberts later added a tennis court and pool.

In 1930 Lambert asked Lindeberg to remodel Carter Hall, a mid-1700s plantation house in Millwood, Virginia, that he bought from his cousin Townsend Burwell. Together, they made the house comfortable while maintaining its Southern character and integrity. While leaving the exterior untouched, Lindeberg modernized the interiors and refined many of the rooms with new paneling and mantels.[6]

In the early 1950s, Lambert and his second wife, Grace Lansing Mull (1900–1993), moved out of Albemarle's main house and into a 15-room cottage on the estate, retaining a riding ring, stables, and dog kennels.[7] The couple sold the main house to the Columbus Boychoir School, which had moved to Princeton in 1950 from Ohio, where it resided until 2012. In financial straits, the American Boychoir School, as it became known after 1980, sold the house to Chinese real estate magnate Jiang Bairong in 2013. He, in turn, opened the Princeton International School of Mathematics and Science (PRISMS). While the school has plans for expansion, Albemarle remains preserved in much of its original condition.

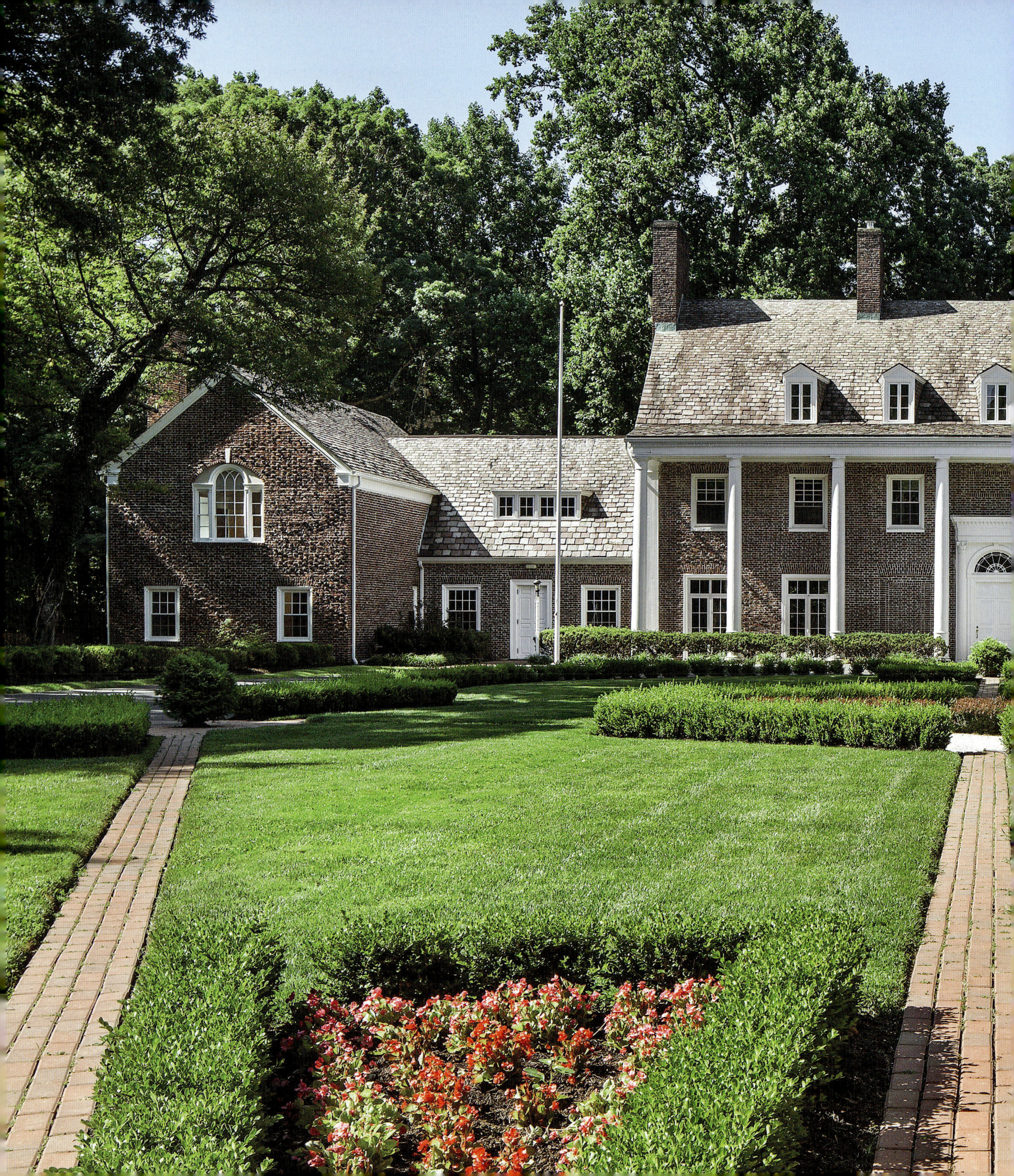

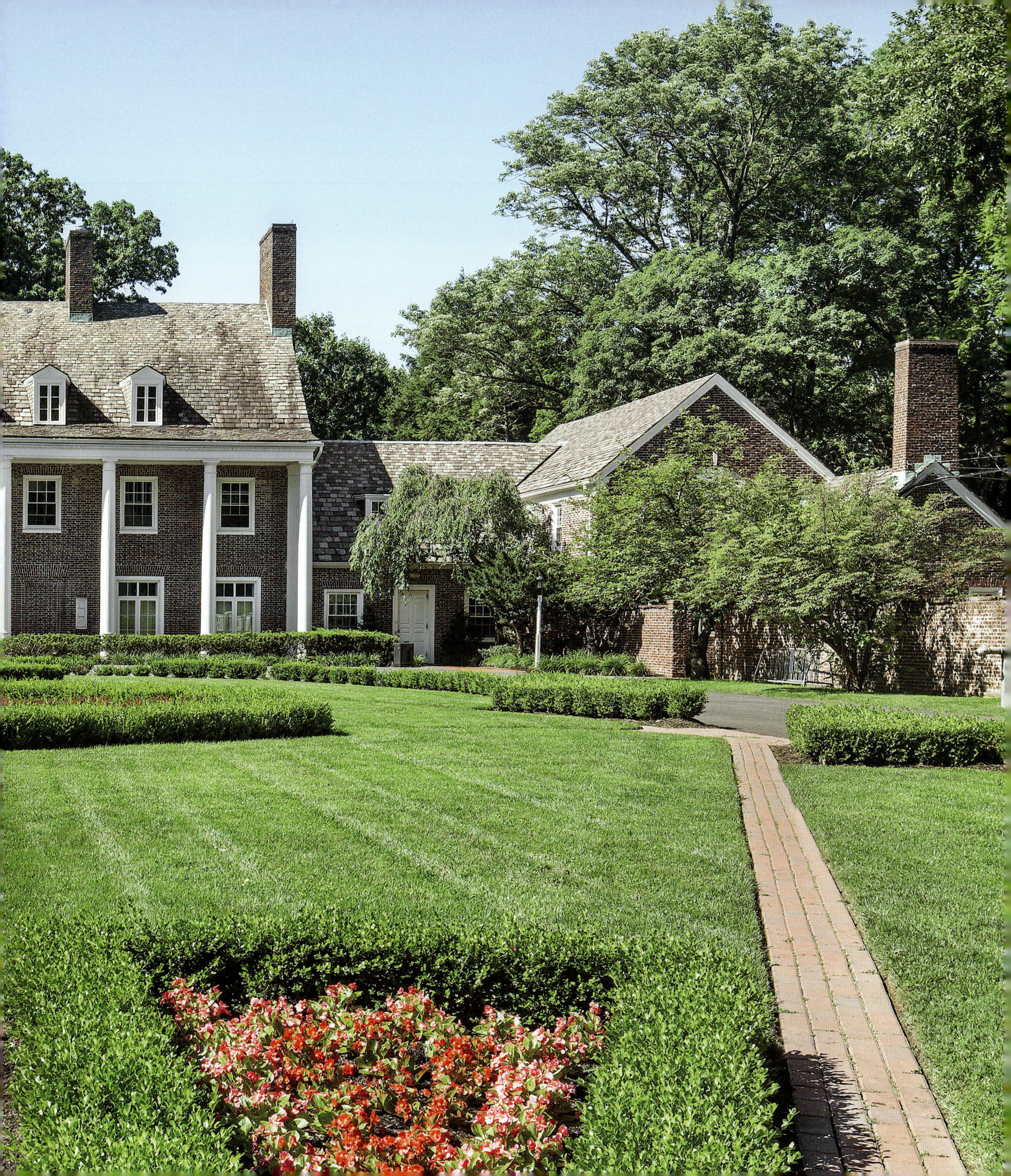

Above: East facade from the vista garden.

Left: Gardens designed by Olmsted Brothers.

Opposite: Engaged Corinthian columns framing the front door.

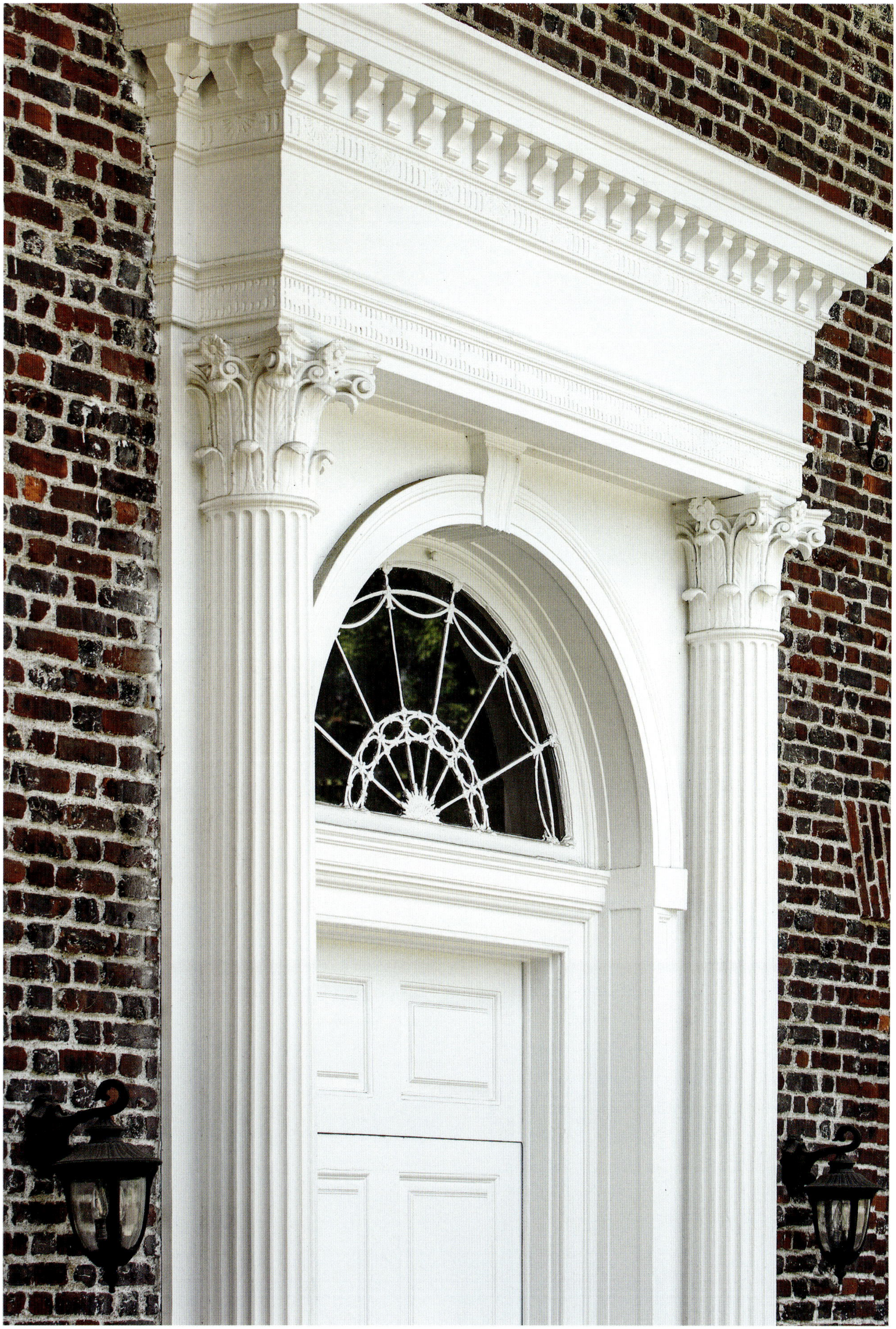

OWL'S NEST
EUGENE DU PONT JR. ESTATE

GREENVILLE, DELAWARE

1915—20

One year after Lindeberg parted with Albro, he won the commission to design an estate for Eugene du Pont (1873–1954) and his wife, Ethel Pyle du Pont (1881–1954), in Greenville, Delaware in the Brandywine Valley. As the family seat, the rolling hills north of Wilmington were peppered with houses and estates belonging to du Ponts, many of which were designed by important Philadelphia architects or New York firms like Carrère and Hastings. A grandson of Éleuthère Irénée du Pont de Nemours, founder of the gunpowder manufacturer E. I. du Pont de Nemours and Company, Eugene was the younger son of Eugene Sr., the last head of the du Pont Company partnership. While he worked in sales for the company after graduating from Harvard in 1897, he retired in 1912 and served on its board from 1917 onward. At the age of 40, a year after his formal retirement, he married Edith Pyle, also of Wilmington, and began to contemplate building a house where he could enjoy farming, horticulture, and hunting and raise a family. After amassing three farms and more than five hundred acres, the du Ponts chose Lindeberg as their architect and Thomas Meehan & Sons of Philadelphia to design the landscape.[1]

In 1915 Lindeberg urged the du Ponts to visit the house he had recently completed for lawyer Paul Moore and his wife, Fanny Hanna Moore, near Morristown, New Jersey, as an inspiration for their project. A large whitewashed-brick house with multiple gables, slate roof, and conical dovecote, Hollow Hill Farm had received many accolades in the architectural press. As critic C. Matlack Price noted, "In the Paul Moore house, at Convent, N. J., there is a great deal that is more than interesting. It astonishes. It would be difficult to find a more picturesque or pleasing roof-line, or a house which naturally falls into so many delight 'compositions' of gables and chimneys and windows."[2] Although Lindeberg proposed the Moore house as a model, Edith du Pont didn't entirely agree. As she noted after the visit:

Mr. Lindeberg built it and as ours has to be on the same order he wanted us to see it. House much larger than our proposed house . . . Very complete but too large. Furnished very expensively but no individuality—living room paneled in blue. Very glary bedrooms. Beautiful loggia, big & airy. Planting of evergreens next to white house very effective.[3]

The du Ponts named their estate Owl's Nest, after a nineteenth-century tavern once located on the corner of the property. Lindeberg incorporated aspects of Hollow Hill Farm into the house, including his characteristic roof—here in shades of purple and green slate laid in diminishing size from eaves to ridge. At 219 feet long, the house rambled across the crest of a rise, its distinctive roof, pierced with eyebrow dormers and chimneys that similarly anchored the sprawling composition to the land. Picturesque details such as a conical ice house/dovecote, a turret containing a loggia and sleeping porch, half-timbering, and irregular clinker bricks added a semblance of age and rootedness to the design. The entrance facade, distinguished by two-story banks of leaded casement windows denoting the double-height great hall within, featured a gabled entrance porch with a round-arch lunette over the front door with a bronze transom grille in the form of an eagle by Oscar Bach. While the German-born craftsman became known for

The rounded southeast end of the house contains a loggia and a sleeping porch.

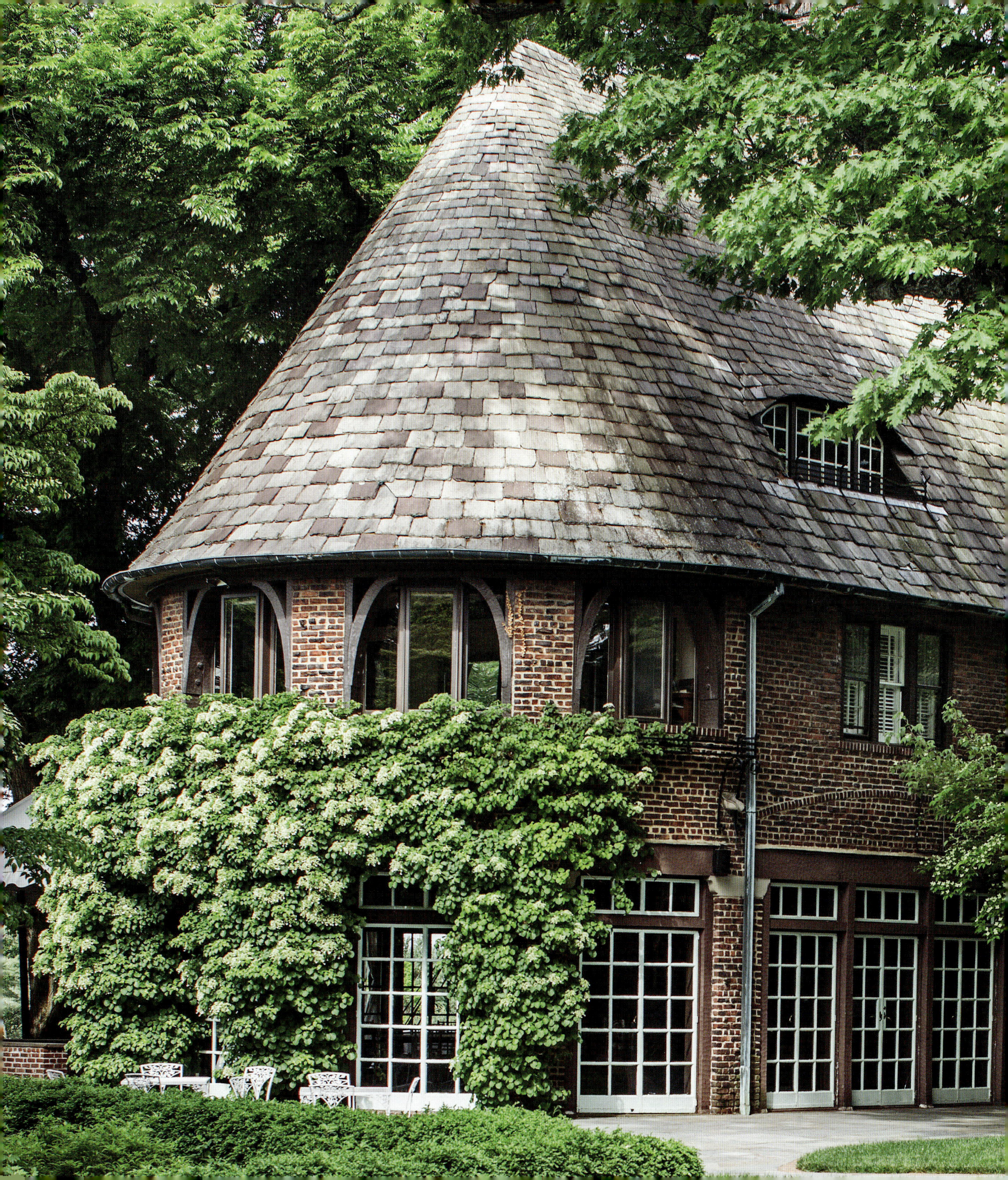

his decorative metalwork for such high-profile commissions as the Woolworth Building, Chrysler Building, Rockefeller Center, and the Empire State Building, he worked frequently with Lindeberg on residential designs; Owl's Nest was one of Bach's first commissions after moving to the United States in 1911.[4]

Inside, Lindeberg evoked a medieval manor hall, creating a space rich in handcrafted elements and details inspired by Northern European vernacular architecture, including limed-oak paneling, rough plaster walls, leaded glass, butterfly-jointed floorboards, beamed ceiling, and artistic metal sconces. Intricately hand-carved wood ornament included heraldic panels and the castle and sailing ship from the du Pont coat-of-arms on the chimney piece, overdoor panels, and strapwork on the balustrade and newel posts. Tucked under the stair leading up to the second-floor balcony lay the entrance to du Pont's den while a secondary hall with an elaborate strapwork ceiling, set on axis with the front door and French doors out to the sloping lawn, connected to the more classical dining room and Georgian living room decorated with walnut paneled walls and a Grinling Gibbons-style overmantel. Here, Lindeberg connected the main rooms with a clear axis that ran from a loggia on one end to an oval-shaped breakfast room wrapped in murals on the other. On the second floor, Lindeberg designed the bedrooms, including two for the du Pont daughters, a night nursery, a guest room and master suite, in a more classical spirit. A dressing room off the master bedroom echoed the shape of the breakfast room below. The steep slope of the roof allowed for full-scale rooms on the attic level where the two du Pont sons had their rooms as well as a billiards room and private apartment. The kitchen and servants' wing extended in a line to the northwest.

The grounds, a park-like setting with a curved entrance drive, sweeping lawns and vistas, and an arboretum, included garages, a potting shed, superintendent's cottage, stucco barns, and a hunting lodge designed by Lindeberg in a modified Tudor style. In 1927 Ellen Biddle Shipman designed a walled boxwood garden and tea house, in a similar Tudor style, to complete the axis extending off of the first-floor loggia.[5]

Above: Entrance facade.

Opposite above: Entrance facade with two-story banks of leaded casement windows.

Opposite below: Tea house designed by Ellen Biddle Shipman, 1927.

Eugene du Pont came to be known as "dirty Gene," as opposed to his first cousin "clean Gene," because of his love of farming and his hands-on approach. A member of numerous hunting associations, he also helped to form the Kinloch Gun Club, a gun club and wildlife preserve on the Santee River in South Carolina.

In 1937 Owl's Nest received national attention when the du Ponts' daughter Ethel married Franklin Delano Roosevelt Jr., the son of the newly reelected president, and a reception for 1,300 was held at the du Pont family home. After the du Ponts' deaths in 1954, the house sat vacant for a number of years. In 1961, the land was subdivided, and the Greenville Country Club,

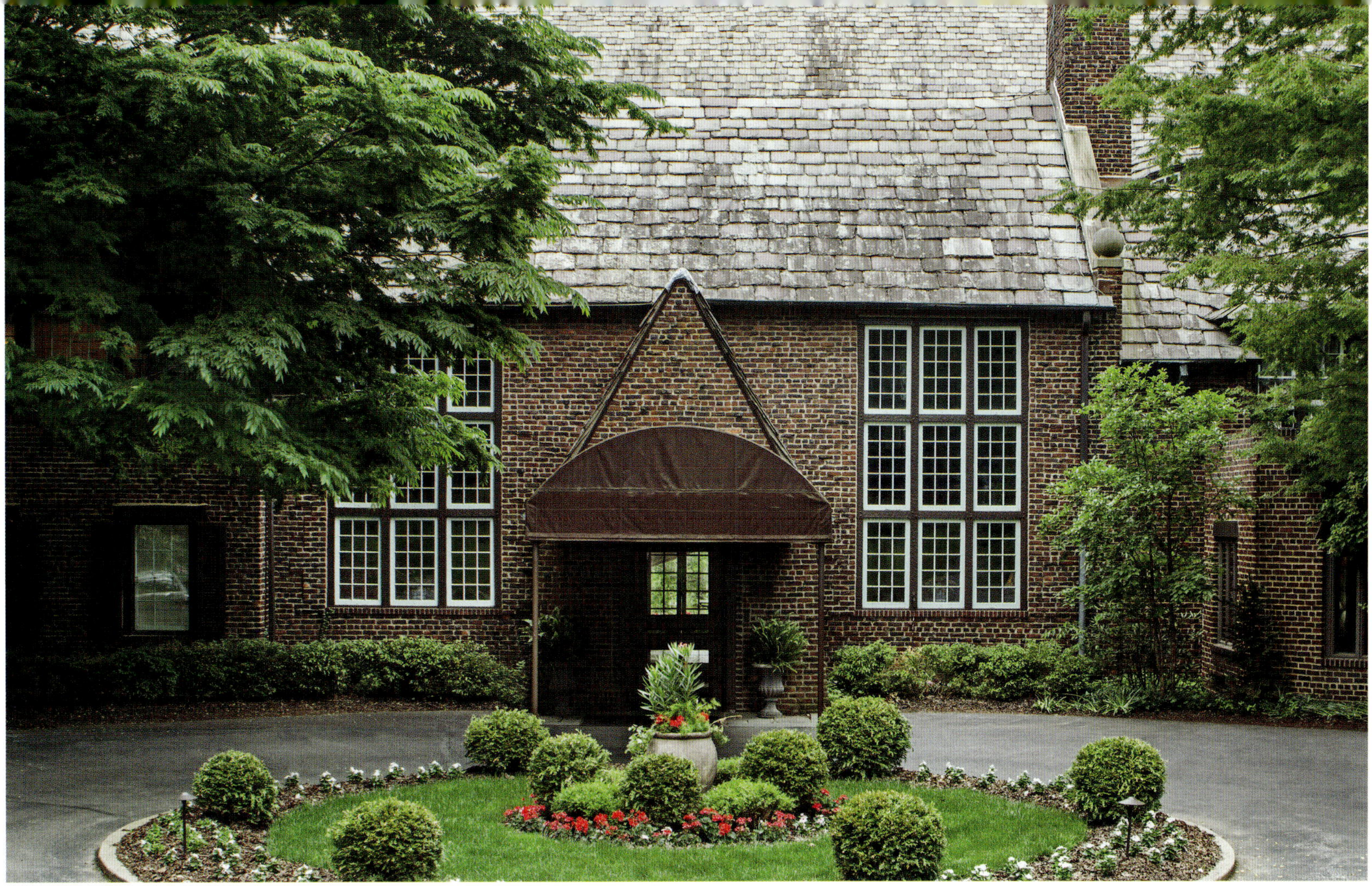

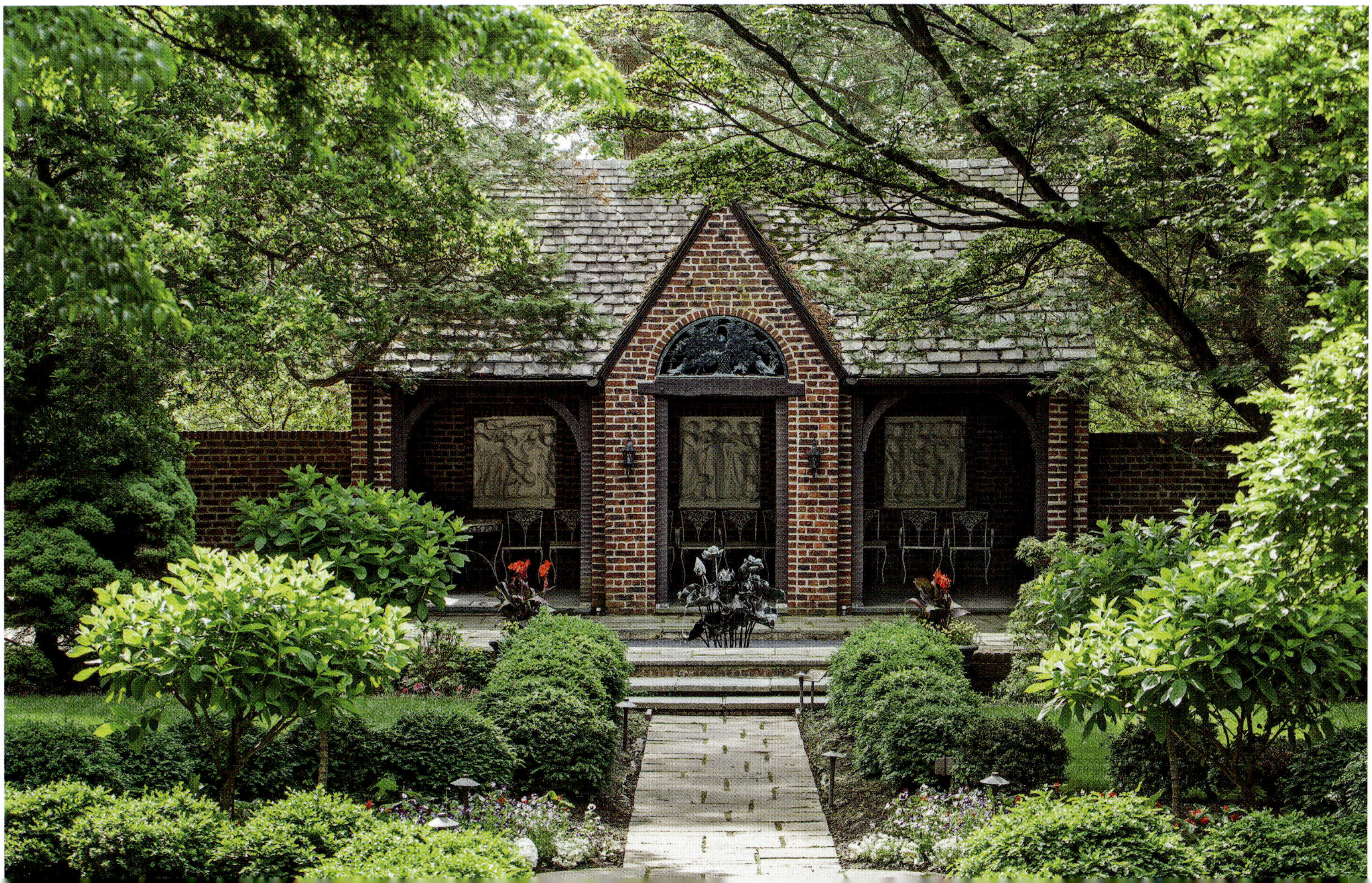

backed by several du Pont relatives, purchased the house and surrounding eighteen acres. The barn, hunting lodge, and superintendent's cottage on Old Kennett Road were sold in separate parcels and are currently maintained as private houses. The Greenville Country Club has upheld the integrity of Lindeberg's design and, with careful research, restored Shipman's gardens; they added a dining and kitchen wing in 1987. In 2010, Owl's Nest was listed on the National Register of Historic Places.

Left: Garden wall capped with slate shingles.

Right above: Gable and chimney detail.

Right below: Bronze transom grille by Oscar Bach over the front door.

Opposite: Conical roof of the ice house.

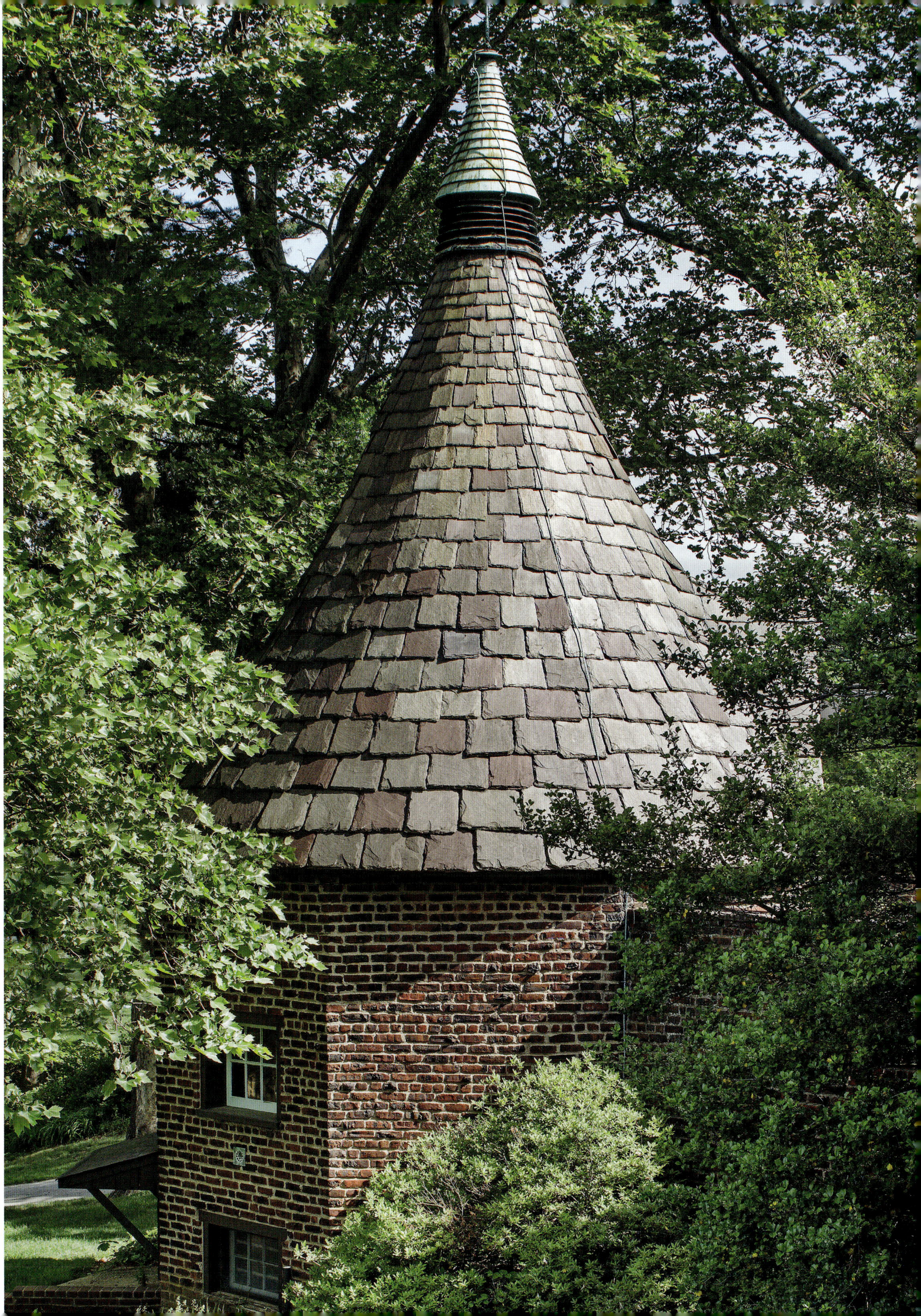

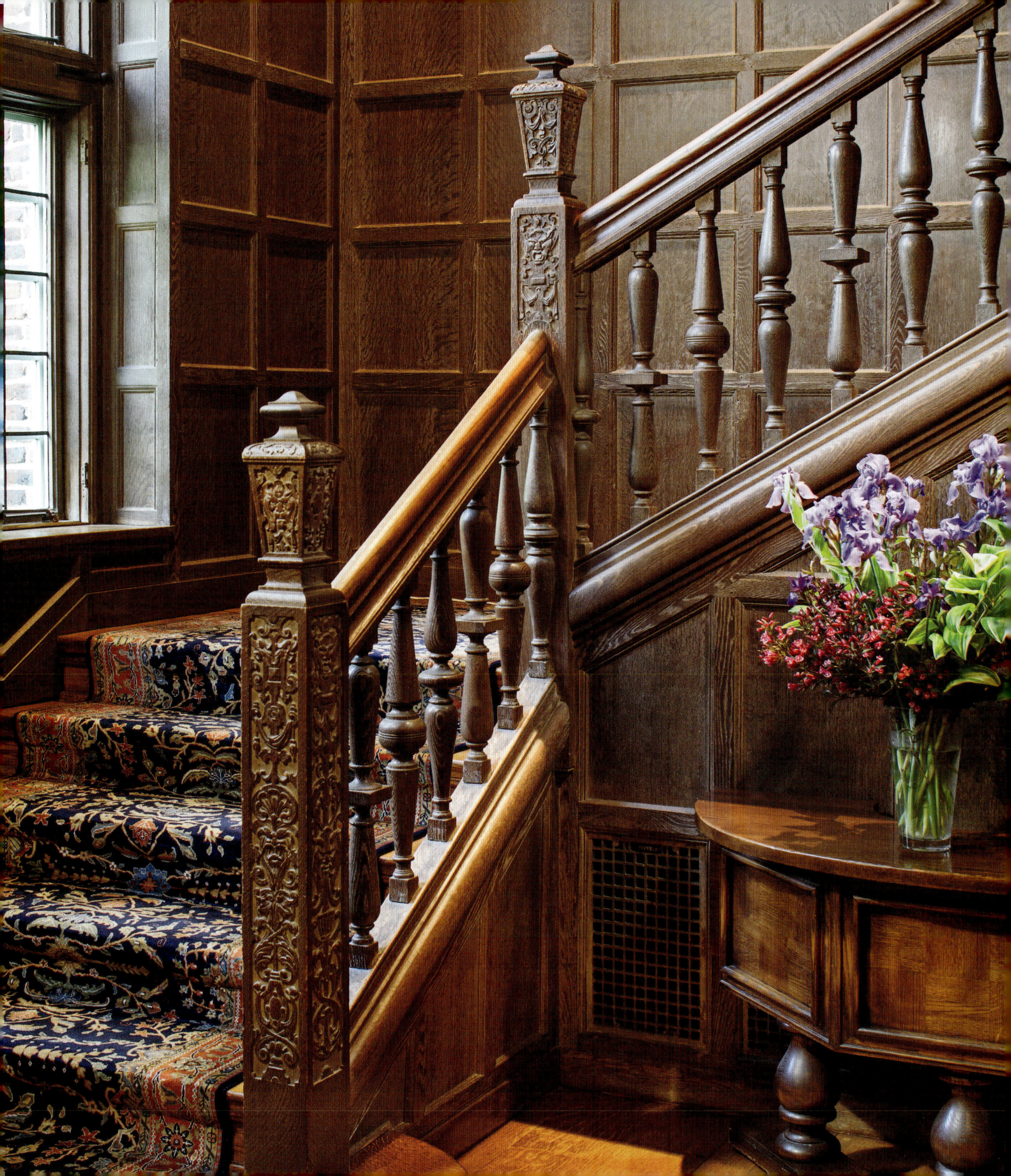

Above: Overmantel in the entrance hall carved with heraldic panels and the castle and sailing ship from the du Pont coat-of-arms.

Right: An original sconce in the entrance hall.

Opposite: Stair with carved newel posts.

Above: Living room fireplace and Grinling Gibbons–style overmantel applied to walnut paneling.

Opposite: Entrance to the dining room from the hall.

Overleaf: Strapwork ceiling in the hall.

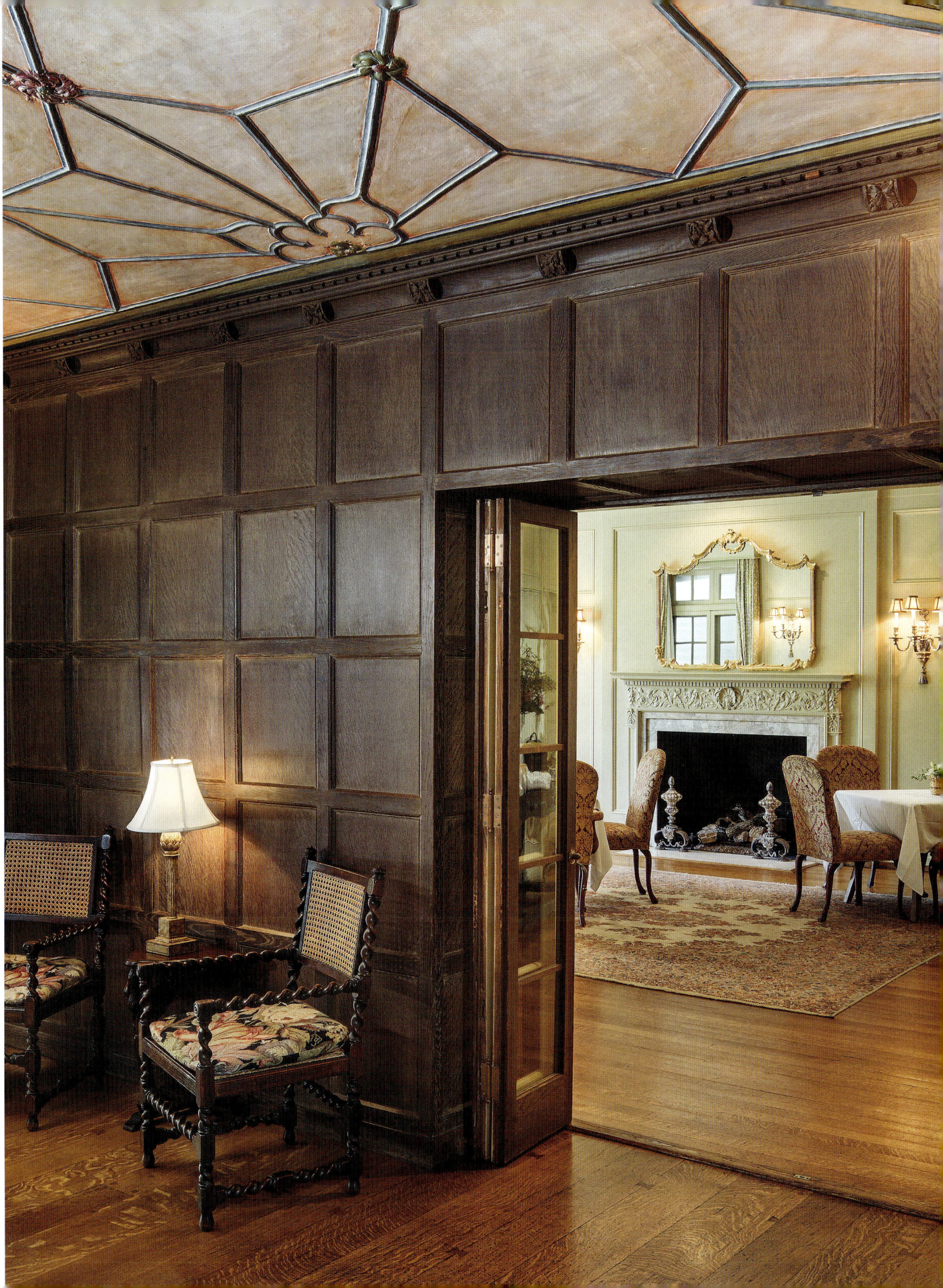

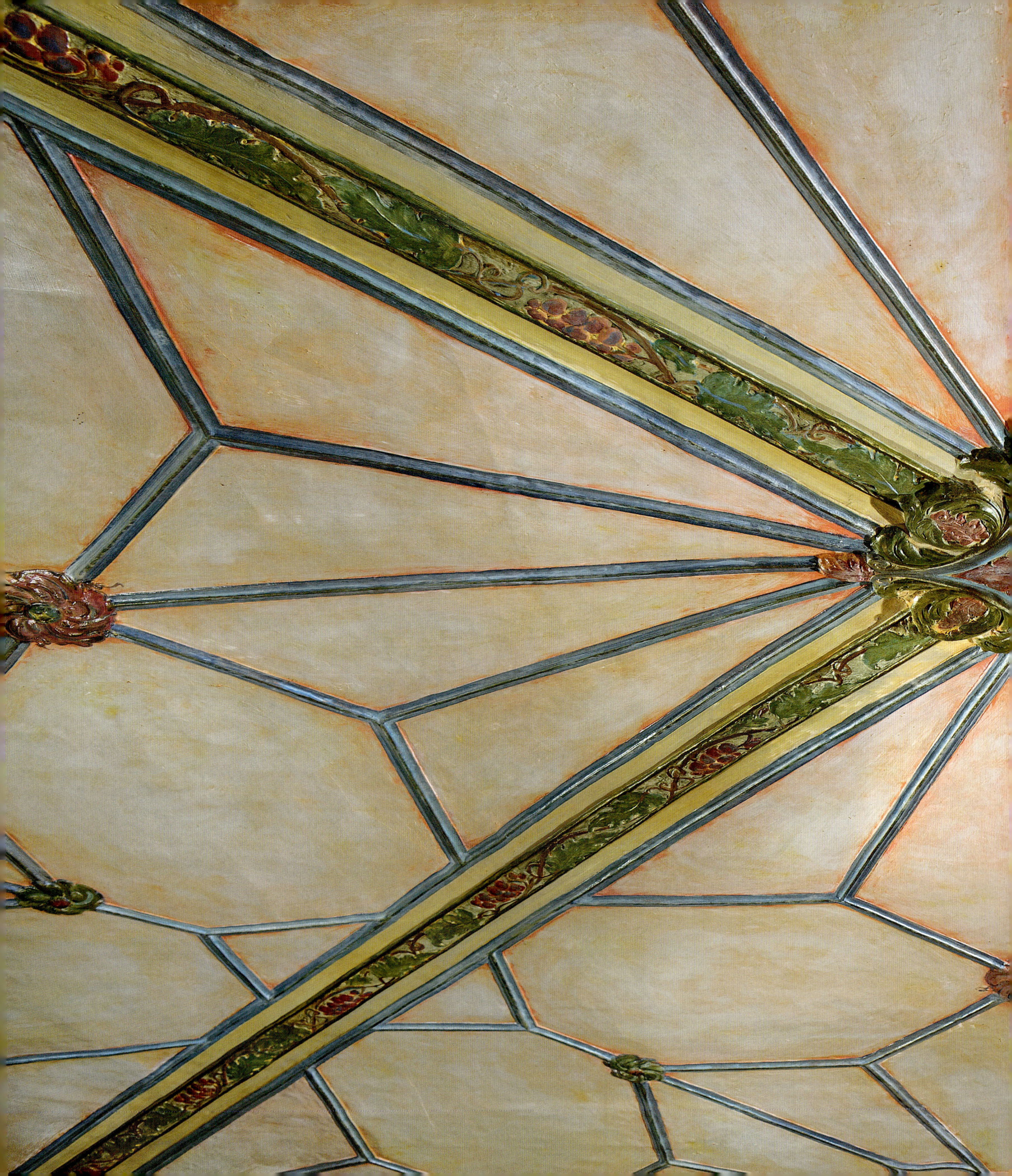

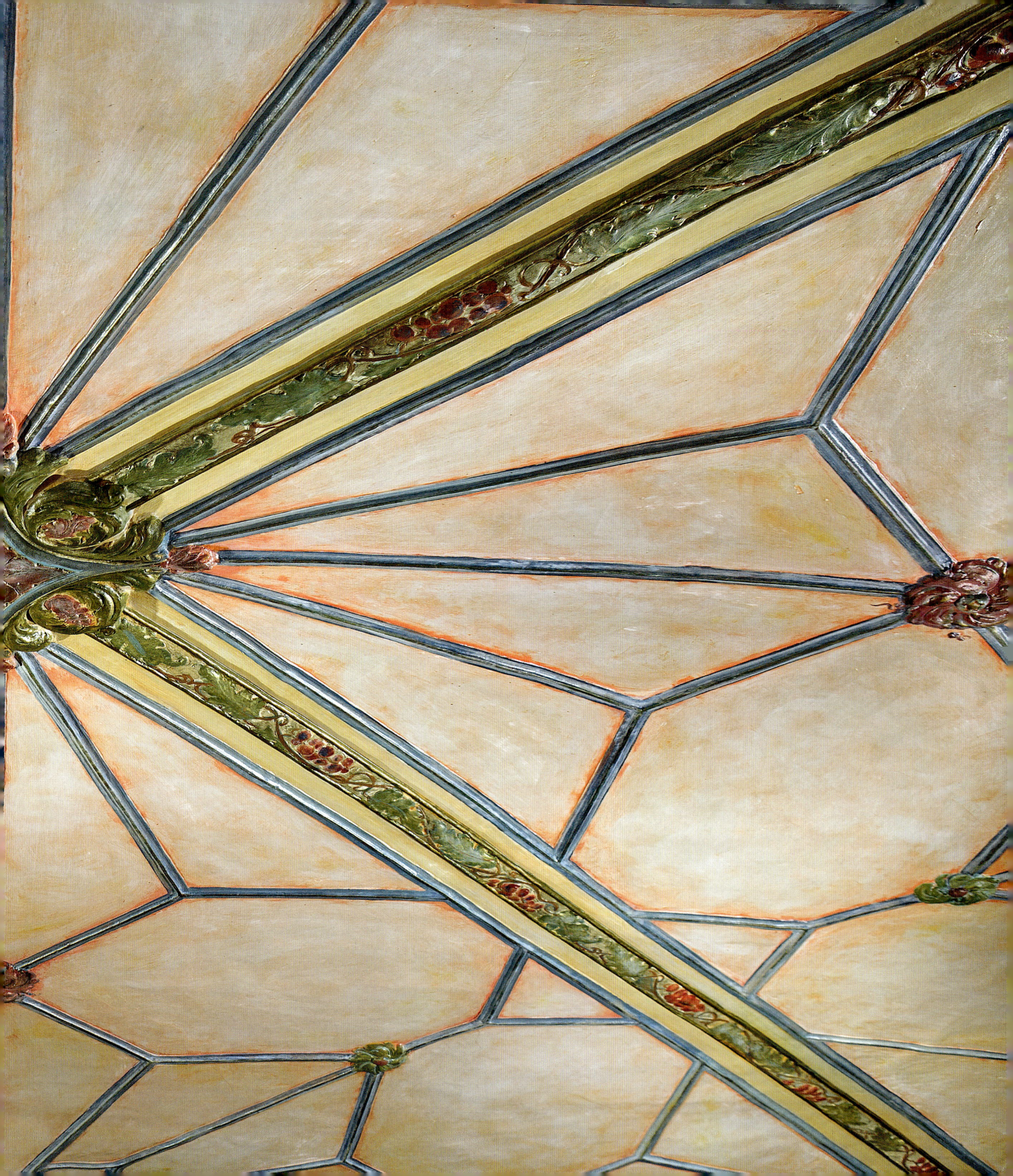

WYLDWOODE
CLYDE M. CARR ESTATE

LAKE FOREST, ILLINOIS

1916–17

During the second half of the nineteenth century, Chicago was the fastest growing city in the country. As a result, it quickly outgrew its boundaries, and the area north of the city on Lake Michigan opened up for new development once the rail line, established in 1855, made the shoreline more accessible. Thirty miles north, a group of Chicago Presbyterians, seeking a refuge outside of the city, discovered Lake Forest's untapped potential and founded the Lake Forest Association to develop the 1,200-acre property they had acquired. In 1857 landscape architect Almerin Hotchkiss laid out an English-style plan for the property with curvilinear roads and three-to-five acre lots centered on an academy and university. Attracted to the beauty of the ravines and wooded bluffs overlooking the lake, some of Chicago's most influential businessmen built summer cottages in Lake Forest and, later, more permanent homes.

By the early 1900s, Lake Forest's high architectural standard had been set. The Onwentsia Club, established in 1895, drew the moneyed elite with leisure sports and local architects such as Jarvis Hunt, Holabird & Roche, Henry Ives Cobb, Howard Van Doren Shaw, and David Adler transformed the area once occupied by Italianate villas and summer cottages into a series of more formal estates surrounding the club. As the architectural tenor of Lake Forest continued to rise, East Coast designers such as Charles A. Platt, Delano & Aldrich, and Olmsted Brothers were drawn to the Midwest. In 1910, while in practice with Albro, Lindeberg designed his first house in Lake Forest for banker Orville E. Babcock (1872–1951) on a nine-acre site. Known as Two Gables, it was a romantic brick and half-timbered manor with a Jens Jensen-designed landscape. Following its purchase by meat-packing scion Laurence H. Armour (1888–1952) and his wife, Lacy Withers Armour (1891–1981), soon after their marriage in 1911, Lindeberg expanded the service wing, and Rose Nichols designed the gardens.

In 1916 Clyde Mitchell Carr (1869–1923) and his wife, Lillian Van Alstyne Carr (1870–1957), asked Lindeberg to design Wyldwoode, the architect's third North Shore commission.[1] A native of Illinois, Carr attended Lake Forest Academy before going East to Princeton for college. Back in Chicago, he rose through the ranks to become president of steel distributor Joseph T. Ryerson & Sons in 1911; he was also president of the Onwentsia Club from 1912 to 1914. The Carrs were dedicated to the artistic and educational development of the city as benefactors of the Chicago Symphony Orchestra and the Art Institute of Chicago. In the city, they lived at 1130 North Shore Drive, the city's first luxury cooperative apartment building designed in 1910 by Howard Van Doren Shaw. Lindeberg designed Wyldwoode—one of his most imaginative designs—as the Carrs' summer house.

As early as 1913, the Carrs asked Jens Jensen to lay out the grounds of their property. Jensen, best known for his work for the West Park System in Chicago, envisioned a long driveway through the woods, revealing a U-shaped house facing the lake. Lindeberg's version was quite different. Using whitewashed brick, Lindeberg designed a large V-shaped plan that presented the visitor no more than a simple high-peaked entrance pavilion facing the arrival court. The architecture created a compelling sequence. He

Entrance pavilion.

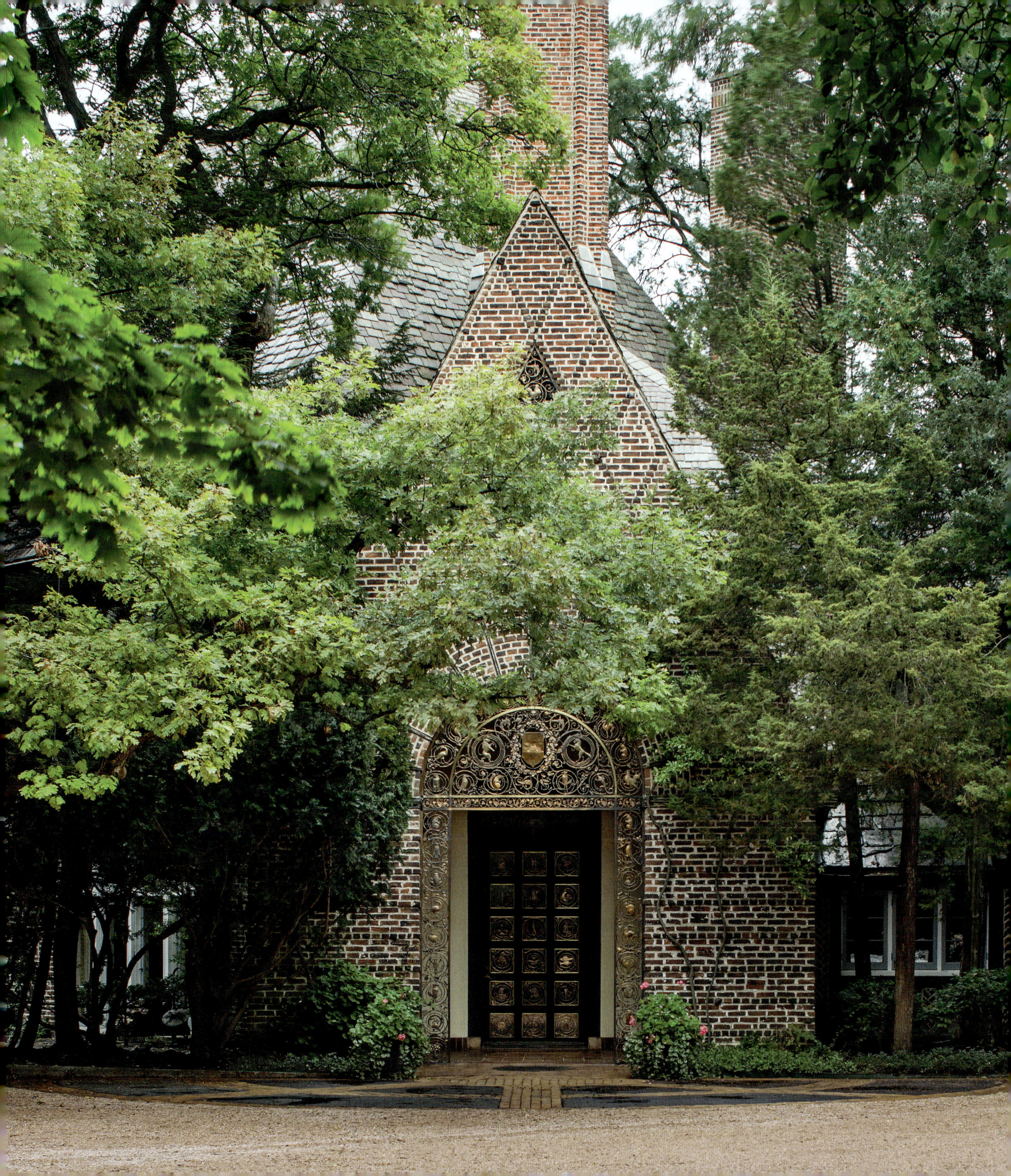

concealed the balance of the house from the initial view, extending the service wing, hidden by a series of trees, to the east, and the wing containing the entertaining rooms to the northwest. As a result, the prospect of Lake Michigan was hidden so that the dramatic views were revealed only from within the rooms. Lindeberg laid the whitewashed brick of the entrance pavilion in a diamond pattern and interspersed radiating slabs of slate into the brick arch over the entrance. With what must have been an ample budget and patient client, Lindeberg lavished his attention on special details. In collaboration with Oscar Bach, he designed an intricate brass fanlight, panels, and a diamond-shaped grille in the gable wrought with animals—birds, deer, fox, crabs—that created a subtle yet ebullient decorative effect. For the front door, he created a series of hammered bronze panels, laid over the glass door, featuring signs of the zodiac as well as other symbols—a sun, ship, and tree—to represent the sky, sea, and earth.

The Carr house created a sensation in the architectural press.[2] As C. Matlack Price remarked, it was the

Above right: Rendering of the entrance facade by William A. Treanor.

Above left: Living room.

Overleaf: Northeast facade.

"direct result of a fearlessly independent spirit, which respects precedent, but is not constrained by it."[3] Indeed, it represented the best of Lindeberg's personal twist on history with its imaginative use of materials, unfolding massing, and unconventional entrance sequence. A mix of whitewashed brick, red-brick trim, and half-timbering, the house unfurled in a sequence of angled wings, bays, and porches pinned down by Lindeberg's extraordinarily steep roof and colossal chimneys.

The entrance pavilion opened into an octagonal hall with a large fireplace and blue-gray tiled floor that served as a hinge between the formal rooms and the service wing. To the northwest, Lindeberg extended a gallery that led to a large stair hall and oriented the paneled dining room with a shallow barrel-vaulted tracery ceiling, oval breakfast room, expansive living

KEY TO SECOND FLOOR

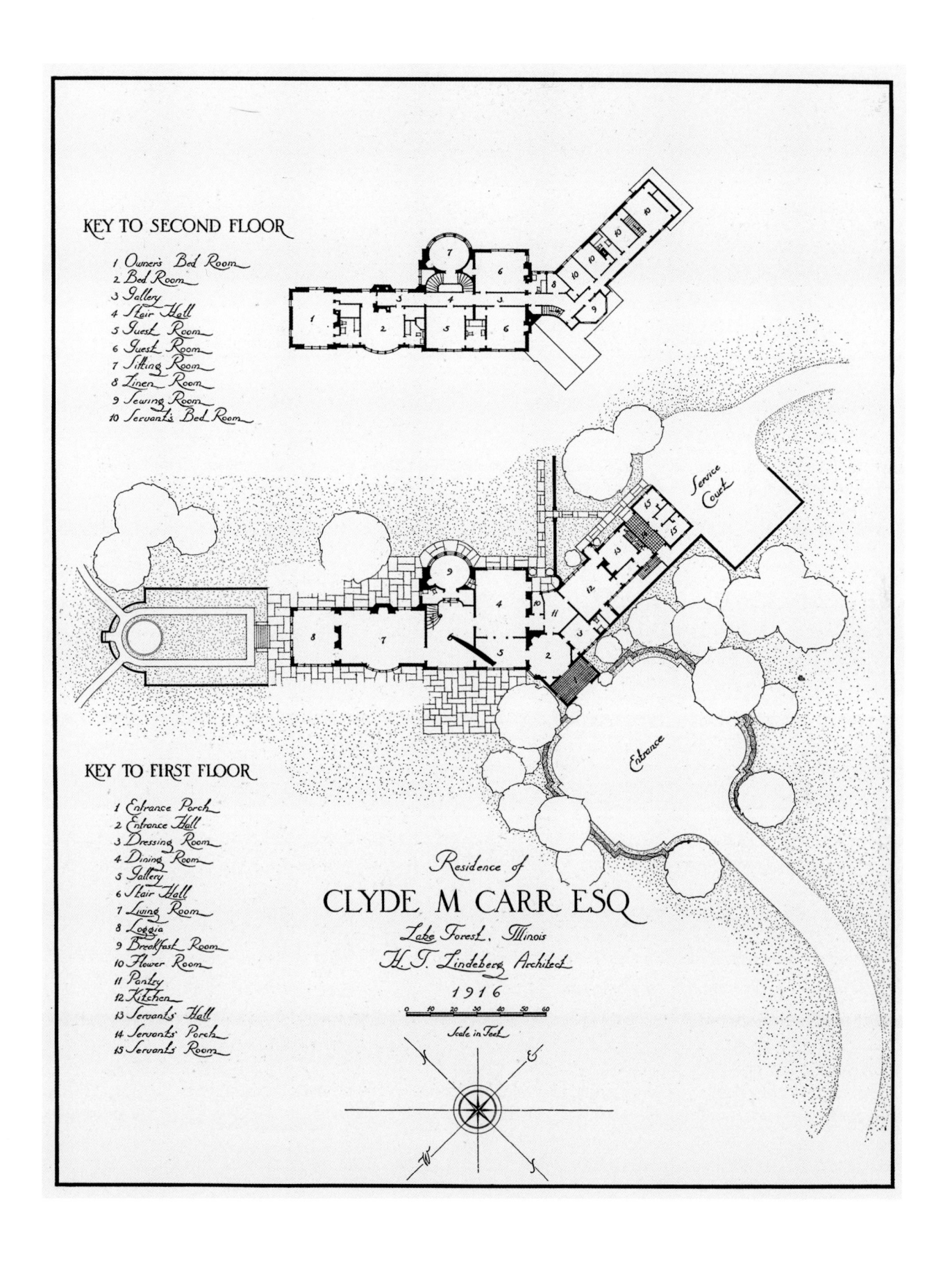

1. Owner's Bed Room
2. Bed Room
3. Gallery
4. Stair Hall
5. Guest Room
6. Guest Room
7. Sitting Room
8. Linen Room
9. Sewing Room
10. Servant's Bed Room

KEY TO FIRST FLOOR

1. Entrance Porch
2. Entrance Hall
3. Dressing Room
4. Dining Room
5. Gallery
6. Stair Hall
7. Living Room
8. Loggia
9. Breakfast Room
10. Flower Room
11. Pantry
12. Kitchen
13. Servants' Hall
14. Servants' Porch
15. Servants' Room

Residence of
CLYDE M CARR ESQ
Lake Forest, Illinois
H. T. Lindeberg, Architect
1916

Scale in Feet

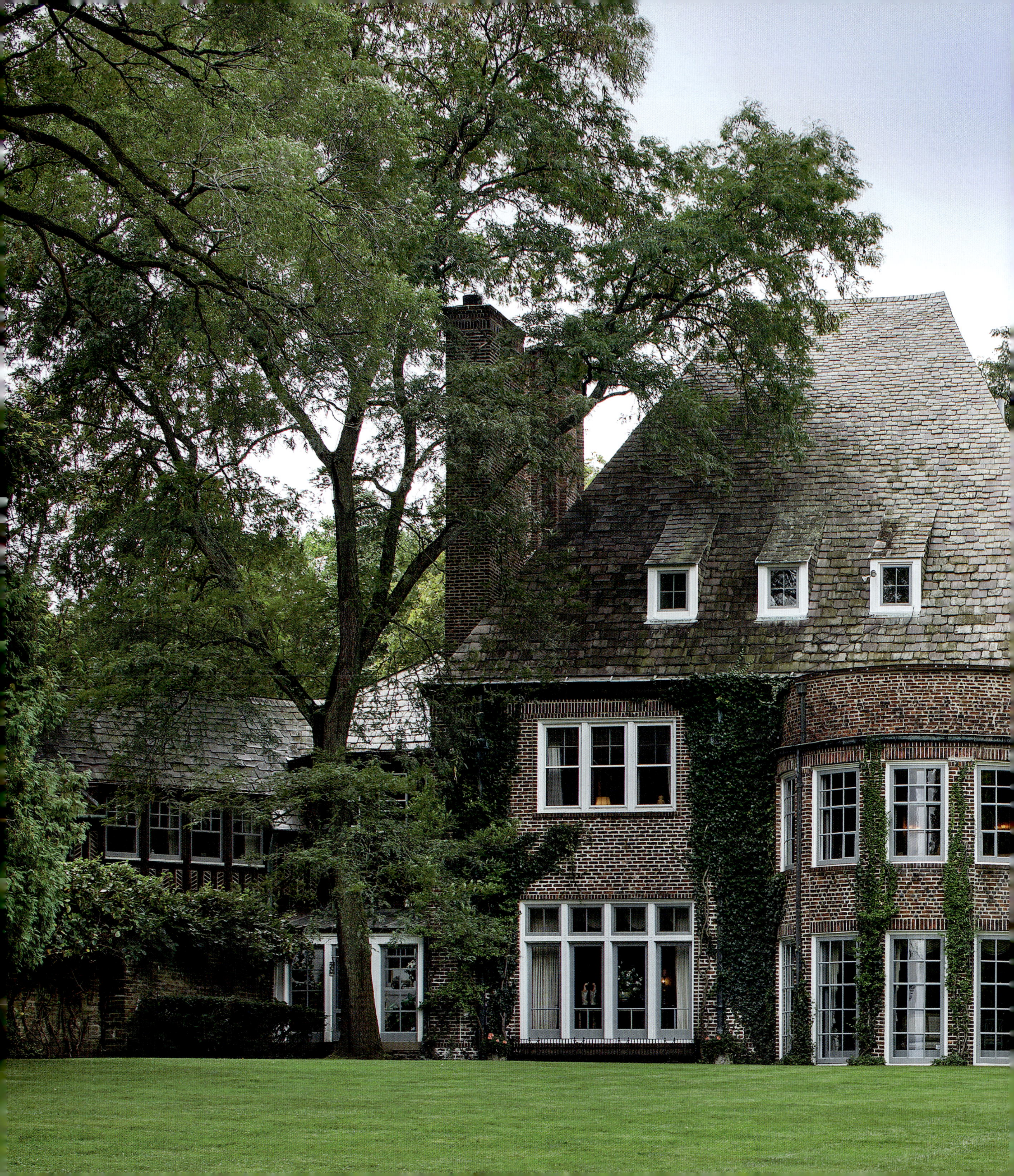

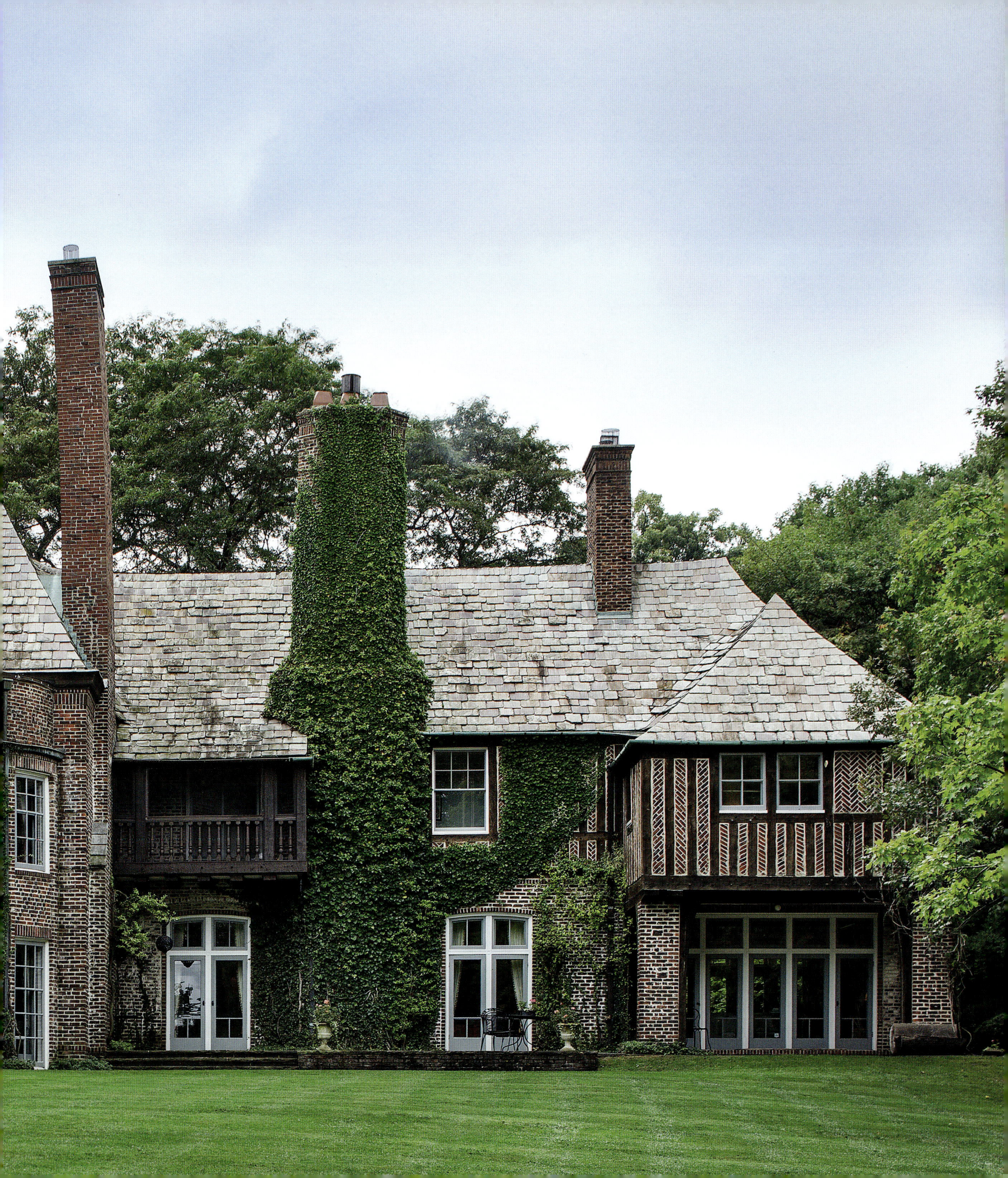

room, and loggia to the northeast with views to the east lawn down the ravine to the lake. With the long, windowed gallery running alongside, the interiors were bright and sun-filled with exposure on two sides. When opened, the floor-to-ceiling windows provided air and breezes and transformed the first floor into an enormous open-air loggia. In the main hall, the stair spilled down over the entrance to the breakfast room terminating in a newel post capped by a crystal globe similar to the one Lindeberg had used at Foxhollow Farm. An oval sitting room above the breakfast room opened onto the landing above and featured curved paneling and mantel. Meanwhile, Lindeberg situated the kitchen and servants' wing to the east where it could catch the morning light. Five bedroom suites and four servant's rooms, linen, and sewing rooms filled out the second floor.

Above: Northwest facade.

Opposite: Hammered bronze panels of signs of the zodiac and bronze fanlight with animals by Oscar Bach.

Overleaf: Breakfast room.

After the house was completed, the Carrs commissioned Olmsted alumnus Warren Manning to design the landscape, including the formal pool and garden to the northwest off of the loggia. Terminating in an abrupt drop down into the ravine, it was defined by low hedges and flower gardens by Rose Nichols. Meanwhile, a series of paths through woodland gardens that

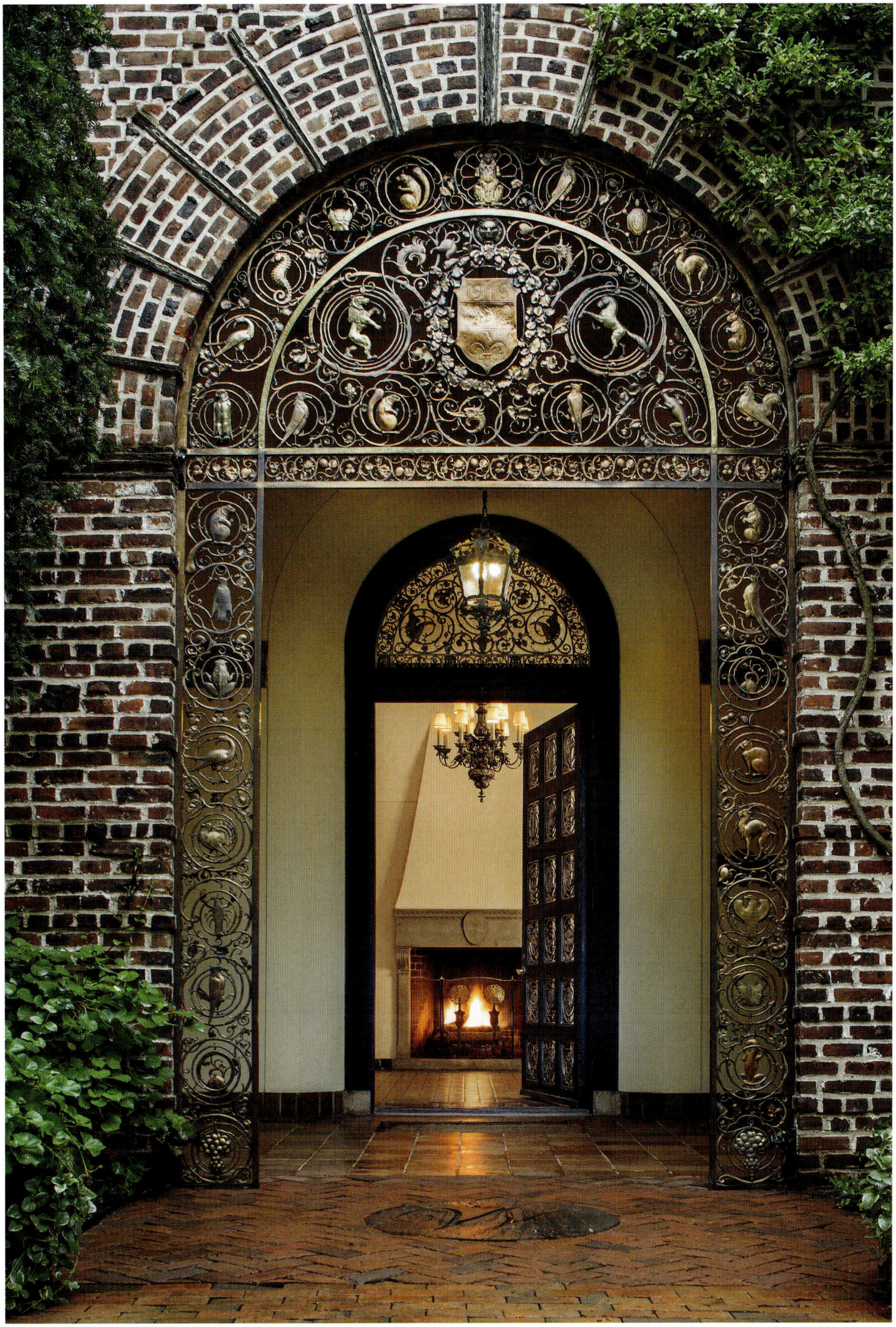

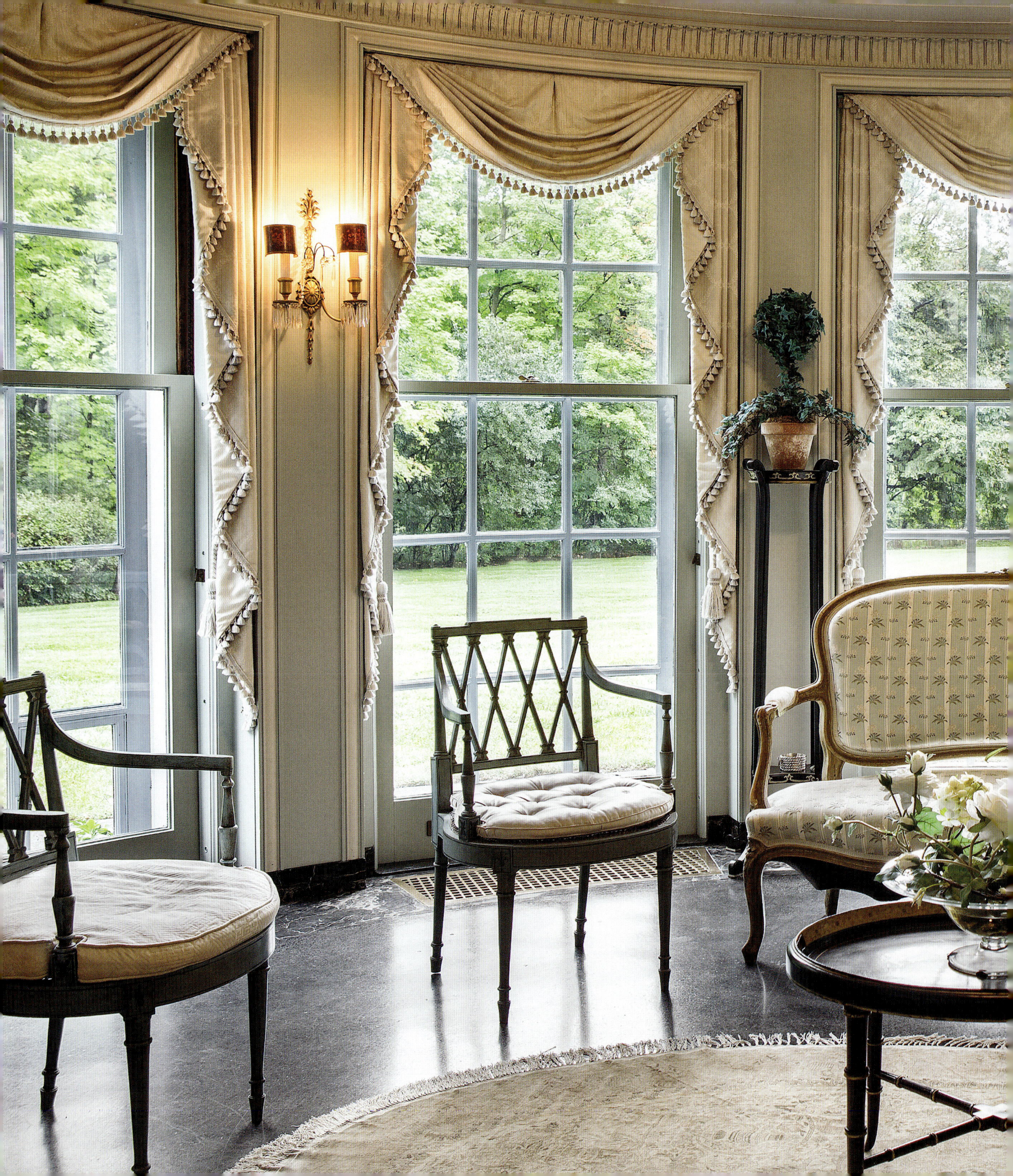

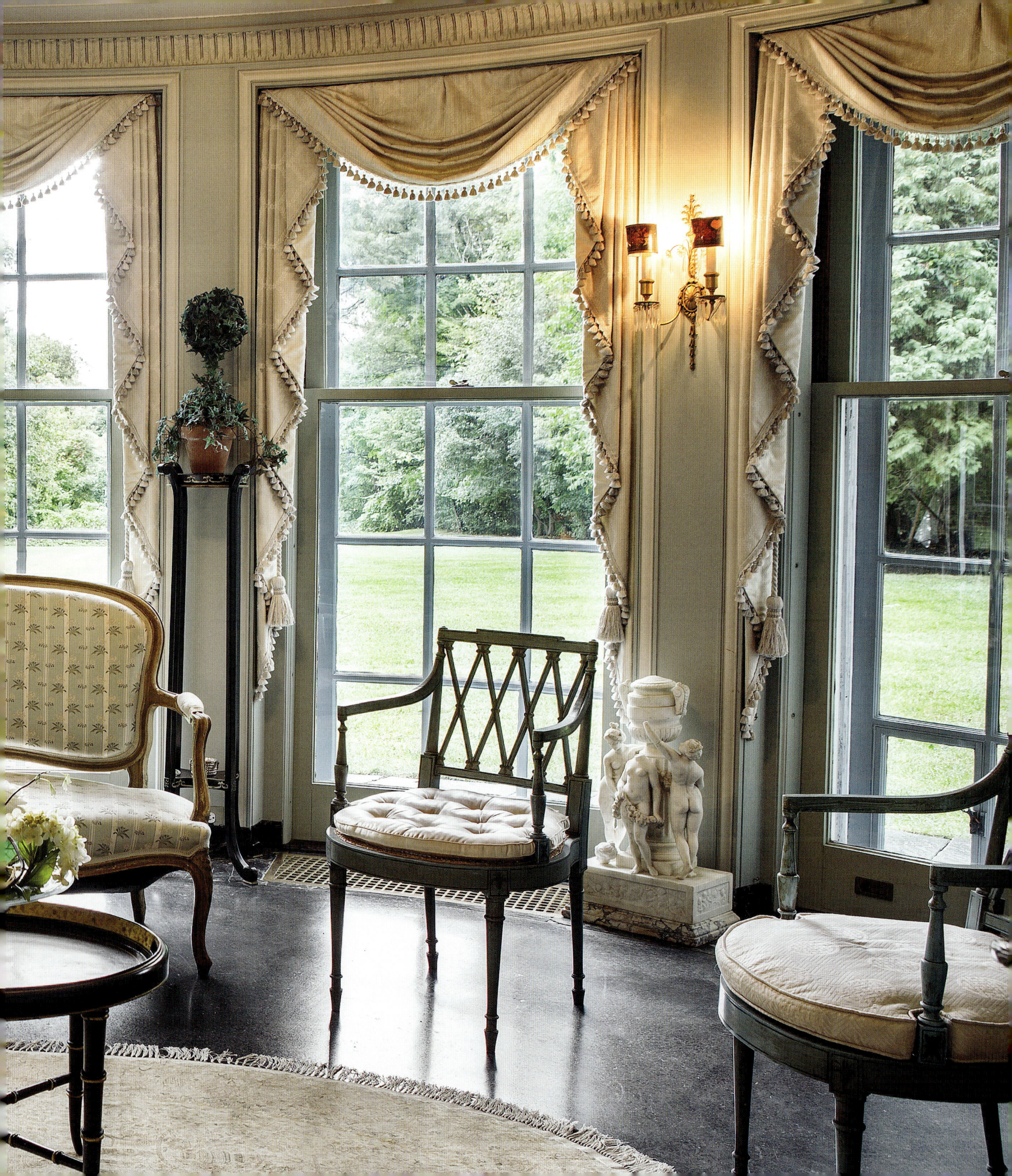

Above: Living room.

Left: Stair with crystal globe newel post.

Opposite: Barrel-vaulted dining room.

surrounded the property offered privacy. Known for his naturalistic approach to garden design, Manning combined informal and more structured techniques to create an oasis overlooking Lake Michigan.

The current owners, the fourth occupants of the house, have maintained and preserved Lindeberg's design. In addition to restoring and slightly raising the decorative metal archway at the entrance to the house, they carefully restored the timber-framed balcony on the east facade—both efforts for which they received awards from the Lake Forest Preservation Foundation. The Carrs' half-timbered cottage and garage building on the western edge of the property is now a separate property.

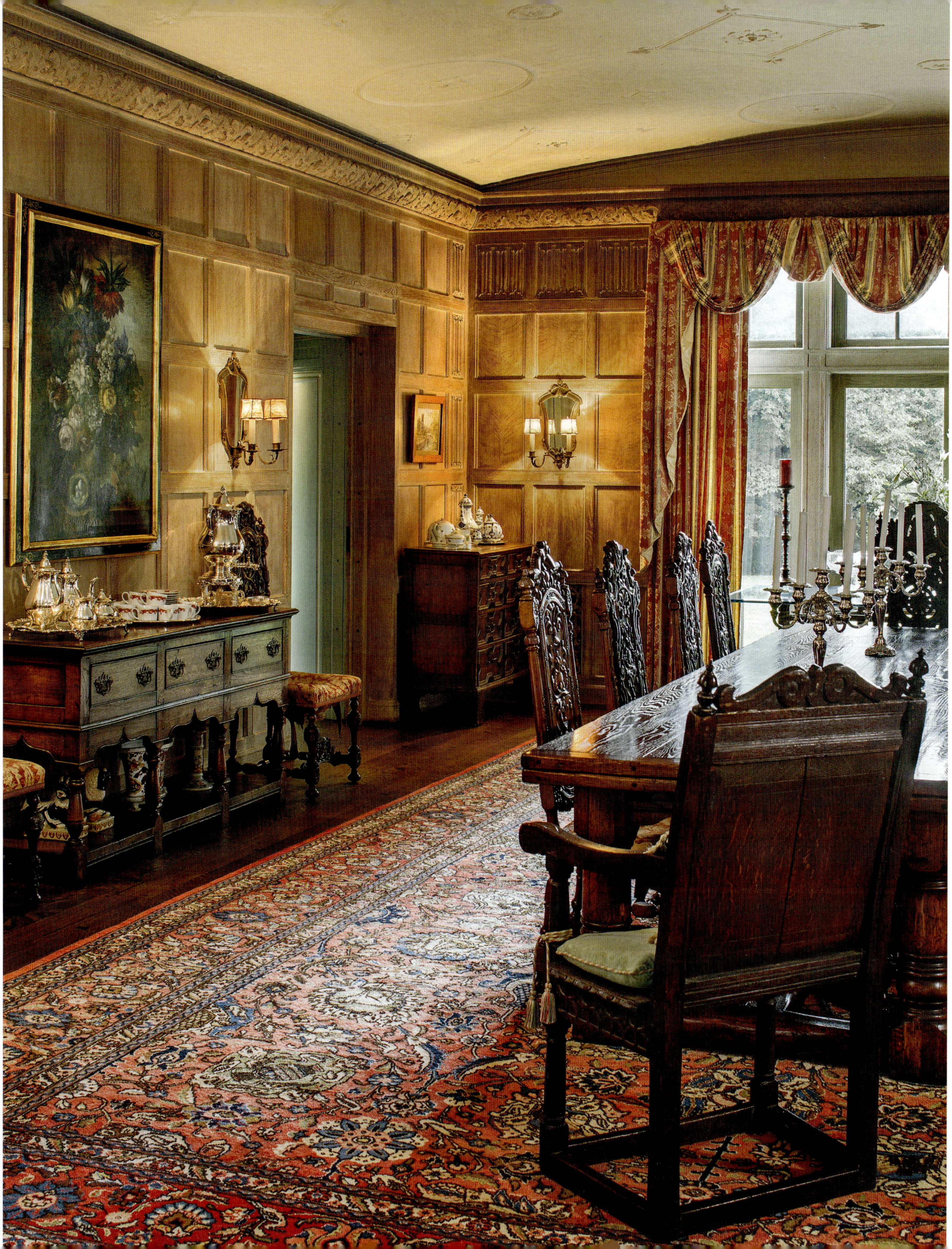

OLYMPIC POINT
HORACE HAVEMEYER ESTATE

ISLIP, NEW YORK

1916–19

As a summer destination, the Great South Bay—a lagoon between Long Island and Fire Island—became increasingly popular in the 1870s after the South Side Sportsmen's Club, an exclusive hunting and fishing club, was established in 1866. The undeveloped waterfront stretching between Bay Shore, Islip, and Oakdale began drawing New York society, offering a low-key alternative to the North Shore. The Havemeyer family was well established in the area and, in part, responsible for developing a portion of it. In the late 1890s, Horace Havemeyer's father, Henry O. Havemeyer (1847–1907), the so-called Sugar King, and his brother-in-law Samuel Peters purchased a strip of land in Islip that became known as Bayberry Point. There, the two developed a colony of inexpensive but stylish Moorish summer cottages designed by Grosvenor Atterbury. Once labeled the "Tuxedo of the Seaside," the enclave initially included ten houses that Havemeyer rented to friends while retaining one for his family.[1]

In the late nineteenth and early twentieth century, the American Sugar Refining Company, founded by the Havemeyer family in the early 1800s, dominated the sugar industry. H. O. Havemeyer was president until his death in 1907, and Horace Havemeyer (1886–1956) worked at the company until 1911, the year he married Doris Dick (1890–1982), also from a sugar-refining family. An avid yachtsman, he then served on corporate boards, including companies in the sugar business, and as a trustee of the Frick Collection and the Metropolitan Museum of Art, to which his mother, Louisine Elder Havemeyer, had bequeathed a large portion of the family's art collection.

Having spent the summers at Bayberry Point, Horace Havemeyer decided to build a house for his young and growing family on the water just west of his childhood home. In 1916, most likely influenced by visiting his friends Paul and Fanny Moore at their Lindeberg-designed estate, Hollow Hill Farm, he commissioned the architect to design a large picturesque house. Built during World War I, Olympic Point was completed in 1919. Due to the war, certain items—for instance, windows imported from France—never arrived. Doris Havemeyer asked Olmsted Brothers to conduct a topographical survey in 1916, but the planting plans were not completed until 1919.

With its long low-lying entrance facade and symmetrical bayfront, the house displayed Lindeberg's ability to successfully synthesize romantic and classical architectural influences.[2] Approached from the north by a driveway that swept across a rolling lawn, Olympic Point rose up as a natural extension of the grassy plain overlooking the Great South Bay. The informal composition gave the impression that the house had been added onto over time. By drawing portions of the roof down to the first floor and incorporating dormer windows on the second story, Lindeberg brought the lines of the house closer to the ground—a stroke that downplayed its size. Meanwhile, Lindeberg opened the south-facing facade to its full two stories, creating a stately and more imposing bayfront. Carried out with weathered whitewashed brick and thin stone window and door frames, the facades were unornamented, with the exception of Oscar Bach's wrought-iron leader heads. Metal casements, leaded glass, and the unbroken lines of the roof, laid in heavy variegated slate, lent a

View of the house from the northeast.

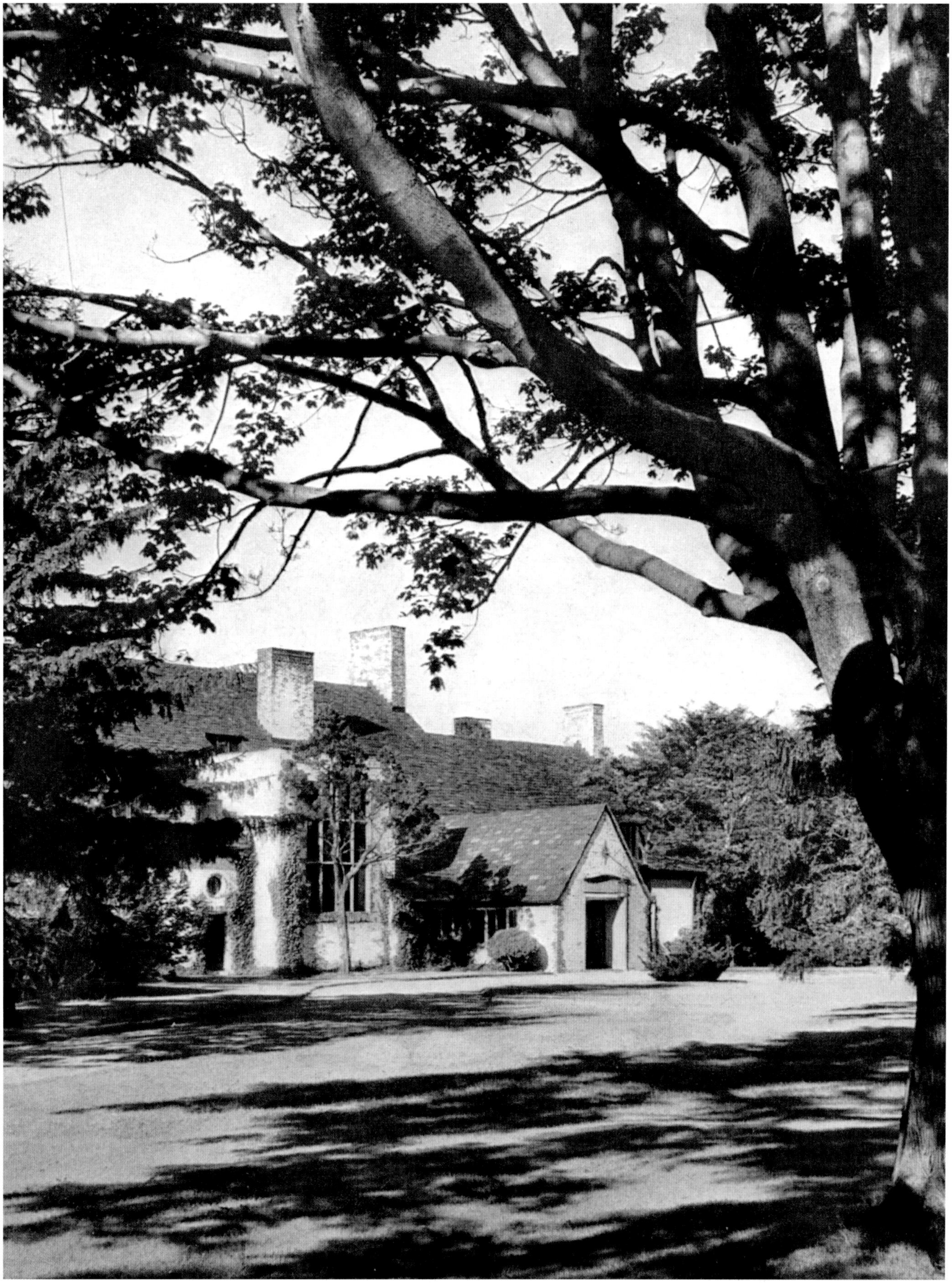

Above: Rendering of the house with the Great South Bay beyond.

Left: Sketch by William A. Treanor.

romantic English quality. Farm designer Alfred Hopkins was put in charge of siting the barns and sheds, several of which were local vernacular structures that he moved to the property and improved with Colonial Revival details.[3]

Inside, Lindeberg's plan was ordered and studied with formal enfilades extending through the main spaces. He extended the primary axis laterally east–west against the southern side of the house from the breakfast porch, gallery, dining room, living room, and vestibule to the loggia, which balanced the breakfast porch on the opposite end. By setting the entrance porch and hall off center, Lindeberg was able to create a lofty square stair hall lit by a double-height casement that included a gracious stair with an elaborately carved stringer and newel post. The second floor held five bedrooms and a sizable master suite with a large bathroom and a dressing room with a rounded bay overlooking a long hedged allée. The upper floor of the servants' wing contained another ten bedrooms for staff.

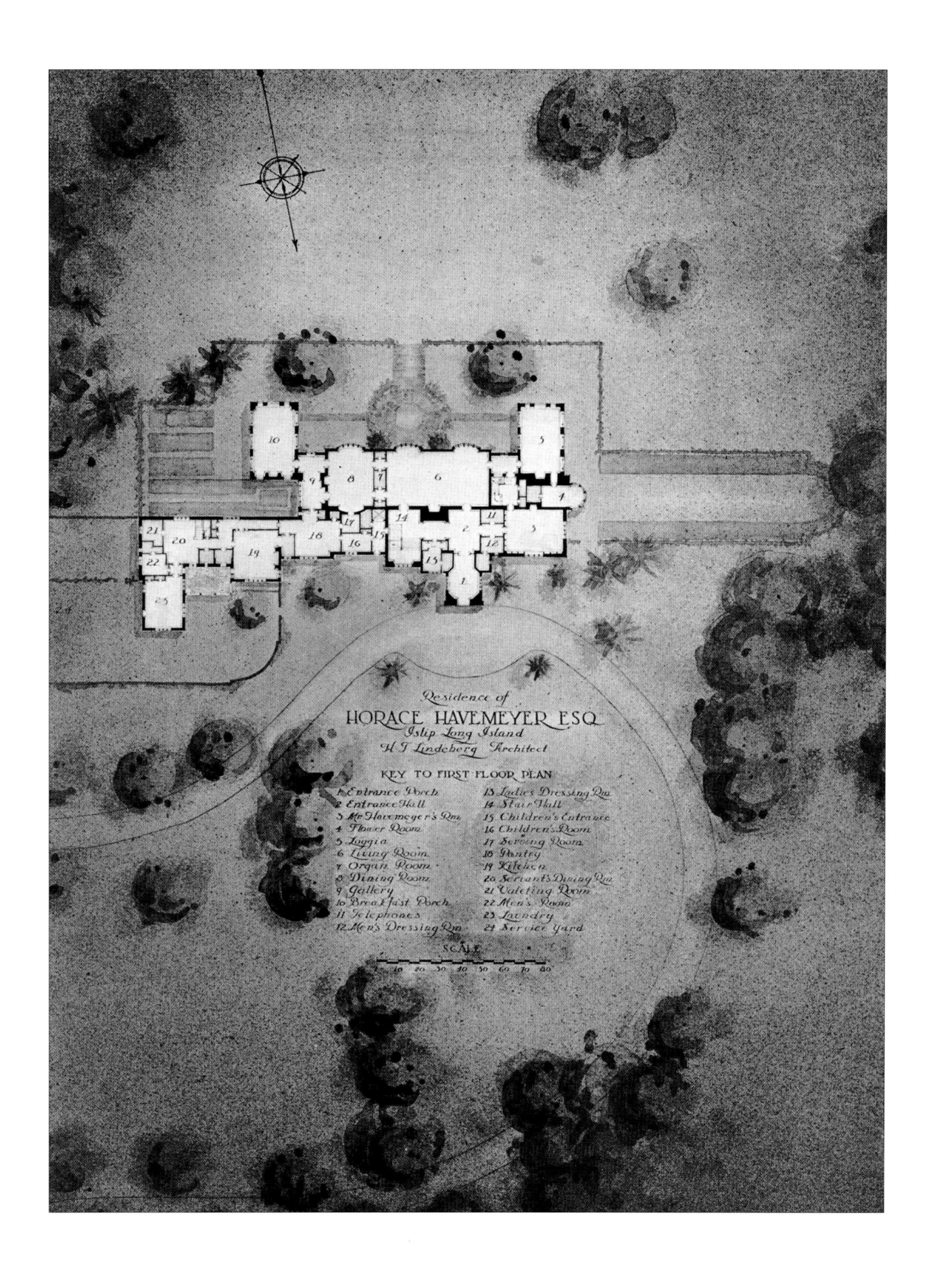

Residence of
HORACE HAVEMEYER ESQ
Islip Long Island
H. T. Lindeberg Architect

KEY TO FIRST FLOOR PLAN

1. Entrance Porch
2. Entrance Hall
3. Mr. Havemeyer's Rm.
4. Flower Room
5. Loggia
6. Living Room
7. Organ Room
8. Dining Room
9. Gallery
10. Breakfast Porch
11. Telephones
12. Men's Dressing Rm.
13. Ladies Dressing Rm.
14. Stair Hall
15. Children's Entrance
16. Children's Room
17. Serving Room
18. Pantry
19. Kitchen
20. Servant's Dining Rm.
21. Valeting Room
22. Men's Room
23. Laundry
24. Service Yard

SCALE

While the family enjoyed Olympic Point for thirty years—mainly as a weekend and summer house—they found its size and upkeep a burden by the 1940s. One descendant recalls that the house was comfortable, but that many rooms, especially the bedrooms located over the breakfast porch and loggia, seemed colossal. In 1948, in a move typical of the simpler tastes of the postwar period, the family demolished Lindeberg's building, replacing it with a more modest Colonial Revival house. Of the original house, only some wide floorboards survive; they were reused in the entryway of the new Olympic Point.

Right: South facade fronting onto the Great South Bay.

Below: Entrance facade.

Opposite: Stair hall.

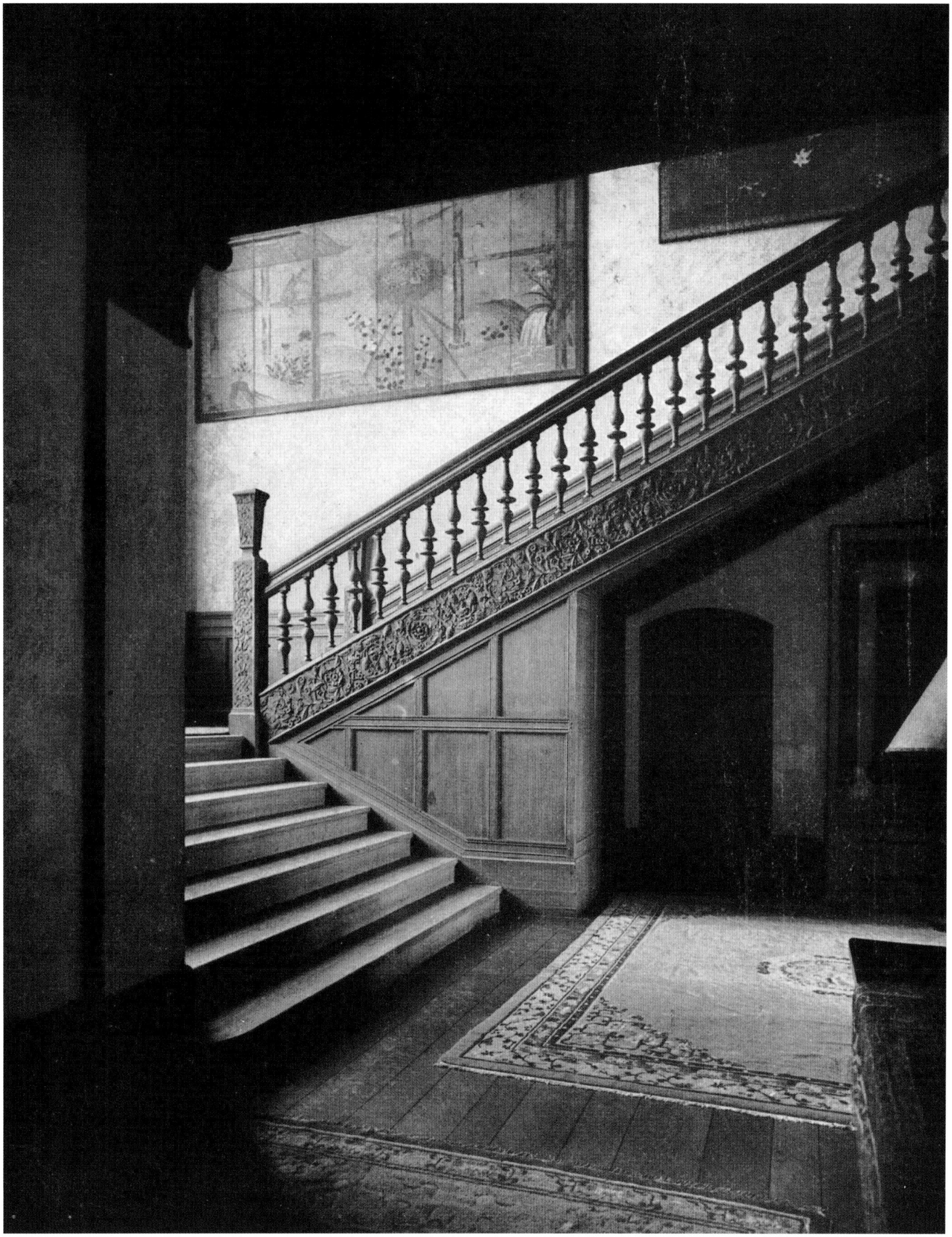

BARBERRYS
NELSON DOUBLEDAY ESTATE

MILL NECK, NEW YORK

1916–19

In 1916—the same year that Nelson Doubleday (1899–1949) married Martha J. Nicholson of Providence, Rhode Island—he planned a new house in Mill Neck near his father's place, Effendi Hill, on Oyster Bay. Doubleday's father, Frank Nelson Doubleday (1862–1934), had founded the family business, Doubleday, Page & Co., in 1899. After dropping out of school to help support his family at the age of 14, he started as an office boy at Charles Scribner's Sons, earning a salary of $3 a week, and rose through the ranks. His son, Nelson Doubleday, completed two years at New York University before entering the business. In 1912 he created his own imprint, Nelson Doubleday Inc., publishing books with profits from selling month-old magazines at half price. After the war, he rejoined Doubleday, Page & Co. as a junior partner, eventually taking over as chairman after his father's death in 1934.

The Doubleday offices and plant were located in Garden City where Frank Nelson Doubleday had moved the company in 1910 after it had outgrown its first two buildings in Manhattan. Nelson Doubleday became known as a brilliant merchandiser, revolutionizing the publishing world by developing distribution channels to make books readily available to everyone. In the words of the novelist Edna Ferber:

He was a genius at devising ways to put books into the hands of the unbookish. He thought that books should not be treated as literature only. He thought they should be food. Not caviar, but bread. He would rather have had 10 million people read a book at 50 cents than one million at $5.[1]

By 1916 Lindeberg had designed a number of houses in Glen Cove and Mill Neck, including Beaver Brook Farm for Henry L. Batterman and a cottage for Irving Brokaw, as well as the Mill Neck train station. The Doubledays' seven-and-one-half-acre property was set on the crest of a hill facing Oyster Bay with distant water views. To capture the vista, Lindeberg employed a butterfly plan with wings angling outward from the central block of the house. The design demonstrated Lindeberg's tendency to combine unexpected materials and forms: the whitewash of the brick walls could be Colonial Revival, but the gently sloping tiled roof and sgraffito around the door suggest a Mediterranean flair. As critic C. Matlack Price noted:

The Doubleday house is more than merely 'Italian'—it has much of the elusive artistry of Maxfield Parrish who can suggest in his work so much of the spirit of a faraway place without committing himself as to a specific time or a specific spot on the map.[2]

Ironwork details, including Oscar Bach's zodiac door, reflected Lindeberg's commitment to the allied arts and added a whimsical touch.

The rooms were scaled for entertaining. Oscar Bach's glass-and-cast-bronze doorway opened into a long hall that stretched the width of the house, connecting the walnut-paneled Georgian library, which angled to the southwest, to the kitchen wing to the north. The stair, cleverly incorporated in the hall stepped up before curving over the front door while the Georgian living room and Colonial Revival dining room opened to the view to the east. Once the house

Scrafitto surround and ironwork wrought in the shape of the zodiac signs by Oscar Bach at the entrance.

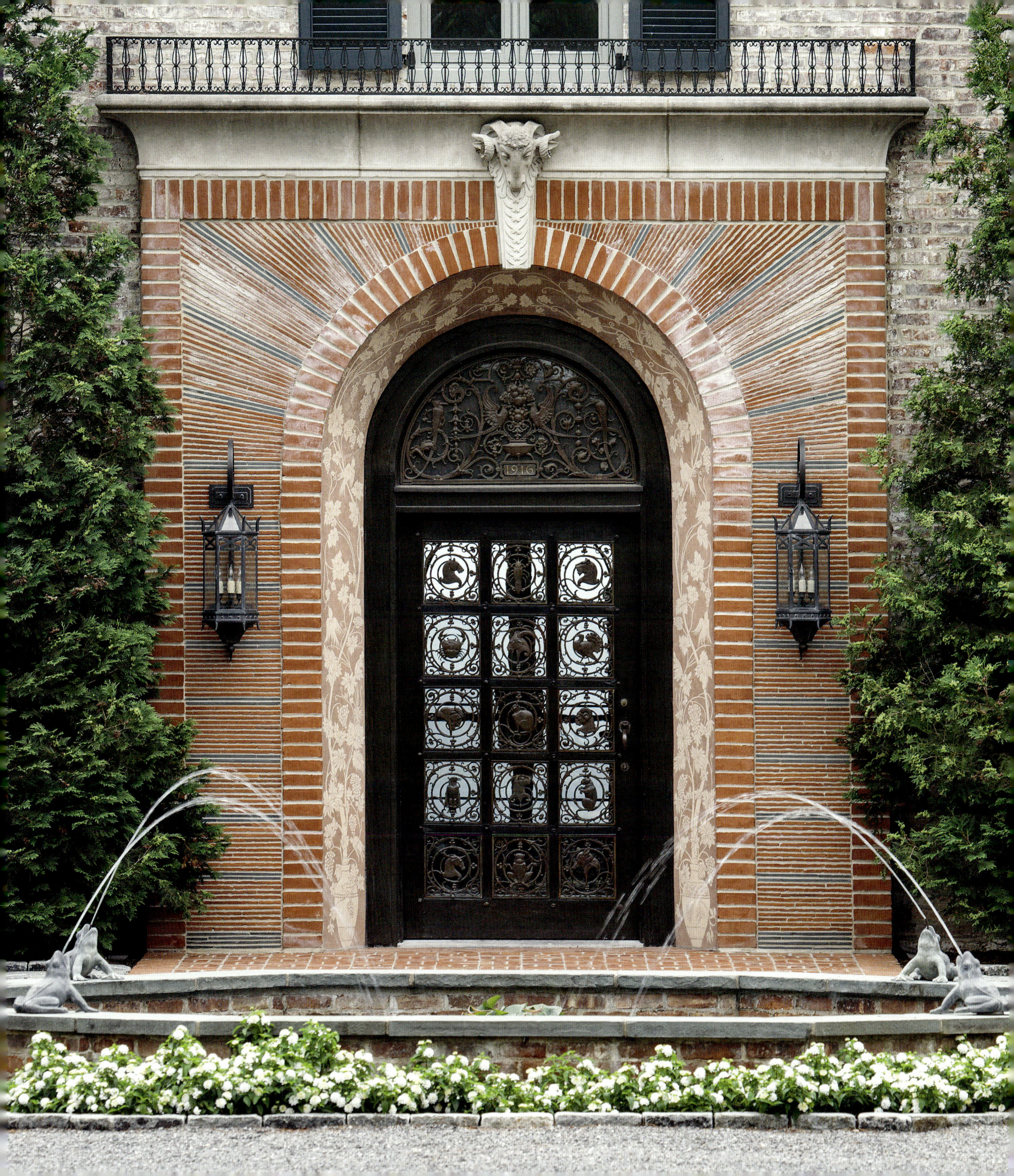
1916

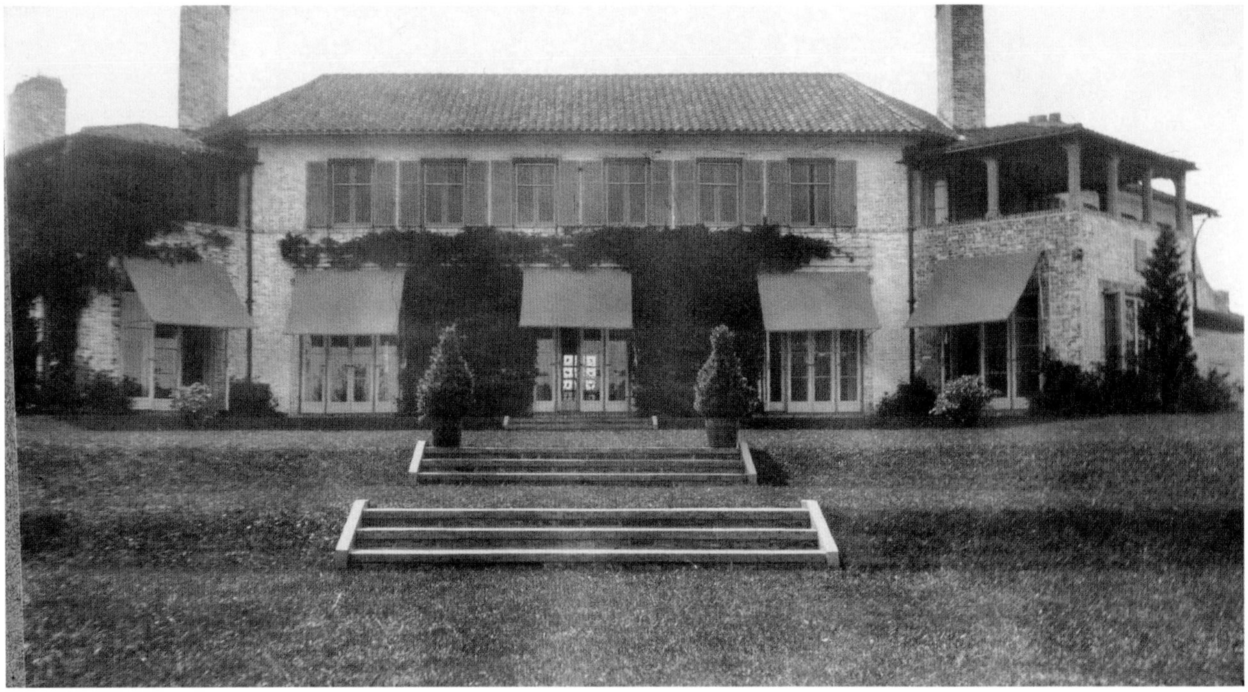

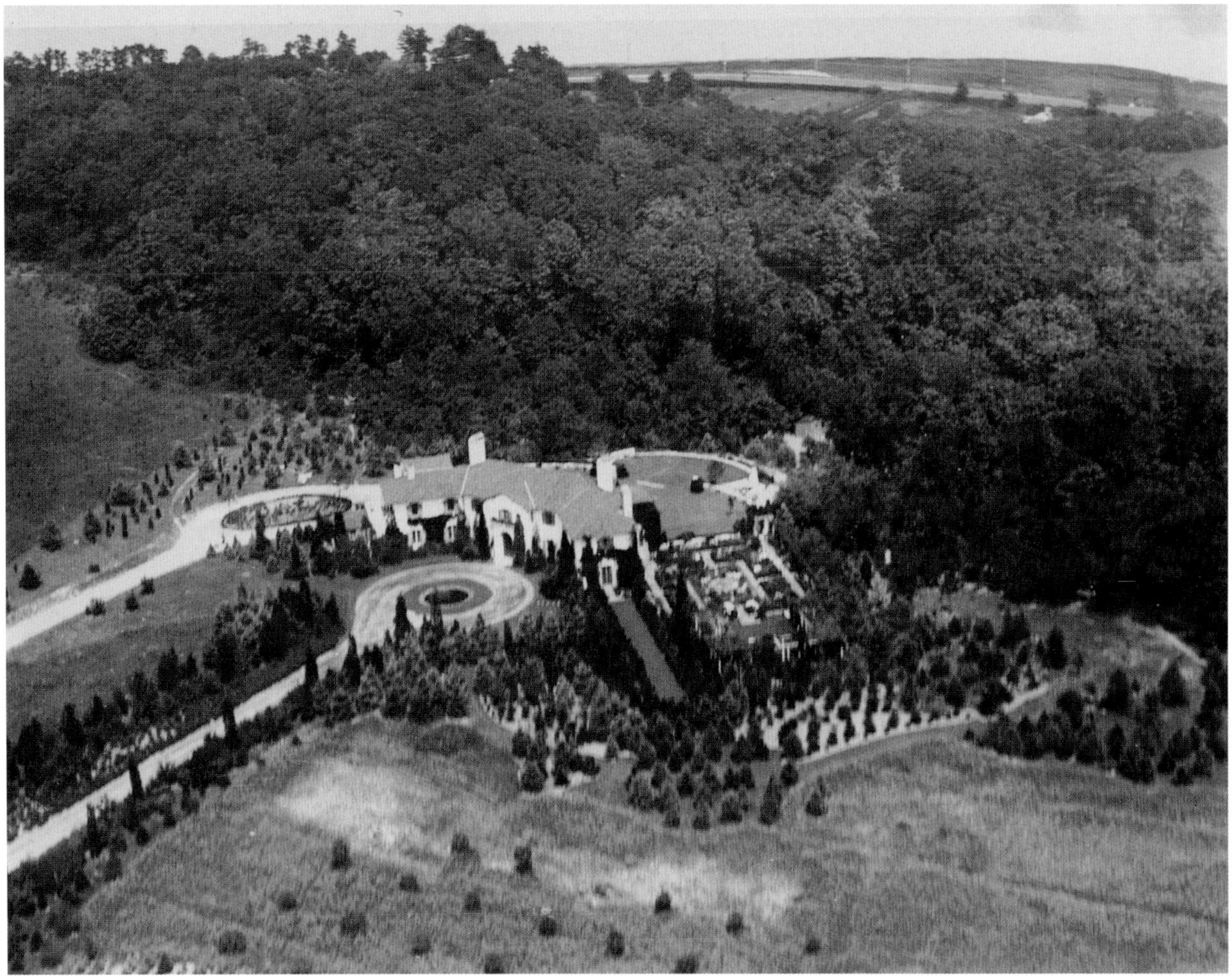

Above: Entrance facade, 1922.

Opposite above: Garden facade, 1922.

Opposite below: Aerial view.

Overleaf: Forecourt and entrance facade.

was completed in 1919, Doubleday contacted Olmsted Brothers for a basic landscape plan and general layout of the property with the idea of carrying out the scheme over time.[3] In addition to a broad terrace stretching out from the living and dining rooms, the Olmsted firm designed a rectangular flower garden running along the rear of the library. Bordered by boxwood and a pergola draped in hardy vines, the garden had a room-like quality with its short side facing a clear view of the water. An allée of cedars, announced by a pair of peacock statues, was centered on the library door and extended to the southwest.

In 1946 Lindeberg returned to Barberrys, adding large bay windows in the dining and living rooms. Lindeberg maintained a friendship with Doubleday and his second wife, Ellen McCarter Doubleday, whom he married in 1932. Around the same time, Lindeberg designed modern classical printing plants for the Doubleday & Company in Hanover, Pennsylvania, and for Country Life Press in Garden City using a light-gauge prefabricated steel module system that he had developed during the Depression.[4]

Barberrys was a frequent stop-over of the acclaimed British author Daphne du Maurier. In the United States to defend her best-selling novel *Rebecca* against claims of plagiarism in 1947, she stayed with Ellen and Nelson Doubleday, her American publisher, and became smitten with Ellen Doubleday. Du Maurier professed her love for Ellen openly, calling her "Rebecca of Barberrys," and while Ellen rejected her advances, the two women remained close friends after du Maurier's return to England. Du Maurier continued to visit Barberrys and eventually based her next novel, *My Cousin Rachel*, on Ellen.

Extremely well preserved, Barberrys is still a private house with its Olmsted-designed garden intact. New owners recently completed a full restoration, working with PBDW Architects and a team of preservationists.

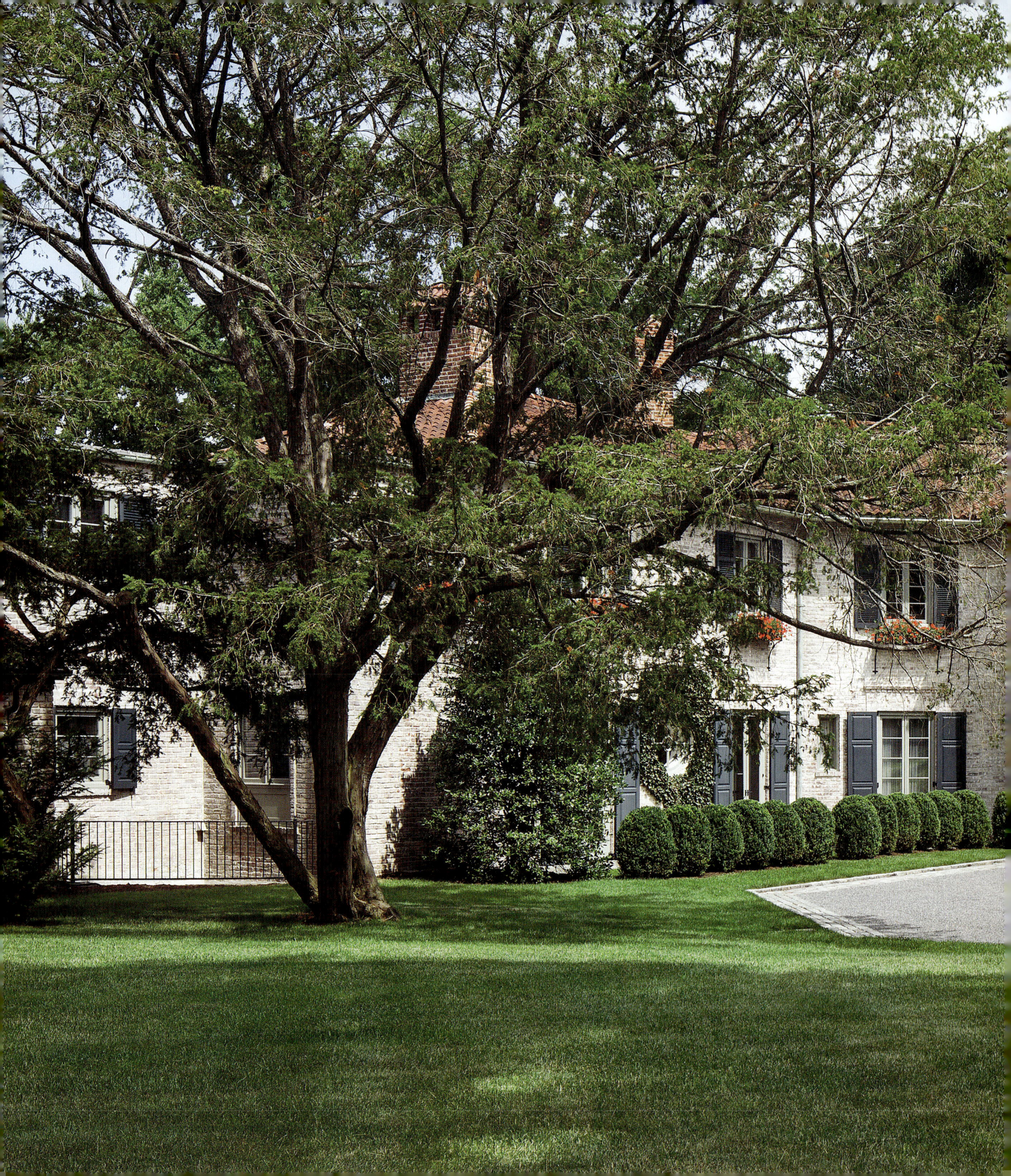

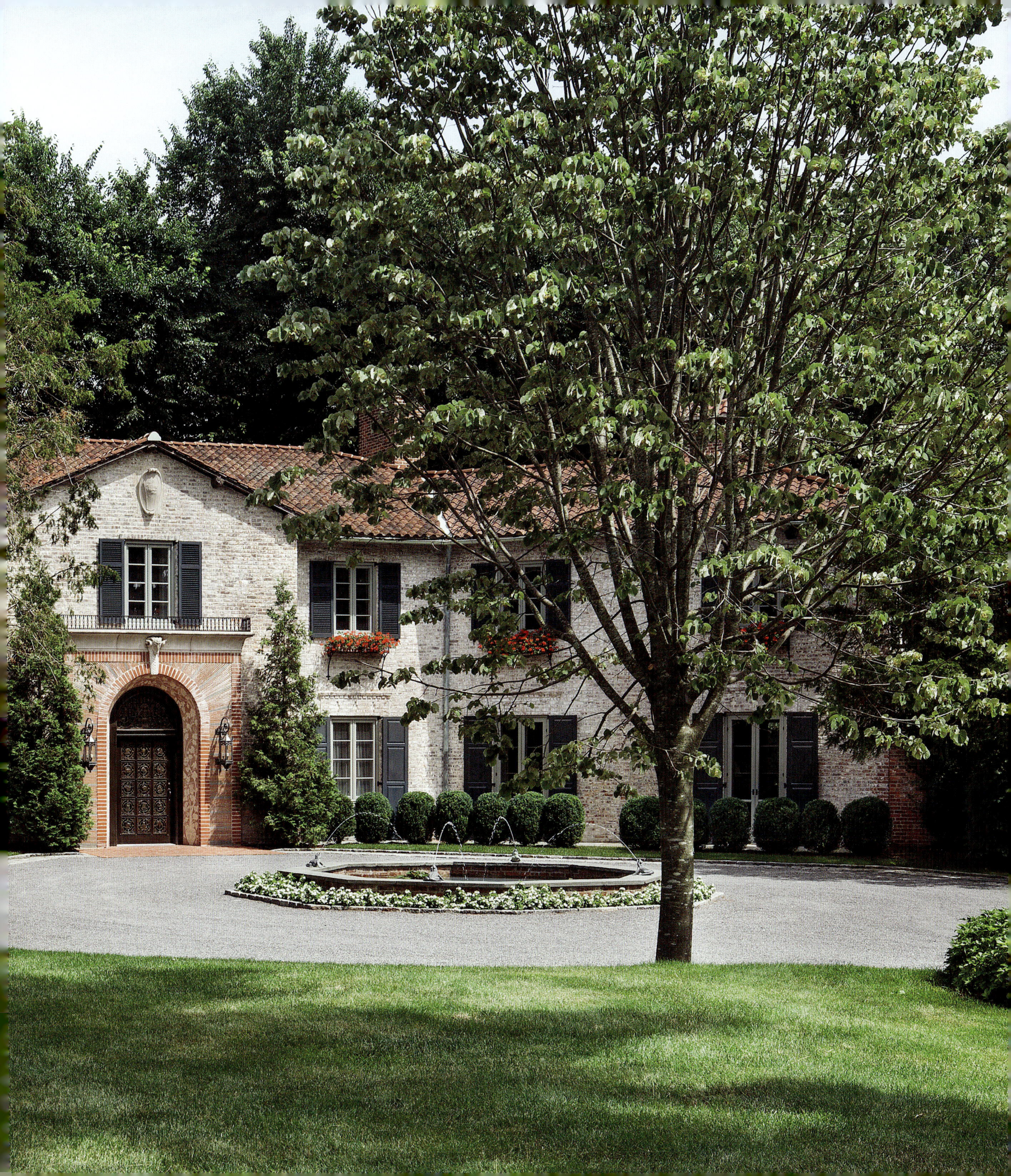

Above: Garden facade.

Far left: Bronze scorpion detail in the front door by Oscar Bach.

Left: Wrought-iron peacock-shaped door hardware.

Opposite: Southeast facade and garden designed by Olmsted Brothers.

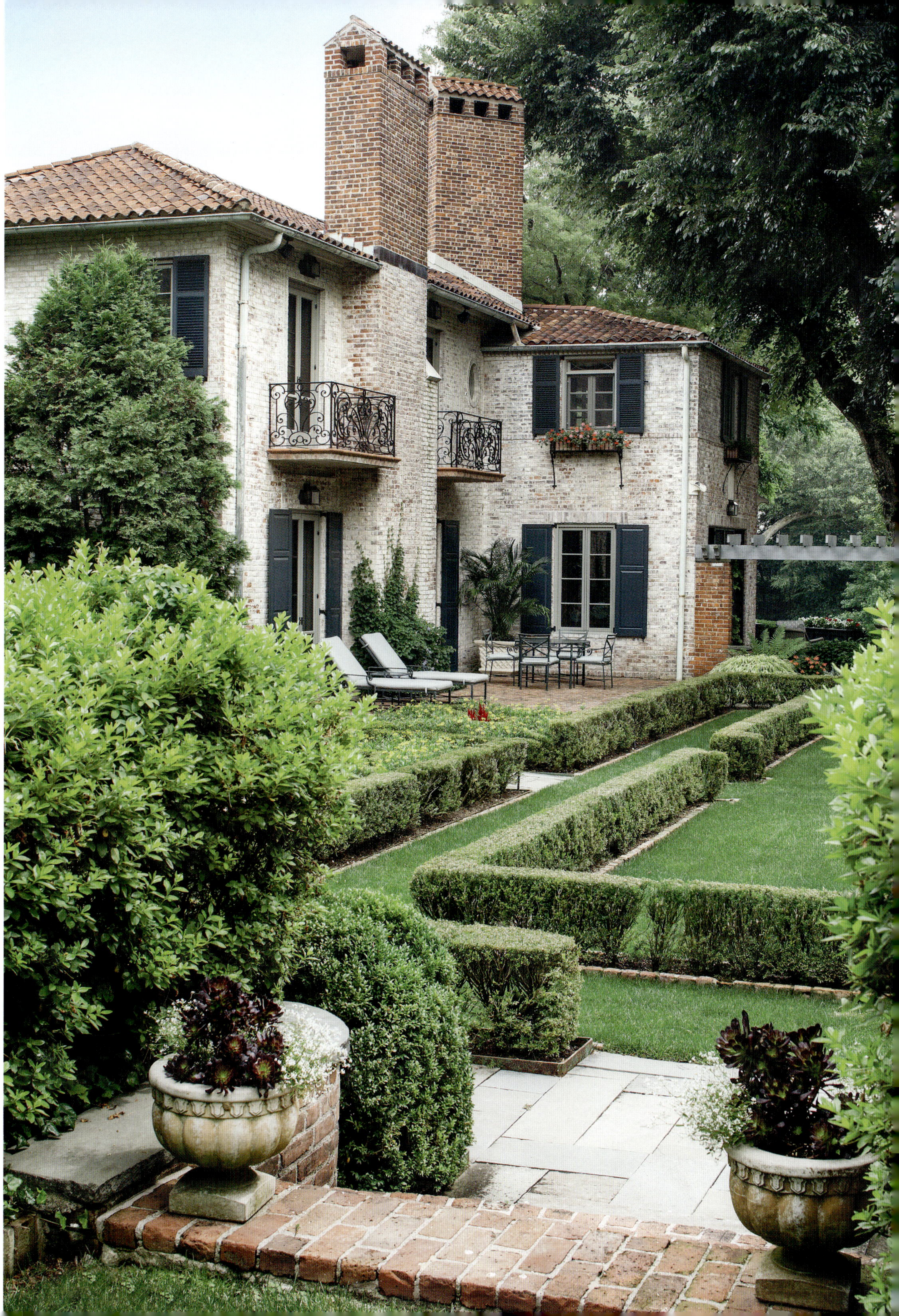

Top: Dining room, 1947.

Above: View from the living room into the dining room, 1947.

Opposite: View from the library into the front hall.

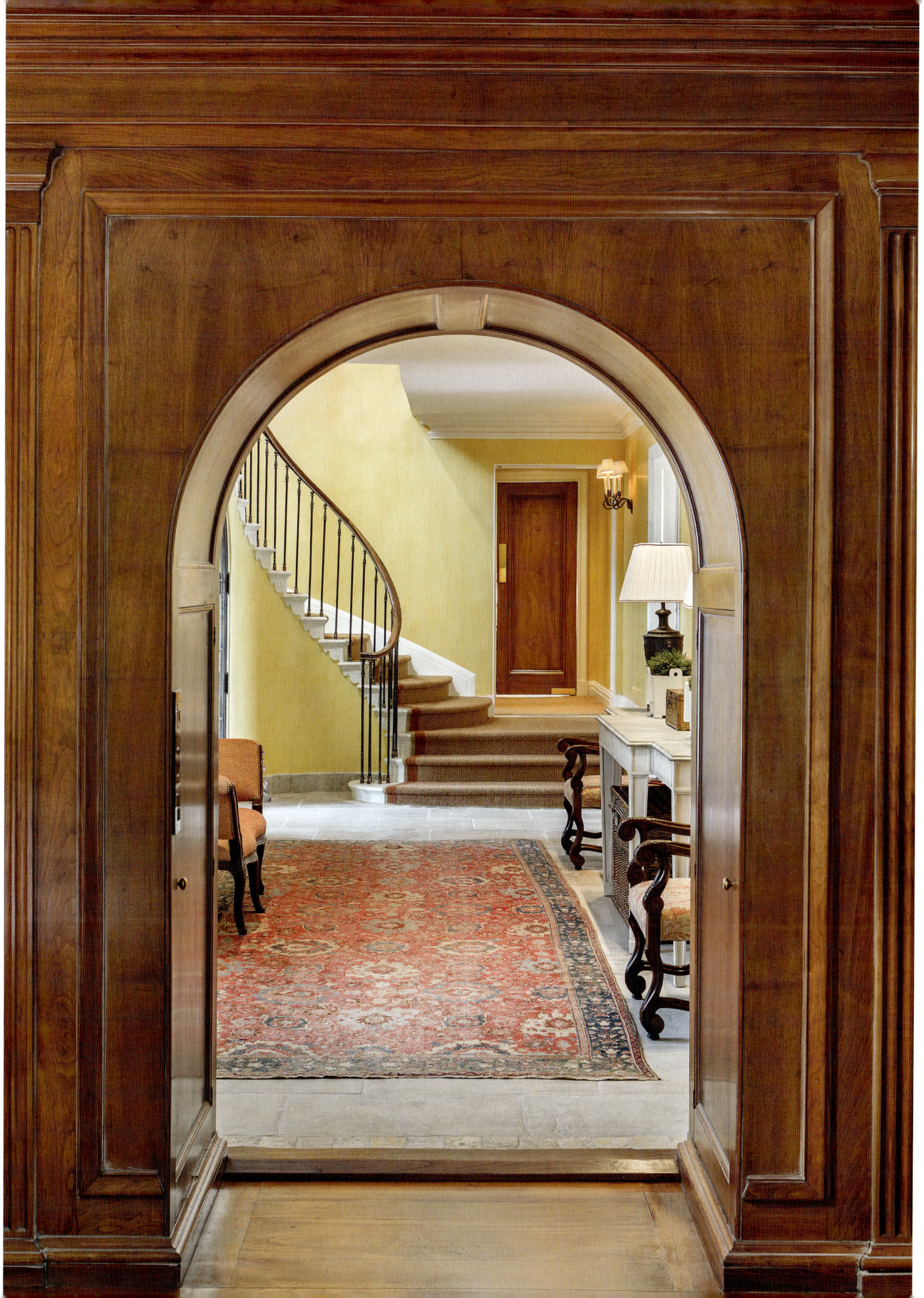

Above: Library.

Opposite: Wrought-iron gate into the garden.

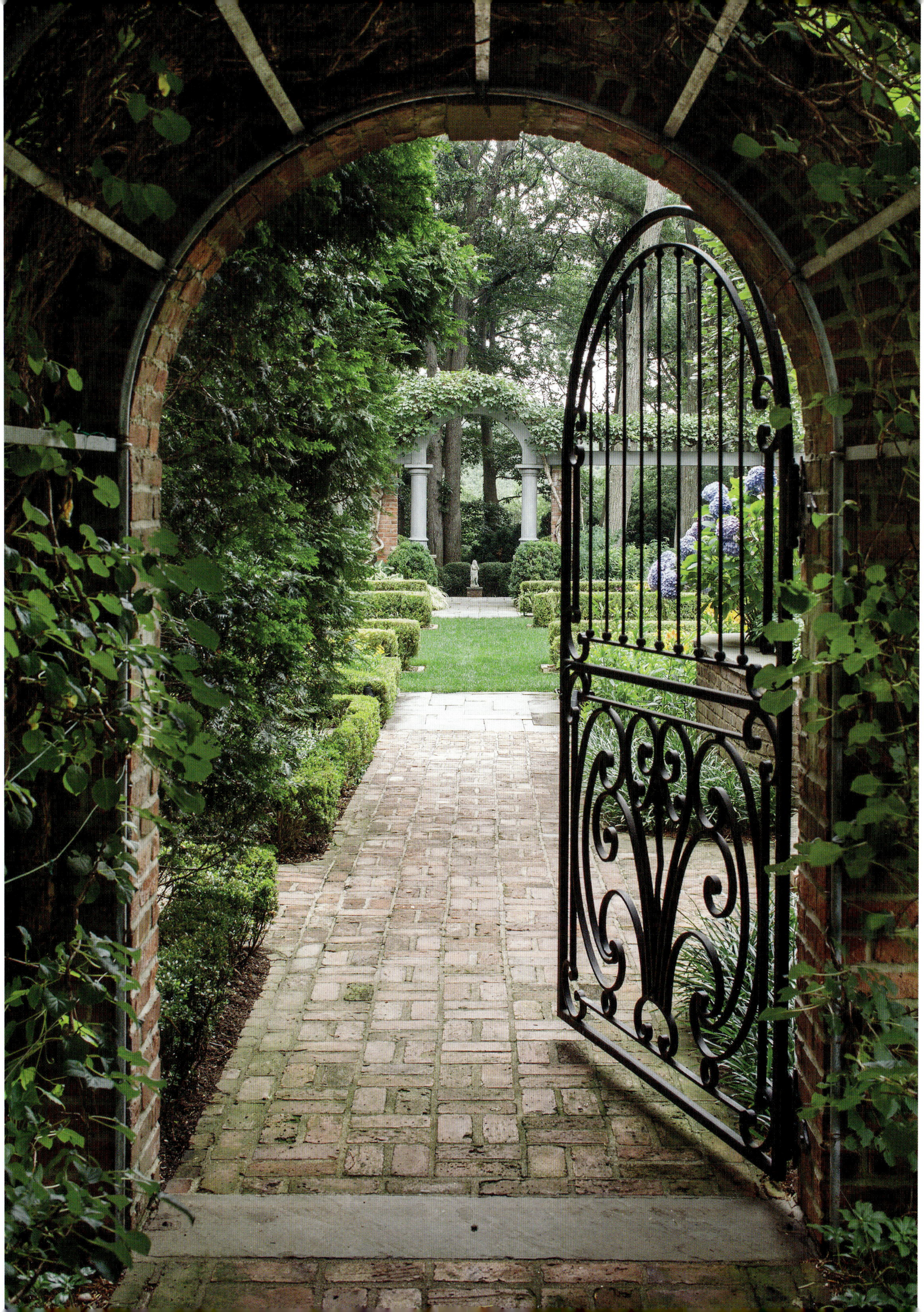

SHADYSIDE

HOUSTON, TEXAS

HUGO V. NEUHAUS HOUSE, 1920–22

KENNETH E. WOMACK HOUSE, 1921

WILLIAM STAMPS FARISH II HOUSE, 1921

DAVID D. PEDEN HOUSE, 1922

HARRY C. WIESS HOUSE,
ALTERATIONS AND ADDITION, 1925

When Lindeberg began working in Houston in the early 1920s, the city was experiencing a wave of economic prosperity and growth due to the state's flourishing oil business and shipping channel. The emerging elite, eager to guide development, began to take an interest in Houston's new shape and direction. Ralph Adams Cram's neo-Byzantine buildings at the Rice Institute, opened in 1912, were emblematic of the new level of architectural sophistication, and the establishment of well-designed parks, including Hermann Park (1914) donated by the estate of oilman and philanthropist George H. Hermann, began a citywide trend. The leading citizens of Houston wanted to improve their city with better planning to include parks, landscaping, and architecture.

Because comprehensive plans guiding residential development did not exist, private citizens took it upon themselves to create their own exclusive neighborhoods, attracting their friends and colleagues. Shadyside, located just northeast of Rice, was an early example of such a proprietary venture. In 1916 Joseph S. Cullinan (1860–1937), an oil operator who had founded the Texas Company (later Texaco), purchased 38 acres from the estate of George Hermann and commissioned the German-born landscape architect George E. Kessler to lay out his enclave. Based in St. Louis, Kessler had gained recognition with his plans for parks, including Hermann Park, and for cities, including Dallas, El Paso, Cincinnati, Cleveland, Terre Haute, Denver, and Syracuse.

Fronting onto Main Street—a newly landscaped boulevard running alongside Hermann Park—Shadyside consisted of two private roads: Remington Lane, which extended off Main and curved around to the southwest to Sunset Road, marking the boundary of Rice; and Longfellow Lane, a shorter stretch between Main and Remington that terminated in a landscaped court; and approximately twenty-two lots. Cullinan hired civil engineer Herbert A. Kipp to supervise Shadyside's development, brought on St. Louis-based architect James P. Jamieson to design his own house, and had restrictive covenants drawn up establishing land use, occupancy, setbacks, and building restrictions—measures that would remain in effect for fifty years before the streets reverted to public use. The lots—offered after World War I—sold extraordinarily quickly. Cullinan also donated land—as had George Hermann—to the Houston Art League for the establishment of a museum, ensuring that the area would continue to remain reputable and relevant.

While a number of architects worked in Shadyside, Lindeberg was the most prolific, designing four houses as well as alterations to a fifth. His first client, Hugo V. "Baron" Neuhaus (1882–1947), had founded Neuhaus & Company, the first brokerage and

Entrance to Hugo V. Neuhaus house.

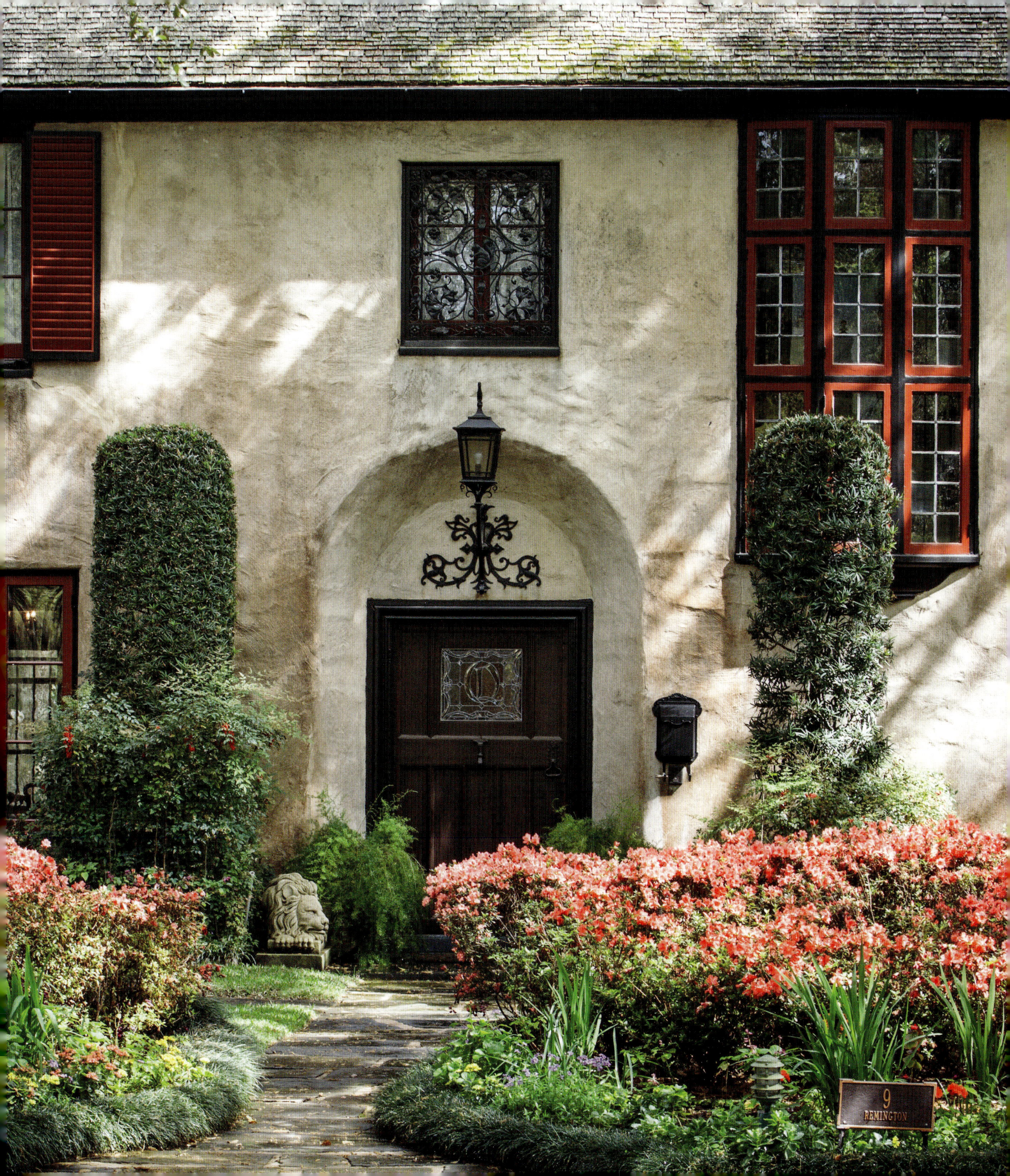
9
REMINGTON

Above: Map of Shadyside.

Opposite above: Rendering of the Kenneth E. Womack house.

Opposite below left: Entrance facade of the Williams Stamps Farish II house.

Opposite below right: Wrought iron gate and owl statues at the Neuhaus house.

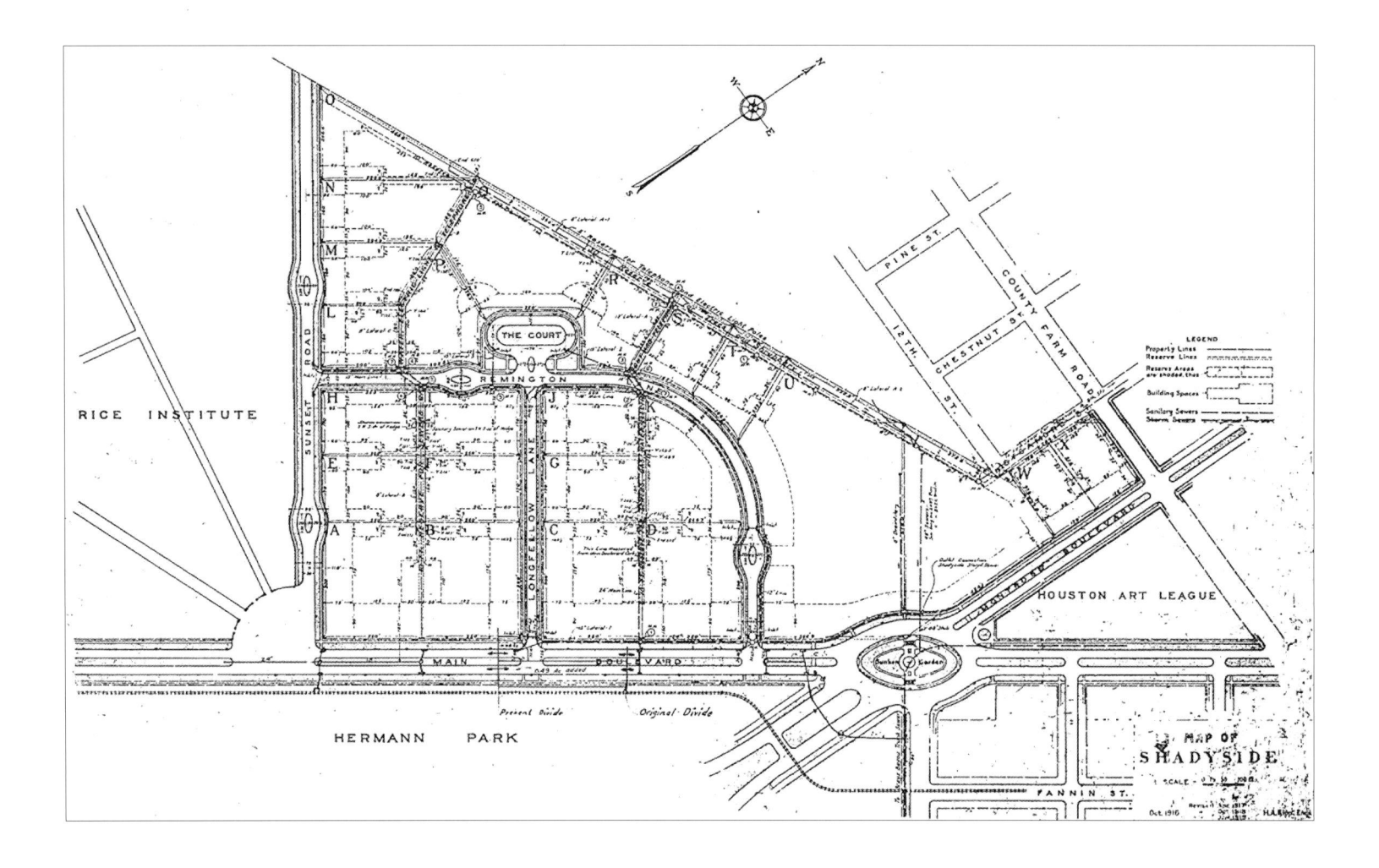

investment house in Texas. In 1919 he and his wife, Katherine Rice Neuhaus—the niece of William Marsh Rice, the benefactor of the Rice Institute—commissioned Lindeberg to design a house at 15 Courtlandt Place in another exclusive development for which Neuhaus's firm served as sole agent. Lindeberg's design however did not fit the site and, after Neuhaus acquired lot I at Shadyside, he was able to use the plans there without any major changes.[1] Neuhaus introduced Lindeberg to two additional clients: Kenneth E. Womack (1870–1946), a cotton exporter, and William Stamps Farish II (1881–1942), a pioneer oilman who helped organize the Humble Oil and Refining Company (later part of Standard Oil). Lindeberg won his fourth Shadyside commission in 1922 from David D. Peden Jr. (1875–1958), head of Peden Iron and Steel, the largest hardware and building supply house in the Southwest. Soon after, Harry C. Wiess, Farish's business partner, asked the architect to renovate his house on lot A, which had been designed by Houston's leading residential architect, William Ward Watkin, in 1919. Lindeberg added a new living room and master bedroom wing and rearranged the ground floor. Lindeberg's designs introduced a new level of sophistication into Houston's architectural scene.

With the flood of new work, Lindeberg opened a Houston office and installed John F. Staub as the

133

manager. A graduate of the Massachusetts Institute of Technology, the Knoxville-born architect had begun working for Lindeberg in 1916—with a break during the war—and in 1921, Lindeberg asked him to go to Houston, a fortuitous decision for Staub's future. With Neuhaus's help, they established an office in the Union National Bank building where the Neuhaus company was also located. Lindeberg operated the Houston office until 1923, bringing in additional commissions for a swimming pool and bathhouse at the Houston Country Club and a house for oil operator John Hamman.[2] After the Lindeberg office closed, Staub stayed in Houston and went on to enjoy a fruitful career creating some of the greatest houses in the city.

Each Lindeberg house in Shadyside was different and yet each seems perfectly expressive of the setting. The picturesque Neuhaus house resembled a medieval Cotswold cottage with rough-plastered walls, leaded-glass details, heavy wood doors, and an organic Lindeberg roof with a double-height oriel lighting the stair hall. Despite the romantic English asymmetry of the facades, the plans were ordered with more formal axes and enfilades. Lindeberg extended the main axis through wrought-iron gates framed by stone posts topped by owl statues, a side door opening into the stair hall, the entrance hall, the living room, and out to the green-tiled loggia; a secondary axis extended from the entrance porch, through the entrance hall into the dining room. Lindeberg kept the interiors simple, adding interest with such details as radiator grills, wrought in the shape of pineapples and flowers, and stout wood balusters. Upstairs, the house contained six bedrooms, several sleeping porches, and a large wood-lined gymnasium in the attic. Since the new site

Opposite: Northwest facade of the Neuhaus house.

Above: Northeast facade.

Right: Garage and cottage.

Far right: Entrance.

required some modifications to the design, Lindeberg's Houston team drew continually to keep up with the pace of work, producing full-scale drawings of details that went directly to the foreman on site.

In 1921 both Kenneth and Alma Womack and William S. Farish and his wife, Lottie Rice Farish —another Rice relative—commissioned houses on adjacent sites across from the Neuhauses on the landscaped court on Remington Lane, at the head of Longfellow Lane. The Farish house on lot Q presented a symmetrical stucco entrance facade to the street, which Lindeberg enhanced with a trellis, ironwork, and an intricate leaded-glass front door. While it was the largest of Lindeberg's houses in Shadyside, the unassuming entrance front masked wings in the rear embracing a large private garden.[3] Meanwhile, the Womack house on lot R resembled a Spanish farmhouse. Lindeberg placed the entrance to the rear of the lot so that the main rooms overlooking the street would capture the prevailing southeast breeze.

Lindeberg used a more formal Georgian style for the Peden house on lot C, at the corner of Longfellow Lane and Main Street, but he stripped the facades of all detail so they appeared planar, almost spare. However, his handling of the entrance front added a singular variation on the theme. He pulled out a central bay, containing the front door and double-height oriel

Above: Entrance facade of the David D. Peden house.

Opposite: Oriel window and wrought-iron entrance porch

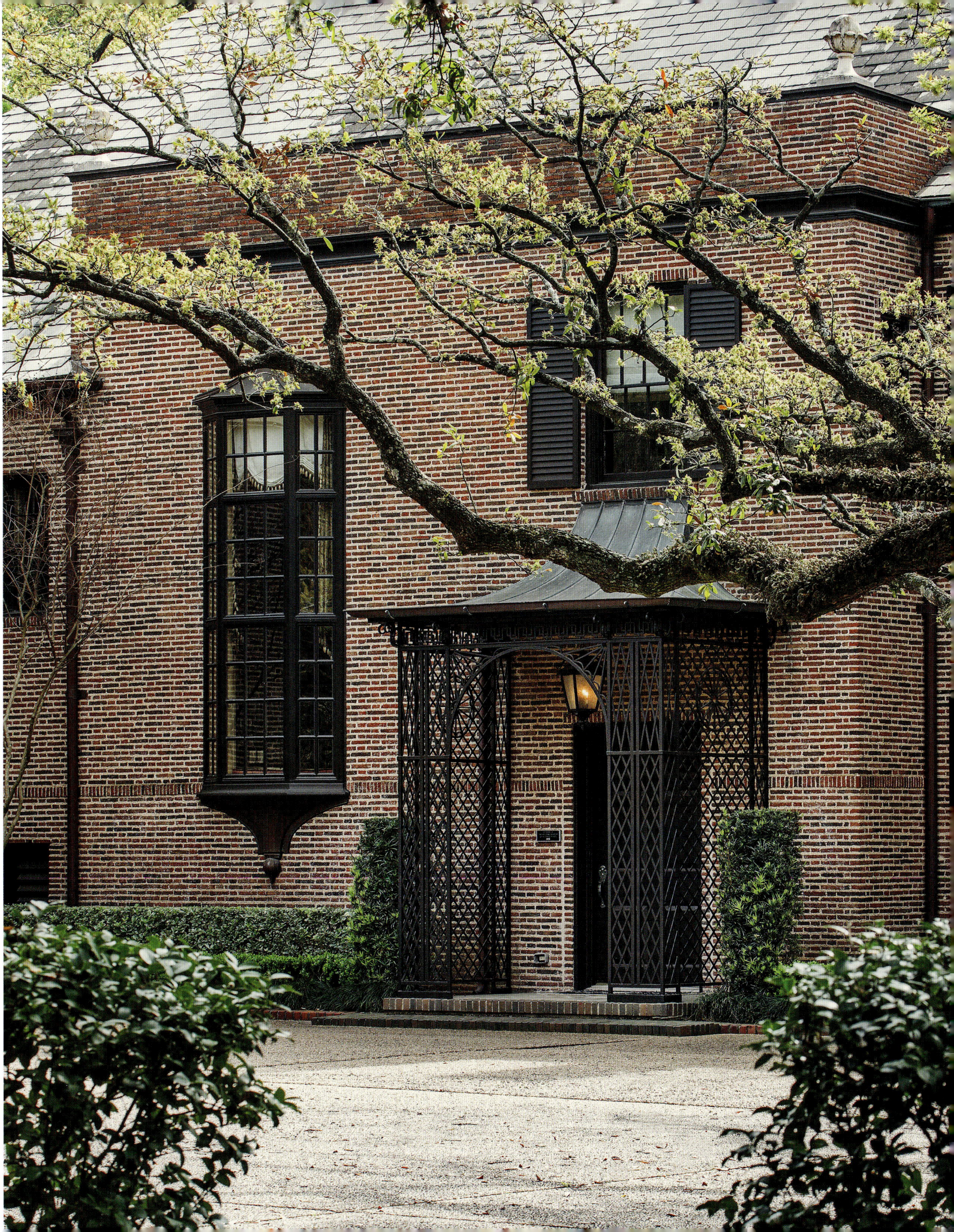

delineating the stair, squaring off its edges and capping the corners with urns—a measure that increased the severity of the design while framing the composition of the entrance facade. By extending the service wing out to the southwest, he was able to divide the entrance and service courts and mask the garage and kitchen area behind walls marked by two eagles perched on ball finials. Compared to the Neuhaus house, the interiors were more formal and grand and included a sweeping spiral stair and an enfilade of public rooms overlooking gardens. Original Jean Zuber et Cie wallpaper still adorns the dining room walls.

In 1983 the property owners' association purchased Remington and Longfellow Lanes from the city, effectively making Shadyside private. Today, it continues as an upscale residential enclave and all of Lindeberg's houses are extant, some with alterations. The Wiess house serves as the President's House of Rice University.

Opposite: An entrance into the kitchen wing at the Peden house built into the backside of the wall separating the service and entrance courts.

Above: Walls capped with eagles perched on ball finials mark the entrance to the service court and garage area.

Right: Garden facade.

Left: View from the Peden house living room into the dining room with the original Jean Zuber et Cie wallpaper.

Opposite: Entrance hall and stair.

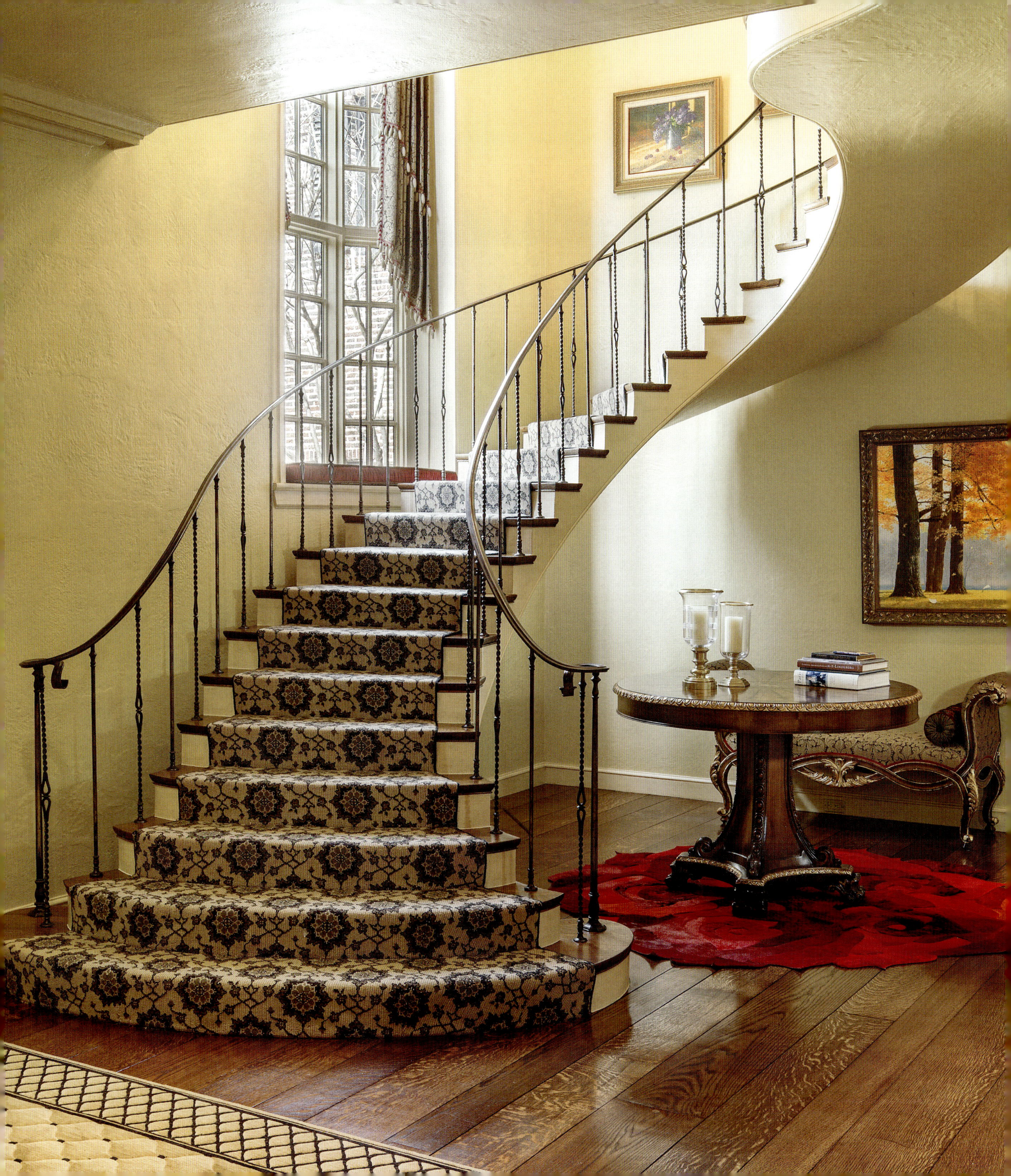

HARRY FRENCH KNIGHT ESTATE

LADUE, MISSOURI

1923–27

A native of St. Louis, Harry French Knight (1864–1933) was a respected banker at A. G. Edwards Sons and well established in the life of the city. In 1887 he married Judith Bertha Brookes (1866–1905), the daughter of a St. Louis doctor, and the couple had four children. After her death, he married Lora Small Moore, widow of James Hobart Moore, in 1922. Moore, with his brother, had built a fortune with such companies as the Diamond Match Co. and the National Biscuit Co. (later Nabisco) and various railroads; together, they were also involved with the founding of U. S. Steel. Having inherited the bulk of his estate, Lora Moore Knight had the resources to commission Lindeberg to design a house on the outskirts of St. Louis.

An aspiring aviator, Knight was president of the St. Louis Flying Club. As the story has it, Knight took Lindeberg up in his plane to view the property's rolling hills from above, enabling him to choose the best spot to locate the house. When it was completed in 1927, the house felt so embedded in its site that critic John Taylor Boyd Jr. commented, "This house in St. Louis . . . is one of the finest architectural achievements in this artist's career—an enchanting place that seems always to have rested on the low hillside dipping into the curve of the entrance road and the hilltop."[1] Long and low, its rambling form followed the rise, with the kitchen and servants wing slung in a curve to fit the contours of the land. With facades of multi-colored Pennsylvania trap rock and a roof of Vermont slate, the exterior was dark but animated with color and varying textures. Lindeberg minimized the size of the house by stepping down the sinuous kitchen wing and tucking additional rooms, as well as the garage, into the backside of the rise.

The interiors were sized for entertaining. A central entrance porch and wide chestnut paneled hall led back to a gallery spanning the width of the house and connecting the dining and living rooms. Lindeberg placed dressing rooms for both men and women off the hall and included a walled garden stretching off the library to the southeast. With Georgian-inspired paneling and pegged oak floors, a series of formal, traditional rooms supported Lora Knight's eclectic mix of French and English furnishings. The staff quarters were extensive, with a series of rooms above the kitchen as well as servants' porch and chauffeur's apartment above the garage.[2]

As president of the St. Louis Flying Club, Knight grew to respect fellow member Charles Lindbergh—at the time living in St. Louis—and chose the pilot as his personal flight instructor. Knight was among a group of wealthy businessmen who backed Lindbergh's solo flight across the Atlantic in May 1927. Knight financed his airplane, the "Spirit of St. Louis," along with Harold Bixby, the head of the Louis Chamber of Commerce, and his son Harry H. Knight. The Knights divorced in 1927, and Knight put the house up for sale in 1928.[3] Over the past sixty years, it has changed hands a number of times and, at some points, sat vacant. In 1966 the property was subdivided and the gatehouse sold as a separate parcel. The current owner has maintained the house and its grounds; San Francisco decorator Suzanne Tucker recently reinvigorated the interiors.

Entrance.

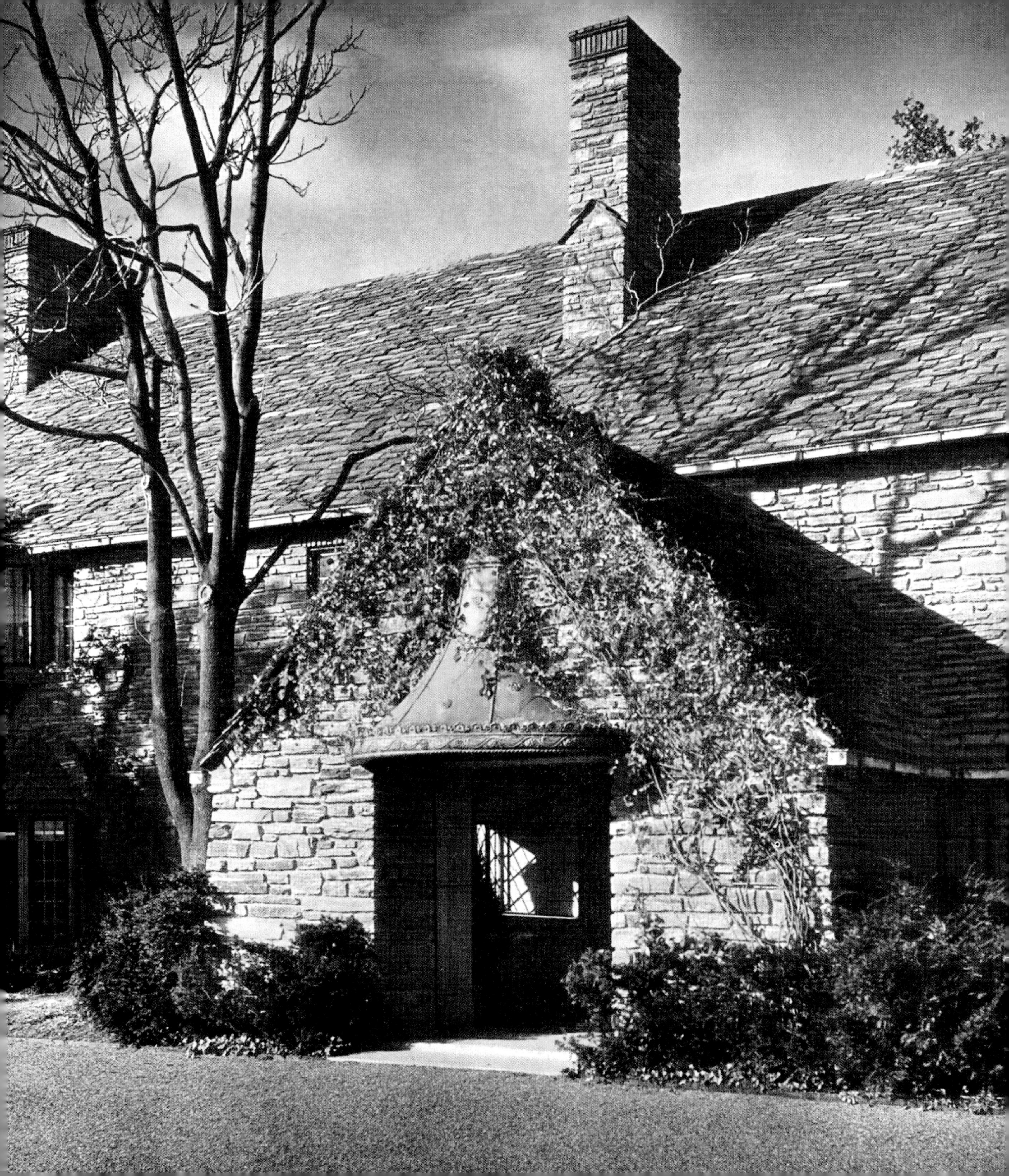

KEY TO SECOND FLOOR

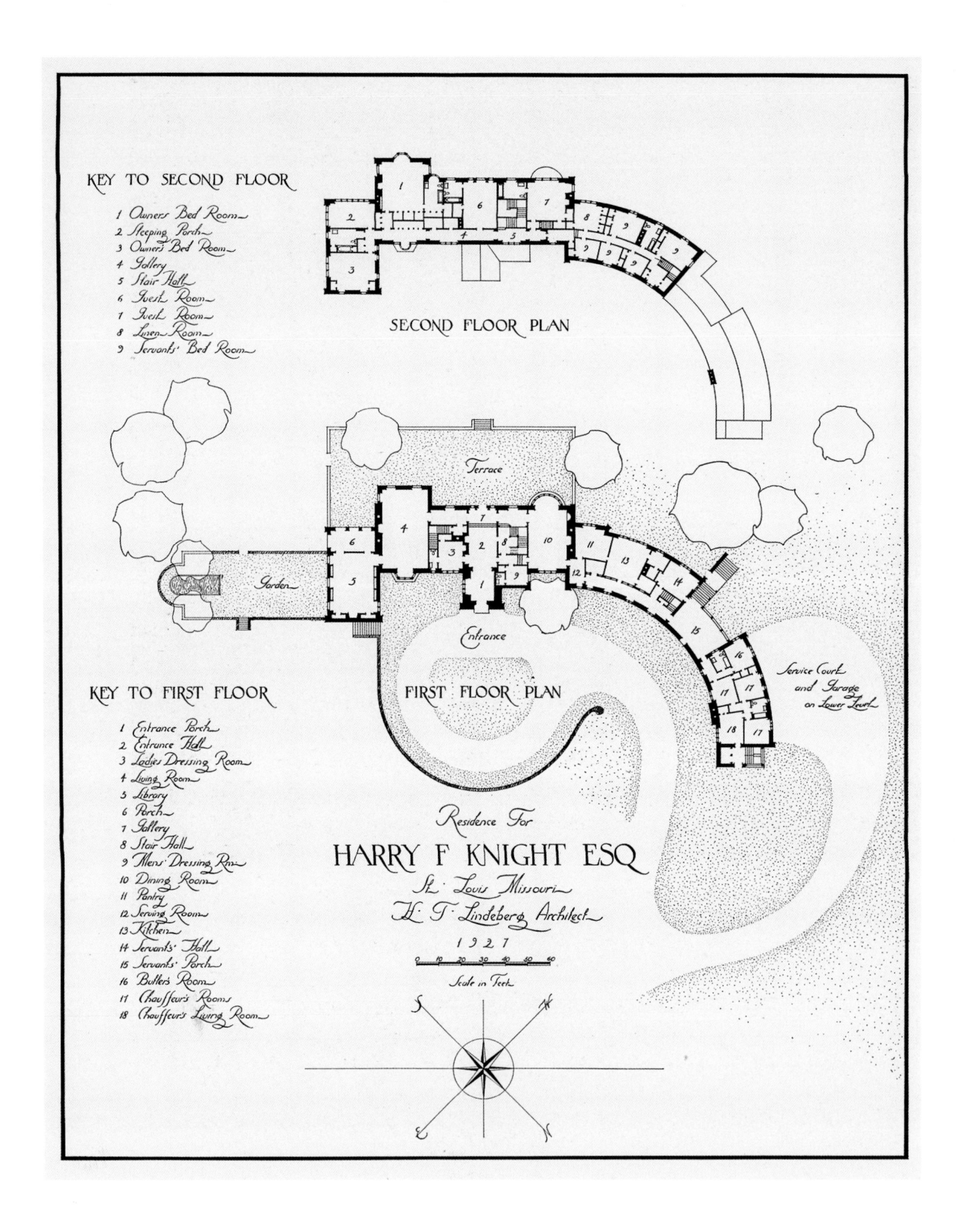

1. Owners Bed Room
2. Sleeping Porch
3. Owners Bed Room
4. Gallery
5. Stair Hall
6. Guest Room
7. Guest Room
8. Linen Room
9. Servants' Bed Room

SECOND FLOOR PLAN

KEY TO FIRST FLOOR

1. Entrance Porch
2. Entrance Hall
3. Ladies Dressing Room
4. Living Room
5. Library
6. Porch
7. Gallery
8. Stair Hall
9. Mens' Dressing Room
10. Dining Room
11. Pantry
12. Serving Room
13. Kitchen
14. Servants' Hall
15. Servants' Porch
16. Butler's Room
17. Chauffeur's Rooms
18. Chauffeur's Living Room

FIRST FLOOR PLAN

Residence for

HARRY F KNIGHT ESQ

St. Louis Missouri

H. T. Lindeberg Architect

1927

Scale in Feet

Right: Curved entrance facade.

Below: Textured stonework and slate shingles of the entrance front.

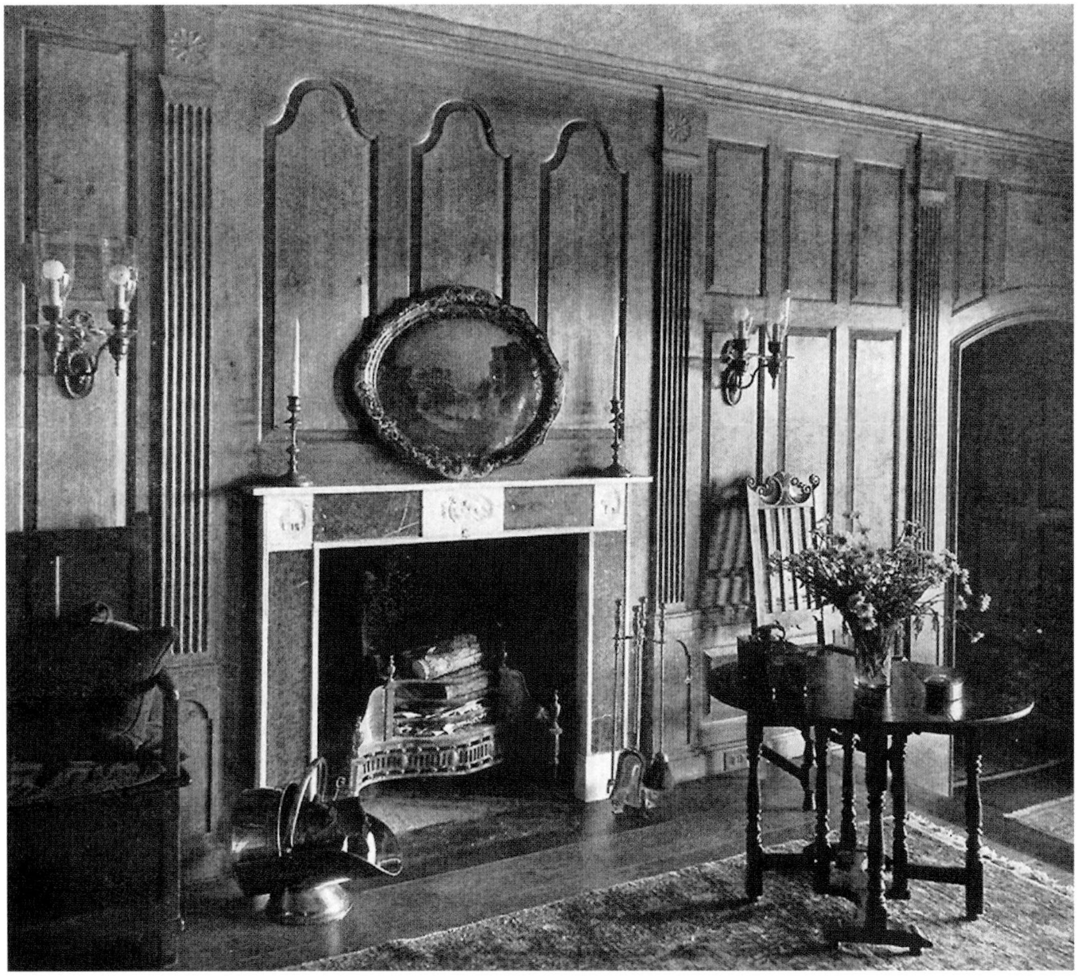

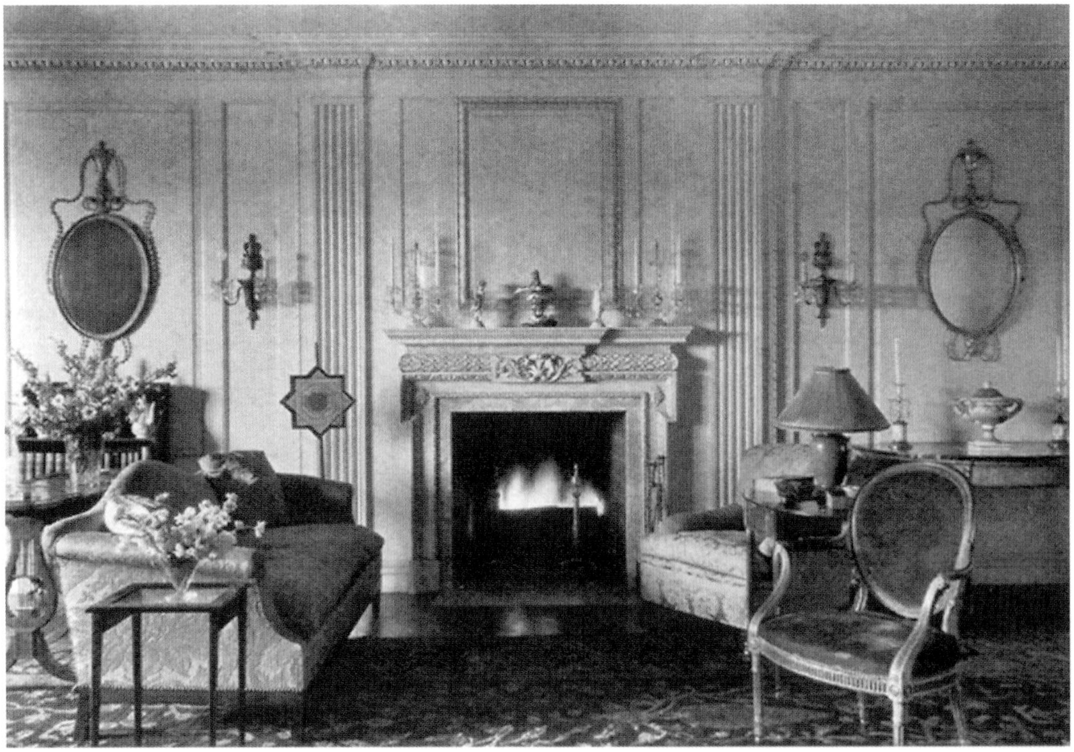

Opposite above: Entrance hall.

Opposite below: Living room.

Above: Library.

GRAY CRAIG
MICHAEL VAN BEUREN ESTATE

MIDDLETOWN, RHODE ISLAND

1924–26

In the mid-1920s, Michael Murray van Beuren (1872–1951) and his wife, Mary Archbold van Beuren (1871–1951), moved from Sunnyfields Farm in Middletown to a storied property nearby with extraordinary views of Sachuest Beach and the Atlantic Ocean.[1] Once home to the Gray Craig Park Association, the land was formerly an exotic zoo—a venture led by Oliver Hazard Perry Belmont, then a flamboyant bachelor and heir to a great banking fortune, with other Newport society leaders, including Cornelius Vanderbilt. In 1892 they stocked the land with exotic animals and birds, including gibbons, Chinese ducks, jungle fowl, pheasants, gazelles, sacred cows from India, mongooses, and antelopes, and Belmont called upon Whitney Warren—a fellow Newporter—to design a fanciful menagerie with a monkey house. Whether Warren's scheme was built is unknown, but plans for a circus with trapeze performers, jugglers, and tight rope walkers never materialized, and the zoo wound down. The association closed soon after, and Belmont laid claim to the title, turning Gray Craig—named after the local pudding stone and its bold rock face—into a farm and horse-breeding facility. In 1901 Belmont—then married to Alva Vanderbilt—sold the property to iron and steel magnate J. Mitchell Clark, who commissioned Abner J. Haydel to build an imposing crenulated stone castle incorporating a porte cochère and old keystones imported from Italy. J. Lawrence Mott III, an iron manufacturer, took over the property in 1917, but, during an extensive remodeling, a fire ravaged the house, leaving it in ruins in 1919.

Michael van Beuren, a broker and Yale graduate, had retired to Middletown in 1910 with his wife, a daughter of John Dustin Archbold, John D. Rockefeller's colleague and president of Standard Oil of New Jersey from 1896 to 1911. In 1924 the van Beurens commissioned Lindeberg to design a new estate on the Gray Craig property. Anchored by the main house, the plans also included a dog kennel, gate house, engineer's cottage, and stable, a complex that took four years to build.

Lindeberg, who had convinced the van Beurens to acquire the extraordinary seaside site, rose to the occasion to produce some of his best work. Gray Craig's dramatic south-facing facade was a powerful abstracted essay in Georgian-influenced architecture expressed in bold lines. Set at the head of Nelson's Pond, the house enjoyed expansive views of the long green slope down to the water.[2] Lindeberg's forms were stripped and elemental—his bold roofline and chimneys, the articulation of volumes—and his handling of materials sculptural and precise.

The warm native stone—quarried next to Gray Craig by the Peckham Brothers—was laid up very tightly in thin courses, the variation in color spread distinctively through the facades, with gray and blues creating a quoining effect at the corners. The sandy color of the limestone details further warmed the facades, as did the variegated roof tiles in shades of brown and orange. The suggestion of piers, capped by urns, softened the center of the block, flanked by one-story pavilions, while the ironwork in the balconies, lanterns, and leader head alleviated the severity of the forms.

From the curving drive, visitors encounter the south facade at an angle before entering though a porte cochère to the west, housed in a separate pavilion.

South facade.

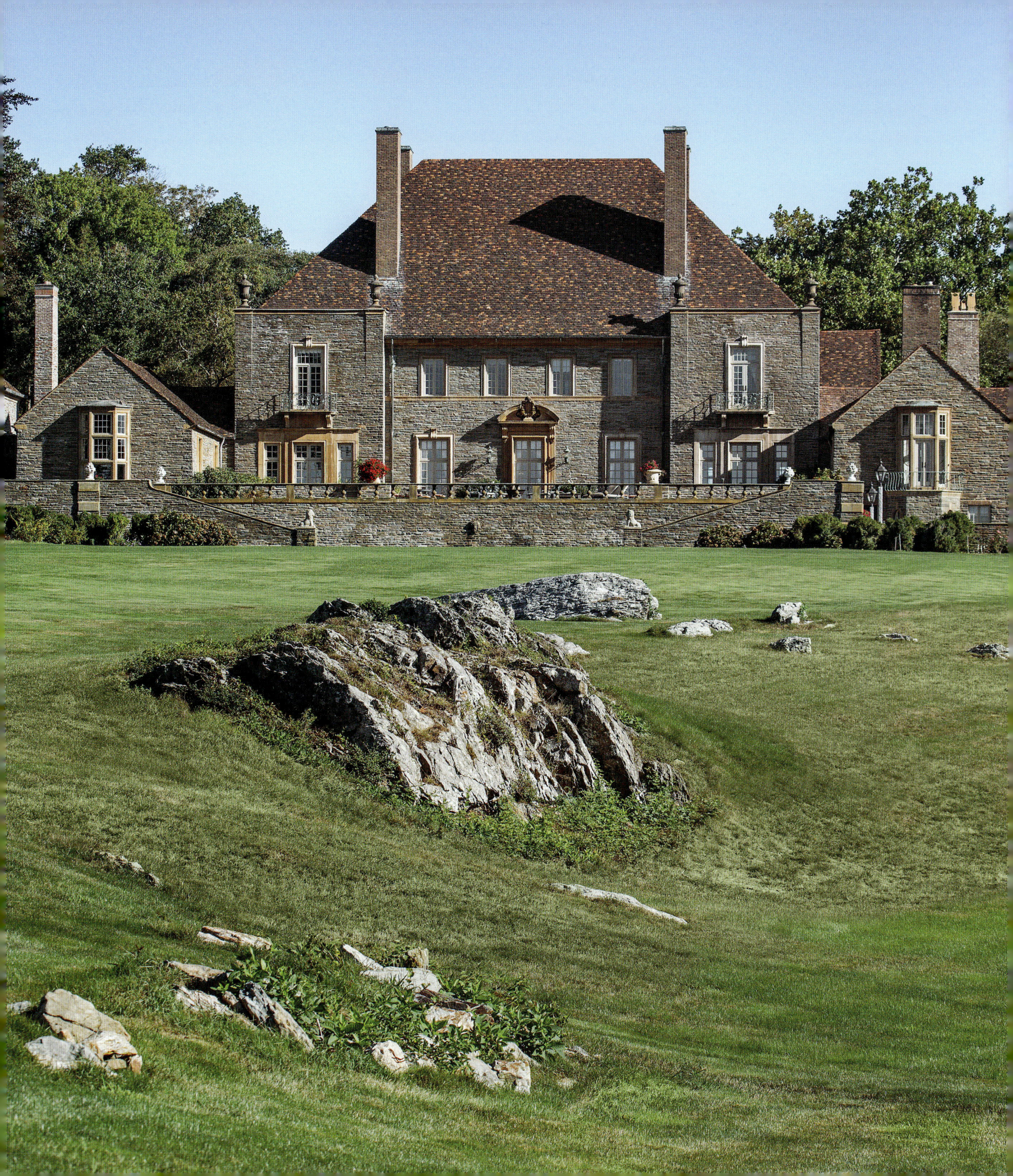

Rendering of the north and east facades showing the interior courtyard and the backside of the entrance pavilion.

Lindeberg embellished the side walls leading up to the entrance with stone peacocks perched on ball finials and bracketed the cornice of the pavilion with abstracted swooping peacocks. An arrival court with a small garage, made to appear monumental with tall wooden doors and urns, overlooked the more conventional elevations on the back of the house. This large false portico revealed within the court extended the axis of the entrance beyond the limits of the porte cochère. The van Beurens commissioned Italian-born landscape architect Ferruccio Vitale to design the grounds. He kept the green slope in the front of the house free to enhance the dramatic views and composed a series of gardens to the north, including a boxwood parterre, a horseshoe-shaped amphitheater, and a reflecting pool. His formal walled garden, once centered on a croquet lawn, bordered by fruit trees and rose-climbing secondary walls, was anchored by Lindeberg's elegant stone teahouse—a simple three-arch structure opening out to the garden.

In the main house, Lindeberg oriented all of the major rooms—the library, reception room, living room, and dining room—toward the water, a plan he achieved by creating a circulation band behind the main rooms along the back of the house. The entrance in the porte cochère opened into the west end of the series of galleries and halls that tied the public rooms together. The first gallery accessed a men's bathroom and ladies' dressing room, decorated with Chinese murals and mirrored panels. To the south, a series of French doors opened into an intimate walled garden—carved into the space behind the library and reception room—that Lindeberg designed to receive sun throughout the day. The entrance gallery stepped up into an elegant oval stair hall with a polychrome marble floor laid in a sunburst pattern and a curving stair embellished with an iron balustrade. Lit by a double-height window, the lofty space, once hung with rare eighteenth- and nineteenth-century tapestries, opened to the reception room with blue-green panels of eighteenth-century hand-painted Chinese wallpaper of birds, butterflies, and flowers that was centered on a scrolling English Rococo pine mantel—said to have been removed from Thomas Chippendale's own home—and a George III style gilt-wood mirror.

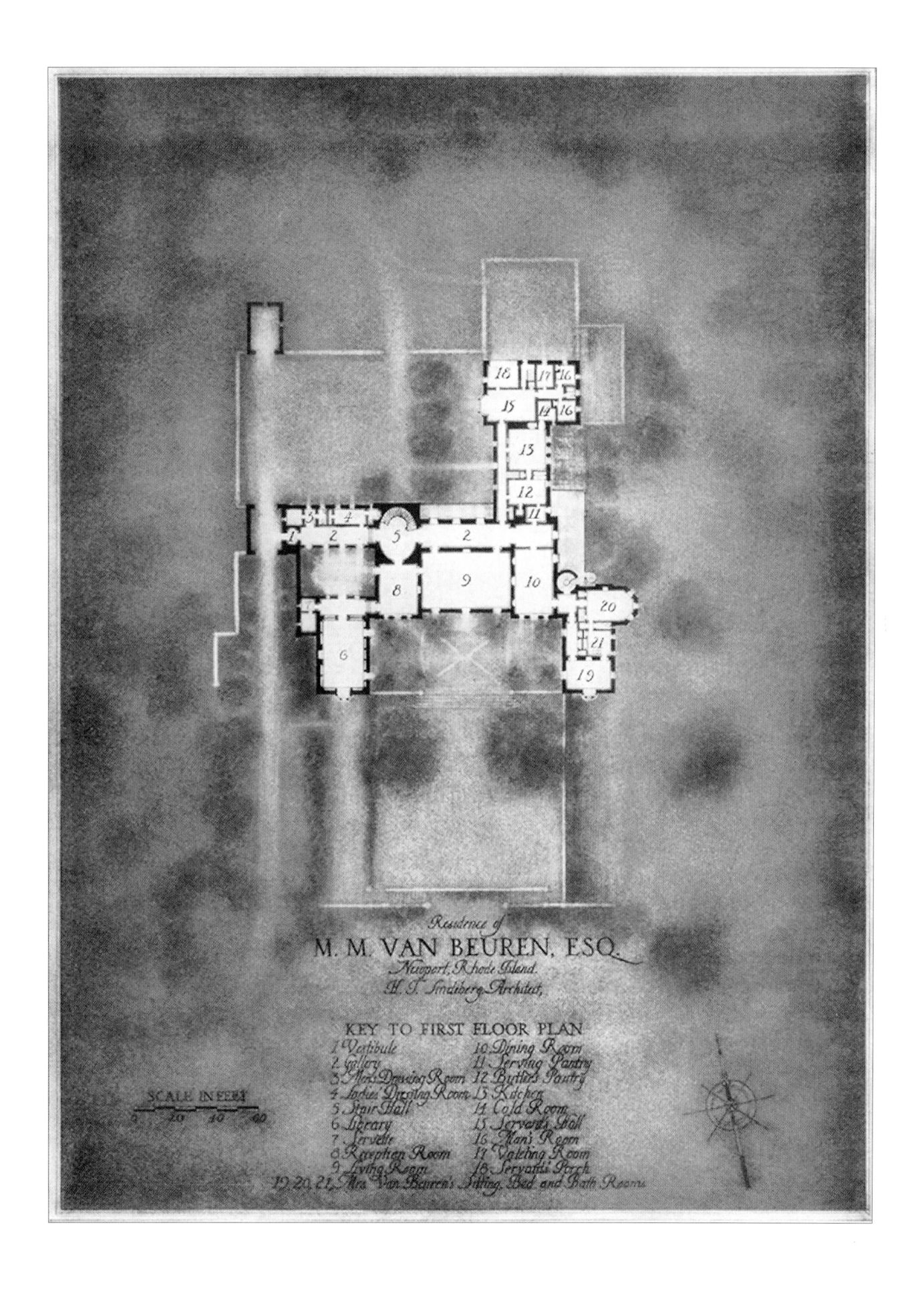

Residence of
M. M. VAN BEUREN, ESQ.
Newport, Rhode Island.
H. T. Lindeberg, Architect.

KEY TO FIRST FLOOR PLAN

1. Vestibule
2. Gallery
3. Men's Dressing Room
4. Ladies Dressing Room
5. Stair Hall
6. Library
7. Servette
8. Reception Room
9. Living Room
10. Dining Room
11. Serving Pantry
12. Butler's Pantry
13. Kitchen
14. Cold Room
15. Servants Hall
16. Man's Room
17. Valeting Room
18. Servants Porch
19, 20, 21. Mrs. Van Beuren's Sitting, Bed and Bath Rooms

The reception room in turn connected to the library housed in one of the one-story pavilions—an expansive bookshelf-lined room with a timbered ceiling and Georgian details. Extending east off the stair hall in line with the entrance gallery, a formal pine-paneled Georgian-inspired gallery connected to the living room and dining room to the south and the kitchen wing to the north. Lit by a series of French windows, the gallery, with its 13½-foot ceiling and polished figured English Wych elm floors, was an ideal setting for the van Beurens' rare set of Gobelin tapestries, c. 1633, depicting the history of Diana. Pedimented doorways led into the large living room, inspired by eighteenth-century France with paneled walls, gently curved doors, and scrolling hardware, and to the bright Federal-style dining room with carved niches, arched window pockets, and a variegated marble mantel incorporating engaged Ionic columns.

The van Beurens had requested that their private bedroom quarters be removed as much as possible from the main house. In effect, Lindeberg designed a separate wing for them in a one-story pavilion, accessible through the dining room. Mary van Beuren's suite of rooms included a bedroom, bath, and sitting room, with a painted chinoiserie door featuring a female figure surrounded by Pekingese and hardware in the shape of a geisha. A George III pine mantel was carved with large foliate scrolls, flowers, and cattle

Above: The entrance pavilion and porte cochère containing the main entrance into the house.

Opposite above: East facade of the stable group.

Opposite below: The teahouse located to the northeast of the house overlooking a walled garden.

Overleaf: The south facade overlooking a great lawn sloping down to the water.

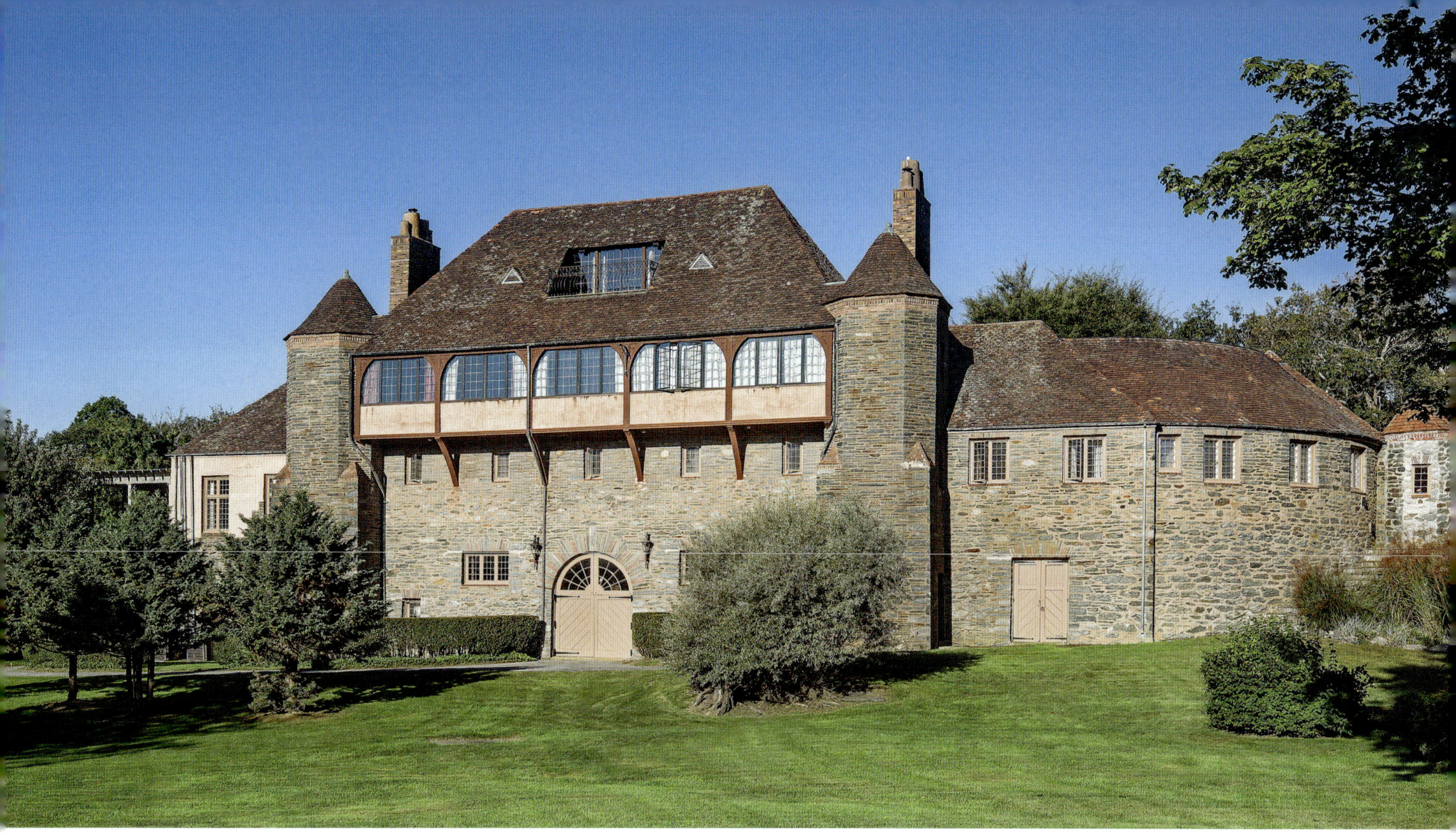

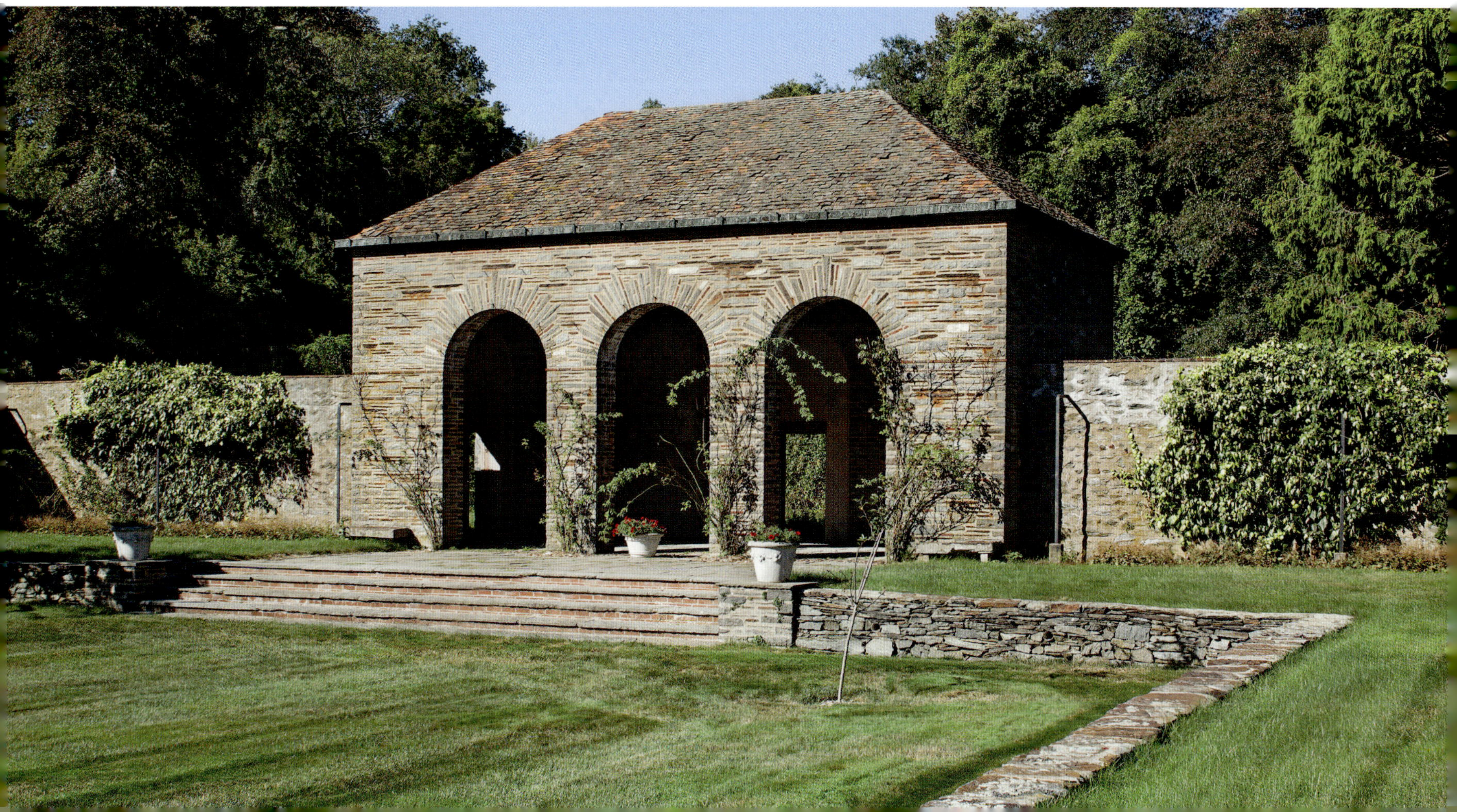

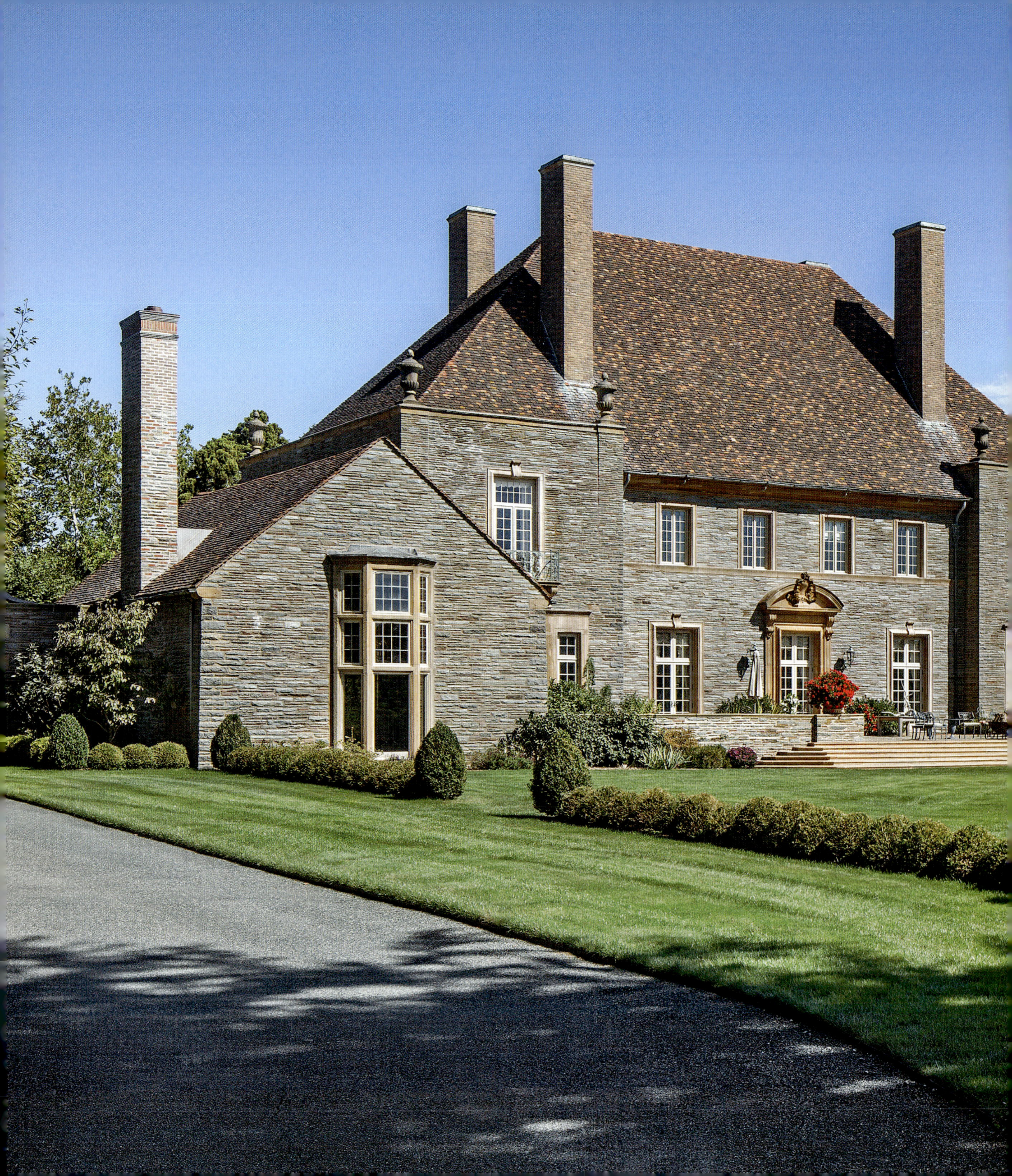

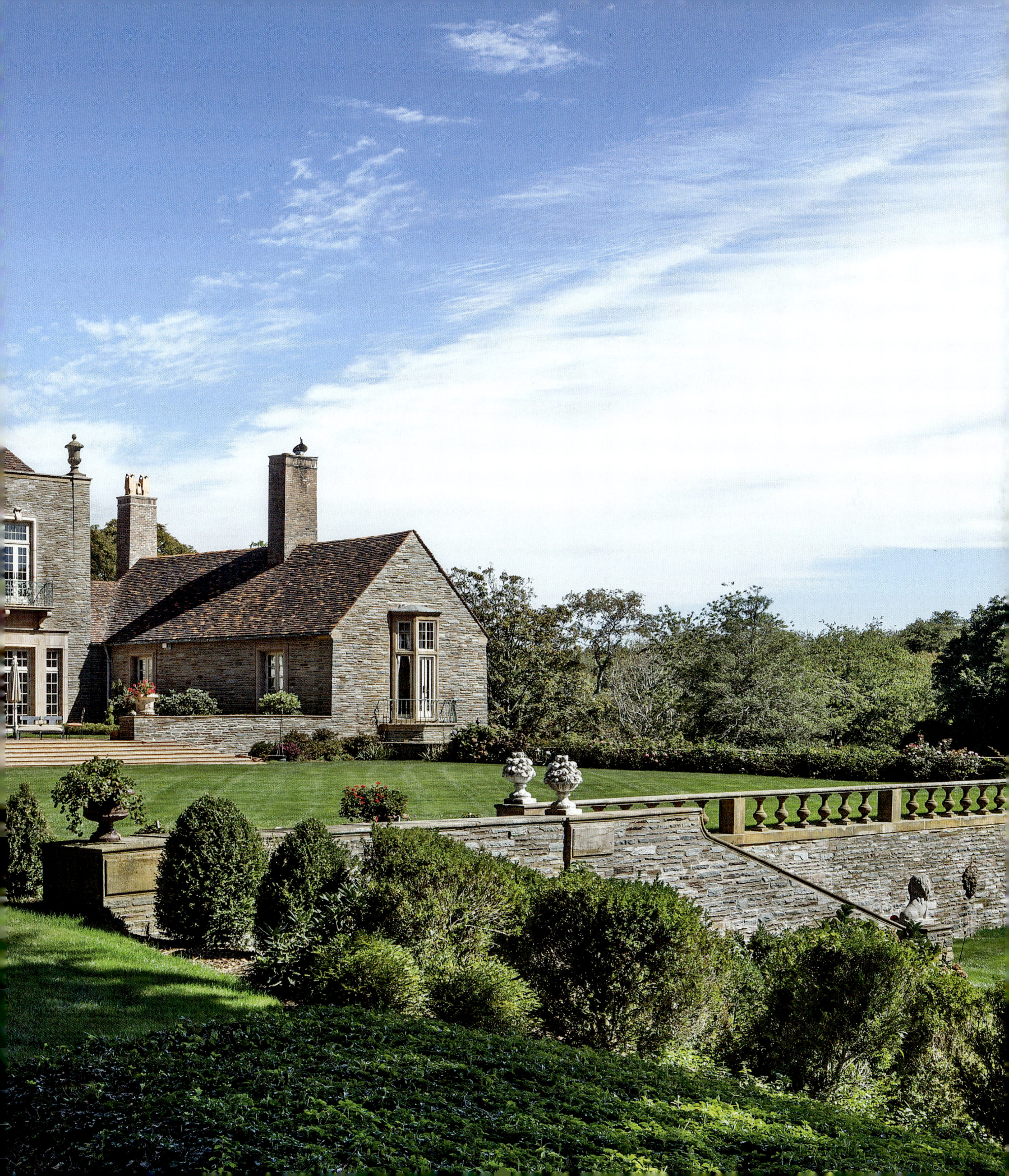

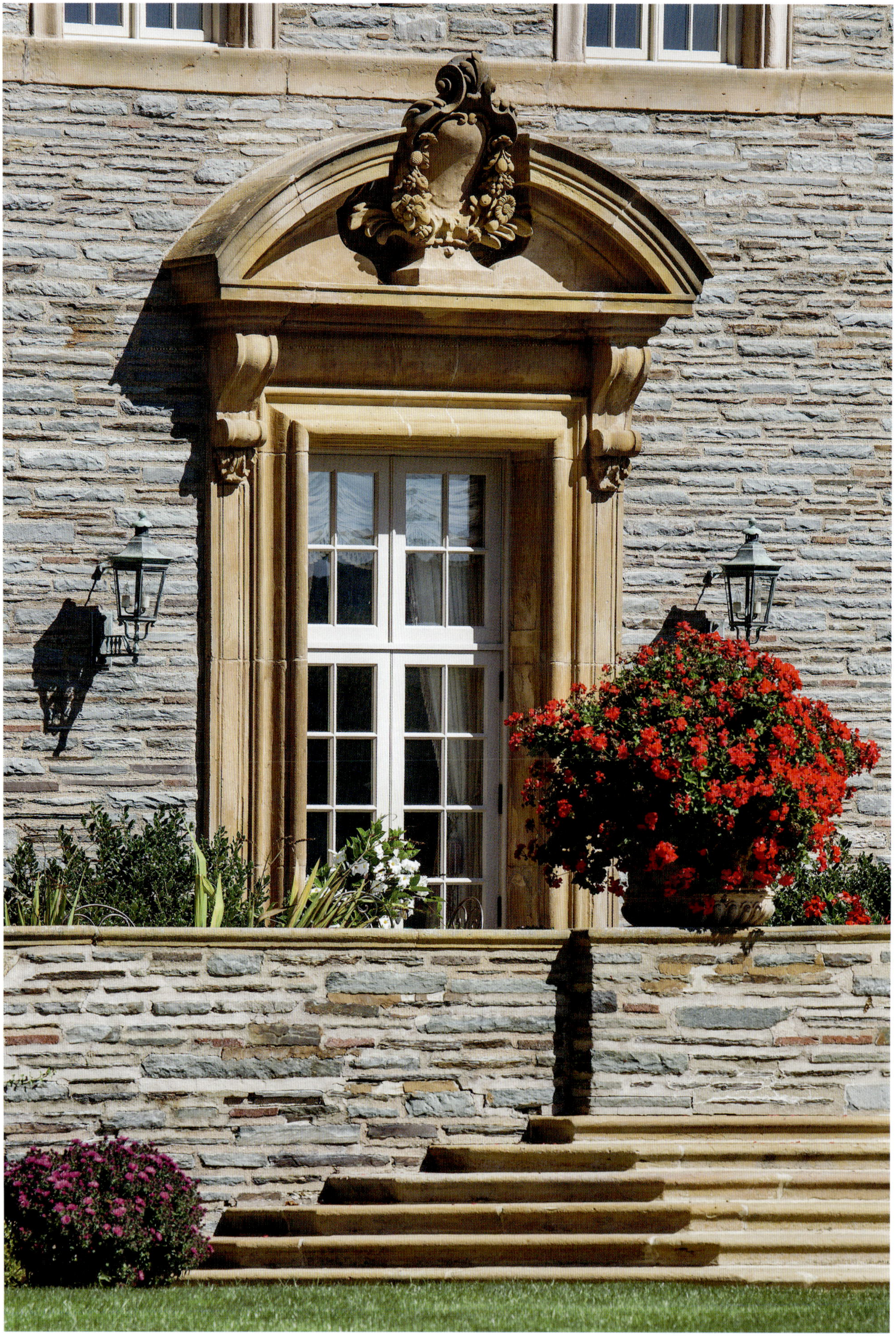

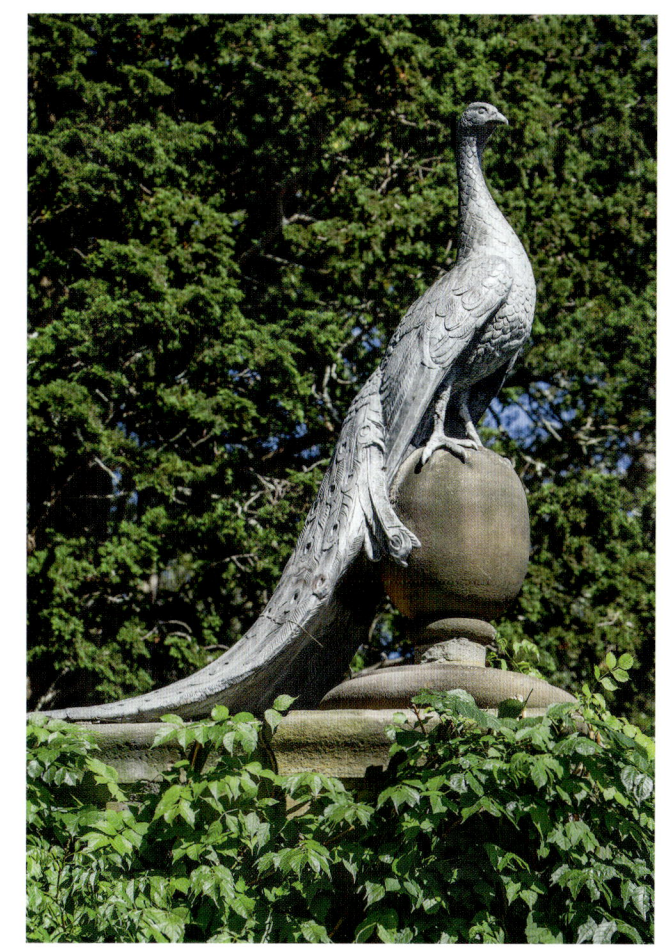

Above left: Ironwork detail on the south facade.

Above right: A peacock perched on a ball finials on the entrance wall.

Opposite: A limestone cartouche and pediment marks the center door on the south terrace.

grazing within an architectural landscape. A spiral stair connected to Michael van Beuren's suite directly below, which Lindeberg laid out along the same lines. Guest rooms possessed even better views of the water from the second floor. And the great attic, housed under the steep roof, contained an expansive play space with elevated stages on either end.

The estate dependencies were located a half mile northwest of the main house. To accommodate a number of diverse functions, many requiring ground-level circulation, Lindeberg clustered the stable buildings around a quadrangle built into a slope of the property. From the west, two low-lying wings enclosed a courtyard, housing wagons, automobiles, and workshops with quarters for the gardeners and staff above. The barn's central block—seemingly an English cottage with dormer windows as seen from the west—transformed into a picturesque turreted affair when viewed from the east. The ground level, accessible from roads set a level lower than the quadrangle, contained stalls for livestock—including blooded Jersey and Guernsey cattle—with a hayloft above. With massive walls of native pudding stone, capped by a steeply pitched roof and bracketed by turrets, the structure had both a whimsical and fortress-like quality. An extensive network of conservatories extended to the south and distant views of the ocean were visible over the tree tops. As president of the Pekingese Club of America, Mary van Beuren was dedicated to the breed and maintained a separate kennel on the estate complete with a dog hospital and veterinarian on staff. Also carried out in an

English-cottage style, the kennel was located due north of the main house while down by the water's edge, discreetly tucked into the woods, she preserved the memory of her beloved dogs in a pet cemetery—still extant—with more than fifty carved gravestones.

The van Beurens' only child, Archbold van Beuren (1906–1974), founder of *Cue Magazine*, and his wife, Margaret Ziegler van Beuren (1909–1987), a daughter of prominent Philadelphia architect Carl Ziegler, inherited the property and resided there until the 1980s. The couple's four children auctioned off the contents of the house in 1985 through Christie's and the property was sold to a group of investors in 1986.[3] Their plans for a condominium development were overridden by preservationists. The estate has since been divided into five separate properties: the main house, the stable, the engineer's cottage, the kennel, and the gate house. As a result, the open acreage has been conserved, and the houses co-exist within a private enclave that feels very much like an estate. The gate house has been recently restored; the dramatic stable transformed into a house; the engineer's cottage expanded; and the kennel sympathetically renovated. The current proprietors of the main house—the third owners since the van Beurens—continue to preserve Gray Craig.

Above: The ladies' dressing room was originally decorated with Chinese murals interspersed between the mirrored panels.

Left: Reception room.

Opposite: The major axis of the house running from the front door, through the entrance gallery and stair hall to a formal pine-paneled gallery beyond.

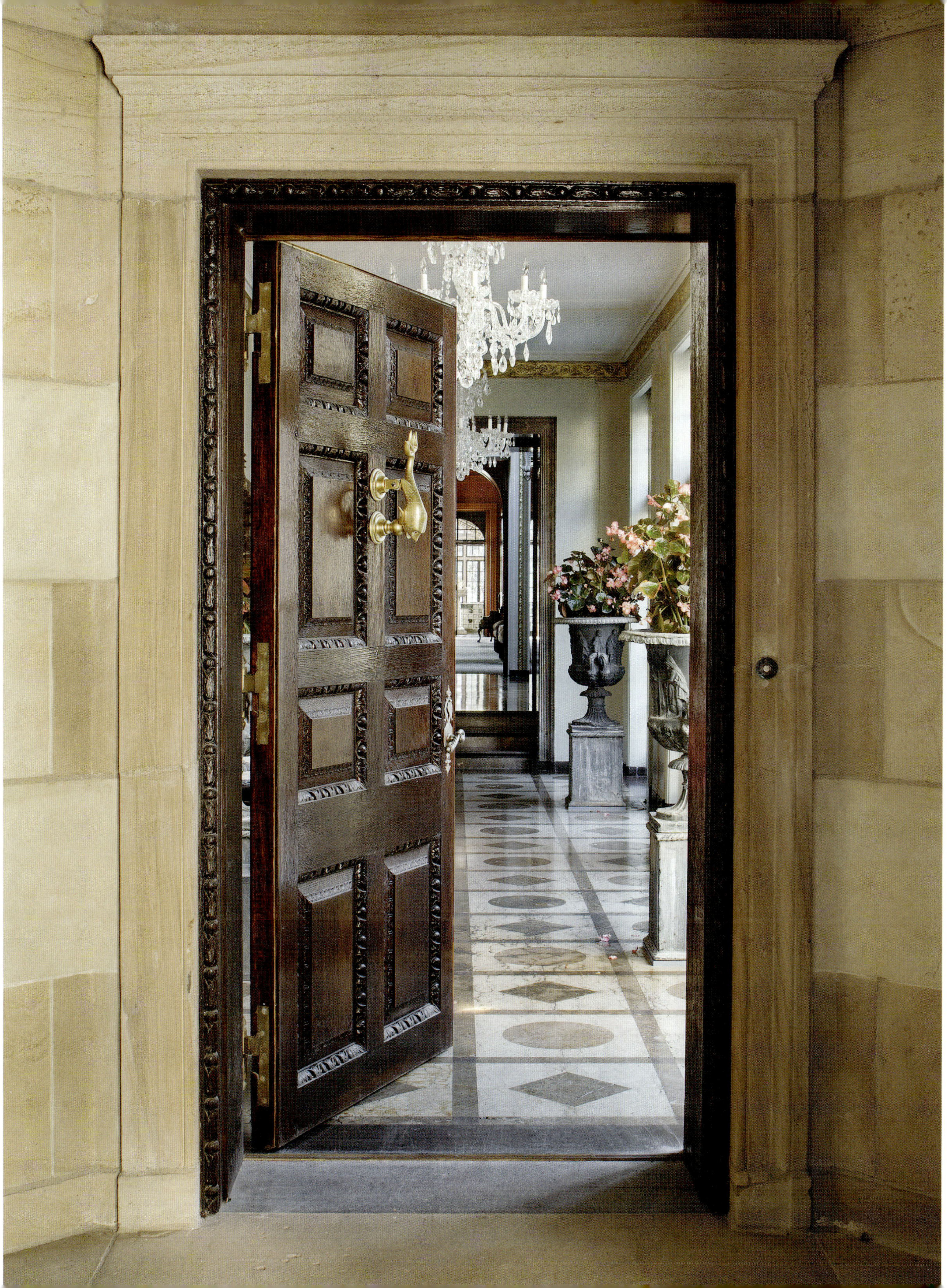

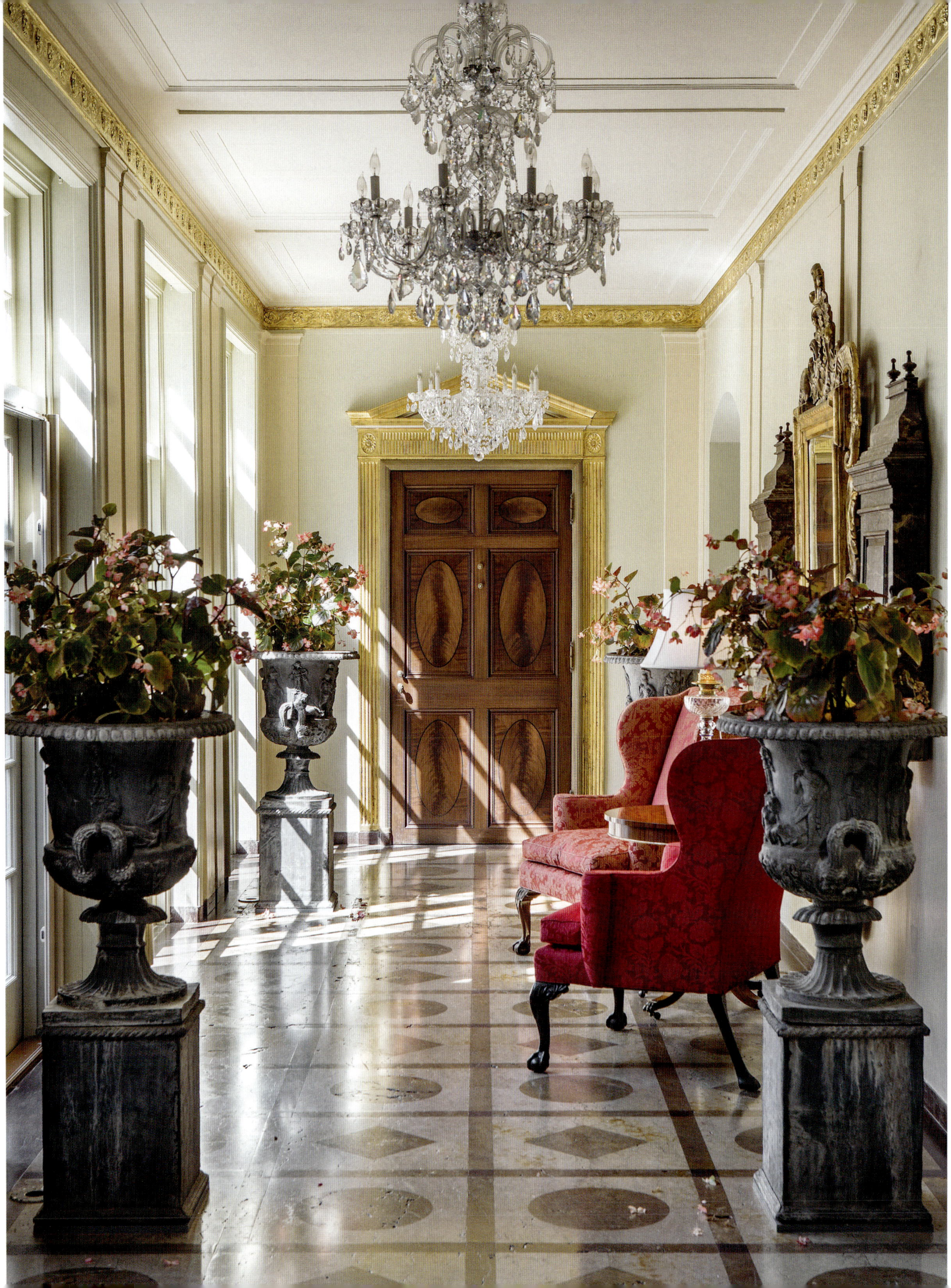

Right: The ladies' dressing room.

Opposite: Entrance gallery looking toward the front door with light streaming in from the walled garden.

Above: Decorative grille in the vestible between the entrance and the stair hall.

Opposite: Stair hall.

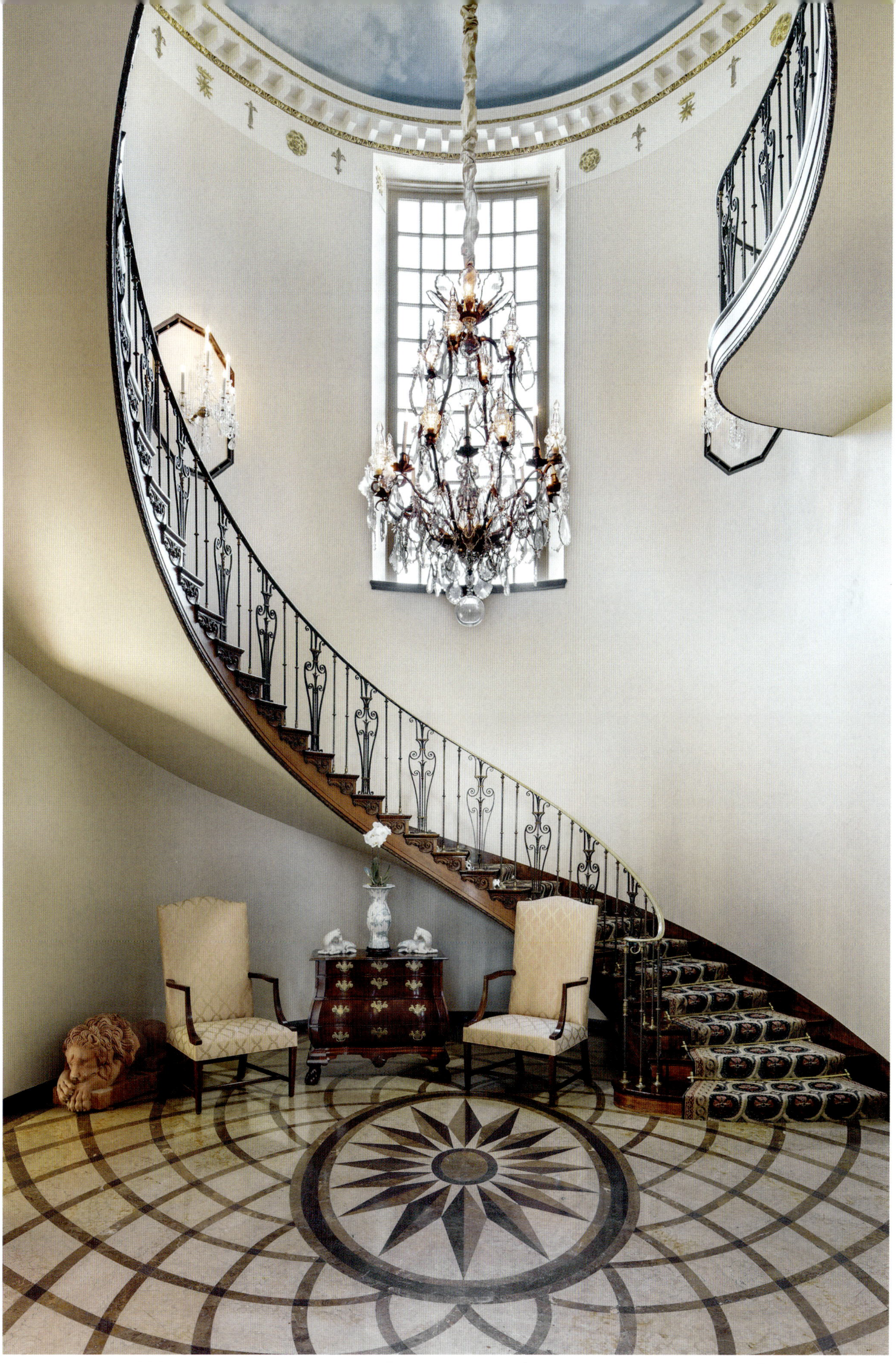

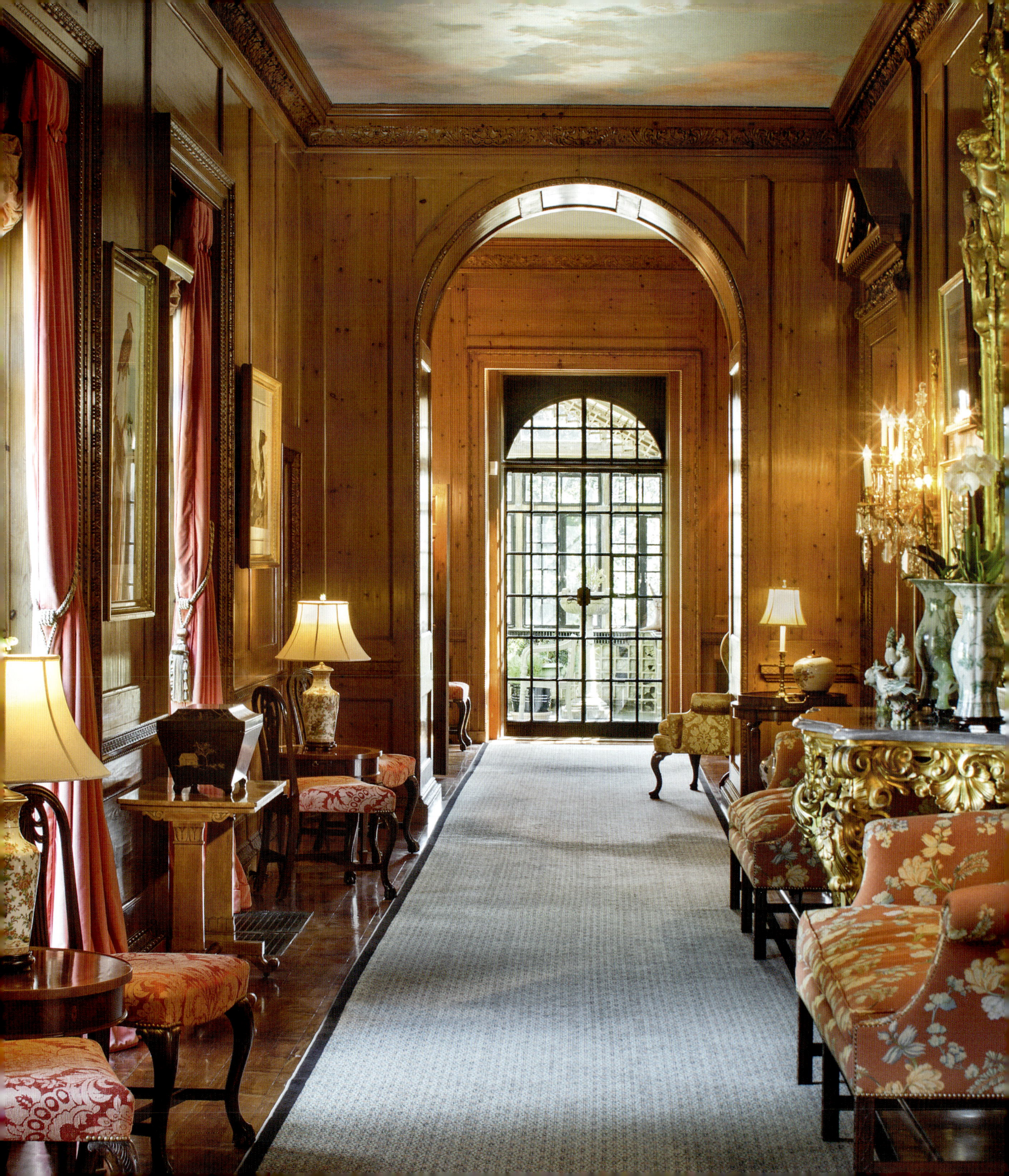

Right: Dining room.

Opposite: Formal gallery connecting the living and dining rooms to the south and the kitchen wing to the north.

JACKSON E. REYNOLDS HOUSE

33 BEEKMAN PLACE

NEW YORK

1925–26

In the 1920s, Beekman Place, a riverfront stretch running from 49th to 51st Street in Manhattan, began to change. Originally, Mount Pleasant, the Beekman family's East River mansion, occupied the area around 50th Street, but after the family sold the land in the 1860s, it was developed with brownstones. Cut off from the city and surrounded by mercantile and industrial concerns, including a coal yard, the once-elegant enclave descended into neglect. By the 1920s, when developers and fashionable society—including banker Van Santvoord Merle-Smith, actress Katherine Cornell, and CBS head William S. Paley—rediscovered the area's potential, Beekman Place was resuscitated, and the brownstones were converted to stylish townhouses and luxury apartment buildings.

Landscape designer Ellen Biddle Shipman transformed 19 Beekman Place into a Georgian style townhouse designed by Butler & Corse that served as her home and office. In 1925 Lindeberg was hired by Jackson E. Reynolds (1873–1958), head of the First National Bank, and his wife, Marion Taylor Reynolds (1879–1950), to design a restrained four-story Colonial Revival house at 33 Beekman Place. Reynolds, a graduate of Stanford University and Columbia Law School, was discovered by George F. Baker when Reynolds was the counsel for the Central Railroads of New Jersey. Baker, then president of the bank, asked Reynolds to join First National; he was promoted to president in 1922.

By 1925 the Reynoldses had already commissioned Lindeberg to design a Georgian Revival style country house in Lattingtown, Long Island. The design was based on a prize-winning entry for a suburban house and garage that several Lindeberg employees had submitted to the White Pine Architectural Competition. The house featured a central block with two wings and center door embellished by a broken Baroque pediment and charming wrought-iron spider-web screen.[1] In comparison, the brick facade of the townhouse was spare, with little ornament except stone window and door surrounds and iron leader heads wrought with foliage. While the building was four stories, Lindeberg tucked the top staff floor into the roofline and extended the cornice above the third level, making the house read as three stories and optimizing the proportions of the facade.

At twenty feet, the building was relatively narrow, but Lindeberg succeeded in making the elegant interiors feel gracious and light. The street facade was understated, but the east facade overlooking the East River was more open, with large bay windows that spanned the width of the house. From the first-floor dining room, a terrace stepped down to a sunken garden facing the river. The living room on the second floor was a double-height space. A lightwell above the oval stair hall brought sun into the center of the house, which, bounded by two party walls, would otherwise not have received natural light. Interior windows on the upper floors allowed light into the halls and service spaces.

Perhaps the most striking aspect of Lindeberg's design, however, was the polish and sophistication of the public rooms. With his graceful doorway arches, the elegant sweep of the stair, and sun streaming in, Lindeberg created a quiet, meditative moment at the center of the house. Both the dining room and particularly the paneled living room received the benefit of

Dining room.

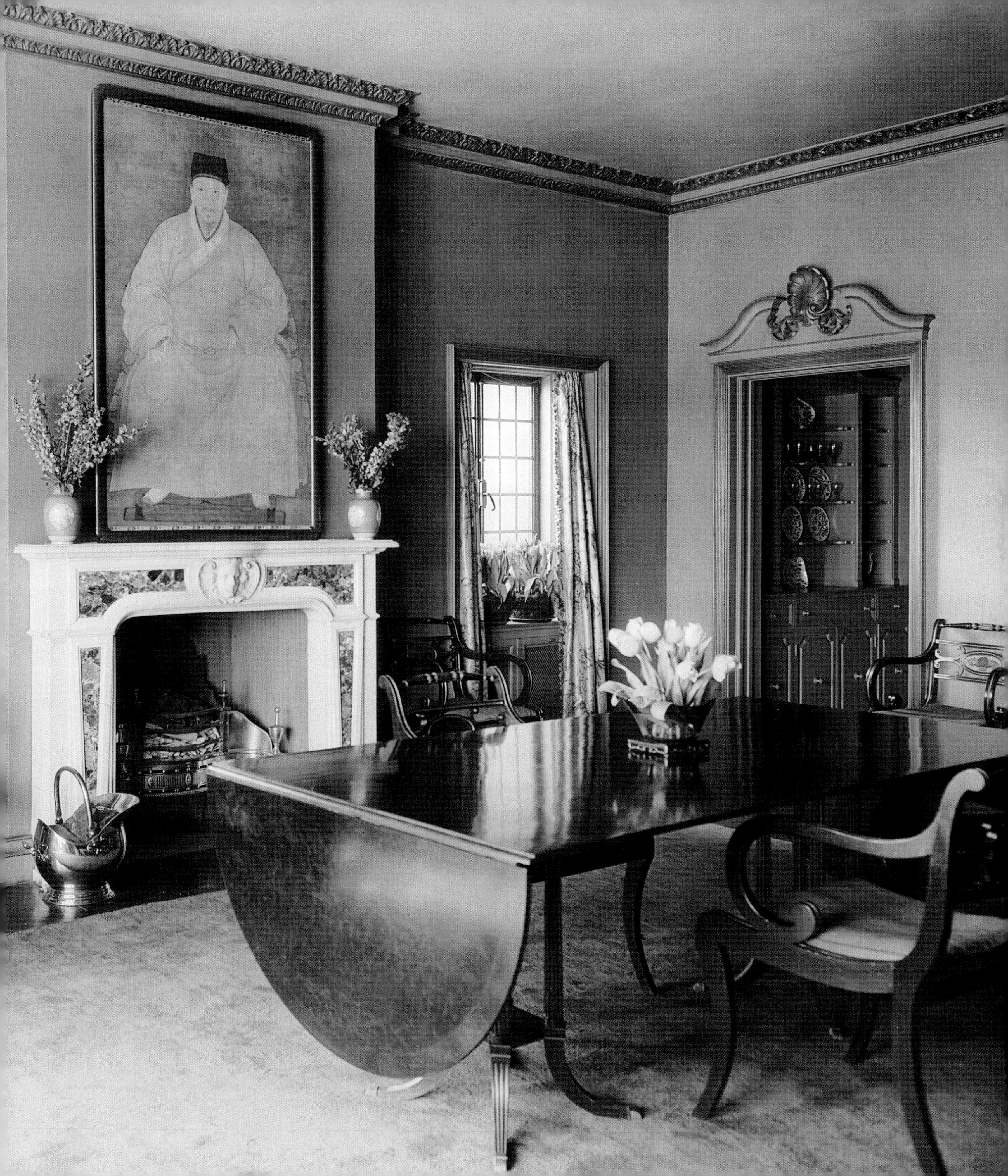

Entrance facade.

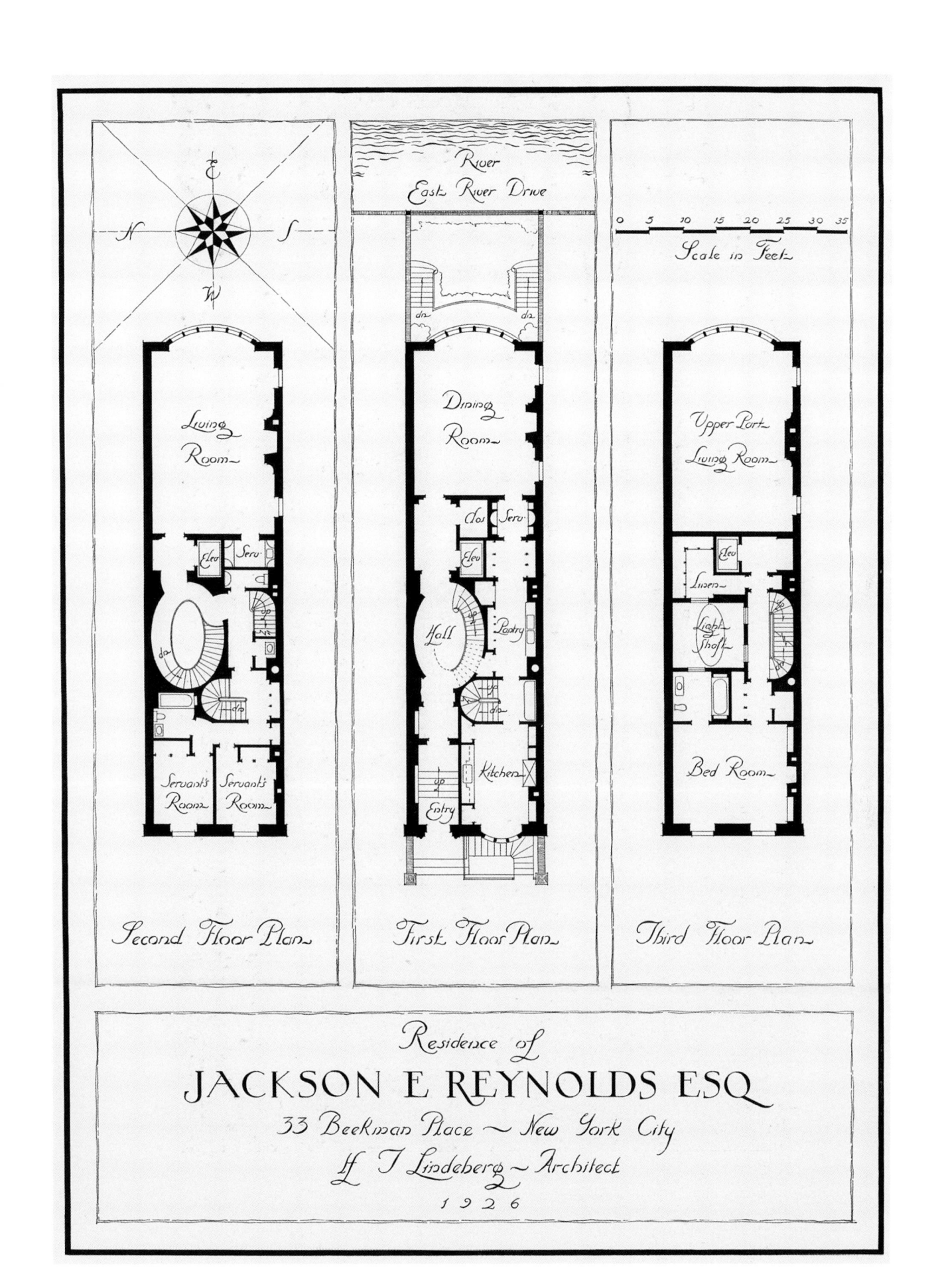

Residence of
JACKSON E REYNOLDS ESQ
33 Beekman Place ~ New York City

H T Lindeberg ~ Architect

1926

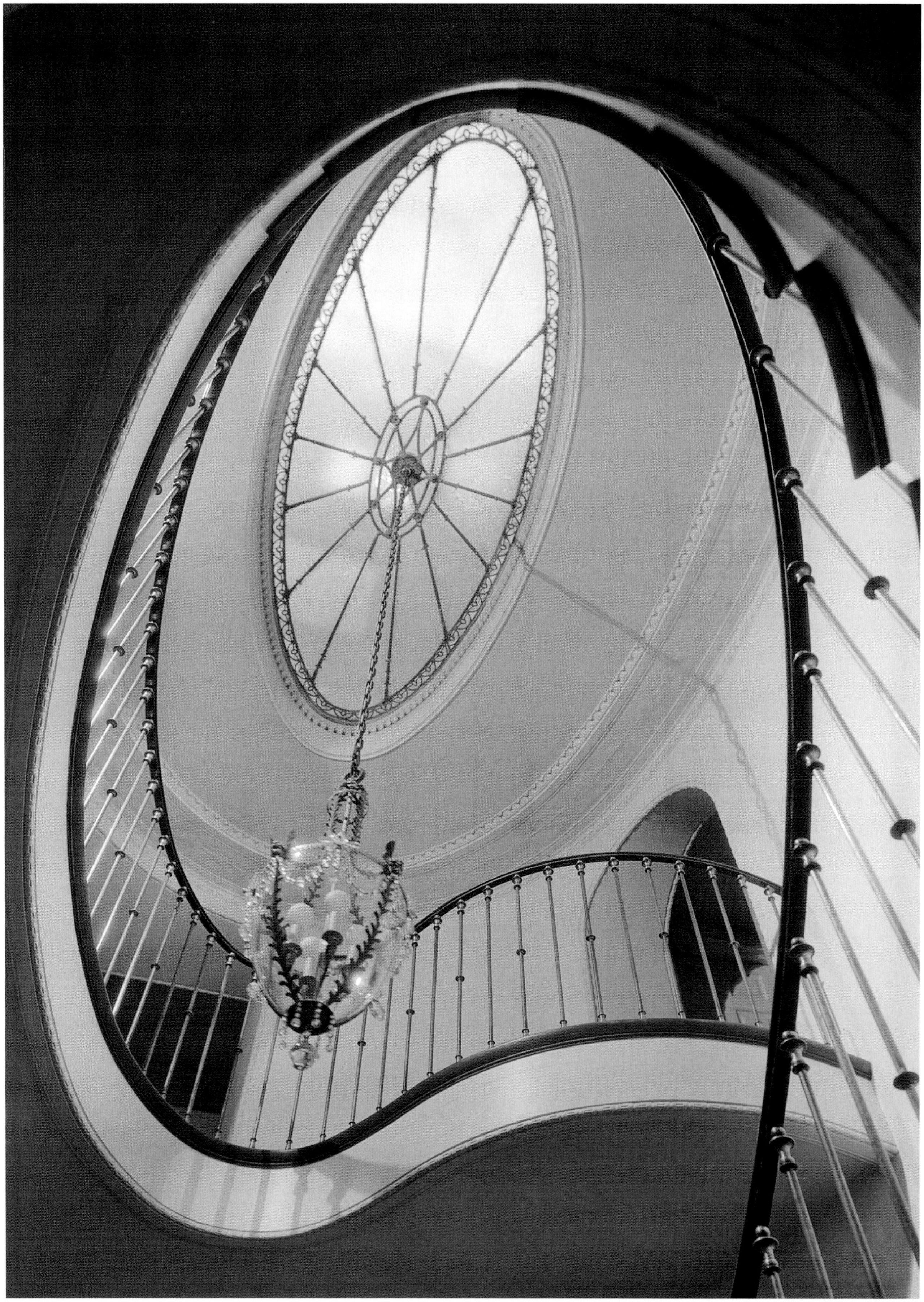

Above: Living room.

Opposite: Stair.

Lindeberg's hand with intricate and delicate woodwork, broken pediments over the doors and moldings perfectly scaled to the rooms. Despite its height, the living room felt warm and comfortable, almost intimate.

Lindeberg designed most of his city houses early in his career while in practice with Albro. The Reynolds house was the only major townhouse project that he carried out as a sole practitioner. In 1939, soon after his marriage to Eleanor Holm, the swimming star of his Aquacade show at the World's Fair, showman Billy Rose bought the house, which he sold in 1954. Currently, the building is the residence of the Ambassador of Kuwait to the United Nations. Now combined with the adjacent 35 Beekman Place, the former home of the aviator and writer Antoine de Saint-Exupéry, 33 Beekman Place has been significantly altered. Lindeberg's casements have been replaced by modern windows and a fifth story has been added.

LOWELL M. CHAPIN/ FRANCIS BEIDLER HOUSE

LAKE FOREST, ILLINOIS

1926–28

In 1926 Lowell M. Chapin (1885–1960) commissioned Lindeberg to design a weekend house on a wooded six-acre site in Lake Forest. Chapin, president of the Zouri Metals Company and treasurer of the Indiana and Michigan Electric Company, was the son of mining and manufacturing magnate Charles A. Chapin. After graduating from Yale in 1909, he married Elizabeth Chalifoux (b. 1890) of Lowell, Massachusetts. The couple lived with their two children in an elegant townhouse on Astor Street in the affluent Gold Coast neighborhood of Chicago.

Lindeberg's summer cottage was informal in comparison. Designed in the French Norman vein, the whitewashed-brick house had subtle medieval references, accentuated by a steeply pitched roof tiled in a deep reddish brown and a turreted stair hall. Lindeberg emphasized the building materials to allow their fullest expression, combining brick laid with slightly raked joints with dressed and natural sandstone. The bold textured mass of the house with its multi-dimensional roofline and undulating shingles stood picturesquely against the greenery of the wooded surroundings.

The L-shaped plan was very different—and smaller—than those of Lindeberg's other houses. He set the entrance in a two-story pavilion to the east, which opened into an intimate hall paneled in knobby Canadian spruce. This led to a great room with an oak-beamed ceiling housed in the main block. The kitchen and several servants' rooms extended to the south and connected back to the garage and chauffeur's quarters. A circular stair to four bedrooms on the second floor was housed in the turret that linked the two legs of the plan. Off the living room was a rustic porch in a hipped-roof pavilion.

Throughout, the details were delightful and exacting. Intricate hardware in the shape of the four suits of playing cards adorned the doors, and iron grilles wrought with garden scenes were curved to fit the walls of the stairwell. The gutters of the owner's portion of the house were embellished with grapes and vines while those on the service wing were plain.

While summering in Lake Forest, Elizabeth Loose Beidler (1868–1948), the recent widow of lumber executive Francis Beidler, and her son Francis Beidler II (1897–1984)—then in his late twenties—noticed the Chapin house under construction. When the Chapins' marriage crumbled in the late 1920s—and ultimately ended in divorce in 1931—mother and son Beidler jumped at the chance to buy the modest yet fanciful cottage, purchasing it in 1929, one year after it was completed. Shortly after, they asked Lindeberg to design an addition that more or less doubled its size with a new entrance hall, living room, and library and two additional bedrooms upstairs. The addition was never realized, but a ravine garden and dining porch, carried out by the Italian-born landscape architect Ferruccio Vitale, were added in 1930.[1]

While Francis Beidler II later built a new house nearby for his family, his mother remained in the cottage until her death in 1948. Beidler held onto the property and rented it out until his son and daughter-in-law took possession in the 1970s. The house has been in the same family more or less from the beginning,

Entrance.

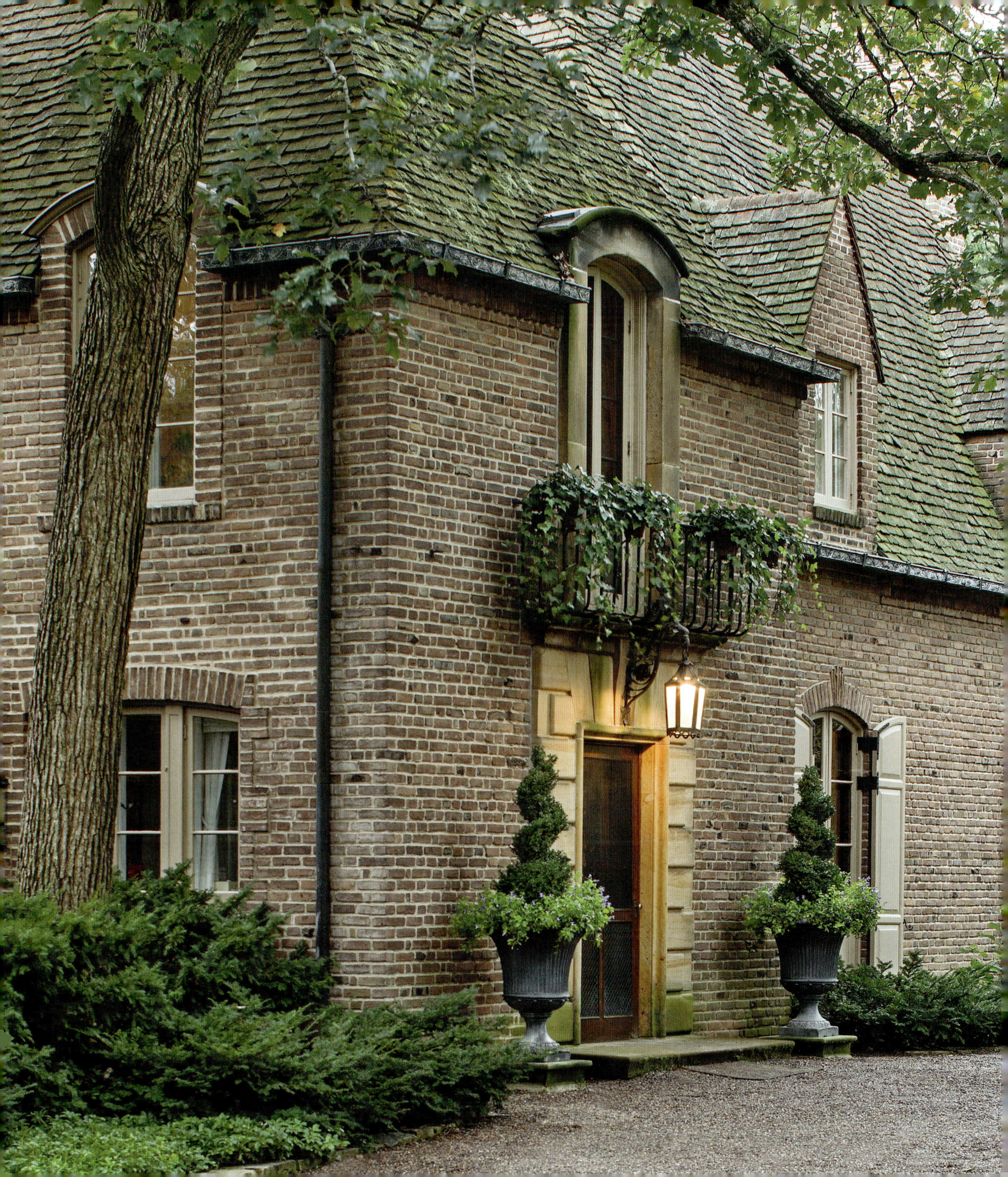

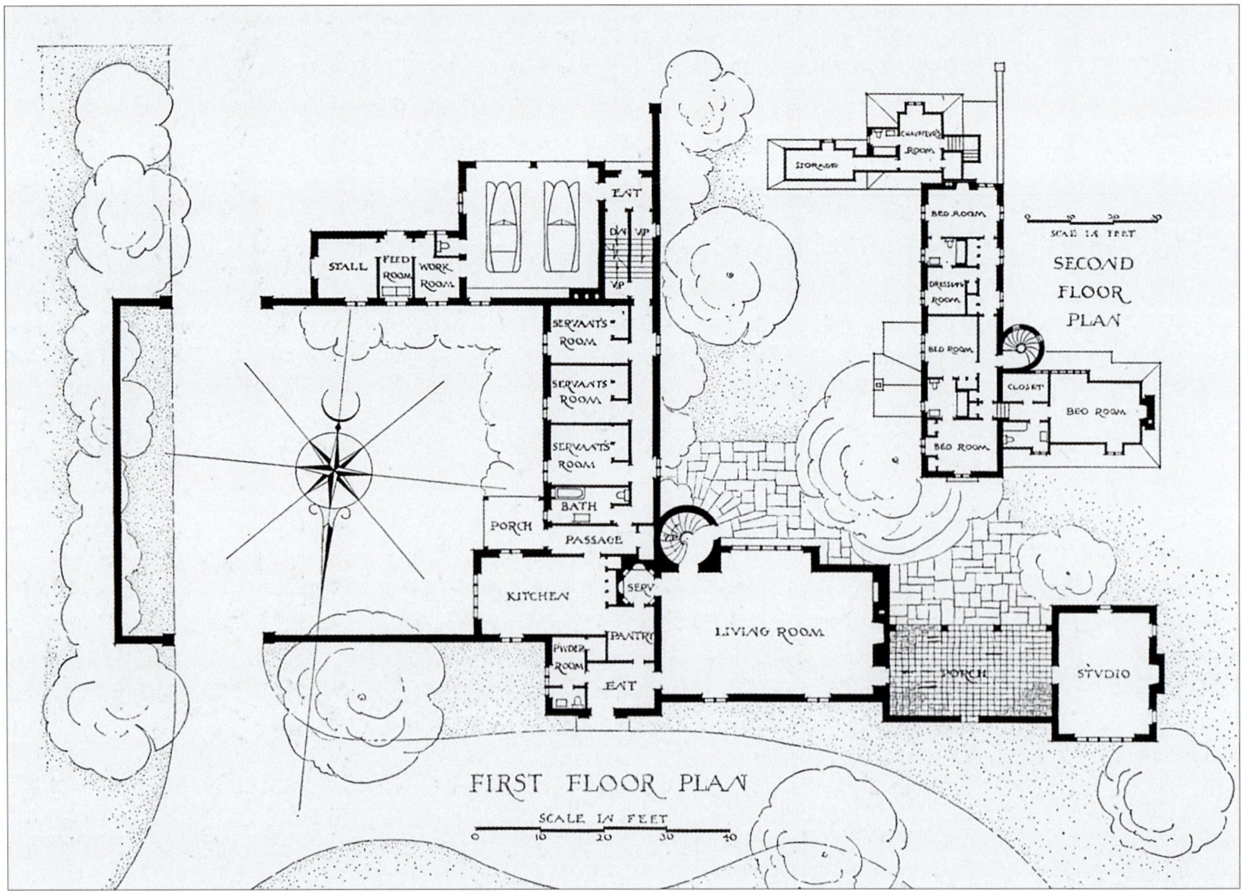
STALL
FEED ROOM
WORK ROOM
EXT
DN
UP
SERVANTS' ROOM
SERVANTS' ROOM
SERVANTS' ROOM
BATH
PORCH
PASSAGE
KITCHEN
SERV
PANTRY
POWDER ROOM
EXT
LIVING ROOM
PORCH
STUDIO
FIRST FLOOR PLAN
SCALE IN FEET
0
10
20
30
40
STORAGE
ROOM
BED ROOM
DRESSING ROOM
BED ROOM
CLOSET
BED ROOM
BED ROOM
SECOND FLOOR PLAN

Above: The turret hinging the south and east facades.

Right: A wooden door built into the curve of the turret.

Opposite above: View from the northwest.

and it has been lovingly and carefully maintained. Furnishings and tapestries, originally acquired by Francis Beidler II and his mother during the Depression, continue to set off Lindeberg's interiors. In 2012 landscape architect Peter Schaudt of Hoerr Schaudt in conjunction with architect Thomas Rajkovich respectfully designed a pool to be set within the original Vitale garden, using Lindeberg's original walls as a guideline.

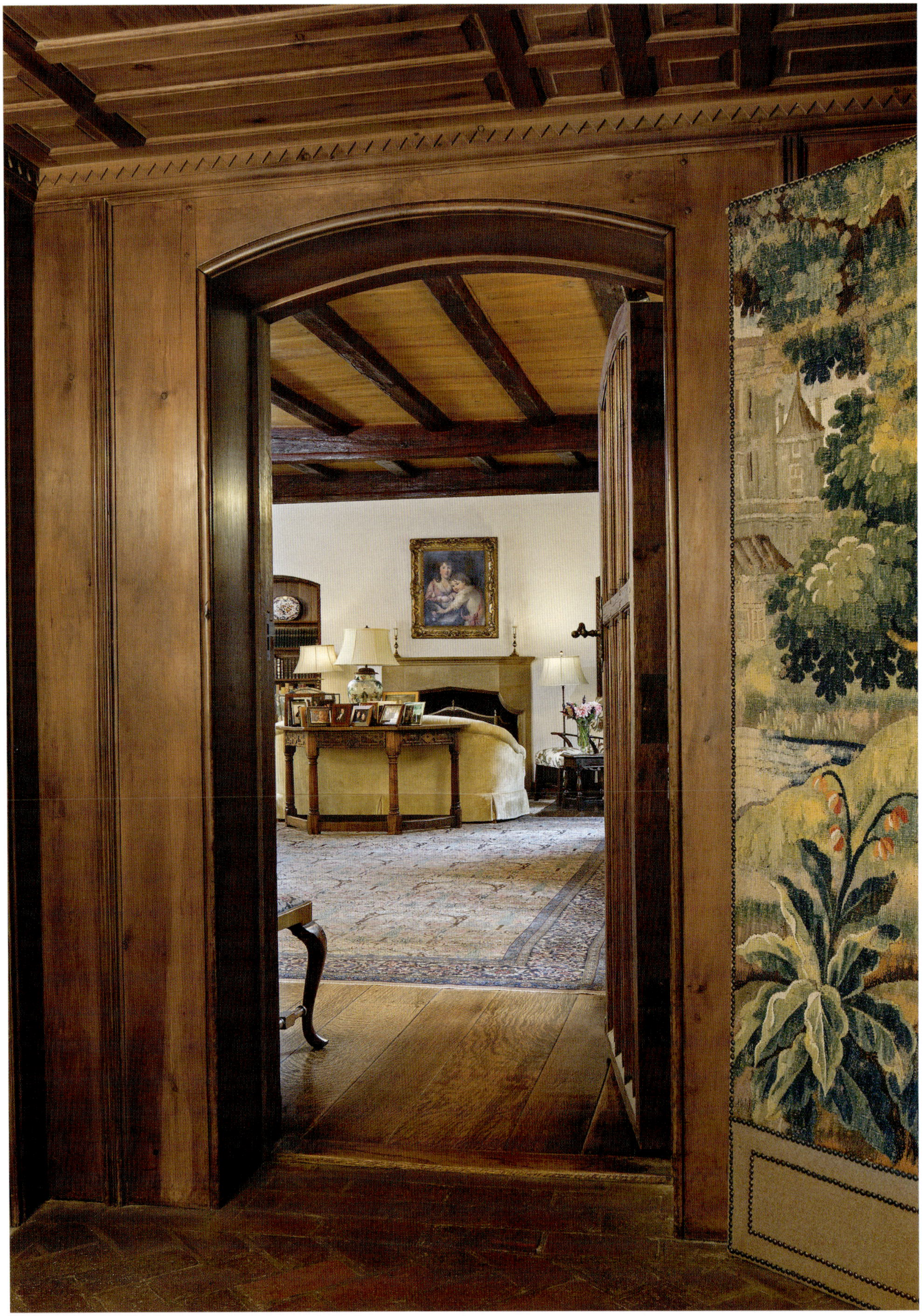

Above left: Grille set into the wall behind the stair.

Above right: The stair curving up inside the turret.

Opposite: View from the paneled entrance hall into the great room.

WEST GATE LODGE
HARRIE T. LINDEBERG HOUSE

LOCUST VALLEY, NEW YORK

1926–27

After Lindeberg's marriage to Lucia Hull in 1914, the couple began spending time in Locust Valley at Wisteria Lodge. By 1920 Lindeberg and his wife were well connected to the social life of the North Shore as members of the Piping Rock Club, the Nassau Country Club, and the Seawanhaka Corinthian Yacht Club. Although the couple divorced in 1925, Lindeberg continued designing and building his own house in Locust Valley, set on eight acres adjacent to the grounds of the Piping Rock Club.

With its crisply articulated facade, modicum of ornament, and steep roof, West Gate Lodge resembled Gray Craig, albeit on a smaller scale. Similarly composed, it consisted of a solid center block flanked by pavilions that extended out to enclose a terrace. Lindeberg wrapped the entrance front in variegated ledgestone, and he used multi-shaded Dutch brick for the sides and rear of the house. He chose the brick for its remarkable tones of pink, violet, red, and yellow that were luminous, even on a rainy day. As critic John Taylor Boyd Jr. remarked, it was a "simple building, almost classic in its center mass and low balanced wings, it was unusual in rich luminous color of orange—tawny ledgestone walls and soft brownish red roofs displayed against billowing green masses of foliage."[1] Peacock statues stationed at the entrance, gutters etched with grapevines and leader heads marked with Lindeberg's initials and "1926" were light-hearted inconspicuous details that relieved the severity of the planar facades. The house had "an effect [that was] at once bold and subtle, but so simple that one could not see so much as one square inch of superfluous ornament, or material, or detail on the whole of it."[2] A long flat expanse of lawn lined with apple and other fruit trees and enclosed by walls draped in climbing roses accentuated the motor court leading to the entrance.[3]

Lindeberg lavished attention on the front entrance, applying a peacock-form ironwork panel over the fanlight and stylized grille work to the heavy wooden door. The entrance led directly into the stair hall, which in turn funneled into a wide gallery with floors of rare quilted fir extending along the west wall down into the expansive story-and-a-half living room set two steps below. As Boyd noted:

Mr. Lindeberg's home is a really remarkable example of interior decoration, distinguished by its restraint of design and its rich harmony of color. Though there is not a period room in it, its repose and maturity make it seem like something out of another country, yet still America. The interior had something of that mellow refinement and strong personality which are making the buildings of the Swedish architects famous throughout the world today.[4]

The bright, airy living room, entered through an opening framed by a scrolling Baroque pediment, was lit by tall leaded-glass casements and a semi-circular bay to the east and decorated with antiques and furnishings of Lindeberg's design. The library, dining room, and kitchen overlooked the east terrace—a favorite haunt of the owner—while the north wing and nearby garage contained staff quarters. Lindeberg furnished the octagonal dining room, painted a striking shade of green with gold trim, with pieces he had designed, including an armoire and a sideboard with

Entrance.

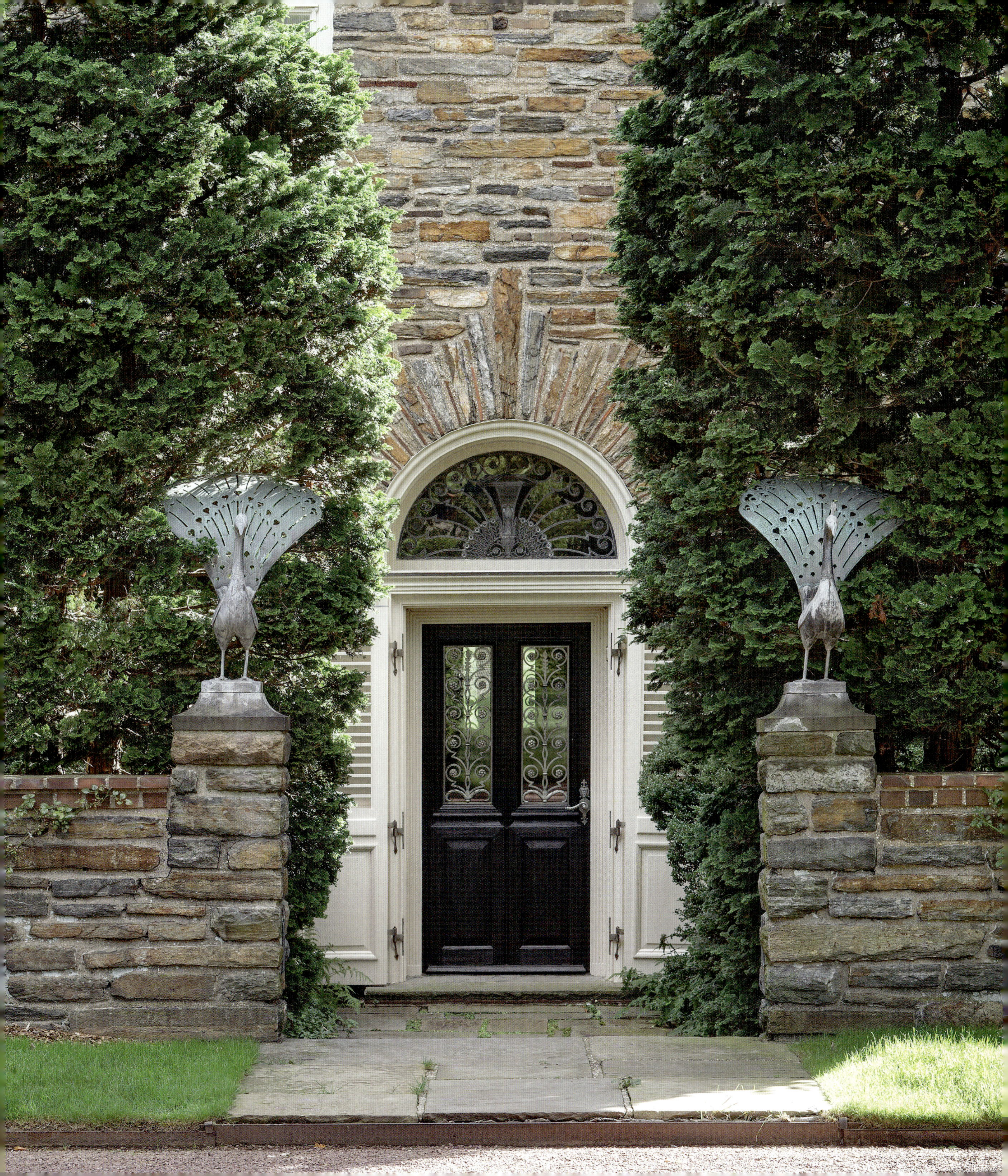

THIRD FLOOR PLAN

SECOND FLOOR PLAN

FIRST FLOOR PLAN

Residence of
MRS · H · T · LINDEBERG
Locust Valley — Long Island
1927

Entrance facade.

slender and refined profiles. His shallow ceiling moldings, stylized crown moldings, and sleek mirrored chimney breast added to the jewel-like ambiance. The adjacent library was similarly sophisticated with one wall given over to a series of bookshelves capped with arched niches, painted green, for statuary, including a model of the peacock finial that he used at Gray Craig. Upstairs, the second floor contained four bedrooms, some of which were furnished with Colonial-style bed niches. The attic accommodated two additional suites with dormer windows and fireplaces.

Lindeberg tucked his studio and a small drafting room behind the south wall of the entrance court. In his later years, he increasingly used the studio, which featured whimsical crown moldings fashioned after thick nautical rope tied in the corners with sailor's knots, as an alternative to his city office. Behind the house, the property fell away with ravines on either side and a steep lawn extended down to the east. From the rear terrace, steps led down to a small circular garden with stone retaining walls. Originally, a pair of life-sized penguins by Gertrude K. Lathrop adorned the walls.

Lindeberg transferred ownership of the house to his third wife, Angeline Krech Lindeberg, in the late 1930s. Today, the estate is in pristine condition. It is occupied by its fourth owner, who has restored the integrity of Lindeberg's design, some of which had been obscured over time.

Left: Living room, 1935.

Below: Library, 1935.

Opposite: Lindeberg's studio.

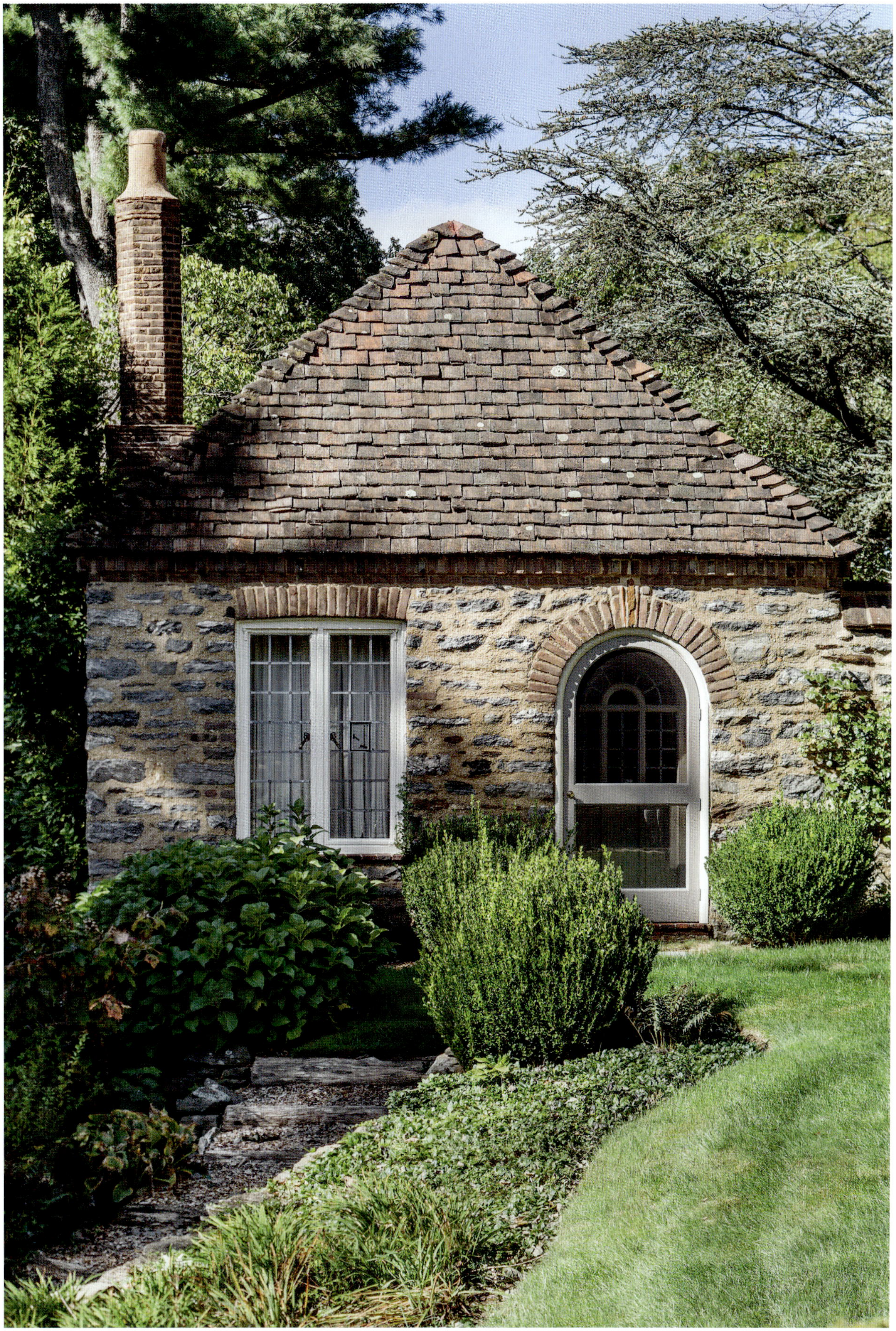

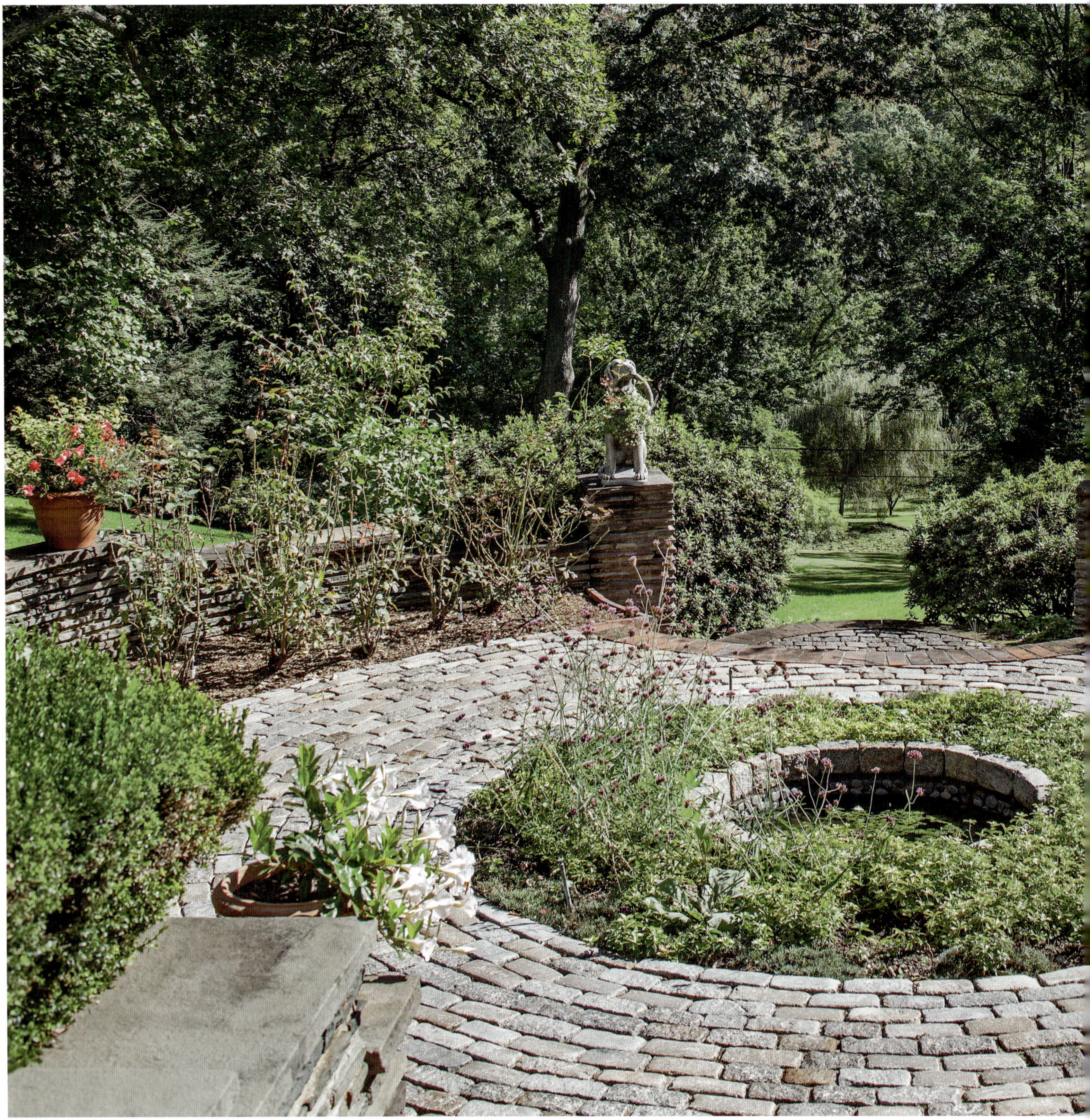

Above: One of a pair of peacocks marking the entrance.

Opposite: Circular garden off the east terrace.

ONWENTSIA CLUB

LAKE FOREST, ILLINOIS

1927–28

The backbone of Lake Forest's social scene, the Onwentsia Club was officially organized in 1895 by a group of Chicago business leaders—men who had begun summering in the area in the late 1800s—headed by Hobart Chatfield-Taylor. At first, the club, known as the Lake Forest Golf Club, was located on the grounds of Senator Charles B. Farwell's estate; his daughter Rose, eventually Chatfield-Taylor's wife, loved to play golf. In 1894 the course moved to a portion of Leander McCormick's farm, and the informal group used a deserted sheep shed as a locker room. In 1895, however, these grounds were deemed inadequate, and Chatfield-Taylor, along with several other prominent Lake Forest residents, founded Onwentsia—an Iroquois word for a meeting place in the country—and moved to a 175-acre farm owned by architect Henry Ives Cobb. Cobb's rambling shingle style cottage served as the clubhouse, and Charles Blair MacDonald, designer of the course at the Chicago Golf Club—the first course in the Midwest—laid out a new course.

Onwentsia occupied the Cobb house for more than twenty-five years, but by 1925, it was clear that the building needed to be substantially upgraded or rebuilt. The club established a committee, headed by pipe manufacturer William Clow, which was charged with finding an architect. To avoid the complications of choosing among the number of reputable Chicago architects within Onwentsia ranks—Clow's own house was designed by David Adler—the committee decided to go with an out-of-town designer. According to Lake Forest architect Alfred Granger, "Mr. Lindeberg came, saw and (by his charm of manner) conquered and was immediately commissioned to design the new club house."[1] Not only had he designed two houses for former Onwentsia presidents—Clyde M. Carr and Albert A. Sprague II—but also he was in the midst of working on a house for Lowell M. Chapin nearby. He had also just completed the Asheville Country Club in the resort town of Asheville, North Carolina.[2]

During the planning, many of the members felt that Lindeberg's new clubhouse was too large, but club president Cyrus Adams and Clow supported the architect's vision. Following the demolition of the Cobb house in 1927, Lindeberg would stay with Adams, and the two would talk about the construction progress before Lindeberg would set out on a narrow path that led through the woods to the building site.[3] The new Onwentsia clubhouse was officially opened on November 3, 1928 with a celebratory dinner of six hundred members and guests.

The brick facades—like many of Lindeberg's houses—were whitewashed, but here they were accented with red brick trim. A change from the shingle style Cobb house, the design was more sophisticated, with both French and English overtones and the characteristic Lindeberg roof, here of quarry tile. In plan, the clubhouse resembled the Piping Rock Club in Locust Valley. Designed in 1911 by Guy Lowell, Piping Rock's Colonial Revival clubhouse featured an interior courtyard circumscribed by a hall connecting to all of the public rooms and a one-story hyphen housing the entrance that linked two-story wings on either side. In Lake Forest, Lindeberg followed a similar formula, incorporating a center court with a hallway surrounding it, paved with bricks laid in a herringbone pattern, as

Governors' Room.

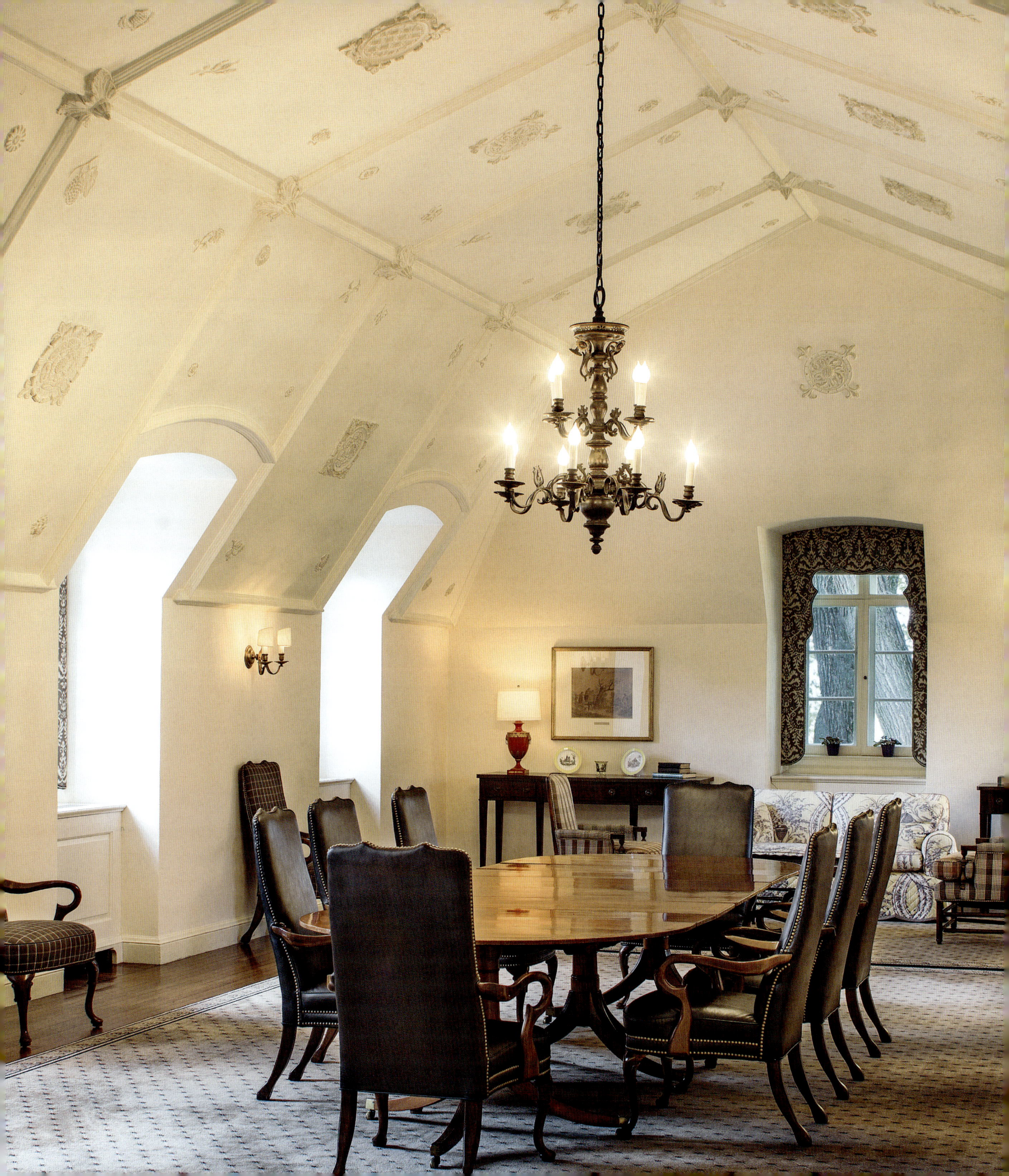

well as a one-story screen bridging his two wings, which he decorated with urns along the ridge. In both instances, the fireplace in the lounge backed up to the courtyard and a chimney rose up through the center of composition in line with the front door. Lindeberg extended the kitchen wing, grill room, and men's lockers off to the southwest, overlooking the swimming pool.

The centerpiece of the club was the two-story lounge with a soaring roof that faced the golf course. Almost sixty feet long, the room had French doors running the length of each side, a minstrel's gallery, hand-plastered walls, and a high knotty-pine sheathed ceiling. Using little extraneous ornament, Lindeberg focused on the light, air, and views, both to the outside and within. Across the width of the building, he created an enfilade between a more intimate library paneled in knotty pine, the lounge, and the formal dining room. Upstairs, set into the slope of the roof, Lindeberg enhanced the Governors' Room with an arched ceiling detailed with tracery and the grill room with knotty pine

Above: West facade fronting onto the golf course.

Opposite: Entrance facade.

paneling and moldings carved with snails, griffins, dragons, and swine. After the club's completion, several members commissioned Lindeberg to design their houses, including amateur golfers Ralph A. Gardner and Dexter Cummings as well as banker Earle Reynolds.

The club's first full year in operation coincided with the stock market crash. Subsequently, the Depression prevented the club from paying the interest on its mortgage bonds for the new building and maintaining the high level of service. In 1940 the club was refinanced and by 1960, it owned all of the land it had formerly leased. While in the beginning, some members missed the Cobb house, Lindeberg's large modern clubhouse has stood the test of time and is both well maintained and cherished by its membership today.

Key To Second Floor Plan

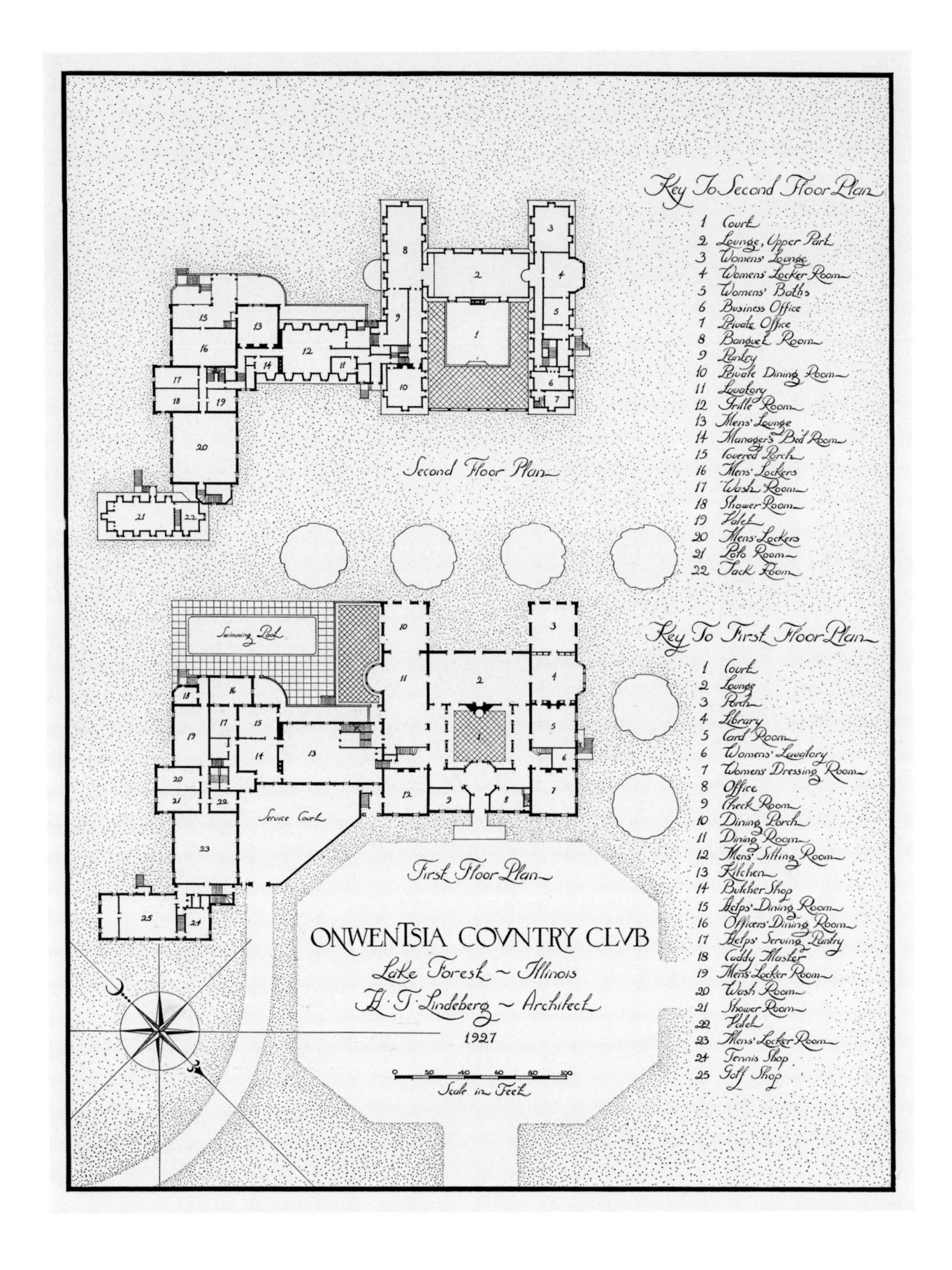

1. Court
2. Lounge, Upper Part
3. Womens' Lounge
4. Womens' Locker Room
5. Womens' Baths
6. Business Office
7. Private Office
8. Banquet Room
9. Pantry
10. Private Dining Room
11. Lavatory
12. Grille Room
13. Mens' Lounge
14. Manager's Bed Room
15. Covered Porch
16. Mens' Lockers
17. Wash Room
18. Shower Room
19. Valet
20. Mens' Lockers
21. Polo Room
22. Tack Room

Second Floor Plan

Key To First Floor Plan

1. Court
2. Lounge
3. Porch
4. Library
5. Card Room
6. Womens' Lavatory
7. Womens' Dressing Room
8. Office
9. Check Room
10. Dining Porch
11. Dining Room
12. Mens' Sitting Room
13. Kitchen
14. Butler Shop
15. Helps' Dining Room
16. Officers' Dining Room
17. Helps' Serving Pantry
18. Caddy Master
19. Mens' Locker Room
20. Wash Room
21. Shower Room
22. Valet
23. Mens' Locker Room
24. Tennis Shop
25. Golf Shop

First Floor Plan

ONWENTSIA COUNTRY CLUB
Lake Forest ~ Illinois
H. T. Lindeberg ~ Architect
1927

Scale in Feet

Above: Library

Right: Double-height lounge.

THE CHURCH HOUSES

MILL NECK, NEW YORK

1930

In 1930 Lindeberg designed a pair of houses for two brothers who married sisters. Charles Thomas Church (1874–1953) and Frederic Edwin Church (1877–1975) were heirs to the Arm & Hammer Baking Soda fortune, a company founded by their grandfather Austin Church and great-uncle John Dwight in 1846. Church & Dwight Co., the umbrella company to Arm & Hammer, is still in business today.[1] After their father, E. Dwight Church, took over as chairman in 1941, Charles T. Church became president. Meanwhile, his brother pursued the arts, studying at Columbia University's School of Architecture, the Académie Julian in Paris, and the Art Students League in New York. To avoid any confusion with the famous Hudson River painter of the same name but of no relation, he signed his work as F. Edwin Church. In 1901 Frederic married Alice Slocum Nichols (1879–1973), a daughter of James Benton Nichols, originally from Virginia, and Elizabeth Slocum Nichols, a descendant of a wealthy Michigan family. Two years later, Charles married Charlotte Sophia Nichols (1881–1961), Alice's younger sister.

Both Church couples lived in New Rochelle, New York, after their respective marriages. In 1927 C. T. Church purchased a tract of undeveloped land at Beaver Brook in Mill Neck from banker Anton Hodenpyl with the intention of building two houses on the 21-acre property. Lindeberg positioned the houses within sight of one another but on separate ridges with a shallow gulley running in between; the houses shared a driveway and swimming pool. Lindeberg used a textured red brick for both, but he introduced enough variation to differentiate the houses as "sisters," rather than "twins." While both had stripped, almost austere, facades and the characteristically brooding roof, the C. T. Church house had a taut character with a center door set within a one-story portico, a large bay window denoting the stair, and a hipped roof. Wings containing a story-and-a-half living room and the kitchen and staff quarters framed the center block of the house to the east and west. The F. E. Church house, on the other hand, featured a flattened turret containing the stair at center with an entrance pavilion on one side and a heavy chimney on the other. In both cases, Lindeberg kept the decoration to a minimum, incorporating ironwork, brickwork, and leader heads effectively into the facades.

The C. T. Churches were keen hunters, traveling to remote locations from Africa to Alaska to indulge in what was one of their favorite pastimes.[2] In addition to Lindeberg's carefully designed light fixtures, some of which were in the shape of flowers, the interiors of the house abounded with hunting trophies, particularly in the living room. This expansive 20-by-30-foot space had a soaring wood ceiling, African hardwood floors, and a great bay window overlooking the rear of the property. The Churches did not have children and, as a result, their house had only three master bedrooms with much of the house given over to service quarters. As in other late houses, moldings profiles, cabinets and wrought-iron stair railings were sleek and stylized. In plan, the house resembled that of Lindeberg's own home completed several years earlier.

For the F. E. Churches, Lindeberg designed a gabled entrance porch that opened into a spacious tiled stair hall that ran through the depth of the house out to the terrace in the rear. The simplicity of the

Studio in the F. E. Church house.

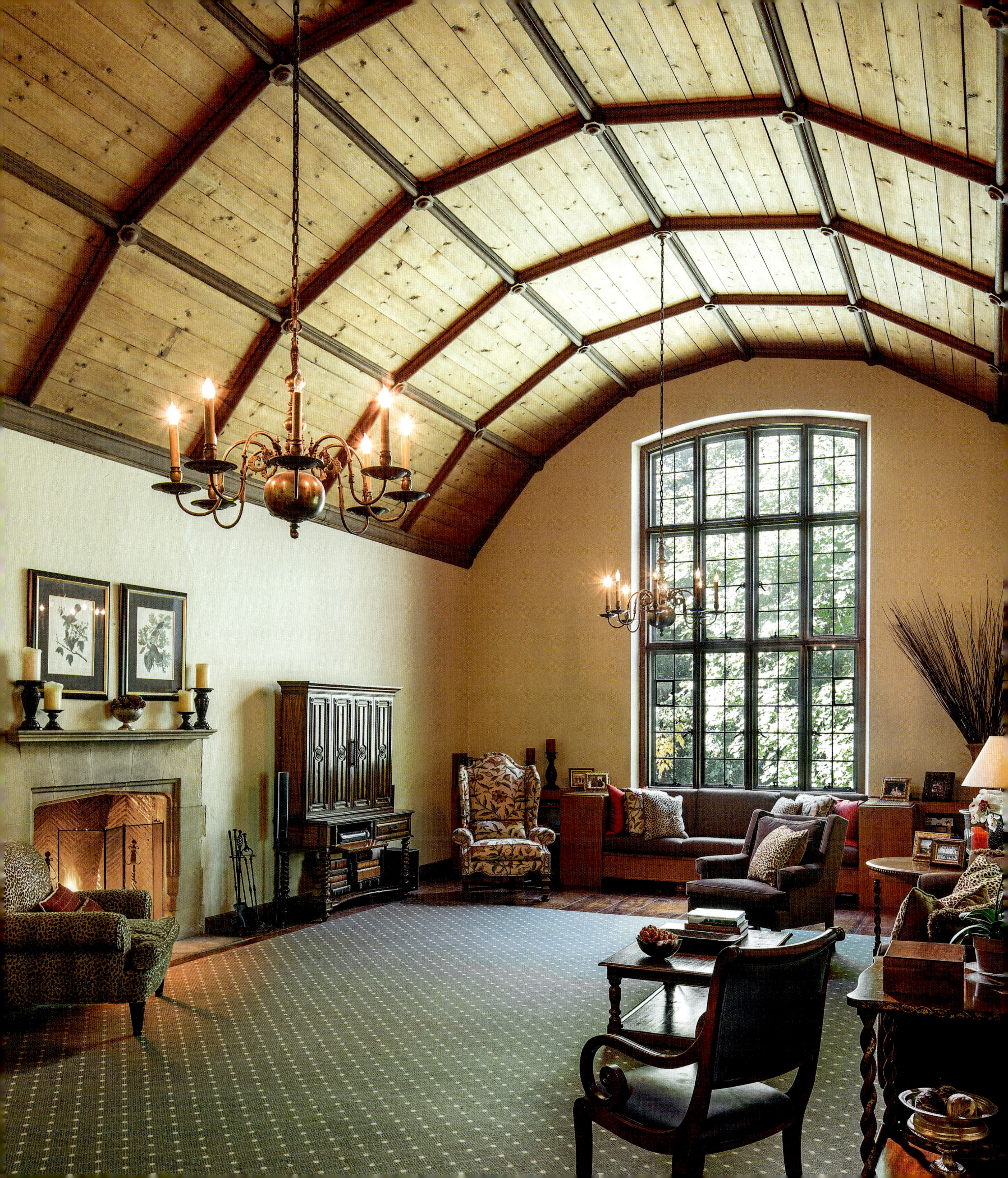

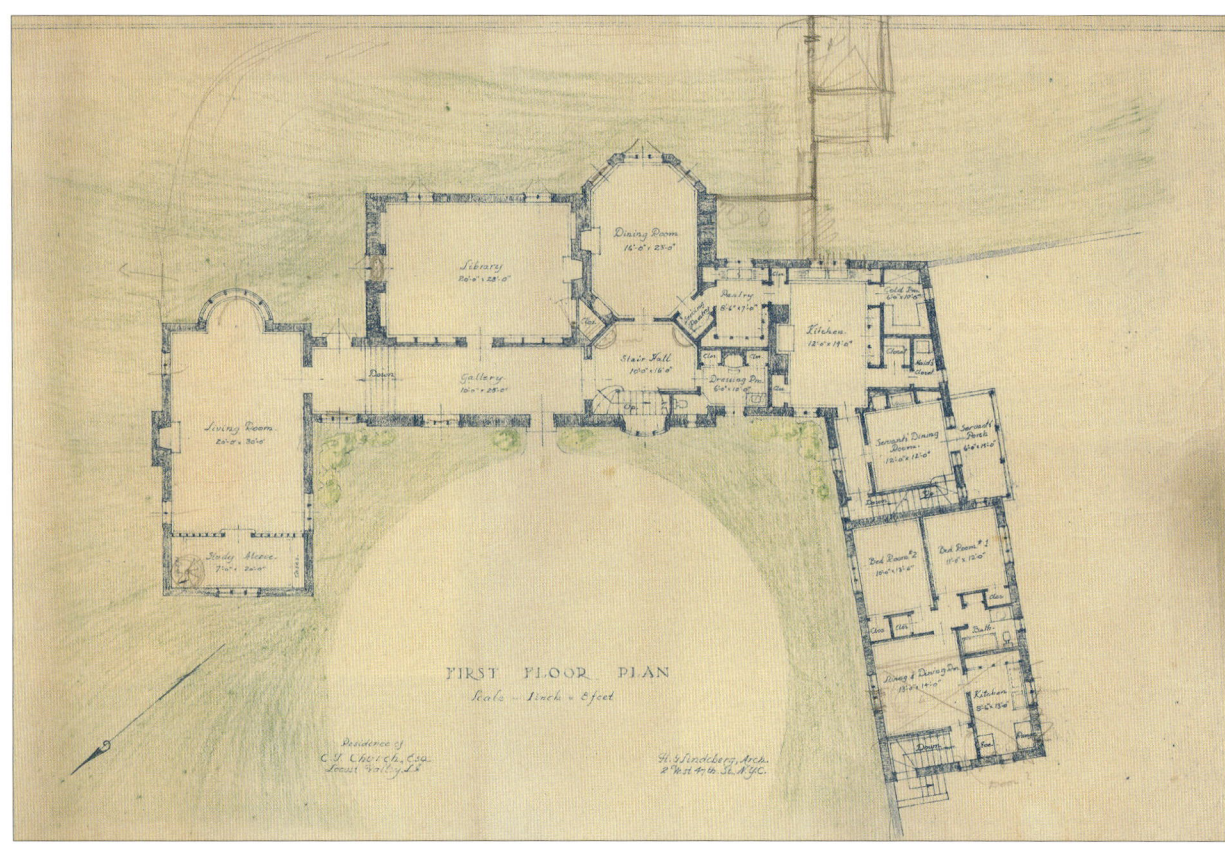

Above: Entrance facade and plan of the C. T. Church house.

Opposite: Entrance facade and plan of the F. E. Church house.

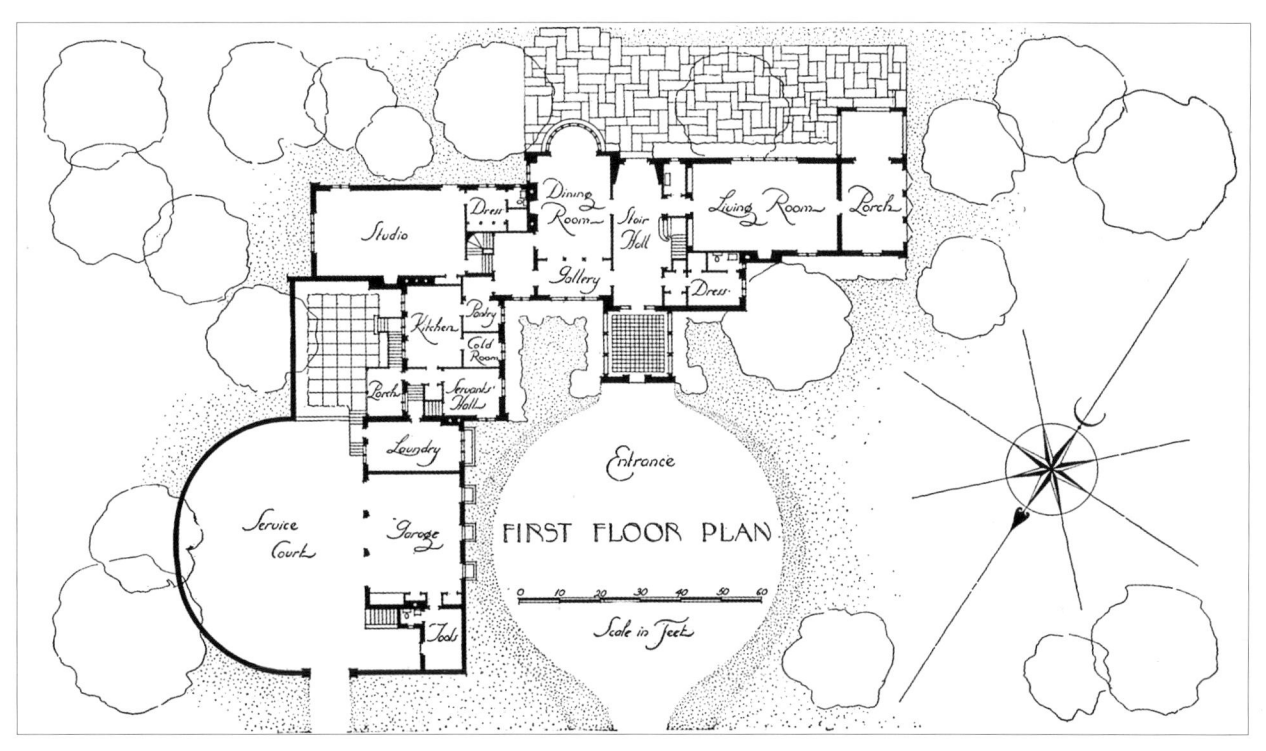

entrance facade concealed a more complicated and sophisticated plan within. A stair wound up from the hall into a turreted space above the dressing room lit by a large window with colored panes while the step-down living room—lit from both the southeast and the northwest—extended behind it. A shallow barrel-vaulted gallery led past the dining room back to an expansive barrel-vaulted studio screened on the entrance facade by the kitchen and service wing. Since the F. E. Churches had four children, their house was slightly larger than its neighbor. Such Lindeberg flourishes as the stepped brick entrance arch with a slender wrought-iron dragon head light fixture above as well as the terra-cotta tiles and oriel with diamond

Above: Entrance facade of the C. T. Church house.

Left: Detail of the entrance and lantern.

Opposite: Entrance, oriel window, and leader head.

panes and leaded repoussé sheathing on the rear, animated the facades.

In the 1950s, the property, now known as Three Brooks after the three streams on the land feeding into Beaver Pond, was divided and another driveway added. In 1963 F. E. and Alice Church deeded part of their property, now known as the Shu Swamp Preserve, to the newly established North Shore Wildlife Sanctuary as a memorial to his brother. Both houses have been preserved and well maintained, and both are on to their fifth owner.

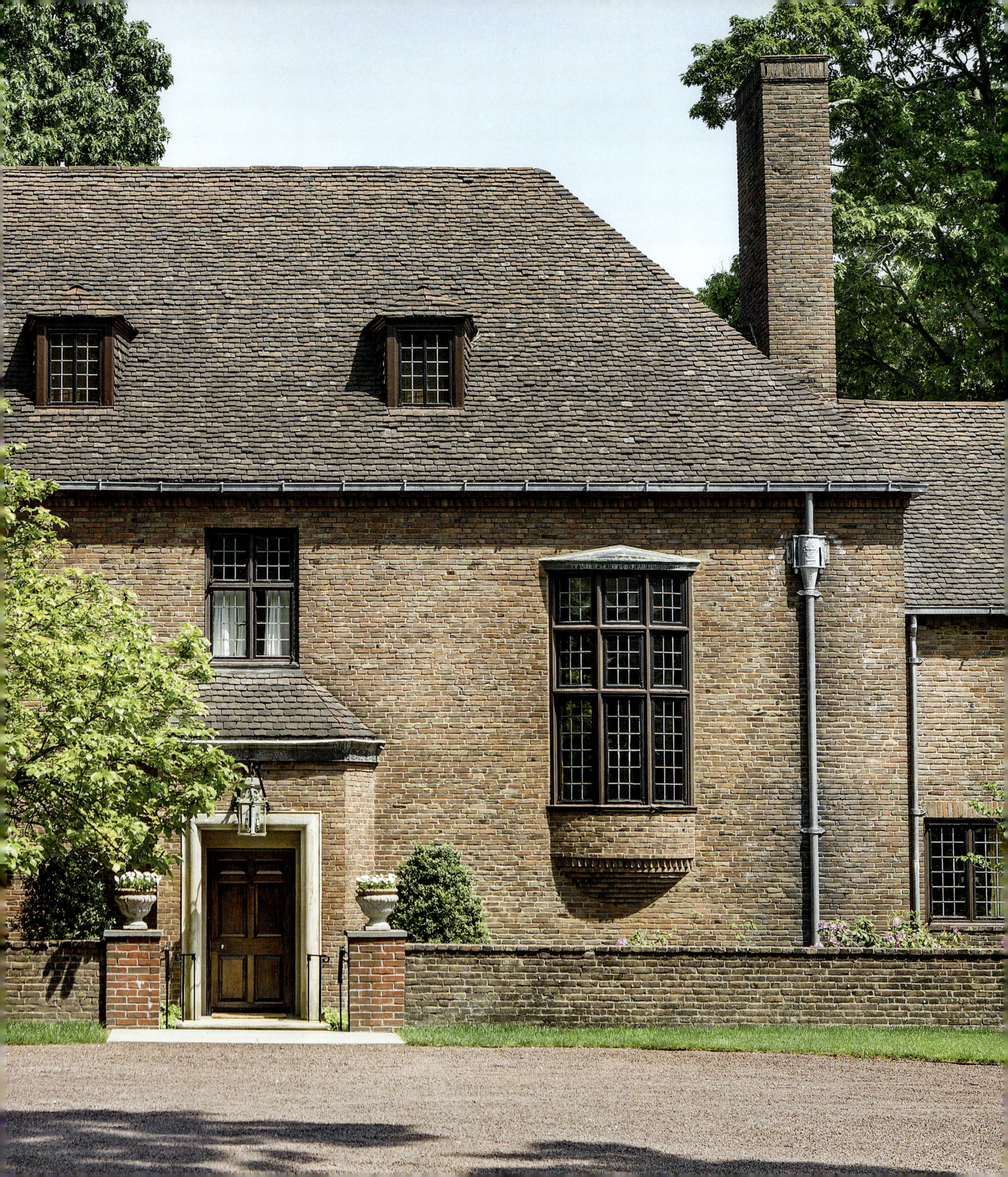

Above: Living room of the C. T. Church house. The interiors were recently decorated by Markham Roberts.

Left: Library.

Opposite: Dining room.

Overleaf: Entrance facade of the F. E. Church house.

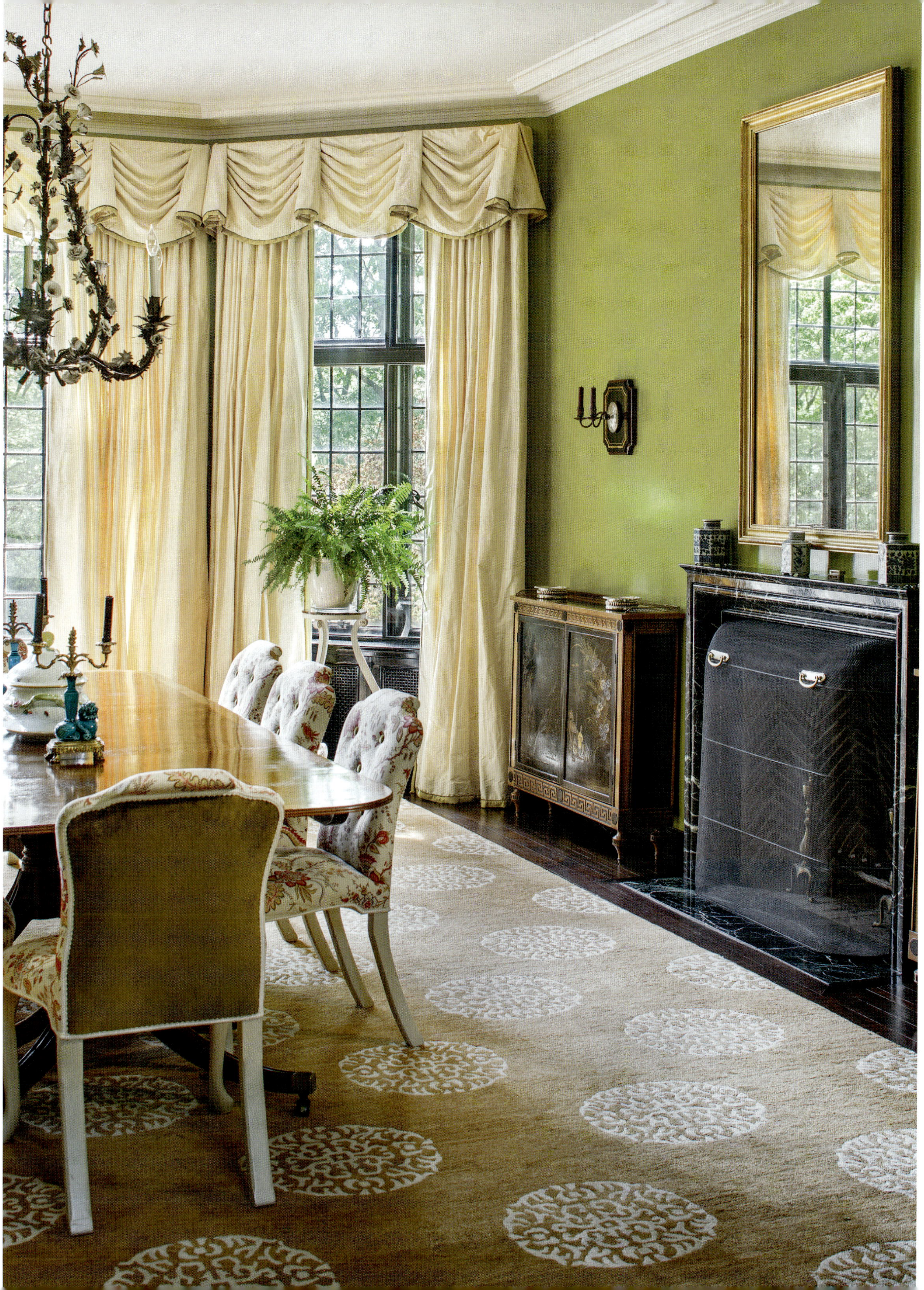

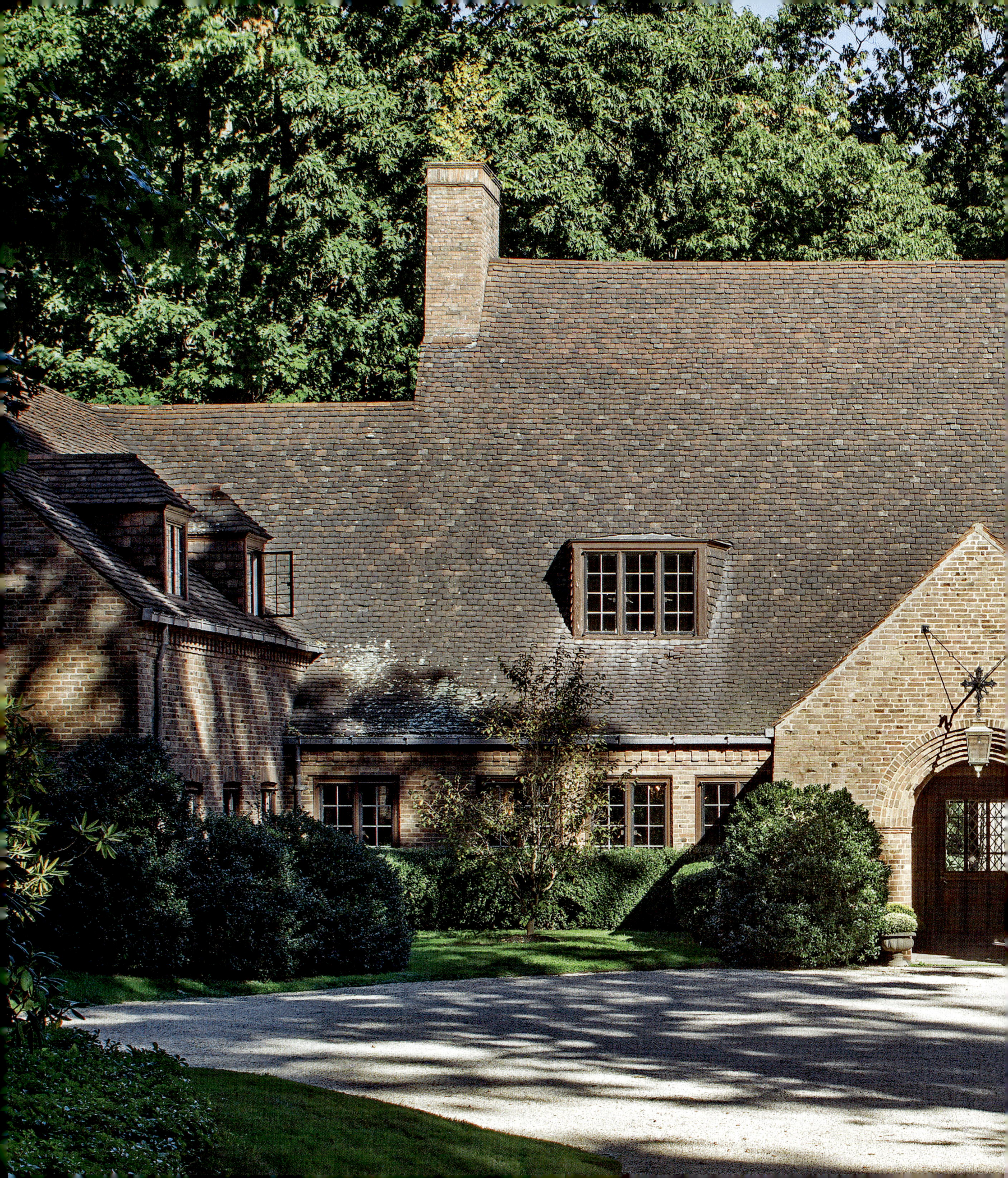

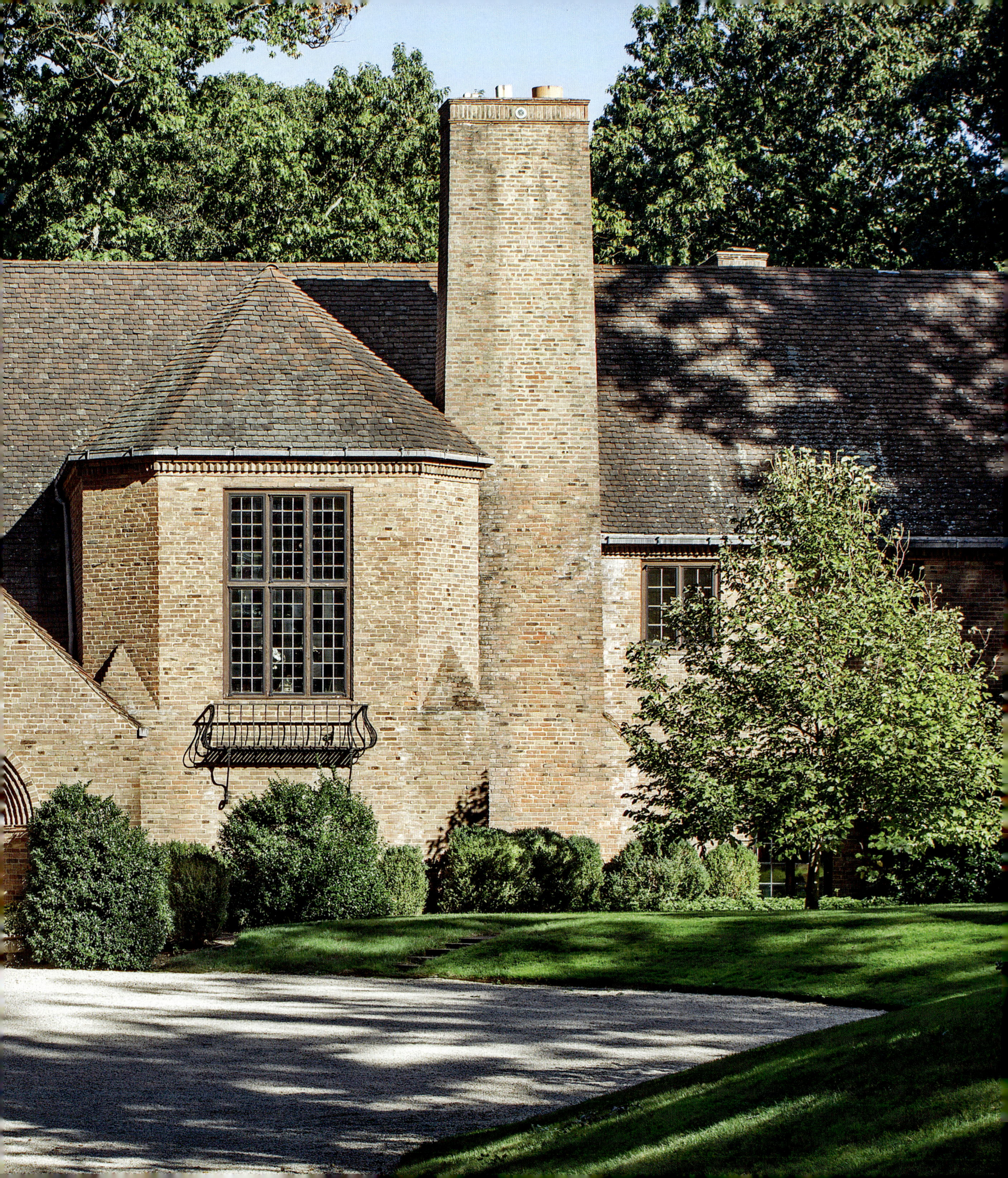

Left: Entrance pavilion, window bank, and chimney of the F. E. Church house.

Below: Lantern bracket wrought in the form of a dragon.

Opposite left: An oriel window with diamond-paned glass and leaded repoussé sheathing at the base.

Opposite right: Loggia and oriel window on the garden facade.

203

TANGLEY OAKS
PHILIP D. ARMOUR III ESTATE

LAKE BLUFF, ILLINOIS

1917– 32

In 1916 Philip D. Armour III (1893–1958) and his new wife, Gwendolyn Condon Armour (1893–1950), purchased a 161-acre tract of land in Lake Bluff, just north of Lake Forest. The grandson of Philip Danforth Armour (1831–1901), Armour was the scion of an important meatpacking family. His grandfather had revolutionized the industry by changing the way meat, grains, and byproducts were used and distributed. Not only did Armour & Company introduce refrigerated railway cars that enabled shipment to the East Coast, but it also utilized all parts of the animals for various byproducts, giving rise to Philip D. Armour's famous slogan: "Nothing of the pig was wasted but his squeal." Armour's uncle, J. Ogden Armour, continued to grow the company into a billion-dollar business.[1]

During the war—around the same time that Lindeberg was working on the Carr house in Lake Forest—the Armours commissioned the architect to design their summer estate. At this point, the Armours were one of the richest families in the country. In 1917 construction began on a temporary eight-room house for the Armours while construction of the manor house was underway. At the same time, Lindeberg designed stables, staff quarters, and a seven-car garage, which were located around a courtyard known as "Armour Court." The garage, a long, low-lying building with a great hipped roof punctuated by two large chimneys, formed one side of the court. By 1922 the couple had three young children and did not anticipate staying in Armour Court very long, but the family's financial situation changed significantly in the wake of the armistice in 1918. Armour & Company was caught off-guard when meat prices plummeted as excess supplies were dumped into market. Paired with a series of bad investments, these difficult conditions led the company—and the Armours—into serious debt. Armour & Company went into trust as J. Ogden Armour, his wife, children, and nephews—including Philip—struggled to meet their obligations, and the family lost control of the company. During the 1920s, these reduced circumstances curtailed any further building campaigns. The Armours stayed in what was built as a temporary house, and Lindeberg's plans for a great Tudor Gothic-style estate remained on the drafting boards.

In the early 1930s, an investment in oil refining restored the family fortune. By the late 1920s, Philip Armour had recovered much of the money he had lent to meet the company debt, while his uncle's investment in Universal Oil Products became exceedingly valuable as automobile use increased exponentially. In 1931 the sale of Universal Oil Products rendered Armour's widow and the extended family wealthy once again. However, when the interim president of Armour & Company retired in 1931, Philip was passed over to head the company. As a result, he resigned, and the business passed out of the family's control.

Meanwhile, Armour's improved financial situation allowed him to continue with Lindeberg's 1916 design with some changes.[2] The expansive manor featured a formal walled entrance court and a picturesque house, with a Ludowici-Celadon tile roof and soft orange and red face brick facades and limestone details, stretching across the south end. While the building was asymmetrical and rambling, the composition was balanced, with oversized casements, oriels, gables, sturdy

View from the living room into the stair hall.

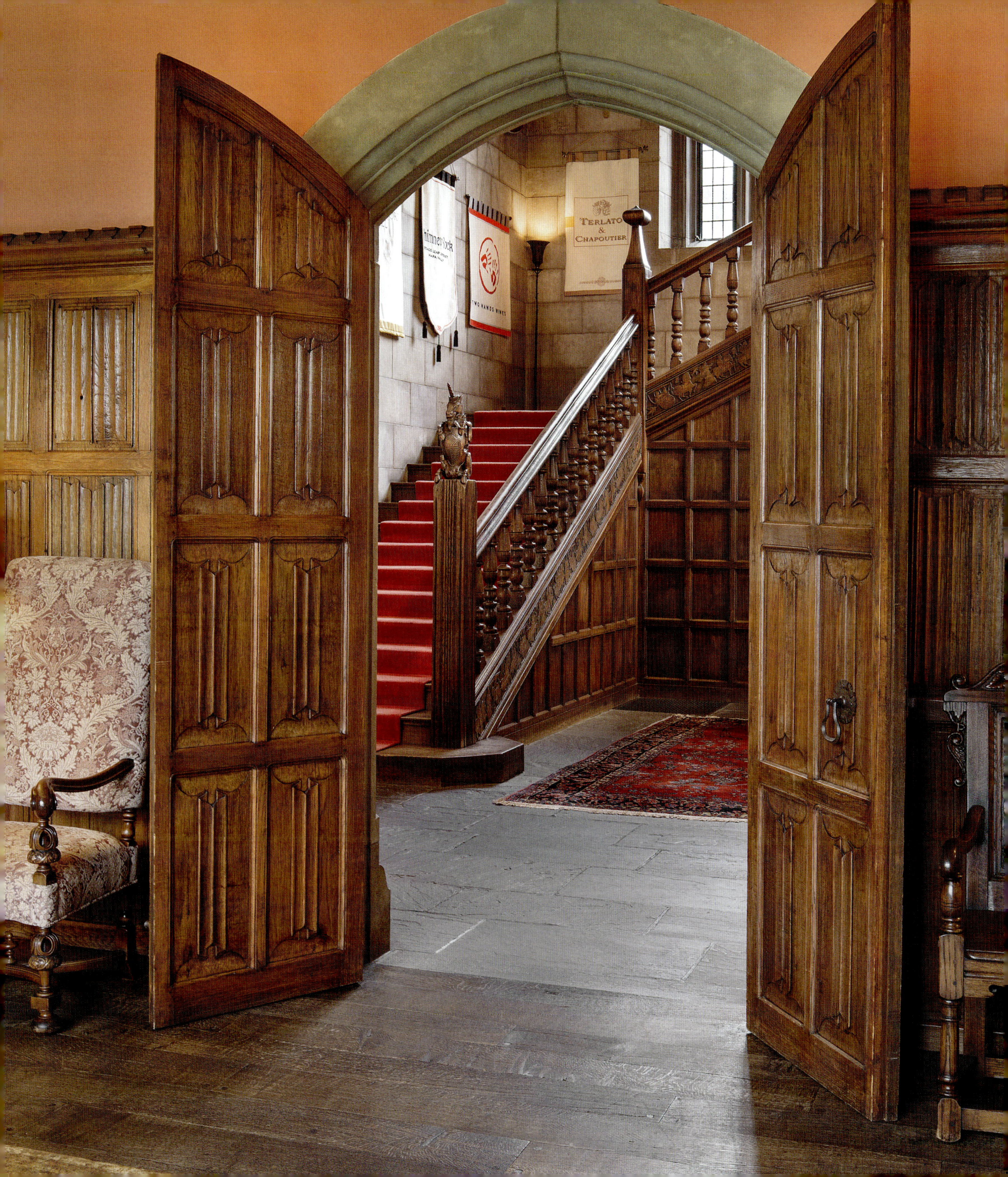
TERLATO
&
CHAPOUTIER
TWO HANDS WINES

First Floor Plan

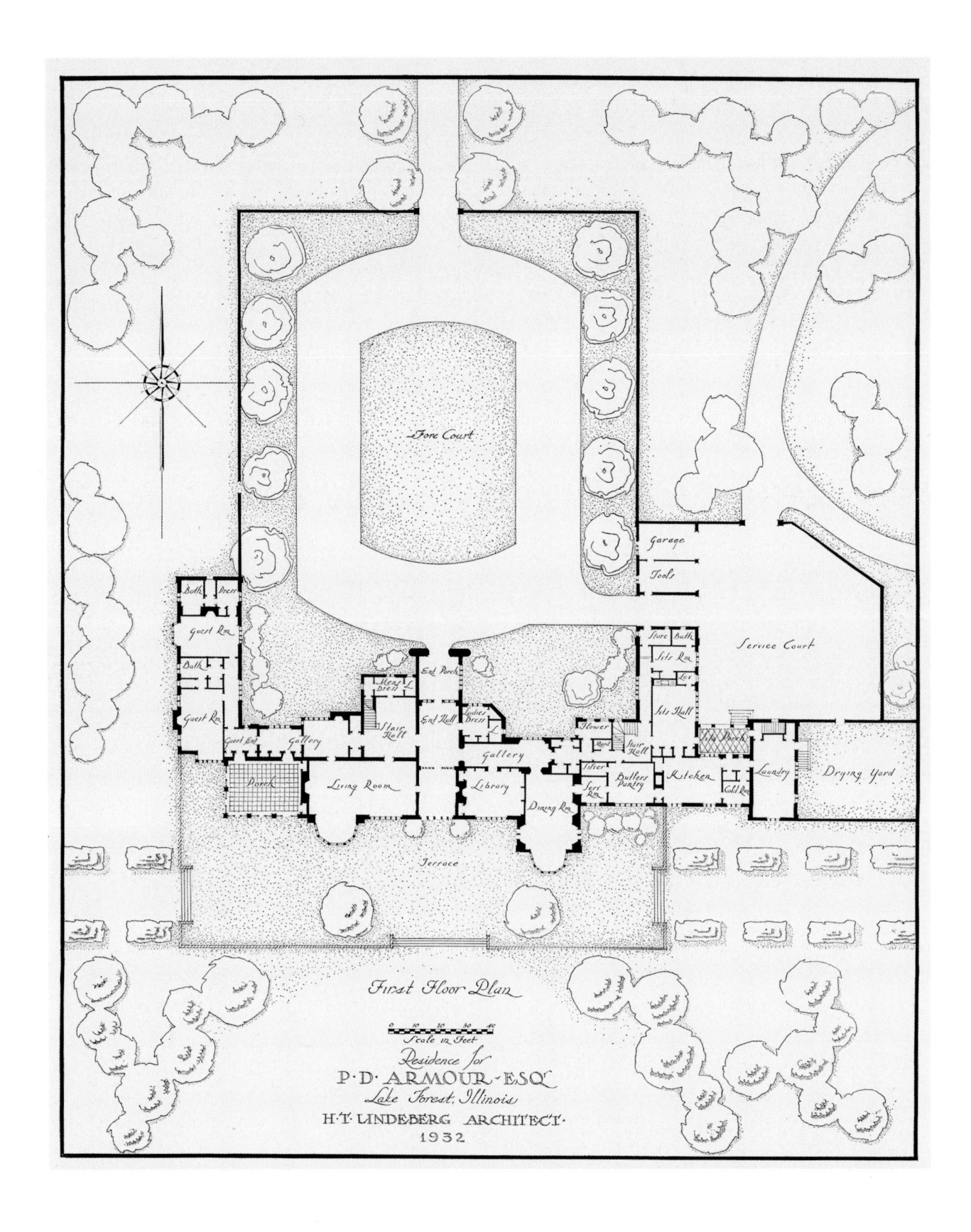

Residence for
P. D. ARMOUR, ESQ.
Lake Forest, Illinois
H. T. LINDEBERG ARCHITECT
1932

Above: Entrance facade.

Overleaf: Garden facade.

chimneys, and two wings—a one-story guest suite to the west and a two-story service wing to the east—that formed a portion of the entry court. On the rear, Lindeberg created a more classically balanced elevation overlooking a meadow and pond in a park-like setting. Decorative lead-coated copper gutters etched with grapevines adorned the formal portion of the house.

Inside, he organized the plan around a wide slate-tiled central hall that extended from the gable-fronted entrance porch through the depth of the house and red-oak choir screen—taken from a church in England—and out to the south-facing terrace. Lindeberg strung the primary rooms—the living room, library, and dining room—along the back of the house and created a series of galleries along the front side to tie the space together, much as he had at Southways, the John S. Pillsbury estate in Orono, Minnesota, and later at Gray Craig.

Lindeberg's ability to fuse conventional enfilade arrangements with shifting axes and galleries was again a key to the success of the plan. At Tangley Oaks, he extended one east–west gallery along the north facade to a porch and the guest suite with two bedrooms, one furnished with a rare eighteenth-century English pine mantel attributed to Robert Adam. Another wide hall to the east accessing the library, dining room, and service wing was lit by a double-height bank of windows that

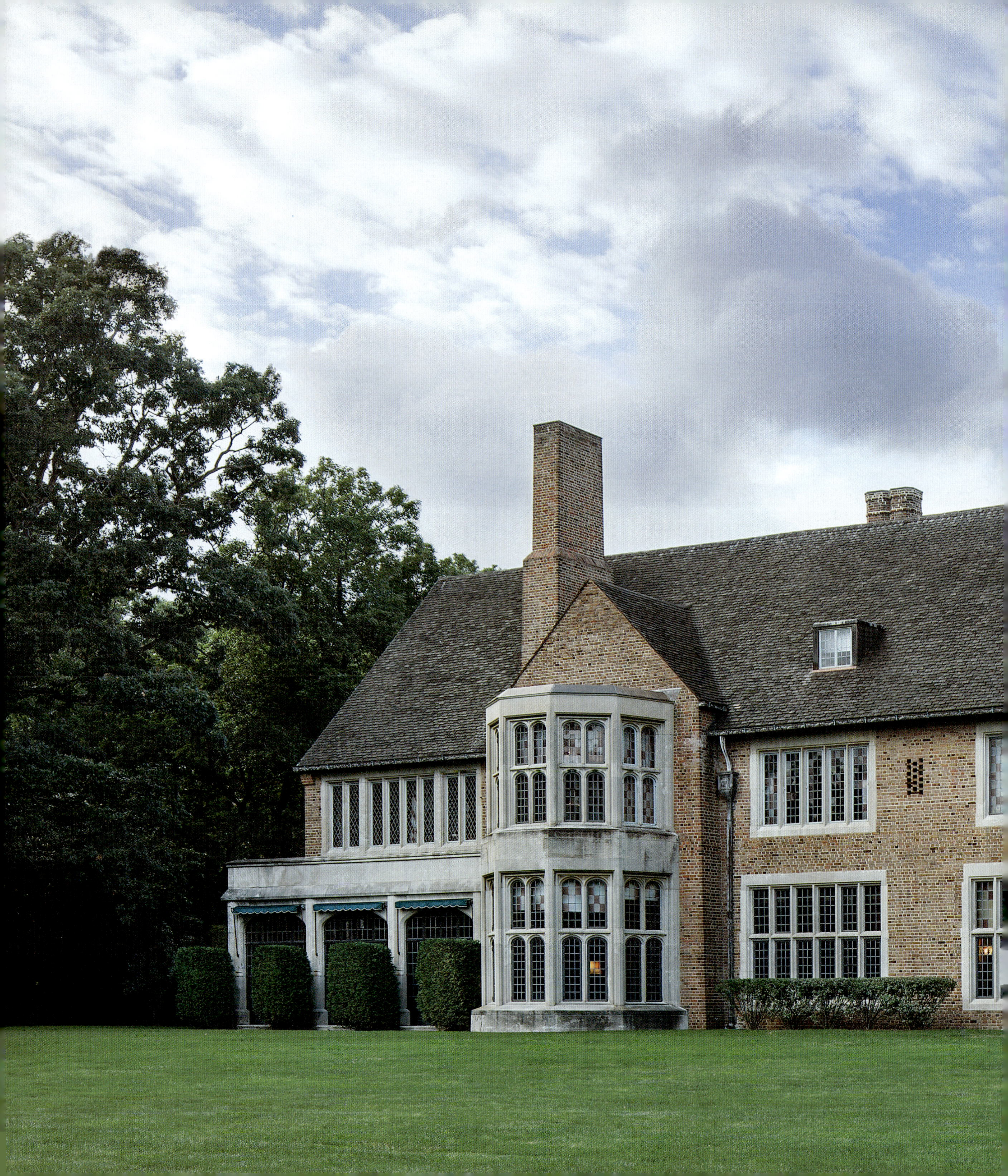

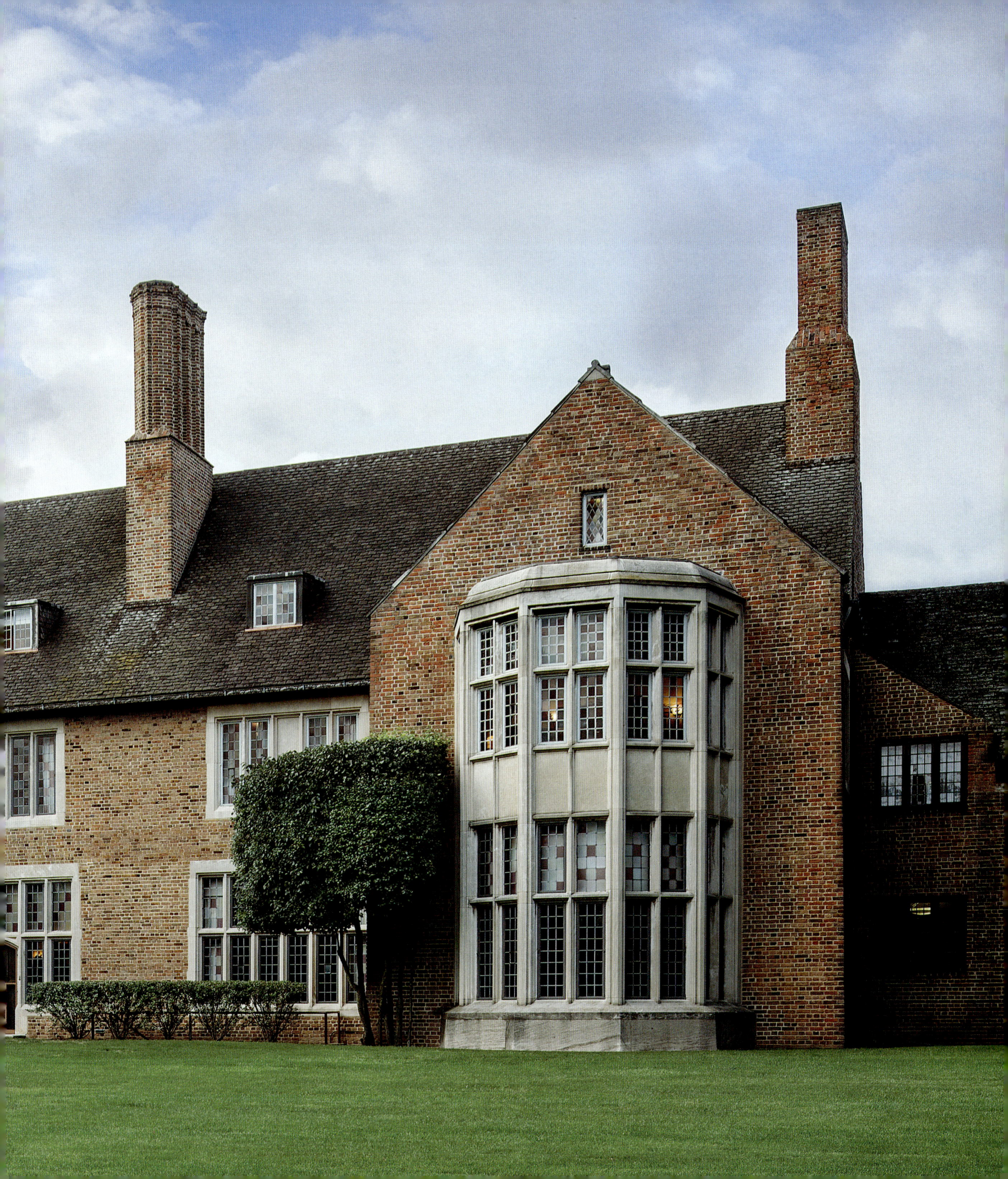

stretched up to the second-floor hallway. The bisecting north–south hall opened onto the great stair hall, which was lit by another double-height casement of colored glass. With oak linen-fold paneling and cut-limestone walls, the stair hall was filled with architectural detail, including a newel post in the form of a bearded unicorn carved out of a solid piece of red oak. An intricately carved frieze of Genghis Khan and his troops riding off to war was carved on the stringer of the walnut stair while a great collar-brace and hammer-beam truss —reportedly repurposed from a wooden bridge in Kentucky—held up the oak ceiling.

Upstairs, Lindeberg located a minstrel's gallery in the hall and an extensive master suite with a sitting room, sleeping porch, two oversized baths, and an octagonal dressing room with a shell molding at the ceiling and seventeenth-century British relief panels inserted above the closets. A guest room, two children's rooms, a governess's room, and nine bedrooms for servants filled out the remainder of the floor.

To furnish the house, Lindeberg and the Armours went on buying sprees in Europe—perhaps after Philip retired from the family business. In addition to acquiring antiques and tapestries, they purchased

Above: Front entrance.

Opposite: Gallery leading to the service wing with the library and dining room to the right.

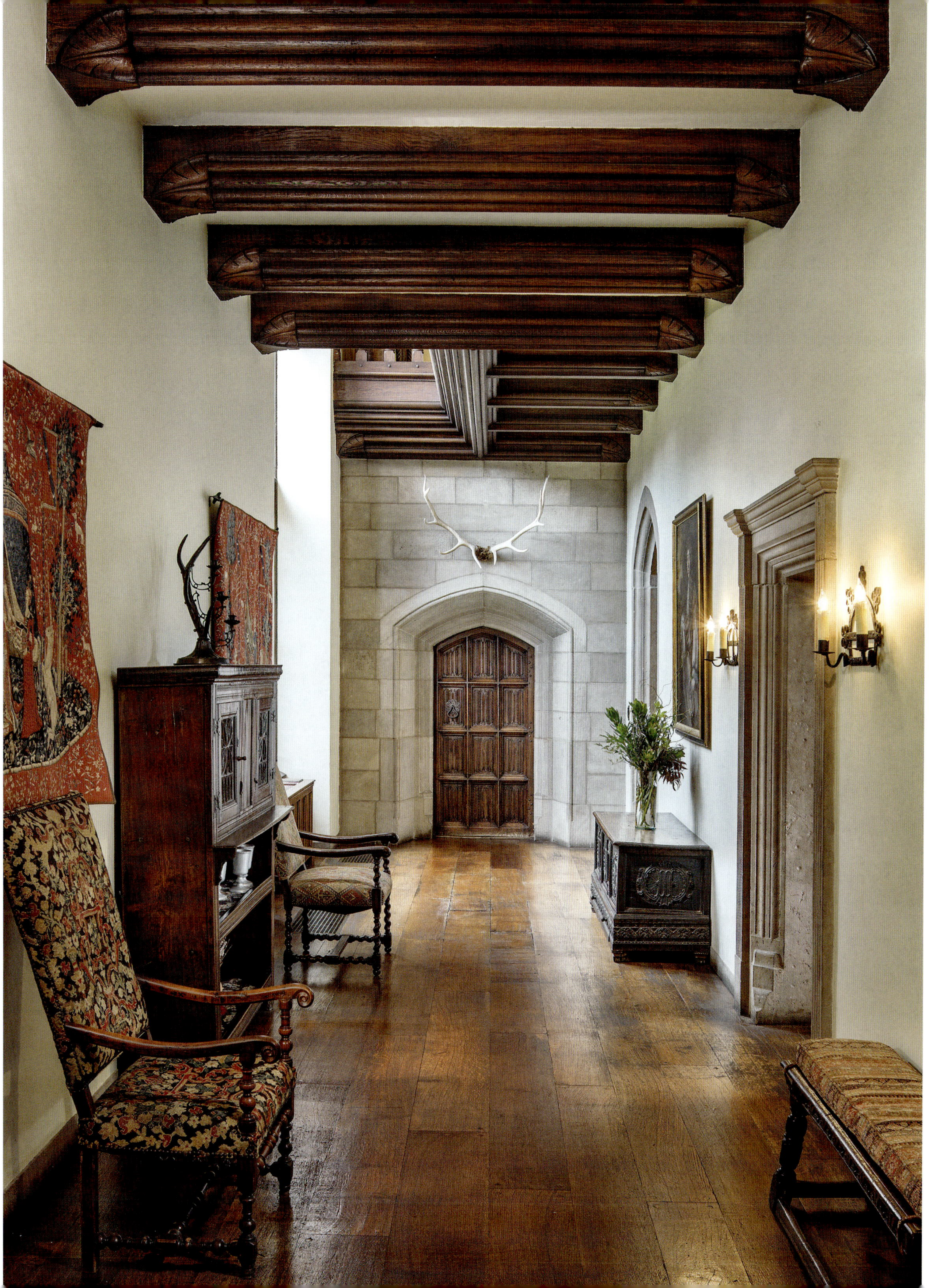

architectural details, fireplace mantels, and entire rooms. The paneled Georgian library was taken from a house in England and combined back at Tangley Oaks with an antique chimney breast from the office of a Lord Chief Justice in the Temple Courts of London. In fact, most of the wooden architectural elements had originally found their place in buildings in France and England. The linen-fold paneling in the living room once graced the walls of a sixteenth-century French chateau; Lindeberg sized the room to accommodate it. For the powder room, the Armours acquired antique hand-painted Chinese rice paper from the late 1600s. Even the exterior bricks were imported, brought over from England as ballast on ships. Lindeberg carried the medieval theme throughout, incorporating light switch plates and hardware that reinforced the Tudor Gothic style of the house.[3]

In 1953, just after the death of his wife, Armour sold Tangley Oaks to the Davis family who maintained the property as the headquarters of their encyclopedia publishing business, United Educators, until 1995. In 1978, they sold off most of the land, which had grown to 220 acres under the Armours, to developers, and Armour Court was torn down. The Terlato family took over the property in 1995 as the center of their wine business, Terlato Wines International. In 1996, they commissioned architect Thomas Rajkovich to restore the main rooms on the ground floor and saw that Tangley Oaks was listed on the National Register of Historic Places. The main house and its immediate seven acres, including the landscape, pond, gardens, and vistas, have survived as the focal point of the new development and Lindeberg's gate house (1925), since parceled off as a separate property, remains extant. All of the Tangley Oaks public rooms are original and still include some of the Armours' furnishings, which amounted to one hundred pieces and twenty Oriental rugs at the time the Terlatos took over as stewards.

Above left: Carved stringer on the main stair.

Above right: Bearded unicorn newel post on the main stair.

Opposite: Carved oak closet door between the stair hall and the galley leading to the guest wing.

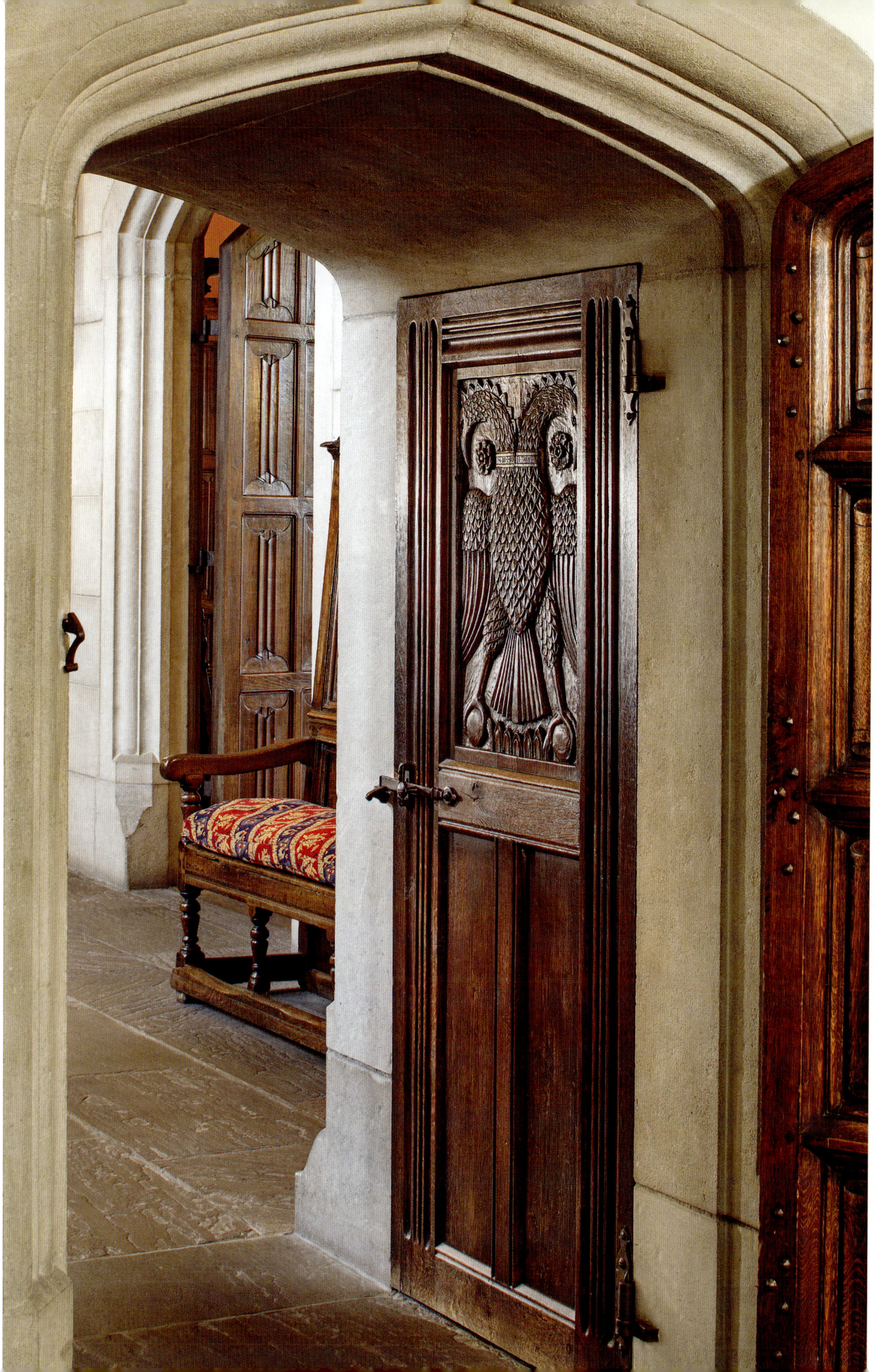

RUBY BOYER MILLER HOUSE

GROSSE POINTE FARMS, MICHIGAN

1935

Lindeberg designed this modest yet stylish house for Ruby Boyer Miller in Grosse Pointe Farms, a suburb just northeast of Detroit fronting on Lake St. Clair. In the late 1800s, this lakefront stretch thrived as a summer colony for the city's newly rich. At that time Detroit, located at the center of the Great Lakes region, began to boom as a manufacturing hub. The industrialists and executives who made fortunes at the end of the nineteenth century were joined by others during the rise of city's automobile industry in the early twentieth century. Areas to the north of Detroit flourished as the city's elite began to build principal houses and estates on the lake and farmland was transformed into golf courses as country clubs were established and leisure sports took hold.

Ruby Boyer Miller (1882–1959), a native of St. Louis, was a daughter of inventor Joseph Boyer, president of the Burroughs Adding Machine Company from 1902 to 1920. In 1904 Boyer moved the company from St. Louis to Detroit as Burroughs grew into the largest adding machine company in the country with an increasing international presence.[1] Four years later, Ruby Boyer married lumber executive William A. C. Miller (1881–1949), a Detroit native and University of Michigan graduate. They settled on Iroquois Street and had three sons, but they divorced in 1921. Eight years later, Ruby Boyer Miller commissioned Lindeberg to design Penguin Hall, an expansive stone house in Wenham, Massachusetts, which she built to pursue her relationaship with the married Arctic and Antarctic explorer Admiral Richard Byrd (1888–1957), who lived on Beacon Hill in Boston. Miller spent summers at Penguin Hall and maintained a residence in Detroit for the winter season.

In 1935 Lindeberg designed a second house for her, this time a smaller structure with custom furnishings designed by his office. Located just one block from Lake St. Clair, it overlooked the golf course at the Country Club of Detroit in a prime residential neighborhood. As a later project, the house represented the aesthetic that Lindeberg began developing in the 1930s based on fixed modules. In his words, "My present study toward a type of house structurally new has taken for its basis of design a module system as definite as any that was set up by the architectural rationale of the Italian Renaissance."[2]

While Miller's house was not composed of steel modules, it reflected the same orderly division of elements as Lindeberg's cellular houses. Here, Lindeberg extended his commitment to simplicity, developing a spare vernacular all his own. Entirely symmetrical, the entrance front featured a central gable with two low-lying boxy wings that framed a small enclosed court. Lindeberg offset the simplicity of the whitewashed gable end with the sinuous lines of the transom, the segmental arch of the pediment, and the globe-like oculus in the attic story. On the garden side, which fronted onto a private road and golf course, Lindeberg followed a taut symmetrical facade of Greek Revival influence, stripped to its essentials.

Inside, he devised a plan more compatible with modern-day living, combining the living and dining space into one large room divided by two large chinoiserie screens. He tucked a small office behind the stair and balanced the kitchen wing and service court to the

Entrance facade.

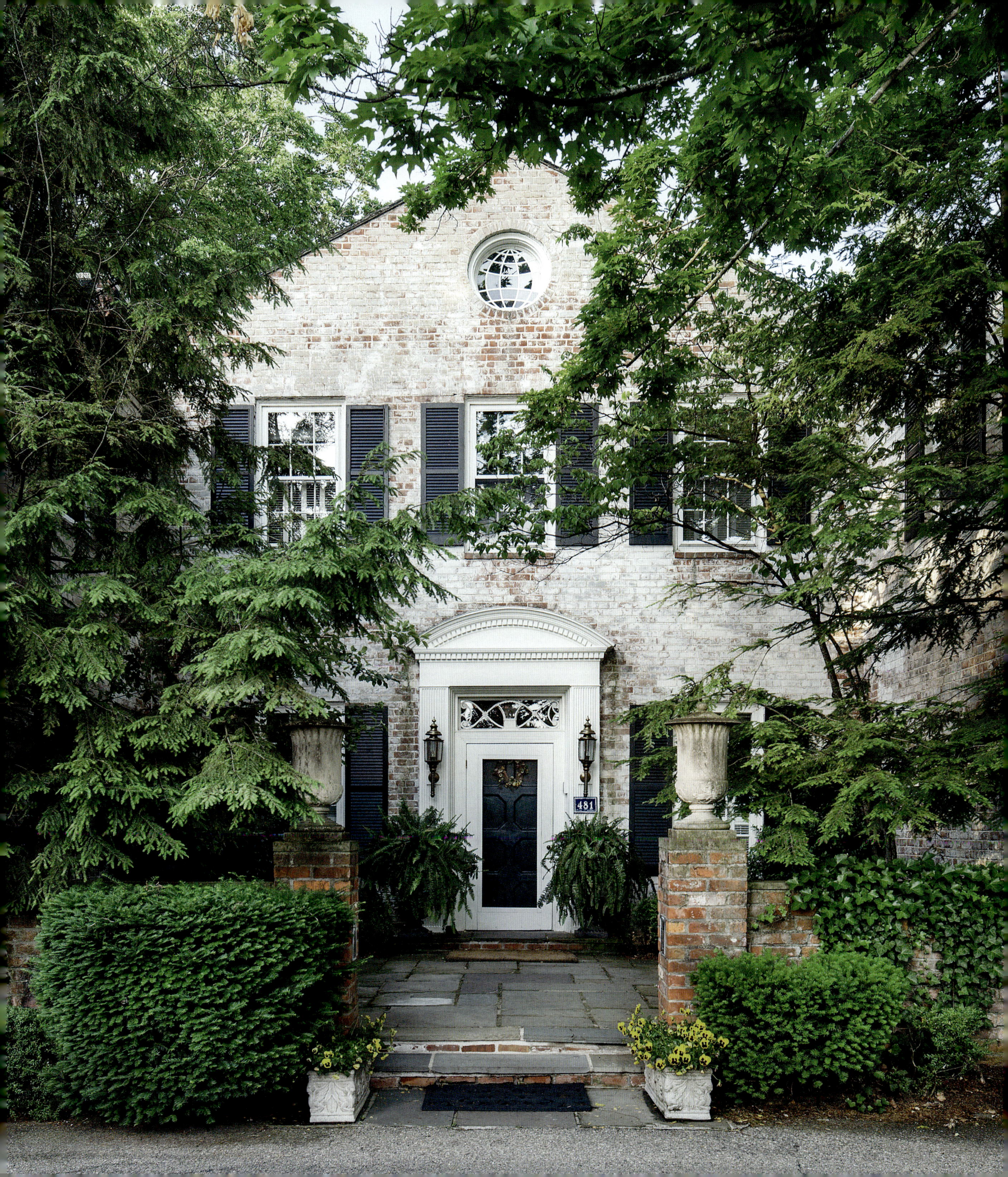
481

MRS. R. BOYER MILLER
GROSSE POINTE, MICHIGAN
1935

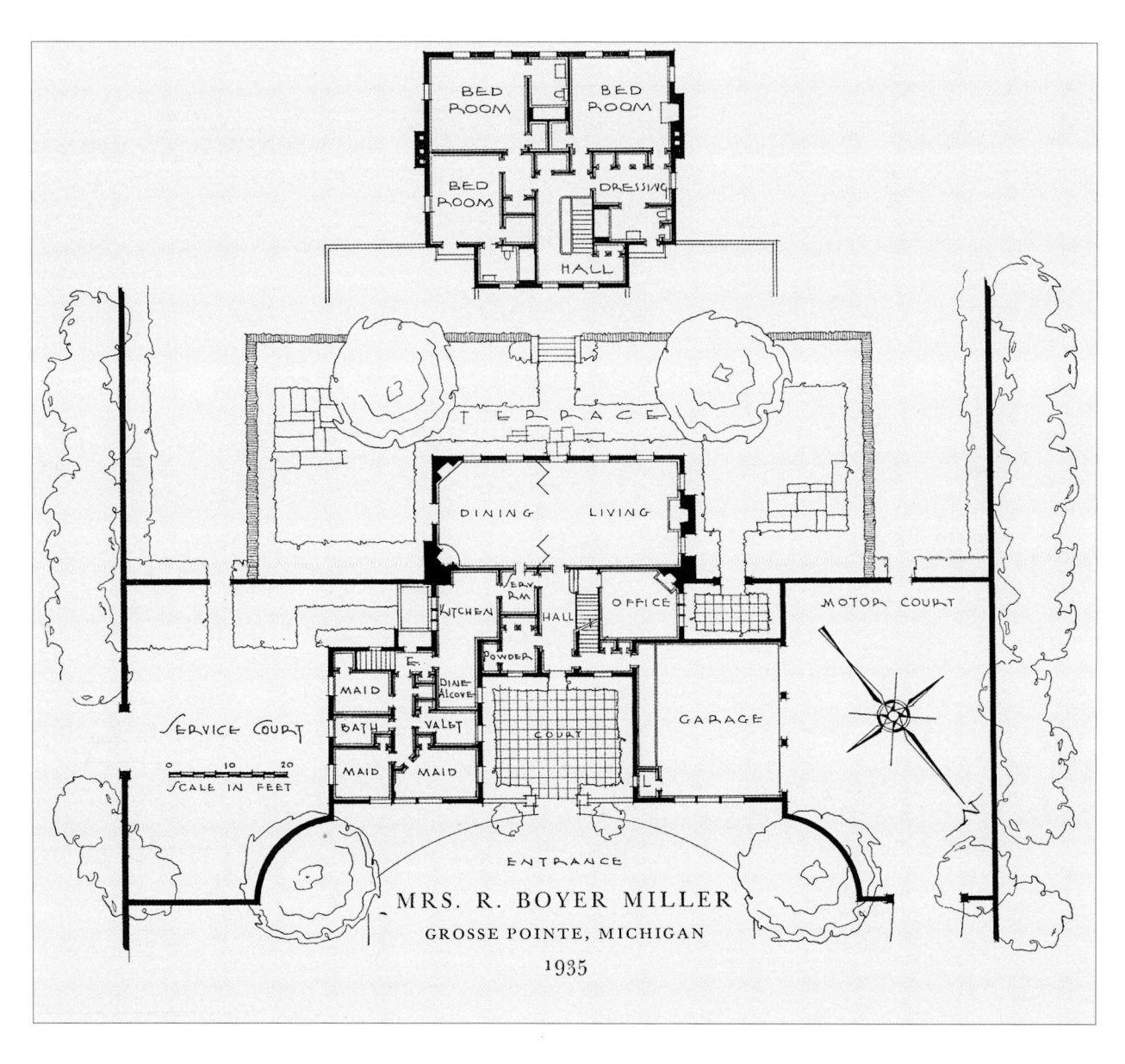

Opposite above: Northeast entrance facade.

Above: Garden facade.

east with the garage and motor court to the west. The second floor contained three bedrooms, each with its own bath. Three maids and a valet could be accommodated on the first floor—a condensed, although still sizable, version of Lindeberg's typical 1920s servants wing. With mirrored panels, stylized architectural details, and an Art Deco stair railing of alternating bars and scrolling curves, Lindeberg emphasized the jewel box quality of the interiors. The mix of Art Deco lamps and mirrors, neoclassical revolving bookcases and chairs, and tables inspired by Émile-Jacques Ruhlmann gave the rooms a glamorous, cosmopolitan flair. In the living room, a framed mirror reflected an Art Deco fantasy verging on the modern baroque sensibility of the well-known New York decorator Dorothy Draper. Meanwhile, the turned-out feet of Lindeberg's night tables pointed to Swedish influences (see page 234).

Miller lived in the house for twenty-five years. In 1961 the Gordon T. Fords bought the house and built two small additions above the garage and kitchen to create more space upstairs. The current owners, who asked architect Karen Swanson, the great granddaughter of Eliel Saarinen, to add two bay windows on the garden front, have lived there since the early 1990s. Despite the changes, the exterior retains much of its original charm and Lindeberg's appealing arched gate, wrought with shapes of shells and flowers, still fronts the drive into the Country Club of Detroit.

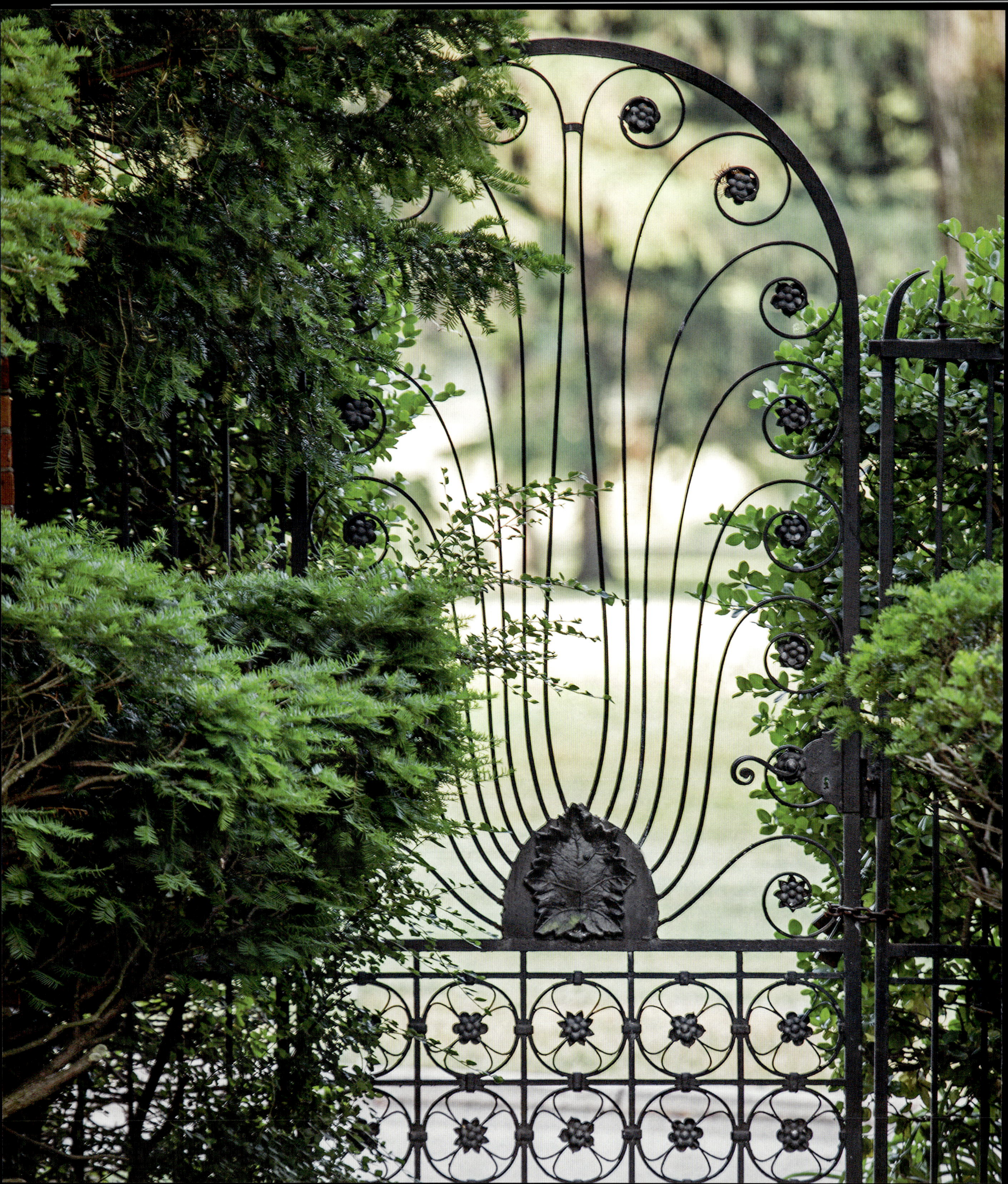

Above: Living room, 1937.

Right: Stair hall, 1937.

Opposite: Wrought-iron gate marking the property line.

UNITED STATES LEGATION

HELSINKI, FINLAND

1936–40

When the austerities of the Great Depression all but destroyed architectural careers based on grand houses, Lindeberg had the good fortune to be chosen to design a number of projects abroad for the United States Foreign Buildings Office, including embassies in Moscow (1934), Shanghai (1936) and Managua, Nicaragua (1937). Unfortunately for American diplomatic architecture, construction was deferred on all but one: the U. S. Legation in Helsinki, Finland. The Foreign Service Buildings Commission, created in 1926 under the jurisdiction of the Secretary of State, was charged with purchasing, constructing, and altering diplomatic buildings abroad, pulling from a newly established fund of $10 million, of which $2 million could be used each year.

During the 1930s, the United States began to assume a more prominent role internationally and the State Department, looking to spread the message of enlightened thinking and democracy, established a new program for America's diplomatic architecture. President Franklin D. Roosevelt had specific opinions of the historic styles of the various embassies, which conveyed a symbolic image he wanted the United States to project, and the new buildings constructed in foreign cities during the 1930s and early 1940s were to be "as typically American as they can possibly be."[1] This period saw a rise in the popularity of Thomas Jefferson, who epitomized enlightened thought; several newly published biographies and the design and construction of the Jefferson Memorial in Washington, D. C., had brought the founding father to the fore. In Moscow, Lindeberg's embassy design, based on the Jefferson's University of Virginia, encapsulated the essence of an American diplomatic building. In the words of Roosevelt:

We can build an embassy on that hill in the city park overlooking the river which will be as simple and as beautiful as Monticello, and I myself should like to see a modern version of Monticello built there with subsidiary buildings patterned after those which fringe the lawn of the University of Virginia. I like the idea of planting Thomas Jefferson in Moscow. For this particular job, I know no one so well fitted as Harrie T. Lindeberg.[2]

Roosevelt, a neighbor of the Dows family in the Hudson Valley, would have likely first encountered the architect through Rhinebeck circles.

While the ambitious Moscow scheme was never realized—due to prohibitive costs and impossible logistics—Lindeberg was able to create an American enclave in Helsinki which stands today as the only Colonial Revival building in the Nordic countries. After construction of the legation and consulate was authorized in 1935, Keith Merrill, the chief of the Foreign Buildings Office, and Ambassador Edward Albright chose a three-acre site in the historic Kaivopuisto neighborhood with views of the Gulf of Finland.[3] Although construction was delayed because supplies were slow to arrive and a factory housing some of the woodwork was bombed during the Winter War, the legation was successfully completed in 1940. Lindeberg's building, designed under Louis A. Simon, Office of the Supervising Architect, evoked Westover, an eighteenth-century Virginia plantation house on the James River.

Living room in the Ambassador's residence.

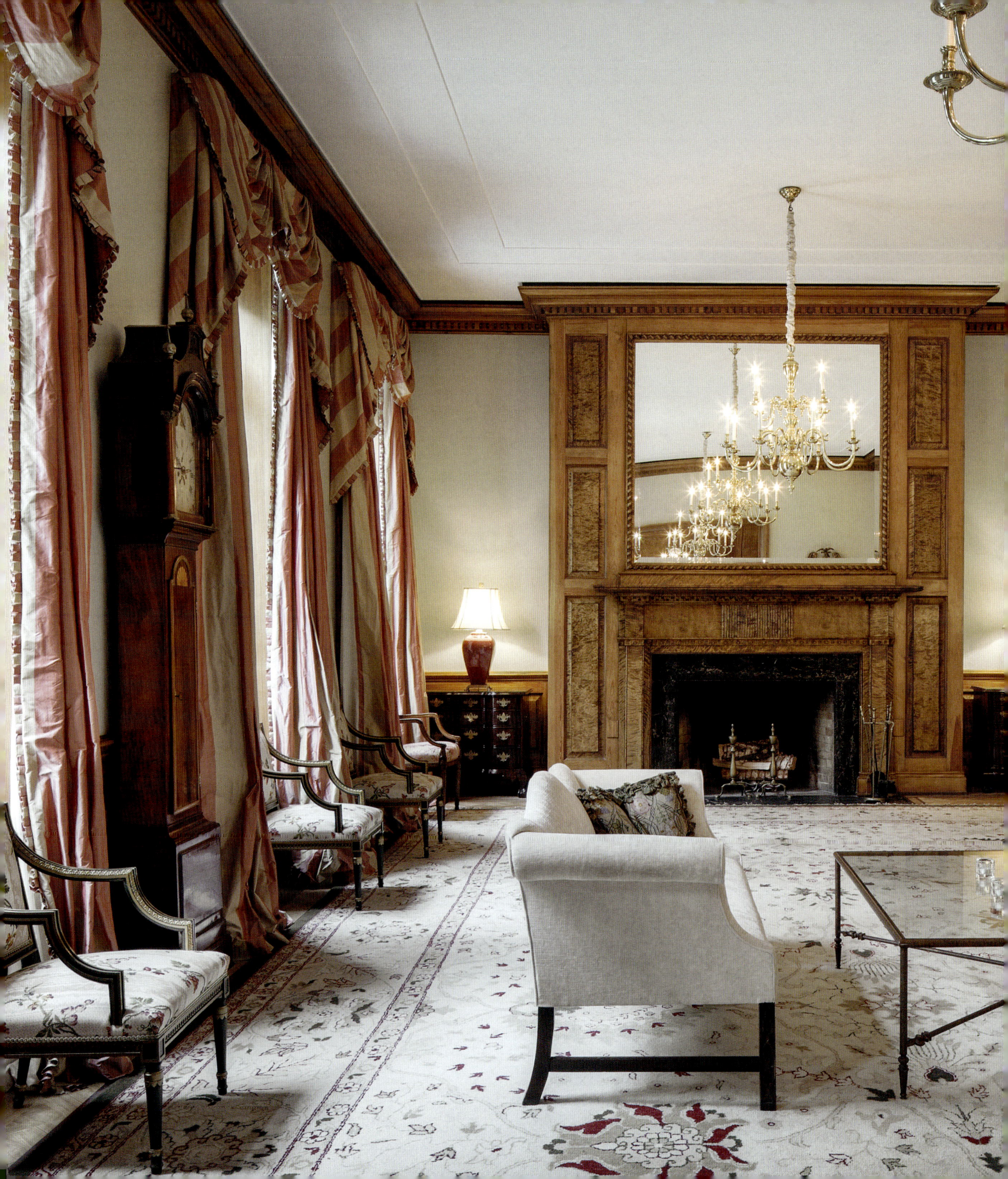

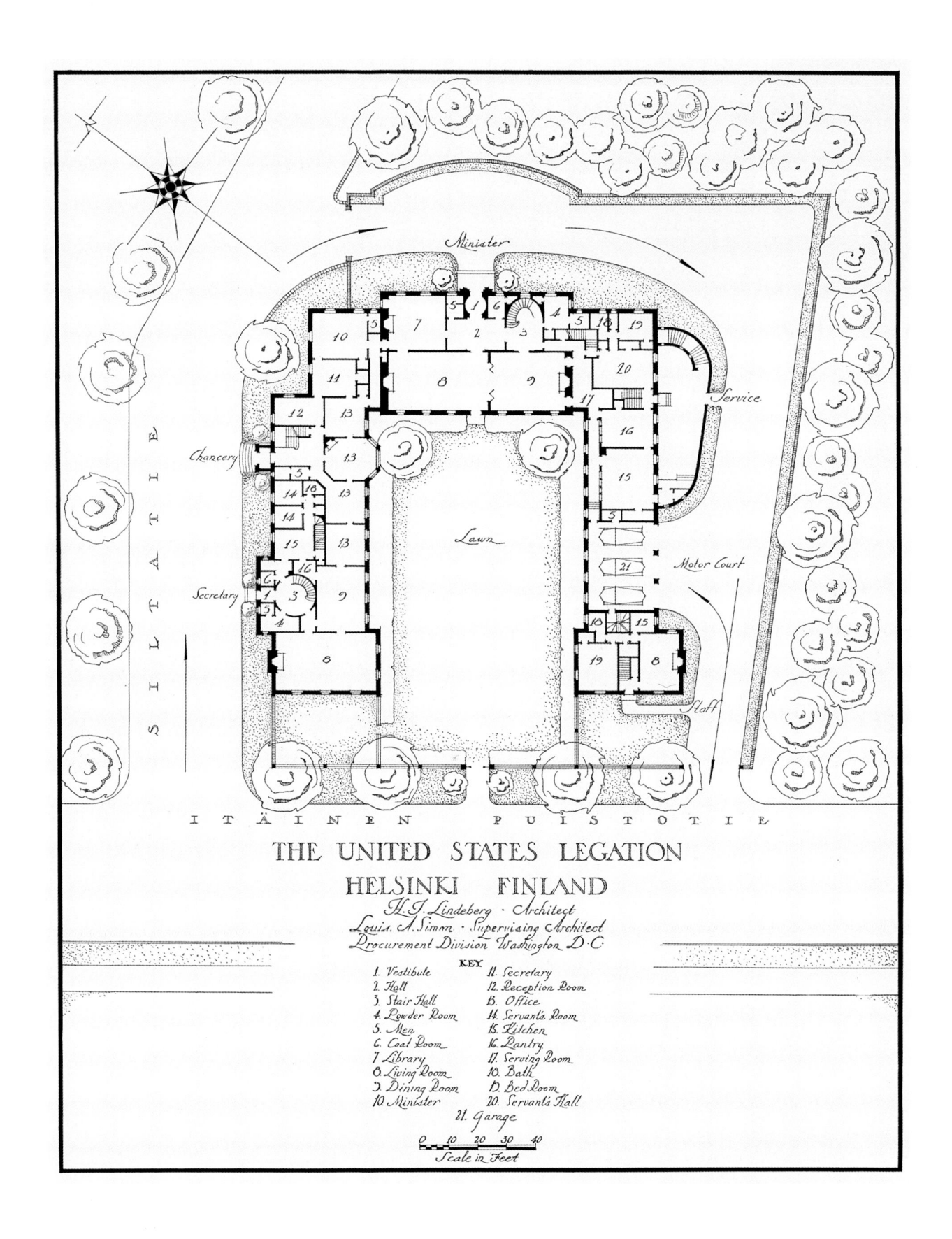

THE UNITED STATES LEGATION
HELSINKI FINLAND
H. J. Lindeberg · Architect
Louis A. Simon · Supervising Architect
Procurement Division Washington D.C.

KEY

1. Vestibule
2. Hall
3. Stair Hall
4. Powder Room
5. Men
6. Coat Room
7. Library
8. Living Room
9. Dining Room
10. Minister
11. Secretary
12. Reception Room
13. Office
14. Servant's Room
15. Kitchen
16. Pantry
17. Serving Room
18. Bath
19. Bed Room
20. Servant's Hall
21. Garage

Scale in Feet: 0 10 20 30 40

Above: Entrance facade.

Set on the banks of the gulf, the central brick portion of the building, housing the Ambassador's residence, rose two stories to a steeply pitched roof punctuated with a row of dormer windows and four stately chimneys—much like Westover. To the southwest, two wings—one of which contained the embassy, the other a garage and staff quarters—extended back to enclose a center lawn. Lindeberg carried out the interiors in a restrained Georgian idiom. In addition to his signature graceful and sweeping stair, he paneled the library and dining room in a rare figured wood from the Karelian Peninsula—a material that was wiped out after Finland was forced to cede Karelia to the Soviet Union after the Winter War in the Moscow peace treaty of 1940.

Lindeberg poured over every aspect down to the living room mantel, which includes a carved detail of the Finnish parliament, pictured upside-down. Lindeberg's plan solved the practical and programmatic issues with rooms that were bright and livable, but more importantly, the complex rose to the challenge set by Roosevelt by bringing an essentially American architecture that was both dignified and welcoming to foreign lands.

Over the years, the embassy complex has grown to include the early 1900s apartment building next door, annexed after World War II. In 2014 a new chancery designed by Moore Ruble Yudell based on the work of Alvar Aalto was completed, and the existing annex was transformed into the Innovation Center for the embassy's public offices. At the same, Lindeberg's historic building was restored. While the wing housing the former chancery has been entirely renovated over time, the Ambassador's residence remains in its original state. Of particular note, the rare Karelian wood—which had come to represent some political importance and pride—was preserved despite being over-painted in the 1970s. In the 2014 restoration, overseen by Ambassador Bruce J. Oreck, Lindeberg's woodwork was uncovered and restored to its former glory.

Above: Dining room.

Opposite above: Rendering of the legation.

Opposite below: Southwest facade overlooking the lawn.

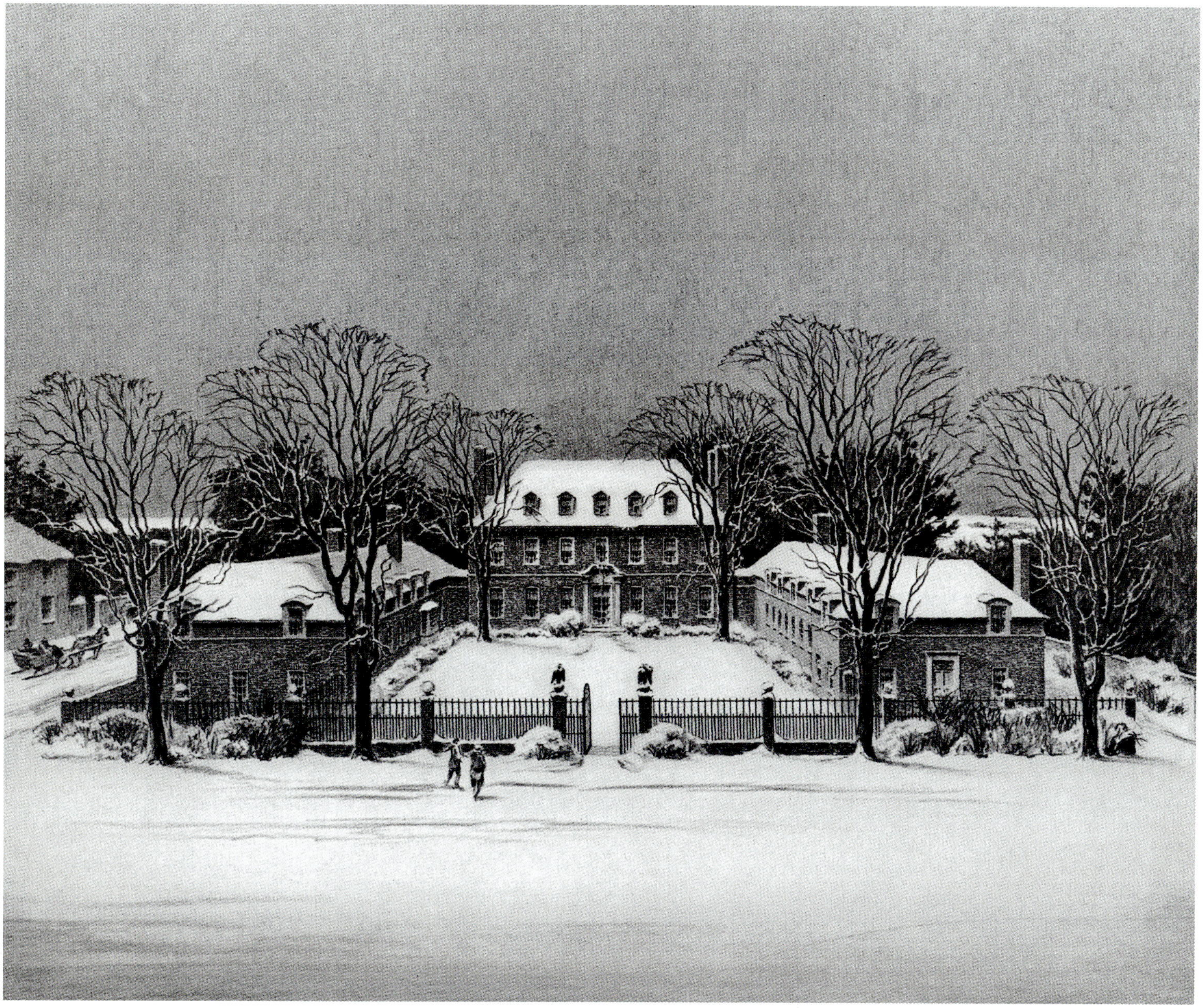

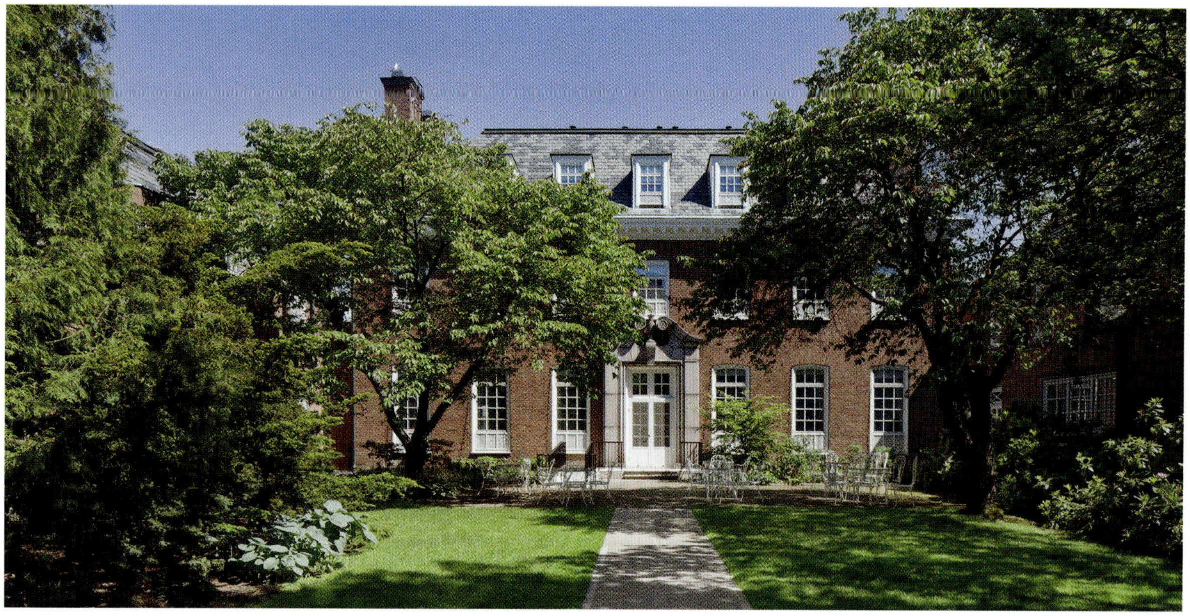

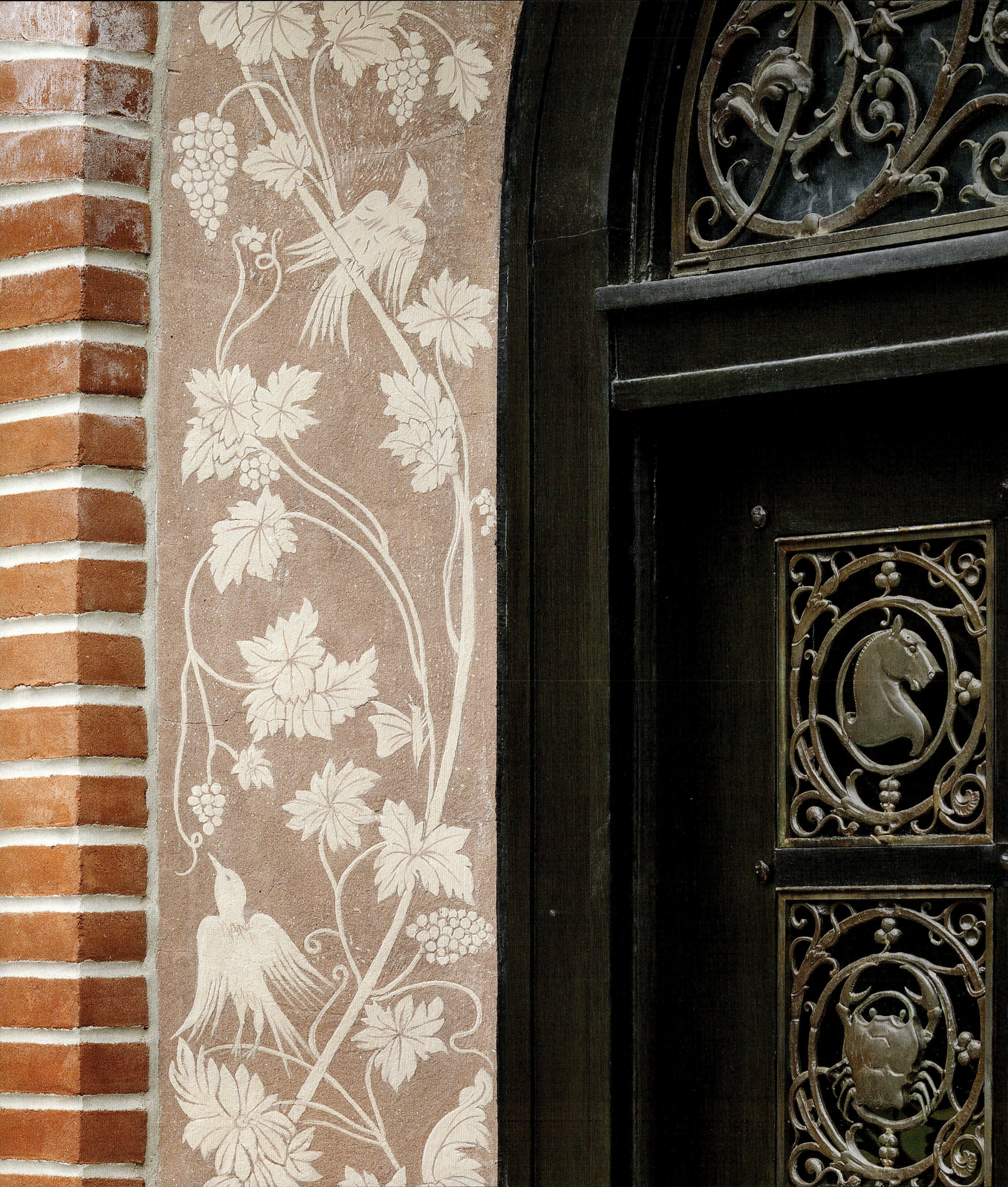

CATALOGUE RAISONNÉ

In 1940 Lindeberg documented his work in the monograph *Domestic Architecture of H. T. Lindeberg*, published by William Helburn Inc. In addition to illustrating a number of his projects, he included a List of Clients—including his clients from Albro & Lindeberg—with geographic locations. Using this list as a starting point, we have attempted to date each project and to determine whether it is extant. Buildings have been ordered chronologically by the year they were started, if known. If the current status of the building is unlisted, it is unknown. Please note that this catalogue raisonné is still a work in progress; there were a number of projects we were unable to track down. Generally, projects dated before 1914 were by Albro & Lindeberg and those dated after were by Lindeberg as sole practitioner.

1906
Edward T. Cockcroft house, Little Burlees, Lily Pond Lane, East Hampton, New York; extant.

J. Langdon Erving house, 62 East 80th Street, renovations, New York; extant.

Tracy Dows house, Foxhollow Farm, Foxhollow Road, Rhinebeck, New York; 1906–10; extant: Samaritan Daytop Village.

Mrs. Stephen H. Olin house, Glenburn, alteration, Southlands Drive, Rhinebeck, New York; 1906–7; extant: remodeled.

North College, Wesleyan University, High Street, Middletown, Connecticut; 1906–8; extant.

James A. Stillman house, Mondanne, Stillman Lane, Pocantico Hills, New York; 1906–10; house razed by fire in 1932, outbuildings extant.

1907
Edward T. Cockcroft house, 59 East 77th Street, renovation, New York; extant.

Russell S. Carter house, Villa Blue, Cedar Avenue, Hewlett, New York; remodeled: 1984.

Caroline (Carroll) Macy house, Birch Corners, Cedar Avenue, Hewlett, New York; demolished.

Carleton Macy house, Meadowwood, Veeder Drive, Hewlett, New York; extant.

Tracy H. Harris house, Wisteria Lodge, East Rockaway Road, Hewlett, New York; demolished; outbuildings now house the Center for Adult Life Enrichment.

Dr. E. H. Pershing house, Broadway, Woodmere, New York; demolished.

John A. Topping house, alteration and addition, Greenwich, Connecticut.

Royal Typewriter Company factory, New Park Avenue, Hartford, Connecticut; demolished by fire: 1992.

1908
Dr. Frederick K. Hollister house, Lily Pond Lane, East Hampton, New York; extant.

F. G. Schmidt house, Manor Lake Farm, N. Manor Avenue, Kingston, New York; 1908–9; extant.

Albert H. Marckwald house, Montview Avenue, Short Hills, New Jersey; extant.

C. E. Van Vleck Jr., House #75, Highland Avenue, Short Hills, New Jersey; extant.

Mount Vernon Public School, Mount Vernon, New York.

John N. Tilden house, Garrison-on-Hudson, New York; 1908–10.

T. Jefferson Coolidge house, enclosed patio, Manchester, Massachusetts; demolished: 1958.

1909
Mary Hale Cunningham house, 124 East 55th Street, renovation, New York: extant.

Richard M. Hoe garage and apartment, 163 East 69th Street, New York; extant: Lisker Congregation.

George Davidson house, Pine Street, Madison, New Jersey; extant.

Levin R. Marshall house, Hawkswood, Waverly Avenue, Hewlett, New York; extant.

Bradish J. Carroll house, Dongan Hills, Staten Island, New York.

William T. Carrington house, Denbigh Farm, Riversville Road, Greenwich, Connecticut; extant.

Scheme for a YMCA, White Plains, New York; c. 1909; unbuilt.

1910
Orville E. Babcock house, Two Gables, North Green Bay Road, Lake Forest, Illinois; extant.

Dr. Ernest Fahnestock house, Shadow Brook Farm, Broad Street, Shrewsbury, New Jersey; extant: Shadowbrook at Shrewbury, an event venue.

Thomas H. Kerr house, Ridgeway, White Plains, New York; extant: Women's Club of White Plains.

Mrs. S. K. Nester house, Lochland Road, Geneva, New York; 1910–14; extant: Geneva of the Lake.

Hugh Chisholm house, Strathglass, Lincoln Avenue, White Plains, New York: extant: SUNY Purchase.

J. H. Ranger house, Quaker Ridge Park, New Rochelle, New York.

Pliny W. Williamson, Heathcote Road, Scarsdale, New York; c. 1910; extant.

Charles S. Brown house, Ardshiel, Mount Kisco, New York; c. 1910.

House for Crestmont Construction Co., house, Montclair, New Jersey (Harold Wilcox), c. 1910.

House #2 for Crestmount Construction Co., Montclair, New Jersey; c. 1910.

1911
Henry L. Batterman house, Barwin Realty, Meadow Spring Lane, Glen Cove, New York; extant.

Arthur W. Rossiter house, Cedarcroft, Cresent Beach Road, Glen Cove, New York; extant.

V. Everett Macy house, Twin Gables, Hewlett, New York; demolished.

Stewart Hartshorn house, House #77, Northern Drive, Short Hills, New Jersey; extant.

1912
Dr. John F. Erdmann house, Coxwould, Lily Pond Lane, East Hampton, New York; 1912–13; extant.

D. G. Gregory house, Hewlett, New York; c. 1912.

Mill Neck Railroad Station, Frost Mill Road, Mill Neck, New York; extant: post office and village hall.

Philip B. Jennings house, Wayside, West Road, Bennington, Vermont; extant: Four Chimneys Inn.

Houses for the Sage Foundation Home Company, Puritan Avenue, Forest Hills Gardens, New York; extant.

Albert A. Sprague house, Forest Cove Road, Lake Bluff, Illinois; extant: extensively remodeled.

Samuel G. Colt house, Overmead, Colt Road, Pittsfield, Massachusetts; demolished: 1960s.

1913
Henry C. Martin house, Meadow Spring Lane, Glen Cove, New York; 1913–14; demolished by fire: 1923.

Holiday Farm for Vincent Astor, Mill Street, Rhinebeck, New York; extant: Astor Services for Children & Families.

Clayton Cooper house, Waldo Avenue, Riverdale, New York; extant.

Nicholas Kelley house, Fieldston Road, Riverdale, New York; extant.

Norman H. Donald house, The Billows, Dongan Hills, Staten Island, New York.

Dr. Archibald R. Gardner house, Dunwoodie Heights, New York; c. 1913.

Edwin Britton Katte house, Lane's End, Dows Lane, Irvington, New York, c. 1913.

Corn Exchange Bank, 375 East 149th Street, New York, New York; extant: altered beyond recognition.

Daniel England house, Wendell Avenue, Pittsfield, Massachusetts; extant: Unitarian Universalist Church.

Gerard B. Lambert house, Albemarle, Lambert Drive, Princeton, New Jersey; 1913–17; extant: PRISMS.

1914
Clarence F. Alcott house, Lily Pond Lane, East Hampton, New York; extant.

Henry L. Batterman house, Beaver Brook Farm, Frost Mill Road, Mill Neck, New York; demolished: 1950s.

Irving Brokaw house, Goose Point, Frost Mill Road, Mill Neck, New York; extant.

Mrs. Horace Irving Brightman house, Waccabuc, New York.

John T. Gillespie house, Ogden Place, Morristown, New Jersey; c. 1914; extant.

Paul Moore house, Hollow Hill Farm, Woodland Avenue, Convent, New Jersey; demolished: c. 1980s.

George Frederick Humphreys house, The Orchards, Normandie Parkway, Morristown, New Jersey; 1914–17; extant.

Arthur I. Keller house, Goodridge Avenue, Fieldston, New York; 1914–15; extant.

George D. Strayer house, West 246th Street, Fieldston, New York; 1914–15; extant.

Hugh Mullen house, Greenway South, Forest Hills Gardens, New York; extant.

Boardman Robinson house, Whitestacks, Continental Avenue, Forest Hills Gardens, New York; extant.

Thomas E. Wing house, Rockledge Road, Bronxville, New York.

Corn Exchange Bank, 124 East 86th Street, New York, New York; alterations; extant: altered.

1915
Elmore Coe Kerr house, Frost Mill Road, Mill Neck, New York; c. 1915; extant.

Eugene du Pont house, Owl's Nest, Owl's Nest Road, Greenville, Delaware; 1915–20; extant: Greenville Country Club.

Thomas F. Vietor house, Rumson Road, Rumson, New Jersey; extant.

Corn Exchange Bank, 139 East 60th Street, New York, New York; alterations; demolished: 1960s.

George Galt Bourne house, Meadow Spring Lane, Glen Cove, New York; c. 1915; extant.

1916
G. W. Baxter house, Glen Head, New York.

Horace Havemeyer house, Olympic Point, Saxon Avenue, Islip, New York; 1916–19; demolished: 1948.

Nelson Doubleday house, Barberrys, Cleft Road, Oyster Bay, New York; 1916–19; extant.

Beekman Arms Inn, renovations, Mill Street, Rhinebeck, New York; 1916–18; extant.

Clyde M. Carr house, Wyldwoode, N. Mayflower Road, Lake Forest, Illinois; 1916–17; extant.

John Sargent Pillsbury house, Southways, Stevens Avenue, Orono, Minnesota; 1916–20; extant.

Henry R. Rawle house, Topsides, Knox Hill Road, Morristown, New Jersey; extant: Community Foundation of New Jersey.

1917
George Allison Armour house, cottage, garage and barn, Stockton Street, Princeton, New Jersey; extant.

Philip D. Armour house, Tangley Oaks, Armour Drive, Lake Bluff, Illinois; 1917–32; extant.

Mrs. Lisbeth Ledyard house, Prospect Hill Road, Stockbridge, Massachusetts; extant.

Frederick L. Lutz house, Laurel Acres, Cove Road, Oyster Bay, New York; extant.

Frances S. Mead house, Tredinnock, Mead Street, Waccabuc, New York; extant.

Halsey Malone house, Weatherhill Farm, Bedford State Road, Mount Kisco, New York; 1917–21.

1918
Stone Barns for Vincent Astor, River Road, Rhinebeck, New York; c. 1918; built by Charles A. Platt; extant.

Herbert Coppell house, Cotswold, Byrne Lane, Tenafly, New Jersey; 1918–25; extant.

1919

Mrs. Frederick G. Achelis house, Round Hill Road, Connecticut; demolished: 2007; carriage house: extant.

Dr. Lee M. Hurd house, 39 East 50th Street, New York; demolished.

Jackson E. Reynolds house, Old Tappan Road, Locust Valley, New York; extant.

Amasa Stone Mather stable group, Chagrin River Road, Gates Mills, Ohio; extant.

1920

Mrs. C. P. Dugmore house, The Gables, renovations, Locust Valley, New York; c. 1920; destroyed by fire.

Richard Everett Dwight house, Valley Road, Matinecock, New York; c. 1920; extant.

Paul Fuller house, 60 East 92nd Street, renovation, New York.

Frederick L. Lutz house, 44 East 66th Street, renovation, New York.

Hugo V. Neuhaus house, Remington Lane, Houston, Texas; 1920–22; extant.

Norman Toerge, The Hitching Post, Piping Rock Road, Locust Valley, c. 1920.

Charles Owen house, Oakwood Place, Lynchburg, Virginia; extant.

1921

William Stamps Farish II house, Remington Lane, Houston, Texas; extant.

Kenneth E. Womack house, Remington Lane, Houston, Texas; extant.

Duncan Harris house, Woodland Road, Wilson Point, Norwalk, Connecticut; extant.

Bertrand L. Taylor Jr. house, Chicken Valley Road, Mill Neck, New York; extant.

1922

Amelita Galli-Curci house, Sul Monte, Galli-Curci Road, Fleischmanns, New York; extant.

J. J. Levison house, Downing Avenue, Sea Cliff, New York; 1922–24: extant.

Henry C. Martin house, Jackson Lane, Glen Cove, New York; extant.

Dr. Samuel McCullough house, Station Road, Mill Neck, New York.

Scott Stewart house, Kimball Avenue, Bronxville, New York; extant: Slonin House, Sarah Lawrence College.

Bertrand L. Taylor Sr. house, alteration and addition, Locust Valley, New York.

Myron C. Taylor house, Killingworth, Bayview Road, Lattingtown, New York; c. 1922; extant.

Seth Thomas house, Red Gate Farm, Van Beuren Road, Morristown, New Jersey; 1922–25; extant.

Orson D. Munn house, Short Hills, New Jersey; c. 1922.

David D. Peden house, Longfellow Lane, Houston, Texas; extant.

Houston Country Club, swimming pool and bathhouse, Capital Street, Houston, Texas.

1923
Harry French Knight house, S. Warson Road, Ladue, Missouri; 1923–27; extant.

Francis L. Wurzburg house, Kimball Avenue, Bronxville, New York; extant.

William N. Dykman house, White Acre, Meadow Spring Lane, Glen Cove, New York; extant.

Scheme for a hospital commissioned by Mrs. George W. Vanderbilt, Biltmore Forest, North Carolina; 1923–24; unbuilt.

1924
Michael M. Van Beuren, Gray Craig, Gray Craig Road, Middletown, Rhode Island; 1924–26; extant.

1925
Jackson E. Reynolds house, 33 Beekman Place, New York; 1925–26; extant.

Edward F. MacNichol house, The Ledges, Grapevine Road, South Hamilton, Massachusetts; 1925–28.

Frederick B. Patterson house, Far Hills, East Thruston Boulevard, Dayton, Ohio; extant: Lutheran Church of our Savior.

Harry Wiess house, alteration and addition, Sunset Boulevard, Houston, Texas; extant: President's House, Rice University.

Asheville Country Club, Club View Road, Asheville, North Carolina; 1925–26; extant: Grove Park Country Club.

The Honorable and Mrs. Cameron Morrison house, Morrocroft, Richardson Drive, Charlotte, North Carolina; 1925–27; extant.

1926
Harrie T. Lindeberg house, West Gate Lodge, Locust Valley, New York; 1926–27; extant.

Lowell M. Chapin/Francis Beidler house, South Stone Gate Road, Lake Forest, Illinois; 1926–28; extant.

John Hamman house, Lovett Boulevard, Houston, Texas; extant: Red House.

Archibald F. MacNichol house, Laurel Court, Khakum Wood Road, Greenwich, Connecticut; 1926–27; extant.

Hugh W. Sanford house, Kingston Pike, Knoxville, Tennessee; extant.

1927

George M. Gales house, Eckington, Overlook Road, Locust Valley, New York; extant.

Robert A. Gardner house, Meadow Lane, Lake Forest, New York; 1927–29; extant.

Joseph H. Kahrs house, Twin Eagles, Oak Bend, Llewellyn Park, New Jersey; extant.

Onwentsia Club, North Green Bay Road, Lake Forest, Illinois; 1927–28; extant.

Henry S. Pritchett house, Garden Street, Santa Barbara, California; extant.

Robert Lee Ellis house, Ellsleigh, Vanderbilt Road, Biltmore Forest, North Carolina; extant.

1928

Wilbur Laing Ball house, Skunks Misery Road, Lattington, New York; extant.

Joseph J. Bodell house, Intervale Road, Providence, Rhode Island; demolished.

1929

Martin L. Cannon house, White Oaks, renovation, Hermitage Road, Charlotte, North Carolina; extant: The Duke Mansion, an event venue.

Dexter Cummings house, North Lake Road, Lake Forest, Illinois; extant.

Dale Parker house, Middle Neck Road, Sand's Point, New York; extant.

J. Arnot Rathbone house, Strathmont, Fassett Road, West Elmira, New York; extant.

1930

Charles T. Church house, Shu Swamp Road, Mill Neck, New York; extant.

Frederic E. Church house, Shu Swamp Road, Mill Neck, New York; extant.

Ruby Boyer Miller house, Penguin Hall, Essex Street. Wenham, Massachusetts; extant: The Academy at Penguin Hall.

Gerard B. Lambert house, Carter Hall, renovation, Carter Hall Lane, Millwood, Virginia; extant: Carter Hall Conference Center.

Ernest A. Randall house, Foreside Road, Falmouth Foreside, Maine; extant.

Earle T. Reynolds house, Green Bay Road, Lake Forest, Illinois; extant: Rosalind Franklin University of Medicine and Science.

1931

F. Burch Ijams house, Country Club Road, Terre Haute, Indiana; extant.

1934

U. S. Foreign Building Commission, Scheme for the Consulate in Moscow; unbuilt.

William Coxe Wright house, Ravenscliff, alteration to Brockie & Hastings' 1904 design, St. David's, Pennsylvania; extant.

1935

Ruby Boyer Miller house, Kercheval Avenue, Grosse Pointe, Michigan; extant.

1936

U. S. Foreign Building Commission, Scheme for the Consulate in Shanghai; unbuilt.

U. S. Foreign Building Commission, Consulate, Itäinen Puistotie, Helsinki, Finland; 1936–40; extant.

1937

Walter T. Douglas house, The Highlands, NW Cherry Loop, Shoreline, Washington; extant.

William L. Hanley Jr. house, Yal Farm, Sterling Road, Greenwich, Connecticut; 1937–40; extant.

Edward C. Mattes house, Bolton's Landing, New York; demolished: 2000s.

U. S. Foreign Building Commission, Scheme for the Consulate in Managua, Nicaragua; unbuilt.

1938

Colonel George S. Patton house, Green Meadows Farm, addition, Asbury Street, South Hamilton, Massachusetts; extant.

House schemes for the Weyerhaeuser Sales Company, St. Paul, Minnesota.

House schemes for McCall's Magazine, New York.

1939

Major David S. Barry house, Kalorama Road, Washington, D.C.; extant.

Sidney Alexander Mitchell house, Crabapple Lane, Brookville, New York; extant.

Richard Thurlow Vanderbilt house, Beachside Avenue, Green Farms, Connecticut; extant: Green Farms Academy.

1940

Robert T. Vanderbilt Company, Laboratory, Winfield Street, East Norwalk, Connecticut; c. 1940; extant.

Monroe Maltby house, 63 East 90th Street, New York, New York; alterations; c. 1940; extant.

House schemes for Jean F. Mesritz house, Grosse Pointe, Michigan; unbuilt.

1941

John C. Blair house, Westover Road, Stamford, Connecticut.

1946

Sidney Alexander Mitchell house, 184 East 64th Street, New York; alterations; extant with changes.

Country Life Press for Doubleday & Co., Franklin Avenue, Garden City, New York; extant.

Doubleday & Co., Ridge Avenue, Hanover, Pennsylvania; extant.

1949

Devereux Milburn Jr. house, Sunridge Hall, Hitchcock Lane, Old Westbury, New York; extant.

1951

Dr. James Lawrence and Angeline Pool house, Closter Dock Road, Alpine, New Jersey; demolished: 2010s.

1955

Mrs. Stedman Hanks house, Matinecock, New York.

1956

Harry LaMontange house, Mill Neck, New York; with William Russell.

1959

Dr. James Lawrence and Angeline Pool house, Pool Road, North Haven, Maine; extant.

Date Unknown

Dr. Warren Sanford Adams house, Atlantic Avenue, Little Boar's Head, New Hampshire; extant.

American Agricultural Chemical Co., Boca Grande, Florida.

Captain William T. Barlow house, Woodstock, Vermont.

Lawrence Bogle house, Seattle, Washington; extant.

Banyer Clarkson house, Riverside Farm, Tyringham, Massachusetts.

F. R. Davis house, Forest Hills, New York.

Paul M. Davis house, Deer Park Drive, Belle Meade, Tennessee; extant.

Gates for the Albert Blake Dick house, Applegate, Green Bay Road, Lake Forest, Illinois.

Walter Gibbs house, Brooklyn, New York.

Rev. Myles Hemenway house, Cedar Hill Drive, Windsor, Vermont; extant: Cedar Hill Continuing Care Community.

Thomas H. Hodgens house, Greenwich, Connecticut.

Edward B. Hough house, Olney Street, Providence, Rhode Island.

Millard C. Humstone house, Clapboard Ridge Road, Greenwich, Connecticut.

Coulter D. Hyler house, Round Hill Road, Greenwich, Connecticut.

Dr. Arnold Knapp house, New York.

Elgood C. Lufkin house, Haderway, Rye, New York.

Clarence H. MacKay, Roslyn, New York and New York office.

C. H. McNider house, Rochester, New York.

Keith Merrill house, Fairfax County, Virginia.

Maxwell S. Mannes house, Upper New Rochelle, New York.

D. Percy Morgan house, New York, New York.

Mrs. L. J. Morehead house, Salem, North Carolina.

Thomas O'Reilly house, Spring Lake, New Jersey.

Charles A. Otis house, Tannenbaum Farm, Willoughby, Ohio.

Ralph H. Perry house, Fishers Island, New York.

Mrs. Evelyn Schley house, Bernardsville, New Jersey.

D. D. Tenney house, Shorewood Farm, Crystal Bay, Minneapolis, Minnesota.

APPENDIX

Known employees of Albro & Lindeberg
and Harrie T. Lindeberg

Lewis Colt Albro*	R. S. Raymond
H. Bartlett	Walter Stuart Pavey
Ernesta Beaux	Christian Persina
Frederick Behr	Burgo Purcell
Karl Bradley	Alberta Raffl Pfeiffer
Herman Brookman**	Richard Perrien Raseman
George Henry Buterbaugh	Lovett Rile*
Maurice Fatio	George Senseney
W. H. I. Fleming	William Shepherd
Irving Harris	Howard Dwight Smith
J. Byers Hays	John Staub
Henry Powell Hopkins	Penrose Stout
Gerald B. Houk	William A. Treanor**
Charles Frederick Houston	William T. Warren
Musgrave Hyde	Henry Ross Wiggs
John Jay Ide	Percy Roy Wilson
Linda Lindeberg	Mary Worthen
Lytle Lindeberg	Addison F. Worthington
Walter McQuade	
R. L. Morin	* Albro & Lindeberg
Daniel Neilinger**	** Both Albro & Lindeberg and
Robert Emanuel Ochs	Harrie T. Lindeberg

NOTES

Foreword

1. Henry-Russell Hitchcock, *Modern Architecture: Romanticism and Reintegration* (New York: Payson & Clarke, 1929), 92.

2. Hitchcock, 103.

Introduction

1. Royal Cortissoz, Introduction, *Domestic Architecture of H. T. Lindeberg* (New York: William Helburn Inc., 1940): 14.

2. William Adams Delano, "Architecture is an Art," *The Architectural Forum* 72 (April 1940): 17.

3. C. Matlack Price, "The New Spirit in Country House Design," *House Beautiful* 57 (February 1925): 128.

4. H. T. Lindeberg, "The Home of the Future: The New Domestic Architecture in the East," *The Craftsman* 29 (March 1916): 603.

5. Albro & Lindeberg, *Domestic Architecture* (New York: privately printed, 1912): 1.

6. G. H. Edgell, *The American Architecture of Today* (New York: Charles Scribner's Sons, 1928): 116.

7. Cortissoz, *Domestic Architecture of H. T. Lindeberg*, 13.

8. Talbot Faulkner Hamlin, *The American Spirit in Architecture* (New Haven: Yale University Press, 1926): 263.

9. In 1962 Lindeberg's third wife, Angeline Lindeberg, donated his collection of over 350 books and periodicals to the C. W. Post library of Long Island University. The collection remains intact in the library's archives and special collections.

10. Henry-Russell Hitchcock, *Modern Architecture: Romanticism and Reintegration* (New York: Payson & Clarke, 1929): 147.

11. Theodore Lindeberg was born in Stockholm. His mother was Birgitta Arvidsdotter Lindeberg (b. 1799), the daughter of Johan Gustaf August and Christina Catharina Elsabeth Österlund of Stockholm's Hedvig Eleanora parish. The tradition of Lindeberg silversmiths was carried forward by Harrie's cousin Carl Otto Lindeberg who continued his father Erik Otto Lindeberg's shop in Stockholm. Harrie's uncle Erik Otto Lindeberg (b. 1827) in Södertälje, apprenticed to Möllenborg in Stockholm, worked in Germany and Paris, before opening his own shop in 1863. Other prominent Lindeberg cousins include Sven Jakob Lindeberg (1896–1944), a lawyer, bank inspector and receiver when the construction and match company, Kreuger and Toll, went into bankruptcy and Otto Lindeberg (1863–1947), an affluent brewer who became the mayor of Nyköping, just south of Stockholm.

At some point, Lindeberg changed the spelling of his name to Harrie but it is hard to say when. Records, such as passport applications show that the spelling fluctuated between Harry and Harrie.

There is a record showing Augusta Mathilda Eleanora Lindeberg (née Österlund) and three children registered to emigrate to North America on May 28, 1867. It seems that the Lindebergs had several children before Frederick and Harrie, none of whom survived to adulthood. The 1870 census shows Theodore, a salesman, and Augusta, keeping house, and a daughter Annie (6) living in Manhattan in the East Village. After Augusta's death in 1896, Theodore married Clara Cohen in 1897 and appears to have worked as a superintendent on East 11th Street.

12. In his passport application of 1923, Lindeberg claims to have lived abroad from from 1884 to 1894 in Sweden, Germany, France and England; however, according to Cedric Larson, "Dean of Domestic Architecture in America," *Bulletin of the American Swedish Institute* 5 (September 1950), by the time he was 9, he was back in the United States.

13. "History of Stevens Institute of Technology, *Stevens Indicator* (1887): 123.

14. Frederick became an organist and a musician but died as a young man.

15. Larson, "Dean of Domestic Architecture in America," 16–17.

16. The Barney house, known as Windy Barn, was destroyed by fire in 1901 caused by a faulty flue—just two years after the ballroom was added.

17. H. Van Buren Magonigle as quoted in Leland Roth, *McKim, Mead & White, Architects* (New York: Thames and Hudson, 1984): 62.

18. "Celebration of the Harvard Club of New York City," *The Harvard Graduates' Magazine* 14 (March 1906): 436–37. According to family lore, Lindeberg also received a gold watch for his work on Harvard Hall.

19. Charles F. McKim to James L. Breese, January 7, 1903. Charles Follen McKim Papers (MSS32243), Library of Congress.

20. "Group of Residences for Professors of University of Chicago," *The Inland Architect and News Record* 45 (June 1905): 56; "A Successful Alteration of a Townhouse," *Town and Country* 61 (February 3, 1906): 10; "Some Pretty Country Houses," *Ladies' Home Journal* 23 (February 1906): 34; *Rochelle Park – Rochelle Heights Historic District*, National Register of Historic Places Registration Form, United States Department of the Interior, National Parks Service, 2008. Web.

21. According to Christopher Gray, "Streetscapes: A 1904 Neo-Federal House, Built by the Gibson Girls," *New York Times* (September 12, 1999), Albro prepared the original design drawings for the house. The

237

Gibsons were later included as guests at Albro's intimate wedding in 1916 to Mrs. Mary Pace Gromer.

22. Information from Frederick Finn, Florence Quin Finn's grandson, January 2015.

23. Information from Eugene H. Pool, Lindeberg's step-grandson, March 2015.

24. As relayed by client Eleanor Lawler Pillsbury in *Southways: Random Reminiscences* (privately printed, 1985).

25. Philip Gustafson, "He Creates an American Style in Architecture," *American Swedish Monthly* 34 (July 1940): 6.

26. "Architect's Shirts," *The New Yorker* (June 11, 1928): 8.

27. In 1993 The National Institute of Arts & Letters, the parent body of the American Academy of Arts & Letters, established in 1904, was dissolved and the organization became known as the American Academy of Arts & Letters.

28. Larson, "Dean of Domestic Architecture in America," 14.

29. A. H. Forbes, "The Work of Albro & Lindeberg," *Architecture* 26 (November 1912): 207.

30. Aymar Embury II, "Current Tendencies in Country House Design in the East," *The Architectural Record* 52 (October 1922): 252.

31. The Albert A. Sprague house (1912) in Lake Bluff, Illinois, and the Gerard B. Lambert house (1914) in Princeton, New Jersey, followed this model.

32. Russell F. Whitehead, "Harrie T. Lindeberg's Contribution to American Domestic Architecture," *The Architectural Record* 55 (April 1924): 341.

33. Harrie T. Lindeberg, "Thatched Roof Effects with Shingles," *The Brickbuilder* 18 (July 1909): 133.

34. Lindeberg, "The Home of the Future: The New Domestic Architecture of the East," 604.

35. Robert Leonard Ames, "A Long Island Country House," *American Homes and Gardens* 9 (January 1912): 3–6.

36. Additional houses included those of Russell S. Carter, Carroll Macy—Macy's sister—and Levin R. Marshall. Carleton Macy also commissioned an Albro & Lindeberg house in Woodmere on a section of land developed by the Woodmere Realty Company. Jared Stuyvesant, "A Long Island Country Home," *Country Life in America* 15 (November 1908): 59–60.

37. Phil M. Riley, "Harmonizing a House and Building Site," *Country Life in America* 19 (January 1911): 236.

38. Report of Special Committee on Building Restrictions, December 30, 1910; Series 3, Box 23, Folder 183, Russell Sage Foundation Records, Rockefeller Archive Center, Sleepy Hollow, New York.

39. "The Home of Mr. Boardman Robinson, Forest Hills, Long Island, N.Y.," *Country Life in America* 27 (November 1914): 58–59; "House of Boardman Robinson, Esq., Forest Hills Gardens, Long Island, N.Y." and "House of Hugh Mullen, Esq., Forest Hills Gardens, Long Island, N.Y.," *The Brickbuilder* 25 (July 1916) 149–50.

40. New York City Landmarks Preservation Commission, *Fieldston Historic District Designation Report* (New York: Landmarks Preservation Commission, 2006): 25.

41. The Delafield Estate developed 4711 Fieldston Road (originally occupied by Nicholas Kelley) and 4682 Waldo Avenue (originally occupied by the Coopers) in 1913. In 1914 and 1915, George D. Strayer, a Columbia University professor, commissioned 417 West 246th Street and Arthur I. Keller, an artist and illustrator, commissioned 5020 Goodridge Avenue and Lindeberg, as sole practitioner, carried them out. The Keller house was later occupied by Fiorella LaGuardia as he finished up his third term as mayor until his death in 1947.

42. "The Home of Mr. Clayton S. Cooper at Fieldston, New York," *Country Life in America* 27 (April 1915): 56–57.

43. Forbes, "The Work of Albro & Lindeberg," 206.

44. This phenomenon is discussed in Brian Lee Johnson, *The Architecture of Harrie T. Lindeberg* (Master's Thesis, School of Architecture, University of Virginia, 1984): 60–65.

45. Andrew Dolkart's book *The Row House Reborn: Architecture and Neighborhoods in New York City: 1908–1929* (Baltimore: The Johns Hopkins University Press, 2009) closely examines this phenomenon.

46. New York City Landmarks Preservation Commission, *Mary Hale Cunningham House*, 124 East 55th Street, Manhattan. New York. Cunningham's husband James had been a partner in an importing and publishing business in San Francisco and also had real estate interests in New York.

47. These houses appear as plates in *The American Architect* 97 (May 4, 1910) and in "The Passing of the Brownstone Front," *International Studio* 40 (April 1910): 37–39.

48. C. Matlack Price, "The Recent Work of Albro & Lindeberg," *Architecture* 31 (January 1915): 2.

49. "Personal and Trade Notes," *Real Estate Record and Builder's Guide* 93 (January 3, 1914) 32.

50. "Cedar Brook Farm," *House & Garden* 37 (June 1929): 30–31; "House at Cedar Brook Farm," *The Architectural Review* 11 (July 1920): pls. 8–10;

51. Information from Mandy Lindeberg, Lindeberg's granddaughter, May 6, 2015.

52. Christopher Gray, "Streetscapes: 2 West 47th Street," *New York Times* (April 16, 2000): RE9.

53. In his 1940 monograph, Lindeberg first thanks Daniel Neilinger "whose skill in design and draughtsmanship has long been an inspiration not only to the members of my organization but to draughtsmen throughout the country." Neilinger often entered designs in competitions (such as the White Pine Architectural Competition) and consistently

won honorable mentions. In 1917, he won first place for the best design of a house for $5,000, held by the *New York Herald*.

54. Letter from Fatio to his parents, November 26, 1920, in Alexandra Fatio, *Maurice Fatio, Architect*, 1992.

55. Letter from Fatio to his parents, June 1921, in Fatio, *Maurice Fatio, Architect*, 1992.

56. Letter from Alberta Raffl Pfeiffer to Laura Katz, 1988. Alberta Pfeiffer Architectural Collection, 1929–1976, Special Collections, Virginia Polytechnic Institute and State University.

57. J. Ernest Gonzales, article from the *New Haven Register* (September 15, 1974) in the Alberta Pfeiffer Architectural Collection, Virginia Polytechnic Institute and State University.

58. Letter from Fatio to his parents, April 10, 1921, in Fatio, *Maurice Fatio, Architect*, 1992.

59. Letter from Alberta Raffl Pfeiffer to Laura Katz, 1988. Alberta Pfeiffer Architectural Collection, Virginia Polytechnic Institute and State University.

60. Others included: R. L. Morin of Portland, Oregon; Burgo Purcell of San Francisco; C. Frederick Houston of Baltimore; H. Bartlett and Mary Worthen of Melbourne, Australia; Christian Persina of Washington, D.C.; George Senseney of Chicago; and P. R. Wilson of Montreal.

61. Ernesta Beaux was born Aimee Ernesta Drinker. She married William C. Bullitt Jr. in 1916 but they divorced in 1923. Bullitt, who as Ambassador to the Soviet Union, later became a client of Lindeberg's. After their divorce, Ernesta took her mother's maiden name. She was frequently painted by her aunt and was the subject of Girl in White in the collection of the Metropolitan Museum of Art.

62. The Linda Lindeberg Papers, 1940–1973, at the Archives of American Art include biographical data, records, photographs and clippings about her career as an artist. Her work—abstract paintings and drawings of landscapes and nudes—were exhibited at the Museum of Modern Art, the Whitney Museum, the Houston Art Museum and the Berkeley Art Museum. She and her second husband, Giorgio Cavallon, were part of the SoHo art scene; their circle of friends included Franz Kline, Jackson Pollack, and Stanley Kunitz. She was previously married to John Carrington Yates (d. 1951), the real estate manager of Vincent Astor's estate.

63. Staub's career is discussed in Howard Barnstone, *The Architecture of John F. Staub* (Austin: University of Texas Press, 1979) and Stephen Fox, *The Country Houses of John F. Staub* (College Station: Texas A & M University Press, 2007).

64. C. Matlack Price, "Thoughts and Thinking in Architecture—Some Comments on the Work of Harrie T. Lindeberg," *The International Studio* 54 (October 1915): 82.

65. Whitehead, "Harrie T. Lindeberg's Contribution to American Domestic Architecture," 343.

66. Gerard B. Lambert, *All Out of Step: A Personal Chronicle* (New York: Doubleday, 1956): 63.

67. Pillsbury, 12.

68. According to www.oscarbach.org, Bach designed exterior and interior fittings for the houses of Eugene du Pont Jr., Greenville, Delaware (1915–20); Thomas Vietor, Rumson, New Jersey (1915); Nelson Doubleday, Mill Neck, New York (1916–19); Clyde Carr, Lake Forest, Illinois (1916–17); Philip Armour, Lake Bluff, Illinois (1917–1932); Lisbeth Ledyard, Stockbridge, Massachusetts (1917); George Humphreys, Morristown, New Jersey (1914–17); Frederick Lutz, Oyster Bay, New York (1917); Horace Havemeyer, Islip, New York (1916–19); John Pillsbury, Orono, Minnesota (1916–20); Herbert Coppell, Tenafly, New Jersey (1918–25); Orson Munn, Short Hills, New Jersey (c. 1922); Harry F. Knight, St. Louis, Missouri (1923–27); and W. L. Hanley, Greenwich, Connecticut (1937–40).

69. C. Matlack Price, "Individuality in Country Homes," *House & Garden* 37 (February 1920): 25.

70. According to the "A History of Sheep's Run," Mrs. Vietor was unable to decide between the three baluster options Lindeberg presented for the main stair. As a result, all three choices were carried out in an alternating pattern. The bedrooms had door knockers with different bird motifs. http://www.rumsonnj.gov/rhpc/history-sheeps-run.

71. Pillsbury, 8, 10, 19

72. This is discussed at length in Johnson, 67–80.

73. Cortissoz, *Domestic Architecture of H. T. Lindeberg*, 15.

74. Pillsbury, 14.

75. Lindeberg, "The Home of the Future: The New Domestic Architecture in the East," 613.

76. Lindberg, "The Home of the Future," 613.

77. Photographs of this house can be found in *Domestic Architecture of H. T. Lindeberg*, 167.

78. Whitehead, "Harrie T. Lindeberg's Contribution to American Domestic Architecture," 319, 369; *Domestic Architecture of H. T. Lindeberg*, 162–63.

79. Amelita Galli-Curci Estate, National Register of Historic Places Registration Form, United States Department of the Interior, National Parks Service, 2010. Web.

80. "Patterson Mansion Open House Dec. 22," *The Oakwood Register* 21 (December 19, 2012). Web. Also: "Modern Architecture That Is Not Modernistic," *Arts & Decoration* 31 (September 1929): 48.

81. *Domestic Architecture of H. T. Lindeberg*, 44–59.

82. H. T. Lindeberg, "A Return to Reason in Architecture," *The Architectural Record* 74 (October 1934): 252–56; 261–313; Curtis F. Columbia, "Cellular Houses: A Revolutionary New Building Idea," *Country Life* 71 (April 1934): 34–37.

83. Alfred Bruce and Harold Sandbank, *A History of Prefabrication* (Raritan, New Jersey: John B. Pierce Foundation, 1945): 48–49.

84. Mark Alan Hewitt, "Harrie T. Lindeberg and Modern Domestic Architecture," *Domestic Architecture of H. T. Lindeberg* (New York: Acanthus Press, 1996): xviii.

85. Larson, "Dean of Domestic Architecture in America," 13.

86. Weyerhaeuser Sales Company, *4-Square Book of Homes* (Saint Paul, Minnesota: Weyerhaeuser Sales Company, 1940).

87. Ron Theodore Robin, *Enclaves of America: The Rhetoric of American Political Architecture Abroad, 1900-1965* (Princeton: Princeton University Press, 1992): 92-94.

88. Bullitt's first wife Ernesta Drinker, known professionally as Ernesta Beaux, had worked in Lindeberg's office as an interior designer.

89. President Franklin D. Roosevelt to Secretary of State Stimson, February 11, 1934, in the minutes of the FSBC as quoted in Robin, 93.

90. Bullitt's attempts to construct Lindeberg's scheme are discussed in Will Brownell and Richard N. Billings, *So Close to Greatness: A Biography of William C. Bullitt* (New York: Macmillan Publishing Company, 1988): 155-57. Also: "U.S. Embassy in Soviet to be Jeffersonian," *Herald Tribune* (May 16, 1934): 17; "Lindeberg to Design Embassy in Moscow," *New York Times* (May 18, 1934): 27; "Plans for Embassy in Moscow Pressed," *New York Times* (February 5, 1935): 10. Lindeberg's schemes are pictured in *Domestic Architecture of H. T. Lindeberg*, 250-55.

91. Lindeberg also designed a laboratory and factory, completed in 1941, for Vanderbilt's chemical manufacturing company, Robert T. Vanderbilt Company, in East Norwalk, Connecticut. In describing the factory buildings, the *Herald Tribune* likened them to a college group.

92. There are drawings of the Mrs. Stedman S. Hanks house in Matinecock, Long Island (1955) and the Harry La Montagne house in Mill Neck, Long Island (1956) in the William Hamilton Russell Architectural Drawings and Papers in Avery Drawings & Archives, Columbia University.

Mondanne

1. Royal Cortissoz, Introduction, *Domestic Architecture of H. T. Lindeberg* (New York: William Helburn Inc., 1940): xiv.

2. A. H. Forbes, "The Work of Albro & Lindeberg," *Architecture* 26 (November 1912): 207.

3. Tom Pyle, *Pocantico: 50 Years on the Rockefeller Doman* (New York: Duell, Sloan and Pearce, 1964): 36, 41.

4. Discouraged by standard roofing materials, Lindeberg remembered a stable roof that McKim had designed in Lenox with shingles laid at varying exposures, giving it a rich texture. He came across another example by H. Van Buren Magonigle—a McKim Mead & White alumnus—in Glen Ridge, New Jersey, that took this one step further with shingles bent sightly at the gables and courses varying from two to five inches. Inspired, he began to experiment with rounded gables and softened eaves and ridges by altering the furring, bending shingles and laying them at varying courses to create a wavelike effect. Lindeberg's interest in shingle coursing became so intense that he would layout the design with his own hand, drawing the pattern on the roof with a soft pencil. To prevent the shingling from becoming too irregular, he interspersed a straight horizontal course every tenth row.

5. Other articles on Mondanne include: "A Thatched Palace," *Architectural Record* 28 (November 1910): 315-28; Harrie T. Lindeberg, "The Design and Plan of the Country House," *The American Architect* 99 (April 12, 1911): 133-7; Horace Allison, "English Cottage Types in America," *Country Life in America* 20 (October 1, 1911): 39-42.

6. "J. A. Stillman's $500,000 Country Home Burns; Valuable Paintings and Antiques Destroyed," *New York Times* (May 24, 1932): 1.

Foxhollow Farm

1. Lewis Colt Albro to Messrs. Olmsted Bros., February 1, 1906. Olmsted Associates Records, Library of Congress.

2. Tracy Dows to Messrs. Olmsted Bros., April 20, 1908. Olmsted Associates Records.

3. John C. Olmsted to Tracy Dows, September 3, 1908. Olmsted Associates Records.

4. Phil M. Riley, "An Example of Harmony in Farm Buildings," *Country Life in America* 21 (March 15, 1912): 28.

5. Henry H. Saylor," The Best Twelve Country Houses in America: Foxhollow Farm at Rhinebeck, N. Y.," *Country Life* 29 (February 1916): 25-8. Other articles include: "An American Manor House," *Architectural Record* 30 (October 1911): 310-25; 367-71; Robert L. Ames, "Foxhollow Farm," *American Homes and Gardens* 11 (November 1914): 363-8.

6. The branches for the Corn Exchange Bank were located at 139 East 60th Street (1915), 127 East 72nd Street (1917), 124 East 86th Street (1914) and 375 East 149th Street (1913).

7. Holiday Farm was built on the site of Bois Doré, the Huntington family home. Vincent Astor's first wife was Helen Huntington. Astor combined resources with Levi P. Morton to establish Holiday Farm, which later became known as the Astor Home for Children.

8. After divorcing Vincent Astor, Helen Huntington Astor surprised society by marrying Lytle Hull in 1941.

Houses on Lily Pond Lane

1. Aymar Embury II as quoted in Robert A.M. Stern, "One Hundred Years of Resort Architecture in East Hampton: The Power of the Provincial," *East Hampton's Heritage* (New York: W. W. Norton & Company, 1982): 100.

2. "Originality in Domestic Architecture," *Town & Country* 63 (March 14, 1908): 22-23; "A Study of Picturesque Roof Construction," *The Craftsman* 14 (September 1908): 679-80; "The Cockcroft Cottage at East Hampton, Long Island," *International Studio* 39 (November 1909): 11-14; Alfred F. Loomis, "A Noteworthy Summer Home on Long Island," *Country Life in America* 20 (June 1911): 61-2; Steven M. L. Aronson, "Before and After: Long Island Lineage," *Architectural Digest* 56 (August 1999): 126-33.

3. This commission may have been a real estate venture since the Cockcrofts sold the newly rebuilt Federal townhouse in 1909.

4. "A Successful House on Long Island," *House Beautiful* 31 (February 1912): 65–9.

5. Robert A.M. Stern, "One Hundred Years of Resort Architecture in East Hampton," 101.

6. "Dr. Erdmann, 80, Reviews Career," *New York Times* (March 27, 1944): 14.

7. "House of Rich Color and Graceful Outline," *Arts & Decoration* 26 (March 1927): 54–5;

Meadow Spring

1. An advertisement in the *New York Times* (June 22, 1913): XX4.

2. "Mrs. R. L. Davisson Risks Life in Fire for Cat; $150,000 Glen Cove Mansion Destroyed," *New York Times* (February 5, 1923): 1.

3. Listings in the 1919 Social Register show Jackson Dykman and his wife residing at White Acre so it is unclear how long Dykman actually occupied the house on lot 3. Susan Merrick Dykman, originally from New Orleans, was the sister of Mrs. Theodore Pratt. The Pratts were also a prominent Brooklyn-based family with houses in Glen Cove.

4. Matlack Price, "Individuality in Country Homes," *House & Garden* 37 (February 1920): 21. This article misattributes the location of the Bourne house as Mill Neck.

5. David E. Tarn, "Architectural Sincerity in a Country House," *Town & Country* 78 (June 20, 1921): 26–7; Matlack Price, "The Ideal of Dignity in Domestic Architecture," *Arts & Decoration* 23 (July 1925): 24–6.

6. Tarn, "Architectural Sincerity in a Country House," 26.

Albemarle

1. "Full-length Portrait of a Country Gentleman," *Country Life* 66 (September 1914): 58–64.

2. Gerard B. Lambert, *All Out of Step: A Personal Chronicle* (New York: Doubleday, 1956): 63. Lindeberg used slate from Olde Stonefield Roofs; Mathews Construction Company built the house.

3. McKim, Mead & White's Colonial Revival Hill-Stead in Farmington, Connecticut, also featured a Mount Vernon-style portico. Like Albemarle, it was a collaboration between architect and client, in this case, the self-taught architect Theodate Pope (Riddle).

4. Lambert, 133.

5. Lambert, 133.

6. Carter Hall is now owned by Project HOPE. It serves as its headquarters and operates as The Carter Hall Conference Center. It was listed on the National Register of Historic Places in 1973.

7. Lambert married Grace Lansing Mull in 1936 after divorcing his first wife in 1933. She went on to marry her former brother-in-law Dr. Malvern Clopton (formerly married to Lambert's sister) in 1934. "Princeton's Grand Dame Reminisces," *New York Times* (December 8, 1974): 134.

Owl's Nest

1. Maggie Lidz, *The Du Ponts: Houses and Gardens in the Brandywine* (New York: Acanthus Press, 2009): 100–6; Daniel DeKalb Miller, *Chateau Country: Du Pont Estates in the Brandywine Valley* (Atglen, PA: Schiffer Publishing Ltd., 2013.

2. C. Matlack Price, "The Recent Work of Albro & Lindeberg," *Architecture* 31 (January 1915): 3.

3. Ethel du Pont, "Motor Runs," H. A. du Pont Acc Group B – Ser B – Box 46 (Box W8-11325-11828), Hagley Library, Wilmington, Delaware as quoted in "Owl's Nest Country Place," National Register of Historic Places Registration Form, United States Department of the Interior, National Park Service, 2009.

4. Bach also designed a bronze mantel ornament with a ship at the center for the du Ponts.

5. Shipman had worked with Lindeberg before, first in 1915 on Philip Jennings house in Bennington, Vermont, followed by a commission for Mrs. Frederick Achelis in Greenwich, Connecticut. Judith B. Tankard, *The Gardens of Ellen Biddle Shipman* (Sagaponack, New York: Sagapress, Inc., 1996): 54, 207.

Wyldwoode

1. Albro & Lindeberg also designed a house for Albert A. Sprague in neighboring Lake Bluff in 1912.

2. "Good Architecture is Made Up of Good Details," *House & Garden* 40 (November 1921): 34–5; Residence for Mr. Clyde M. Carr, Lake Forest, Illinois," *The Western Architect* 31 (April 1922): pl. 3; "The Estate of Mr. C. M. Carr," *Country Life* 37 (November 1919): 30–1. Other reading on the Carr house includes: Kim Coventry, Daniel Meyer and Arthur H. Miller, *Classic Country Estates of Lake Forest: Architecture and Landscape Design, 1856–1940* (New York: W. W. Norton & Company, 2003): 212–17; Stuart Cohen and Susan Benjamin, *North Shore Chicago: Houses of the Lakefront Suburbs, 1890–1940* (New York: Acanthus Press, 2004): 165–70; "Wyldwoode: An Unexpected Treasure," *Lake Forest Preservation Foundation* (Summer 2014): 2, 7; and Lake Forest-Lake Bluff Historical Society, *The Estate House in Lake Forest as Seen in the Works of Harrie T. Lindeberg*. (Lake Forest: privately published).

3. C. Matlack Price, "The True Spirit of the American Country House," *Arts & Decoration* 12 (January 20, 1920): 158.

Olympic Point

1. In 1930, Horace Havemeyer organized the Bayberry Point Corporation to sell the original houses and the additional 117 lots that comprised the property that his father and Peters had purchased. By 1950, they were all sold.

2. "The Home of Horace Havemeyer, Islip, L. I.," *House Beautiful* 41 (May 1922): 46–7; Brian Lee Johnson, *The Architecture of Harrie T. Lindeberg* (Master's Thesis, School of Architecture, University of Virginia, 1984): 66–70; Mark Alan Hewitt, *Domestic Architecture of H. T. Lindeberg* (New York: Acanthus Press, 1996): 164–6.

3. Alfred Hopkins, "The Remodeled Farm Group," *The Field Illustrated and System on the Farm* 31 (July 1921): 531–33, 566.

Barberrys

1. As quoted in Terry Considine Williams, "Once Doubleday Was a King, Now House

Gets a New Look," *New York Times* (October 6, 1996): LI1.

2. C. Matlack Price, "The True Spirit of the American Country House," *Arts & Decoration* 12 (January 20, 1920): 157.

3. Leonard Barron, Editor, *The Garden Magazine* to Percival Gallahger, Olmsted Brothers, April 23, 1919. Series B, Box 369, Olmsted Associates Records, 1863–1971, Library of Congress.

4. The Gottscho-Schleisner Collection at the Library of Congress includes a series of interiors taken at Barberrys in 1947 and of the Doubleday plant in Pennsylvania in 1948. Both include Lindeberg's name as the photographer's client.

Shadyside
1. As described by Stephen Fox, "Public Art and Private Places: Shadyside," *Houston History Magazine* (Winter 1980): 51. Additional information about Shadyside can be found in Stephen Fox, *The Country Houses of John F. Staub* (College Station: Texas A & M University Press, 2007): 5-12.

2. Lindeberg was displeased with the Hamman house because his client had turned his architectural drawings over to a contractor and there was no architect supervision. Other houses for John H. Kirby and J. F. B. Rawcliffe near Brays Bayou did not come to fruition. Howard Barnstone, *The Architecture of John F. Staub* (Austin: University of Texas Press, 1979): 13.

3. At Lindeberg's suggestion, both Womack and Stamps purchased extra land west of their lots to increase their size. Fox, "Public Art and Private Places: Shadyside," 52.

Harry French Knight Estate
1. John Taylor Boyd Jr., "Modern Architecture That Is Not Modernistic," *Arts & Decoration* 31 (September 1929) 50.

2. Florence Shinhle, "The Strange House on the Hill," *St. Louis Dispatch* (October 30, 1977): 27–30; Cydney Millstein and Carol Grove, *Houses of Missouri: 1870–1940* (New York: Acanthus Press, 2008): 194-99.

3. Meanwhile, Lora Knight went on to build Vikingholm on Lake Tahoe's Emerald Bay. She commissioned Lennart Palme, a Swedish architect and nephew by marriage, to design a Scandinavian castle, that is now considered one of the finest examples of Scandinavian architecture in the United States.

Gray Craig
1. Colin Carroll, "Newport's Classic Home," *Arts and Decoration* 45 (October 1936): 12–16; Rhode Island Historical Preservation Commission, *Historic and Architectural Resources of Middletown, Rhode Island*, June 1979; Michael C. Kathrens, *Newport Villas: The Revival Styles, 1885-1953* (New York: W. W. Norton & Co., 2009): 301-9.

2. Nelson's Pond was created during the World War II era when the road along the beach was added to access the U.S. Navy's communications center on Sachuest Point.

3. The house sale, held by Christie's on July 23 and 24, 1985, also included Maxfield Parrish's *The Sandman*, mounted in a frame that likely served as a child's headboard. It also included fine furniture, silver, porcelain, paintings, tapestries, and rugs as well as mantels from the reception room and master bedroom and murals from the reception room.

Jackson E. Reynolds House
1. Lindeberg employees R. S. Raymond and Herman Brookman submitted a design to the White Pine Architectural Competition for which they won first prize. The annual competition, initiated to uncover the talents of younger architects in the profession, was established by Russell F. Whitehead, the editor of the White Pine Monograph Series. This series, a well-respected reference tool, was sponsored by Weyerhaeuser Mills.

Lowell M. Chapin/Francis Beidler House
1. Sherry Thomas, "The Country House," *Forest & Bluff* (September 2016): 61-3; also: "Where Texture Plays No Mean Part," *House Beautiful* 68 (December 1930): 628-9; Lake Forest-Lake Bluff Historical Society, *The Estate House in Lake Forest as Seen in the Works of Harrie T. Lindeberg*. (Lake Forest: privately printed).

West Gate Lodge
1. John Taylor Boyd, Jr., "Modern Architecture that is not Modernistic," *Arts & Decoration* 31 (September 1929): 49.

2. Boyd., 49.

3. Additional readings on West Gate Lodge include: Matlack Price, "Fine Tradition in a Modern American Country House," *Country Life* 71 (November 1936): 47–51; Paul Mateyunas, *North Shore Long Island* (New York: Acanthus Press, 2007): 150-7.

4. Boyd, "Modern Architecture that is not Modernistic," 94.

Onwentsia Club
1. Alfred Granger, *Chicago Welcomes You* (Chicago: A. Kroch, 1933): 218.

2. Lindeberg also designed a house for Robert Lee Ellis (1927) in the Biltmore Forest section of Asheville. Mrs. George W. Vanderbilt, of the Biltmore estate, was also listed as a client. In 1923, she and other Biltmore officials asked Lindeberg to design a new hospital in Biltmore Forest. Lindeberg did initial sketches and plans but construction of the hospital was later suspended.

3. Moris T. Hoversten, ed., *Onwentsia Club, 1895-1995: A Centennial History* (Lake Forest: Onwentsia Club, 1995): 75. Additional reading includes: Bill Poole, *The History of Onwentsia: 1895–1945* (Lake Forest: Onwentsia Club, 1984) and Lake Forest-Lake Bluff Historical Society, *The Estate House in Lake Forest as Seen in the Works of Harrie T. Lindeberg* (Lake Forest: privately printed).

The Church Houses
1. Church & Dwight, based in New Jersey, is a major manufacturer of household products, including Arm & Hammer products, various brands of toothpaste, OxiClean, vitamins, etc.

2. "Country House of a Sportsman," *Country Life in America* 65 (November 1933): 54-5. According to legend, the Churches had shooting tunnels in their basement.

Tangley Oaks

1. Armour's father, Philip D. Armour Jr., had assumed a similar role in the company as his father but died unexpectedly in 1900 at the age of 31.

2. Arthur Miller, "Lake Forest Country Places, XXX: Philip D. Armour III's Tangley Oaks, 900 Armour Drive, Lake Bluff," *The Lake Forest Journal* 5 (July 1997): 33-5; Kim Coventry, Daniel Meyer and Arthur H. Miller, *Classic Country Estates of Lake Forest: Architecture and Landscape Design, 1856-1940* (New York: W. W. Norton & Company, 2003): 230-33; Stuart Cohen and Susan Benjamin, *North Shore Chicago: Houses of the Lakefront Suburbs, 1890-1940* (New York: Acanthus Press, 2004): 271-75.

3. Information about furnishings and the design are culled from the Terlato Wines International promotional materials as well as "Armour, Philip D., III, House" National Register of Historic Places Registration Form, United States Department of the Interior, National Park Service, 1996.

Ruby Boyer Miller House

1. This company still exists as the Burroughs Corporation and continues to manufacture business equipment.

2. H. T. Lindeberg, "A Return to Reason in Architecture," The *Architectural Record* 74 (October 1933): 255.

United States Legation

1. President Franklin D. Roosevelt to Secretary of State Stimson, February 11, 1934, in the minutes of the FSBC as quoted in Ron Theodore Robin, *Enclaves of America: The Rhetoric of American Political Architecture Abroad, 1900-1965* (Princeton: Princeton University Press, 1992): 93.

2. Robin., 93.

3. A sum of $300,000 was allotted for the building and the land was purchased in February 1936 for $48,000. Keith Merrill also commissioned Lindeberg to design a cottage for him near Great Falls, Virginia.

BIBLIOGRAPHY

Albro, Lewis Colt and Harrie T. Lindeberg. *Domestic Architecture*. New York: Privately Printed, 1912.

Barnstone, Howard. *The Architecture of John F. Staub: Houston and the South*. Austin: University of Texas Press, 1979.

Boyd, John Taylor Jr., "Modern Architecture That Is Not Modernistic," *Arts & Decoration* 31 (September 1929): 18–22, 92, 94, 96, 100.

Broderick, Mosette. *Triumvirate: McKim, Mead & White, Architecture, Scandal and Class in America's Gilded Age*. New York: Knopf, 2010.

Brownell, Will and Richard N. Billings. *So Close to Greatness: A Biography of William C. Bullitt*. New York: Macmillan Publishing Company, 1988.

Bruce, Alfred and Harold Sandbank. *A History of Prefabrication*. Raritan, New Jersey: John B. Pierce Foundation, 1945.

Byars, David. *Our Time at Foxhollow Farm: A Hudson Valley Family Remembered*. Albany: State University of New York Press, 2016.

Cohen, Stuart Earl. *North Shore Chicago: Houses of the Lakefront Suburbs, 1890–1940*. New York: Acanthus Press, 2004.

Coventry, Kim, Daniel Meyer and Arthur H. Miller. *Classic Country Estates of Lake Forest: Architecture and Landscape Design, 1856–1940*. New York: W. W. Norton & Company, 2003.

Edgell, G. H. *The American Architecture of Today*. New York: Charles Scribner's Sons, 1928.

Fatio, Alexandra, ed. *Maurice Fatio: Architect*. New York: A. Fatio, 1992.

Fox, Stephen. *The Country Houses of John F. Staub*. College Station: Texas A & M University Press, 2007

_____, "Public Art and Private Places: Shadyside," *Houston History Magazine* (Winter 1980): 27–60.

Griswold, Mac and Eleanor Weller. *The Golden Age of American Gardens, Proud Owners, Private Estates, 1890–1940*. New York: Abrams, 1991.

Gustafson, Philip. "He Creates an American Style in Architecture," *American Swedish Monthly* 34 (July 1940): 6–8, 30–1.

Hamlin, Talbot Faulkner. *The American Spirit in Architecture*. New Haven: Yale University Press, 1926.

Hewitt, Mark Alan. *The Architect and the American Country House 1890–1940*. New Haven, Conn.: Yale University Press, 1990.

Hitchcock, Henry-Russell. *Architecture: Nineteenth and Twentieth Centuries*. New York: Penguin Books, 1971,

Hitchcock, Henry-Russell. *Modern Architecture: Romanticism and Reintegration*. New York: Payson & Clarke, 1929.

Howe, Samuel. *American Country Houses of To-day*. New York: Architectural Book Publishing Company, 1915.

Kathrens, Michael C. *Newport Villas: The Revival Styles, 1885–1935*. New York: W. W. Norton & Company, 2009.

Kelly, Nancy V. *Rhinebeck's Historic Architecture*. Charleston, SC: The History Press, 2009.

Lambert, Gerard B. *All Out of Step: A Personal Chronicle*. New York: Doubleday, 1956.

Larson, Cedric. "Dean of Domestic Architecture in America." *Bulletin of the American Swedish Institute* 5 (September and December 1950): 14–21;12–16.

Lawrence, Gary and Anne Surchin. *Houses of the Hamptons*. New York: Acanthus Press, 2007.

Lidz, Maggie. *The du Ponts: Houses and Gardens in the Brandywine*. New York: Acanthus Press, 2009.

Lindeberg, H. T. with an introduction by Mark Alan Hewitt. *Domestic Architecture of H.T. Lindeberg*. New York: Acanthus Press, 1996.

_____, "The Home of the Future: The New Domestic Architecture in the East," *The Craftsman* 29 (March 1916): 602–4, 609–10, 613, 675–77.

MacKay, Robert B, Anthony K. Baker and Carol A. Traynor, eds. *Long Island Country Houses and Their Architects, 1860–1940*. New York: W. W. Norton & Company, 1997.

Mateyunas, Paul J. *North Shore, Long Island: Country Houses, 1890–1950*. New York: Acanthus Press, 2007.

Mellor, Meigs & Howe with an introduction by Daniel Wilson Randle. *A Monograph of the Work of Mellor, Meigs & Howe*. Boulder, CO: Graybooks, 1991.

Miller, Daniel Dekalb. *Chateau Country: Du Pont Estates in the Brandywine Valley*. Atglen, Pennsylvania: Schiffer Publishing Ltd., 2013.

Millstein, Cydney and Carol Grove. *Houses of Missouri, 1870–1940*. New York: Acanthus Press, 2008.

Patterson, Augusta Owen. *American Houses of To-Day*. New York: MacMillan Company, 1924.

Pennoyer, Peter and Anne Walker. *The Architecture of Delano & Aldrich*. New York: W. W. Norton & Company, 2003.

Platt, Charles A. with an introduction by Charles D. Warren. *The Architecture of Charles A. Platt*. New York: Acanthus Press, 1998.

Pillsbury, Eleanor Lawler. *Southways: Random Reminiscences*. Privately Printed, 1985.

Robin, Ron Theodore. *Enclaves of America: The Rhetoric of American Political Architecture Abroad: 1900–1965*. Princeton: Princeton University Press, 1992.

Roth, Leland M. *McKim, Mead & White, Architects*. New York: Harper & Row, 1983.

Schnadelbach, R. Terry. *Ferruccio Vitale: Landscape Architect of the Country Place Era*. New York: Princeton Architectural Press, 2001.

Spinzia, Raymond E. and Judith A. *Long Island's Prominent North Shore Families: Their Estates and Their Country Houses*. College Station, TX: Virtual Bookworm, 2006.

_____. *Long Island's Prominent South Shore Families: Their Estates and Their Country Houses in the Towns of Babylon and Islip*. College Station, TX: Virtual Bookworm, 2007.

Stern, Robert A. M. "One Hundred Years of Resort Architecture in East Hampton: The Power of the Provincial," in *East Hampton's Heritage*. New York: W. W. Norton & Company, 1982.

Tankard, Judith. *The Gardens of Ellen Biddle Shipman*. Sagaponack, New York: Sagapress, 1996.

Unpublished Sources:

Archives of the American Institute of Architects, Washington DC.

Brian Lee Johnson. *The Architecture of Harrie Thomas Lindeberg*. Thesis presented to the faculty of the School of Architecture, University of Virginia, 1984.

Harrie T. Lindeberg, Architect, Collections, 1910–1930s, Lake Forest College Library Archives and Special Collections.

Harrie Thomas Lindeberg Architectural Drawings, 1920 MS 312, Woodson Research Center, Rice University, Houston, Texas.

Linda Lindeberg Papers, 1940–1973. Archives of American Art. Smithsonian Institution.

Charles Follen McKim Papers, 1838–1929, Manuscript Division, Library of Congress, Washington, D. C.

McKim, Mead & White Architectural Records and Drawings. Dept. of Drawings & Archives, Avery Architectural and Fine Arts Library, Columbia University, New York, New York.

Olmsted Archives, Frederick Law Olmsted National Historic Site, Brookline, Massachusetts.

Olmsted Associates Records, Manuscript Division, Library of Congress, Washington, D. C.

Alberta Pfeiffer Architectural Collection, 1929–1976, Special Collections, Virginia Polytechnic Institute and State University.

William Hamilton Russell Architectural Drawings and Papers, Dept. of Drawings & Archives, Avery Architectural and Fine Arts Library, Columbia University, New York, New York.

INDEX

Aalto, Alvar, 223
Adams, Cyrus, 186
Albro, Lewis Colt, 11, 20, 22, 30–31, 64
Albright, Edward, 220
Albro & Lindeberg, 11–12, 20, 21–30, 50, 52, 56, 58, 59, 61, 64, 66, 72, 76, 100
Alcott (Clarence F.) house, East Hampton, N.Y., 33, 68, 70–71, 229
Arents (George, Jr.) estate (Hillbrook), Rye, N.Y., 30
Armour, Laurence H., 100
Armour (Philip D. III) estate (Tangley Oaks), Lake Bluff, Ill., 32, 204–13, 230
Astor, Helen, 31, 63
Astor, John Jacob V., 63
Astor, Vincent, 31, 63
Astor (Vincent) estate (Ferncliff), Rhinebeck, N.Y., 63, 229, 230
Atterbury, Grosvenor, 26, 41, 112
Auerbach, Joseph, 23

Babcock (Orville E.) house (Two Gables), Lake Forest, Ill., 27, 28, 29, 100, 228
Bach, Oscar Bruno, 33, 34, 88, 90, 92, 102, 112, 118, 119
Bacon, Henry, 18
Barney, Charles T., 17–18
Barry (David S., Jr.) house, Washington, D.C., 45–46, 47, 234
Barwin Realty, 72
Batterman, Henry Lewis, 72, 74, 76
Batterman (Henry Lewis) house (Beaver Brook Farm), Mill Neck, N.Y., 76, 118, 229
Batterman (Henry Lewis) house, Glen Cove, N.Y., 228
Bayberry Point cottage colony, Islip, N.Y., 112
Beaux, Ernesta, 32, 38
Beekman Arms, Rhinebeck, N.Y., 63, 230
Beidler (Francis)/Lowell M. Chapin house, Lake Forest, Ill., 172–77, 186, 232
Belmont, Oliver Hazard Perry, 148
Bottomley, William Lawrence, 32
Bourne (George Galt) house, Glen Cove, N.Y., 74, 76, 77, 230
Boyd, John Taylor, Jr., 142, 178
Brandt, Edgar, 16
Breese (James L.) house, Southampton, N.Y., 19, 20, 22, 58, 80
Brokaw (Irving) house, Mill Neck, N.Y., 118, 229
Brookman, Herman, 31
Bullitt, William C., Jr., 43, 44
Burnett, Edward, 56
Byrd, Richard, 39, 214

Carr (Clyde M.) estate (Wyldwoode), Lake Forest, Ill., 32, 100–111, 186, 204, 230
Carrière & Hastings, 18, 88

Chapin (Lowell M.)/Francis Beidler House, Lake Forest, Ill., 172–77, 186, 232
Chatfield-Taylor, Hobart, 186
Chippendale, Thomas, 150
Church (Charles Thomas) house, Mill Neck, N.Y., 192, 194, 196, 197–99, 233
Church (Frederic Edwin) house, Mill Neck, N.Y., 192, 193, 195–96, 200–203, 233
Clow, William, 186
Cobb, Henry Ives, 186
Cockcroft (Edward T.) house (Little Burlees), East Hampton, N.Y., 64, 66, 70, 227
Cockcroft (Edward T.) house, N.Y.C., 29–30, 66, 227
Coolidge (Thomas Jefferson, Jr.) house (Marble Palace), Manchester, Mass., 19, 20, 228
Cooper (Clayton) house, Riverdale, N.Y., 27, 229
Corn Exchange Bank, N.Y.C., 61, 229, 230
Cortissoz, Royal, 11, 12, 14, 35, 50
Country Life Press building, Garden City, N.Y., 43, 121, 234
Cram, Ralph Adams, 130
Crestmount Realty houses, Montclair, N.J., 25, 26, 228
Cret, Paul, 45
Cullinan, Joseph S., 130
Cummings (Dexter) house, Lake Forest, Ill., 32, 189, 233
Cunningham (Mary Hale) house, N.Y.C., 29, 30, 228

Davis, Alexander Jackson, 56
Delafield Estate, Riverdale, N.Y., 27
Delano, William Adams, 13
Delano & Aldrich, 32, 43, 45, 100
de Wolfe, Elsie, 31
Doubleday & Company printing plant, Hanover, Pa., 41, 43, 121, 234
Doubleday (Nelson) estate (Barberrys), Mill Neck, N.Y., 118–29, 230
Dows, Alice Olin, 31, 56, 58, 61
Dows, Tracy, 21–22, 30, 31, 56, 58, 61, 63
Dows (Tracy) estate (Foxhollow Farm), Rhinebeck, N.Y., 21, 22, 23, 30, 56–63, 106, 227
Draper, Dorothy, 217
du Maurier, Daphne, 121
du Pont (Eugene, Jr.) estate (Owl's Nest), Greenville, Del., 33, 88–99, 230
Dykman (Jackson Annan) house, Glen Cove, N.Y., 72, 74
Dykman (William Nelson) house (White Acre), Glen Cove, N.Y., 72–74, 76, 78–79, 232

Edgell, G. H., 14
Embury, Aymar II, 22, 26, 32, 64
Erdmann (John F.) house (Coxwould), 65, 66–68, 69, 70, 228
Ericsson, John, 17
Erving (J. Langdon) house, N.Y.C., 29, 227
Eyre, Wilson, 26

Farish (William Stamps, II) house, Houston, Texas, 132, 133, 136, 231

Fatio, Maurice, 31, 32
Ferber, Edna, 118
Finn, James Wall, 20
Forbes, A. H., 22, 50, 52
Foreign Service Buildings Commission (FSBC), 44, 45, 220
Forest Hills Gardens, Queens, N.Y., 26, 229
Frankfort, F. L., 41
Freeman, George A., 17, 18

Gabriel, Jacques-Ange, 43
Galanti, Charles, 74
Galli-Curci (Amelita) house (Sul Monte), Highmount, N.Y., 36, 37–38, 231
Gardner (Robert A.) house, Lake Forest, Ill., 32, 189, 233
Gibson, Charles Dana, 20, 21–22, 30, 56
Gibson (Charles Dana) house, N.Y.C., 20, 29
Goodhue, Bertram Grosvenor, 31
Gracie Mansion, N.Y.C., 32
Granger, Alfred, 186
Gray Craig Park Association, 148
Gray, Eileen, 41
Gregory (G. D.) house, Hewlett, N.Y., 24, 228

Hamlin, Talbot, 14
Hamman (John) house, Houston, Texas, 134, 232
Harris (Duncan) house, Norwalk, Conn., 63, 231
Harris (Tracy H.) house (Wisteria Lodge), Hewlett, N.Y., 24, 227
Hartshorn, Stewart, 25, 228
Harvard Club, N.Y.C., 18–19
Havemeyer (Horace) estate (Olympic Point), Islip, N.Y., 33, 34, 112–17, 230
Haydel, Abner J., 148
Hays, J. Byers, 32
Hering, Henry, 59
Hermann, George H., 130
Hermann Park, Houston, Texas, 130
Hewitt, Mark Alan, 11, 41
Hewlett Bay Park, Long Island, N.Y., 23–25
Higginson, James K., 19
Hitchcock, Henry-Russell, 15
Hoe (Richard M.) apartment/garage, N.Y.C., 30, 61, 228
Hollister (Frederick Kellogg) house, East Hampton, N.Y., 66, 70, 227
Hopkins, Alfred, 56, 114
Hotchkiss, Almerin, 100

Jackson, W. H., 31
James (Oliver B.) house, N.Y.C., 40, 46, 47
Jamieson, James P., 130
Jefferson, Thomas, 43–44, 220
Jennings (Philip B.) house, Bennington, Vt., 27, 28, 29, 228
Jensen, Jens, 100

Kerr (Thomas H.) house, White Plains, N.Y., 27, 28, 29, 228
Kessler, George E., 130

246

Kipp, Herbert A., 130
Klint, Kaare, 16
Knight (Henry French) estate, Ladue, Missouri, 142–47, 232

Lake Forest Association, 100
Lalique, René, 16
Lambert (Gerard B.) estate (Albemarle), Princeton, N.J., 33, 80–87, 229
Lambert (Gerard B.) house (Carter Hall), Millwood, Va., 83
Lathrop, Gertrude K., 182
Lindbergh, Charles, 142
Lindeberg, Angeline Krech James (third wife), 40, 182
Lindeberg, Augusta Österlund (mother), 16
Lindeberg, Eugenie Lee Quin (first wife), 20
Lindeberg, Frederick (brother), 16, 17
Lindeberg, Fredric Eriksson (grandfather), 16
Lindeberg (Harrie T.) house (West Gate Lodge), Locust Valley, N.Y., 31, 39, 40, 178–85, 232
Lindeberg, Linda (daughter), 31, 32, 46
Lindeberg, Lucia Hull (second wife), 31, 63, 178
Lindeberg, Lytle (son), 31, 32
Lindeberg, Theodore Ferdinand (father), 16
Loos, Adolf, 41
Lothrop, Beverly, 39
Lowell, Guy, 186
Lurçat, André, 51
Lutyens, Sir Edwin, 14, 15, 30, 36, 38
Lutz (Frederick) house (Laurel Acres), Oyster Bay, N.Y., 36, 230

MacDonald, Charles Blair, 186
MacNeille, Perry R., 20
Macy (Carleton) house, Hewlett, N.Y., 24, 227
Macy (Valentine E.) house (Twin Gables), Hewlett, N.Y., 24, 228
Magonigle, H. Van Buren, 18, 43
Mann, Horace B., 20
Mann, MacNeille & Lindeberg, 20
Manning, Warren, 106, 110
Marckwald (Albert H.) house, Short Hills, N.J., 25
Martin (Henry C.) house, Glen Cove, N.Y., 72, 74, 229
Masqueray, Emmanuel L., 18
Mather (Amasa Stone) stable group, Gates Mills, Ohio, 36, 231
Maugham, Syrie, 46
McCormick, Anne Potter Stillman "Fifi", 50, 52, 54
McKim, Charles Follen, 18, 19–20, 50
McKim, Mead & White, 11, 18–20, 21, 22, 23, 25, 50, 56, 58, 80
Meadow Spring, Glen Cove, N.Y., 72–79
Meehan (Thomas) & Sons, 88
Mellor, Meigs & Howe, 12, 13
Merrill, Keith, 220
Milburn (Devereux, Jr.) house, Old Westbury, N.Y., 47
Miller (Ruby Boyer) estate (Penguin Hall), Wenham, Mass., 38, 39, 214, 233

Miller (Ruby Boyer) house, Gross Pointe Farms, Mich., 45, 214–19
Mill Neck Railroad Station, Mill Neck, N.Y., 118, 228
Mitchell (Sidney A.) cottage, Brookville, N.Y., 45
Moore (Paul) house (Hollow Hill Farm), Convent, N.J., 88, 112, 229
Moore Ruble Yudell, 223
Mullen (Hugh) house, Forest Hills, N.Y., 26, 230

Neilinger, Daniel, 31
Neuhaus (Hugo V.) house, Houston, Texas, 130–32, 133, 134–36, 231
Nichols, Rose, 100, 106

Olin (Stephen H.) house (Glenburn), Rhinebeck, N.Y., 61, 227
Olmsted Brothers, 83, 86, 100, 112, 121, 124, 125
Olmsted, Frederick Law, Jr., 26
Olmsted, John C., 56, 58–59
Onwentsia Club, Lake Forest, Ill., 32, 100, 186–91, 233
Östberg, Ragnar, 15

Patterson (Frederick B.) house (Far Hills), Dayton, Ohio, 37, 38, 232
Peden (David D.) house, Houston, Texas, 132, 136–38, 139–41, 232
Perrine, Van Dearing, 17
Pfeiffer, Alberta Raffl, 31–32
Phipps, Paul, 30
Pillsbury (John S.) house (Southways), Orono, Minn., 33, 34–35, 207, 230
Piping Rock Club, Locust Valley, N.Y., 31, 186
Platt, Charles A., 12, 22, 63, 66, 100
Pool, Angeline and James, 47, 235
Price, C. Matlack, 13, 30, 32, 33, 88, 102, 118
Pyle, Tom, 52

Rajkovich, Thomas, 175, 212
Raymond, Antonin, 43
Reynolds (Earle) house, Lake Forest, Ill., 32, 189, 233
Reynolds (Jackson E.) house (19 Beekman Place), N.Y.C., 161–71, 232
Reynolds (Jackson E.) house, Lattingtown, N.Y., 166
Rice University (Institute), Houston, Texas, 130, 132, 138
Richardson, H. H., 36
Riley, Phil M., 59
Robbins, E. F., 20
Robinson (Boardman) house, Forest Hills Gardens, N.Y., 26
Rockefeller estate, Pocantico Hills, N.Y., 50
Roosevelt, Franklin D., 43, 45, 220
Rossiter (Arthur W.) house, Glen Cove, N.Y., 27, 28, 29, 228
Ruhlmann, Émile-Jacques, 16, 217
Runyon, Clarkson, Jr., 76
Russell, William, 47

Saarinen, Eliel, 14

Sage (Russell) Foundation houses, Forest Hills, N.Y., 26, 229
Schmidt, Mott B., 76
Sears, Thomas W., 24
Shadyside, Houston, Texas, 130–41
Shipman, Ellen Biddle, 90, 92, 166
Simon, Louis A., 43, 220
Sprague (Albert A. II) house, Lake Bluff, Ill., 186, 229
Staub, John F., 31, 32, 132, 134
Stern, Robert A.M., 66
Stillman, Anne Potter "Fifi", 50, 52, 54, 56
Stillman, James A., 50, 54, 56
Stillman (James A.) estate (Mondanne), Pocantico Hills, N.Y., 12, 13, 21, 22, 23, 50–55, 58, 217
Stillman, James J., 21, 50
Swanson, Karen, 217

Tengbom, Ivar, 14
Treanor, William A., 31
Tubby, J. T., 26

U.S. Consulate, Shanghai, China, 44–45, 234
U.S. Embassy, Moscow, Russia, 43–44, 234
U.S. Legation, Helsinki, Finland, 45, 220–25, 234
U.S. Legation, Managua, Nicaragua, 45, 234

van Beuren (Michael) estate (Gray Craig), Middletown, R.I., 38–39, 148–165, 178, 232
Vanderbilt (Robert T.) estate, Green Farms, Conn., 45, 46, 234
Van Vleck (Charles E., Jr.) house, Short Hills, N.J., 25, 228
Vietor (Thomas) house, Rumson, N.J., 33–34, 230
Vitale, Ferruccio, 150, 172, 175
Voysey, C. F. A., 36

Warren, Whitney, 148
Warren, William, 32
Watkin, William Ward, 132
Wesleyan University (North College), Middletown, Conn., 61, 227
Weyerhaeuser Sales Company model houses, 42, 43, 234
Wheeler, Albert E., 27
White, Stanford, 18, 20
Whitehead, Russell F., 22, 32
Wiess (Harry C.) house, Houston, Texas, 132, 138, 232
Womack (Kenneth E.) house, Houston, Texas, 132, 133, 136, 231

Yellin, Samuel, 33, 34, 74
York & Sawyer, 18

PHOTOGRAPHY CREDITS

The American Architect: 23 right, 29–30, 74 right, 227 middle center

American Country Houses of To-day: 25 top, 28 bottom left, 228 left, 228 bottom right

American Homes and Gardens: 63, 229 top center

The Architect: 232 center

The Architectural Record: 23 top, 24 top, 54, 55 top, 62 top, 227 top center, 228 top right

Architecture: 26 middle, 27, 28 bottom right, 67 top, 229 top left and bottom left, 229 bottom center, 229 middle right, 230 left

The Architecture of John F. Staub: Houston and the South: 132

Architecture: Nineteenth and Twentieth Centuries: 15 bottom

Arts and Decoration: 24 right, 74 left, 102, 114 left

The Brickbuilder: 52, 66 top, 227 top right, 228 bottom center

Country Life in America: 25 right, 38, 75, 194 top

Domestic Architecture of H. T. Lindeberg: 26 bottom, 28 top right and right, 34, 35 bottom, 36, 39 right, 40–1, 42 left, 43–7, 51, 53, 55 bottom, 57, 60, 66 left, 67 bottom, 68, 82 bottom, 83, 90, 103, 114 top, 115, 117, 133 bottom right, 143–44, 146–47, 151, 158 top, 168–69, 174 bottom, 180, 190, 195, 206, 216, 222, 225 top, 229 top right and bottom right, 230 middle center, top right and bottom right, 231 top and bottom left, top center, and middle and bottom right, 232 bottom left and middle right, 233–34

Dows Collection, Courtesy of Hudson River Heritage: 21, 22, 62 left, 227 bottom right

Frederick Law Olmsted National Historic Site, National Park Service: 58–59, 61, 82 top, 86 bottom, 120–21

Grovewood Gallery: 232 top right

Havemeyer Family: 116 bottom

House Beautiful: 113, 232 top left

House & Garden: 28 top left, 77 bottom, 230 bottom center

Houses and Gardens by E. L. Lutyens: 15 top right

Houston Public Library, HMRC: 133 bottom left

Werner Huthmacher: 221, 223–24, 225 bottom

Library of Congress Prints and Photographs Division: 37, 42 top, 126, 167, 170–71, 182, 219, 235 middle left (Gottscho-Schleisner)

Manchester Historical Museum: 19 top

Paul Mateyunas: 235 top left

Mellor, Meigs & Howe Collection, The Athenaeum of Philadelphia: 13 left

Modern Architecture: Romanticism and Reintegration: 15 top left

Museum of the City of New York: 18, 20 (McKim, Mead & White); 26 top (Wurts Bros.)

National Design Academy: 10

Timothy O'Neill: 194 bottom

© Peter A. Juley & Son Collection, Smithsonian American Art Museum: 17, 35 top, 39 left, 116 top, 133 top, 145 top, 150

Picssr.com: 13 top

Redwood Library and Athenaeum, Newport, Rhode Island: 158 bottom (Gottscho-Schleisner)

Southern Architecture Illustrated: 145 bottom

Jonathan Wallen: Jacket, 2, 5, 6–7, 9 right, 48–49, 65, 69, 70–71, 73, 76, 77 top, 78–79, 81, 84–85, 86 top, 87, 89, 91–99, 101, 104–11, 119, 122–25, 127–29, 131, 134–41, 149, 152–57, 159–65, 173, 174 top, 175–77, 179, 181, 183–85, 187–89, 191, 193, 196–203, 205, 207–13, 215, 217–18, 226, 231 top right, 243

Western Architect: 227 bottom center, 228 top center

Woodson Research Center, Fondren Library, Rice University: 33

Copyright © 2017 The Monacelli Press,
Peter Pennoyer, Anne Walker
Color photographs copyright © 2017 Jonathan Wallen

First published in the United States by
The Monacelli Press.
All rights reserved.
Library of Congress Control Number:
2017949272
ISBN 9781580934497

PAGE 3 View of the loggia and sleeping porch from the garden deigned by Ellen Biddle Shipman, Eugene du Pont estate, Owl's Nest, Greenville, Delaware.

PAGE 6 A window bay on the garden facade, Philip D. Armour estate, Tangley Oaks, Lake Bluff, Illinois.

PAGE 7-8 Stairs at the William Nelson Dykman house, White Acre, Glen Cove, New York (above left), Clyde M. Carr house, Wyldwoode, Lake Forest, Illinois (below left), Michael van Beuren house, Gray Craig, Middletown, Rhode Island (above right) and Francis Beidler house, Lake Forest, Illinois (below right).

PAGE 48-9 Carved overmantel in the entrance hall, Eugene du Pont estate, Owl's Nest, Greenville, Delaware.

PAGE 221 Sgraffito and ironwork wrought in the shape of the zodiac signs by Oscar Bach, Nelson Doubleday Estate, Barberrys, Mill Neck, New York.

PAGE 237 View from the tea house, Michael van Beuren estate, Gray Craig, Middletown, Rhode Island.

DESIGN: Bessas & Ackerman
Printed in China
The Monacelli Press
6 West 18th Street
New York, New York 10011